THE JAPANESE LETTERS OF
LAFCADIO HEARN

1   2

Robert T. Hearn   *Daniel J. Hearn*

3   4

Charles Bush Hearn   *Lafcadio Hearn*

Four Generations

THE JAPANESE LETTERS
OF
LAFCADIO HEARN

EDITED WITH AN INTRODUCTION BY
ELIZABETH BISLAND Wetmore
7

WITH ILLUSTRATIONS

BOSTON AND NEW YORK
HOUGHTON MIFFLIN COMPANY
The Riverside Press Cambridge
1910

15815

PREFACE

SHORTLY after the death of Lafcadio Hearn, Edmund Clarence Stedman said: —

"Hearn will become in time as much of a romantic personality and tradition as Poe now is."

If this prophecy is to be fulfilled 't is desirable that the tradition should be based on truth.

The Poe legend springs in the main from the impression conveyed by his first biographer, Griswold, and it is now generally accepted that Griswold's unfriendly animus so distorted the facts of the poet's life as to give of the man an idea both false and injurious.

A tradition, however, once set on foot and made viable, dies hard. Our poor humanity is ever willing to fancy a biographer more impartial and accurate when he reveals and analyzes faults, than when he dwells on the virtues and nobility of his subject. Lombroso, Nordau, and their school, have inclined the multitude to believe every man of genius more or less morbid and abnormal, and when the ordinary "defects of the qualities" of a famous man are interpreted as signs of degeneracy the public is prone to feel it is at last getting "The Real John Smith," "The Real Robert Robertson." As if there were some greater veracity in faultiness than in goodness, in weakness than in strength!

In the preface to "The Life and Letters of Lafcadio Hearn" occasion was taken to say — "the
intention of such part of the book as is my own is
to give a history of the circumstances under which a
great man developed his genius. I have purposely
ignored all such episodes as seemed impertinent to
this end, as from my point of view there seems a sort
of gross curiosity in raking among such details of a
man's life as he himself would wish ignored. These I
gladly leave to those who enjoy such labours."

Others, since that paragraph was published, have
apparently found pleasure in this squalid industry,
and lest the public should build upon false suggestions an unveracious legend concerning a good man
I have considered it necessary to touch upon and
explain certain events in Lafcadio Hearn's life. Also
to restate in brief the facts concerning him. It is
unfortunate that this should be requisite, but the
duty of those who were really acquainted with
Hearn to puncture any evilly blown bubbles of suggestion and innuendo, cannot rightfully be ignored.

1. First as to his birth and origin: — The story of
these, as related by himself, was carefully investi-
gated at the time of the publication of his "Life and
Letters." It was confirmed in every detail by means
of family papers and through information obtained
directly from his half-sisters, his brother and his
cousins. Without undue credulity it may be supposed that he himself and his immediate family
knew the facts better than some whose entire personal acquaintance with Lafcadio Hearn extended
over the period of exactly five months.

2. His youth and early influences: — I have been personally acquainted with the Hearns for many years. They are people of birth and breeding, and up to his sixteenth year — the formative period of life — Lafcadio Hearn lived in an atmosphere of wealth and refinement. That he quarrelled with his guardian and left home is not remarkable, as many famous and obscure men have done the same thing in the heat and inexperience of youth.

3. As to his sight: — The testimony of his schoolmates and family is that it was good until his sixteenth year, when he injured one eye in playing a game. And while the health of the other eye was much affected by the strain of incessant study and work and he was obliged to use a powerful glass when reading, yet his vision, with its aid, was acute and accurate for such things as did not require the close concentration demanded by print.

Among the legends is a great deal of fanciful nonsense wrapped up in the technical verbiage of the specialist, which always daunts and convinces the ignorant. But as a fact Lafcadio Hearn's eye troubles were not the result of disease, and no more affected his character and writing than the deafness of one ear would have done.

4. His relations with women have been treated with equal inaccuracy and malice in this mass of absurd "Hearn legends." From the tone of many of these aforementioned "legends" and the press comments one would suppose that any irregularity in the relations of the sexes was something hitherto unheard of. To put it simply, no doubt Lafcadio

Hearn did not lead the life of a Galahad up to the time of his marriage. But soon as he had the smallest hope of being able to support a family he married a lady of rank and high character, and was a devoted husband and father to the day of his death. Professor Basil Hall Chamberlain, whose testimony will hardly be questioned, declares the Hearn marriage to have been singularly pure and happy.

5. There has been much whispering of terrible "scandals," but when analyzed by those who know the facts and who cling to some shreds of common sense these scandals resolve themselves into this: When Hearn first went to Cincinnati his poverty was so extreme he slept for a time in an abandoned boiler in a vacant lot. After he secured work his home was a garret room in a cheap boarding-house. It was winter, his room unwarmed, and his hours, owing to the nature of his work, were irregular. The cook in this boarding-house was a handsome, kind-hearted mulatto girl, who kept his dinner warm, and allowed him to sit by her fire when he came in wet and chilled. He was not yet twenty; he was fresh from England, where the racial prejudices of America were unknown and where the sentimentalities of the Abolition party about "the images of God in ebony" had not been instilled into his mind. He apparently drifted into some connection with this girl, and with characteristic chivalry felt that he owed her legal rights and applied for a license to marry her. This was Hearn's own account of the matter, and has been confirmed by the testimony of those who were best fitted to know whether his statement was true.

It was a pathetic, high-minded piece of quixotism. Would that no man had ever been less tender and honest with the women of the African race!

Hearn's life in New Orleans has been referred to as base and gross, but the only specific charge brought is that he was allied to a Voodoo priestess. I happen to know that this charge rests on the fact that he was ordered to see her for the purpose of writing an article about her and that he met her exactly once. When examined, most of these whispered scandals are found to have an equally valuable and accurate basis.

Several times during his various changes of lodgings in New Orleans Hearn occupied rooms rented to him by coloured people. Such lodgings were common enough in that day, and were no more unusual or scandalous than are lodgings kept by Irish or German people in New York. The same was true of the West Indies, and in such lodgings in Martinique he fell ill of yellow fever and was nursed with great kindness and his rent allowed to remain in arrears until he was able to repay it, though he always declared that no money could discharge the debt of gratitude. These are the facts on which are based the charges that he "lived with negroes."

6. Certain portions of these legends were given currency in a recent book about Hearn, the author of which appears to have accepted them without due investigation, or to have lacked the means of verifying his statements. The writer is perhaps hardly to be held responsible for his rather regrettable ignorance of the facts, as his acquaintance with Hearn

was very short-lived. It began through a somewhat desultory correspondence, and included a visit
which ended in a serious rupture. The author of the
book appears to nurse the impression that he "gave
Lafcadio Hearn a soul." Hearn, however, seems
never to have been aware of this debt, or else to have
proved ungrateful, since the acquaintance so soon
and so abruptly ended was never renewed.

So brief a friendship would naturally render it
impossible for the writer of the book to acquire a
very correct idea of the character and antecedents
of his subject, and his confusion as to the facts may
therefore be passed over with proper regret and
indulgence.

To sum up the facts of Lafcadio Hearn's life as
contrasted with these myths: — He was of gentle
birth and lived amid refined surroundings in his
early years. He left home at sixteen and after many
years of poverty and hard work raised himself to the
position of an honoured teacher in one of the world's
greatest universities. He married well and happily
and was a devoted father and husband, and he enriched English literature with valuable and permanent contributions.

There is the real story of the man's life. That he
had some faults and some peculiarities only proves
him to be like all the rest of us, but those who knew
him intimately — not for five months but for the
greater part of his life — remember Lafcadio Hearn
with profound affection and respect.

CONTENTS

ILLUSTRATIONS

INTRODUCTION

INTRODUCTION

WHEN the biography of Lafcadio Hearn was planned
— shortly after his death — such a wealth of his
letters was accumulated, and these so fully and bril-
liantly revealed the nature of the writer, that the
work of the memorialist was reduced to little more
than explaining and arranging the rich material
ready to hand.

The reception by the public of this self-told me-
moir set him at once in the foremost ranks of the
world's great letter-writers. Since its appearance
new stores of his correspondence have come to light,
sufficient to justify adding a third volume to the two
previously published.

So unflagging was Hearn's zest, so instinctively
did he turn to each of his friends a different phase of
his mind, that these additions to the previous collection have none of the quality of those "sweepings"
too often put forth to dim a writer's fame after his
best has been garnered.

The bulk of these newly discovered letters was
addressed to Professor Basil Hall Chamberlain, to
whom, more than to any of his correspondents, he
gave his best and richest efforts. And in them is
shown perhaps better than anywhere else, the wide
range of his mental excursions, his insatiable intellectual curiosity, the dignity and beauty of his char-

acter, the gradual deepening and purifying with time of the graver aspects of his thought. Also they demonstrate how inexhaustible to this "literary monk" was the delight and inspiration of intimate communion and spiritual fellowship. Their mutual interests in all things Japanese permitted Hearn to write to Professor Chamberlain with full assurance of comprehension and sympathy. It was unnecessary to interrupt the flow of his thought for explanations to one so familiar with the environment in which he moved and felt, and though their opinions and convictions varied on many points, Professor Chamberlain, he knew, had that fine mental hospitality capable of welcoming with warm pleasure tenets foreign to his own trend of conclusions.

The greater number of these Chamberlain letters were sent from Kumamoto, where Hearn was teaching in the Government schools and was becoming acquainted — much to his own disgust — with the newer, occidentalized Japan. He was revising those first delighted impressions received in old-world Izumo, where the feudal life of the pre-Meiji period still lingered, with its honourable sweetness and simplicities. He was meeting again the hardness of modern competitive life, from which he had escaped a while in a remote province; and was gradually forgetting that all too brief faëry episode in which, for the only time in his life, he found himself at home and at peace.

One of the intimate charms of letters lies in their freedom from any "body of doctrine." Through all the more formal literature a man may create runs instinctively, and of necessity, a thread of consistency. Having maintained a certain thesis, the consciousness of having once assumed an attitude, or announced an opinion, constrains the omission of any expression of a contradiction of it. Yet the very act of announcing and defending a position exhausts the impulse momentarily, and a reaction inevitable ensues. In these letters this apparent inconsistency is frankly displayed. Having written two volumes of his first impressions and delights in the land of his adoption, one sees the enthusiast stretch himself after the long, cramping task, and exclaim with whimsical heartiness, "D—n the Japanese!"

How little he ever anticipated publicity for these frank outpourings of his feelings and thoughts is proved by just such outbursts. And, no doubt for that very reason, it has been through these fluent, unbridled expressions of the mutabilities of his moods that he has found so much wider and more appreciative an audience than he was able to reach in his life-time. Those who have come to know the richly human nature of the man have turned with new appetite to his serious, purposeful works.

Great letter-writers, like other artists, must needs have the original birth gift; but this gift, to ripen to complete fruition, requires certain fostering circumstances. Lacking these compelling forces, possessors of this charming art let it languish for want of constant use. Some loneliness of character or of circumstance there must be to make it a needed resource. Either shyness or a lack of the power of oral expression drives the letter-writer to his pen for the expression of his intimate self; or lack of sympathetic companionship obliges him to send his fancies far afield for that echo without which his thoughts seem to him as unresonant as "ditties of no tone."

Madame de Sévigné and Lord Chesterfield were both reputed stiff and dry in conversation. FitzGerald was exaggeratedly diffident. Lamb's family sorrows forced him to turn to others for intimate intercourse; and the same was true of Thackeray. Stevenson's long exile made his pen his best means of fellowship.

All these conditions combined to make of Lafcadio Hearn a creator of famous letters. His shyness was extreme. His life, from his nineteenth year, was a sojourn in foreign lands. Without family ties for twenty years, those ties, when formed in middle age, bound him to aliens in race and tongue. He never mastered Japanese sufficiently to express his thoughts freely and completely in the language of his wife and children. Though, as with most of the great letter-writers, literature was his profession, the writing of books is a formal expression: an episode in which the artist walks on cothurns, and speaks through a mask to a large, dimly realized audience. Intimate communication, mental companionship, could be had only by letters. Through this medium only could he find an adequate outlet for the crowding flood of his emotions, observations, and reflections. And through this vent he let them flow with astonishing fulness and intensity.

For one who wrote with such conscientious labour, such almost agonized care, the number and richness

Aet. 16

Lafcadio Hearn

of his letters is the more surprising. At times he wrote to some one of his correspondents almost daily, and at great length. After a day of teaching, or of many hours of drudgery at uncongenial journalism, he would bend himself to further long hours of intense toil at creative work, and at the end of all throw off page after page to some friend, describing his travels, retailing the touching or amusing incidents of the life about him, or discussing the books recently read; analyzing the condition of public affairs (some of his political predictions have been curiously verified), the trend of education, the characters of his associates. Little vignettes of men he had known would be sketched in a few lines of subtle and conclusive portraiture. Reminiscence of past impressions and experiences, philosophic speculation, daring psychological conjecture, criticism, comment, suggestion, were poured out, according to his mood, without stint or haste — as only the born letter-writer can find the energy and desire to do.

It has been maliciously suggested that Hearn "used his correspondent as a method of exercising his own fancy, as a gymnastics in putting his imagination through its paces, or for a preliminary sketching in of notes to be of possible use in later serious work." What is plainly evident is that he wrote in the "profuse strains of unpremeditated art," and as he wrote there was foreshadowed in these flying moments many of the points of serious interest occupying his attention, which in time fructified in his published work.

Certainly no one ever so completely revealed

every quality of his mind, his character, his modes
of thought, his opinions, interests, affections, and
convictions in a correspondence as did Lafcadio
Hearn. From his letters it would be possible for one
who had never known him to entirely reconstruct an
accurate account of his origin, early life, adventures, tendencies, and the gradual growth of his
mental and spiritual life. All that the average individual dissipates in spoken words is here indelibly
recorded. He painted his own portrait, builded his
own imperishable monument. The very fulness and
completeness of the record might, however, easily
leave him the prey of misinterpretation. Moods of
discouragement, of listlessness, of bitterness, of
doubt, of resentment, all find their expression.
Those black hours of self-chastisement, of acknow-
ledgement of failure and wrong, through which all
candid souls must pass when contemplating the
height of their generous ideals as contrasted with
the spiritual achievements realized, — which with
most of us evaporate in silence, — were by Hearn
set down in black and white. The rebellion of youth
against the old careful, dry wisdom of the world
instead of escaping in the froth of boy's talk, was
crystallized by his pen. Juvenile, unripe criticism
was thus saved. The ardours and passions, the
restlessness under middle-aged pudencies which
young men boastfully exchange, with hot cheeks
and shining eyes, over their first cigars, were dashed
down by this lonely lad at midnight in solitary
lodgings, to be preserved for as long as the world
remembers his name. All the languors, the curiosi-

ties, the wild flights of youthful fancy, all the fatigues, the disenchantments, the bitternesses of middle age,—such as volatilize with others in careless spoken confidence, — were given permanent form in his correspondence. It will always be possible for the stodgy or the malicious to misconstrue these intimate self-revelations. But happily alongside of these — to enlighten the wise and the sympathetic — are recorded as well the humilities, the reverence, the enthusiasms of youth; the constant growth toward nobility and strength as the years fled. And as time passes the ever-flowing deposition shows how the young soul sloughed its ignorances and weaknesses, and yearly grew calmer, larger, wiser, and tenderer.

It is very probable that in time these letters will come to be considered the greatest, the most valuable work of Lafcadio Hearn's life. Since in them is recorded, in a fashion very rare, very remarkable, a *Man*. They will be valued as one of the great human documents, one of the great human portraits of literature. Greater than the self-revealment of Rousseau's " Confessions," or Amiel's "Journal," because any "Confession" must be limited by a certain self-consciousness, a certain sense of literary form and continuity. Only in such letters — expressing the emotions and interests of the moment, thrown off with no sense of continuity, written to so many and various correspondents, and covering so long a period of time — could have been so artlessly and completely expressed a man's inmost, and always changing self. They are more interesting too than

the self-revelations of either Rousseau or Amiel,
because recording a so much more lovable, a so
much stronger character; depicting a man, despite
his marked personality, so much nearer in sympathy
with the average than either of his predecessors.
No parent can read Hearn's record of his love and
anxious care for his son without emotion — the
parental emotion that neither Amiel nor Rousseau
ever knew. No wife can become familiar with
Hearn's sacrifices for the happiness and safety of
his wife, his constant, tender, and reverent references to her, read his little affectionate daily notes,
when absent, to "Mama San," without respect and
admiration. No woman can read his letters to a
Japanese friend (pp. 415–422, Vol. II) without astonishment at his insight into the hearts of women.

His letters to his sister — unfortunately absent
from this collection — are a poignant revelation of
his long-expressed yearning for the ties of blood —
those ties worn so carelessly by the general. Though
seemingly recklessly abandoned by his mother his
every reference to her is instinct with protective,
forgiving love.

His letters to his friends, both men and women,
display a thousand charming qualities: — modesty,
affection, sympathy, gaiety, humour, and an unre-
flecting richness of giving of his mental and spiritual best, never stinted by the indolence or aridity
that desiccates so much of human intercourse.

The very highest notes of his capacity for both
good and error will probably never see the light.
Such complete revelations of the innermost quali-

ties of a human soul should, perhaps, always be spared the cold glare of printed publicity. Yet these deep lines "bring up" the self-painted portrait into the rounded vivid truth, and it is almost possible to regret that it is not desirable to give the pages in which he lays bare the potentialities of renunciation and courage within him, or to print the vitriolic resentment of which he was capable under a sense of injustice and wrong. — Both were very characteristic of his temperament — the capacity to sacrifice passion for an ideal of beauty and truth — the power of concentrated fury at offences over which the ordinary man would merely shrug an ironic shoulder.

It is one of the quaintest pranks of that incorrigible Jester, Fate, that this intimate portrait of Lafcadio Hearn should have unwittingly been drawn with his own pen. Nothing could have been further from his intention. Publicity was abhorrent to him in all matters relating to his own personality. He would have liked to be for the public only a voice issuing from the privacy of invisibility. He says somewhere, "I should wish to be merely a handful of dust in a little earthen pot, hid under the grass where no one knows." And had he ever dreamed that his letters might become famous they would never have been written. It would have seemed incredible to him that he could become a subject for myths; that his own voice should have been the one to arouse the critical world to open his books, and that his personality should so appeal to other men that it will probably remain a source of endless con-

tention, of ever-fresh interest, as the vivid personalities always do. Those strong peculiarly vital
natures for which death has no sting — over whom
the grave has no victory; in even whose ashes "live
their wonted fires."

It has been asked by those, not subjected to the
spell of his personality, in what consisted this compelling element? And what did he give to the world
in his completed work which constitutes a claim
upon its serious attention?

To endeavour to answer these quite legitimate
queries is the purpose of this introduction to the
third volume of his letters.

To analyze personality is always a difficult task.
It is a savour that must be tasted, a perfume inhaled,
a colour seen for one's self. — Neither perfume,
flavour, nor hue can be adequately conveyed by
words. — But the two most salient qualities of Lafcadio Hearn's personality may be separated from
the whole gamut of notes and defined as artistic
rectitude, and an unusual sensitiveness.

From the first his calling and election was sure.
Many find their life's real purpose by accident.
Their craft is driven by baffling airs along a half
dozen courses until the wind of destiny fills their
sails and sets them towards the preordained goal of
their being, but Hearn seems never to have suffered
from any uncertainty as to his task as an artificer in
words. Even his queer, helpless little endeavours at
business were only undertaken in the hope of buying
leisure for his real vocation; — he says in one place, —

"The problem of mere daily existence has all my life stared me in the face with eyes of iron." He was hardly more than a boy when he had formed an ideal of using the English language to express the warmth and colour of his thoughts, as he felt the modern masters of French prose had done in their own tongue. Gautier, Flaubert, de Musset, Hugo, were his models. The Victorians, with their large, careless, unacademic manner, had no charm for him. His desire was towards the ornate, the floriated, the exotic, but he wished to convey his sense of it by means exquisite, highly wrought, and perfectly finished. The creators of the French Gothic had the same spirit. Images monstrous, bizarre, grotesque, fascinated their imagination, but this was from no instinct of morbidness; they had the joy of the artist in these things; shaping them perfectly, delicately, lovingly, so that their great monuments had their large majestic lines wreathed with a thousand fantasies strange, terrible, and wholly beautiful. Hearn says, by the way, of Gothic architecture: — "It is the only architecture that is really alive. Victor Hugo perceived one phase of it; — not the beautiful, but the awful, — the sense it gives one of its being the skeleton of some tremendous animal. Certainly within it is all bone and tendon, jointings, articulations, ribbings, vertebræ, — processes fantastic and innumerable. Without, it is a hymn whose strophes rise and burn to heaven as flame, — it is a conflagration of aspirement in stone." The Japanese, whom he was to know so well, had also this sense of the strange and grotesque married with a love of perfection and exquisiteness in detail. Pater, speaking of this love of the romantics for the exotic, the grotesque, says: — "If the union of strangeness and beauty, under very difficult and complex conditions, be a successful one, if the union be entire, then the resultant beauty is very exquisite, very attractive. With a passionate care for beauty, the romantic spirit refuses to have it unless the condition of strangeness first be fulfilled. Its desire is for a beauty born of unlikely elements, by a profound alchemy, by a difficult initiation, by the charm which wrings it even out of terrible things."

The self-discipline of the artist who begrudges no pains for perfection, has grown rare, even in Japan. To our hurried age, which clamours for immediate, ponderable results, such patience seems wasteful and absurd. — (Noguchi speaks of his "spendthrift habit of thought and art.") — But Lafcadio Hearn appears never to have doubted of his real purpose. Throughout all his self-revelations, through the turmoil of the wavering dreams of youth, through discouragements, despairs, ill health, through the lapse of years, he never lost the vision of his ideal to do whatever he did perfectly. That he could count upon no recognition in his life-time, that what he had laboured upon seemed destined to be forgotten and ignored could not alter his intent. Another man driven in like manner inexorably by the Spirit had cried, "God help me, I can do no other !" . . .

This concentration, this intensity, this willing passionate labour to an end that brought him neither worldly goods (about $500 a year was the average income from his writings), nor in his life-time more than the slightest modicum of fame, is the vertebra of Lafcadio Hearn's character. Upon it all the rest of his personality is built. And this integration of purpose for an ideal end is so rare that the personality of which it is a dominant factor cannot be ignored. It is the same stuff out of which are made great scientists and great saints. To those who can see no purpose in giving one's whole life to attain artistic excellence in the expression of thought and emotion Lafcadio Hearn's personality will convey no meaning, in them it will awake no enthusiasm. All such feel a certain restlessness and resentment at the emotion this quality arouses in others. But those capable of being touched and stirred by such a nature will brush away the "impertinences" and find inspiration and stimulus in the personality of Lafcadio Hearn.

His sensitiveness — of which so much has been said — was an essential factor of his artistic conscience. What he felt with such extraordinary emotion, perceived with such clearness and intensity, could be adequately expressed only by supreme endeavour. No slovenly, careless methods could at all convey the depth and subtilty of such perceptions.

He was abnormally responsive to the faintest wind of beauty.

> Mon coeur est un luth suspendu,
> Sitôt qu'on le touche il resonne.

But those lute strings of his heart, keyed to an exquisite pitch, answered to the breathings of life only in the most delicate and intricate harmonies. No slurring, no slackness was tolerable to him. Nothing but pure tone — what the musicians call the just, or perfect temperament — was accepted.

The labour expended in trying a phrase over and over till it could express things seemingly inexpressible, was almost inconceivable to one who had never seen his original working manuscripts.

A friend wrote to him to express the peculiar pleasure awakened by the concluding paragraph of the paper on dragon-flies in the volume called "Kottō."

. . . "Then let me hope that the state to which I am destined will not be worse than that of a cicada or of a dragon-fly: — climbing the cryptomerias to clash my tiny cymbals in the sun, or haunting the holy silence of lotus pools with a soundless flicker of amethyst and gold." He replied that he had written and rewritten that conclusion seventeen times before he had been able to express to his own satisfaction the impression in his mind. And in one of his letters to Professor Chamberlain he says: —

"I could not make 150 printed 12mo pages in less than four months under very favourable circumstances and with the hardest work. Besides I was speaking of forced composition. Inspirational work, emotional work, is just twenty times harder if it can be measured at all. Too much importance cannot be attached to the value of emotion, — the 'kernel,' as you so aptly term it. But this comes only as a feeling. To perfectly disengage it (*le dégager*), develop it, discover its meaning, focus it, is killing work. There is delight in looking at the result, but that is obtained only by actually giving one's blood for it." . . .

Noguchi says of Hearn: —

"Writing was for him no light work, *he wrote with his life and blood.*"

How steeped he became in words, how they grew for him to have the quality of actual objects with form and colour, he explains in one of his letters — a letter which, by the way, is a delightful example of his gay intoxication with an idea. A verbal inebriation more often exhibited in conversation with his intimates towards the small hours of the night, when the fumes of words mounted to his brain, and he bewitched his hearers with the bubbling flow of his talk — his shyness momentarily forgotten.

. . . For me words have colour, form, character: They have faces, ports, manners, gesticulations; — they have moods, humours, eccentricities: — they have tints, tones, personalities. That they are unintelligible makes no difference at all. Whether you are able to speak to a stranger or not, you can't help being impressed by his appearance sometimes, — by his dress, — by his air, — by his exotic look. He is also unintelligible, but not a whit less interesting. Nay he is interesting BECAUSE he is unintelligible. — I won't cite other writers who have felt the same way about African, Chinese, Arabian, Hebrew, Tartar, Indian and Basque words, — I mean novelists and sketch-writers.

To such it has been justly observed: — "The

readers do not feel as you do about words. They can't be supposed to know that you think the letter A is blush-crimson, and the letter E pale sky-blue. They can't be supposed to know that you think KH wears a beard and a turban; that the initial X is a mature Greek with wrinkles; — or that ' — NO—' has an innocent, lovable, and childlike aspect." All this is true from the critic's standpoint.

But from ours, — the standpoint of —

> — the Dreamer of Dreams
> To whom what is and what seems
> Is often one and the same, —

to us the idea is thus: —

Because people cannot see the colour of words, the tints of words, the secret ghostly motions of words; —

Because they cannot hear the whispering of words, the rustling of the procession of letters, the dream-flutes and dream-drums which are thinly and weirdly-played by words; —

Because they cannot perceive the pouting of words, the frowning and fuming of words, the weeping, the raging and racketing and rioting of words; —

Because they are insensible to the phosphorescing of words, the fragrance of words, the noisomeness of words, the tenderness or hardness, the dryness or juiciness of words, — the interchange of values in the gold, the silver, the brass and the copper of words, —

Is that any reason why we should not try to make them hear, to make them see, to make them feel? —

Surely one who has never heard Wagner, cannot appreciate Wagner without study. *Why* should the people not be forcibly introduced to foreign words, — as they were introduced to tea and coffee and tobacco?

Unto which the friendly reply is, — "Because they *won't* buy your book, and you won't make any money."

And I say: — "Surely I have never yet made, and never expect to make any money. Neither do I expect to write ever for the multitude. I write for beloved friends who can see colour in words, can smell the perfume in syllables in blossom, can be shocked with the fine elfish electricity of words. And in the eternal order of things, words will eventually have their rights recognized by the people."

All this is heresy. But a bad reason, you will grant, is better than — &c.

Faithfully,
LAFCADIO HEARN.

All of his published works, the whole of his great mass of letters is a record of sensitiveness of perception of life, of ideas, of the visible and invisible world.

Maimed in his vision while still a lad almost to the point of blindness, Hearn struggled the rest of his years with myopia, and walked always in terror of imminent darkness. Yet the general sense left upon the mind by his whole body of work is of colour. The brain behind those eyes so near to incompetence was a *seeing* mind, and through an in-

INTRODUCTION

efficient medium he perceived, as few men have done, every iridescence of his surroundings. Not a shimmer or a glory escaped him. From his books might be gathered a delightful anthology of the beauty of tint, of form, of shadow, of line. No loveliness was too subtle, too evanescent, too minute, to be recognized by those dim and straining eyes.

And in his letters, again and again, some fairness, so fine as to go unperceived by the stronger-visioned, is commented upon with pleasure. His perception of the delicate groove in the Japanese eyelid, mentioned in one of the letters of this volume, is one of those feats of observation which so often startled his better-sighted but duller-visioned friends. Again, note his "living statues of gold, with *blue hair*, like the Carib half-breeds."

One with the patient curiosity to follow up these revelations of a sort of "second-sight," of delicate intensity, throughout his writings, might find almost sufficient testimony to prove that only through his myopic eyes could one learn wholly to see the complete beauty of our earth.

Nor was it alone the things small and near he saw. What Mrs. Hearn quaintly calls his "nose-glass" was in constant use for immediate objects, and she comments upon the extreme quickness of his observation. One glance through it appeared to give him a thousand details. In his pocket he constantly carried a small, but quite powerful folding telescope, which also made him intimate with the distance. Through it he marked all the aerial glories of tropic

days, all the "sweet glamours," the "translucence
milky and soft" of Japan. Pages 140–141 in the first
volume of "Glimpses of Unfamiliar Japan," show
how he could see and feel a landscape.

. . . "Roused thus by these earliest sounds of the
city's wakening life, I slide open my little Japanese
paper window to look out upon the morning over a
soft green cloud of spring foliage rising from the
river-bounded garden below. Before me, tremu-
lously mirroring everything upon its farther side,
glimmers the wide glassy mouth of the Ohashigawa,
opening into the great Shinji lake, which spreads
out broadly to the right in a dim grey frame of
peaks. Just opposite me across the stream, the
blue-pointed Japanese dwellings have their *to* all
closed; they are still shut up like boxes for it is not
yet day.

"But oh, the charm of the vision, — those first
ghostly love colours of a morning steeped in mist
soft as sleep itself resolved into a visible exhalation!
Long reaches of faintly-tinted vapour cloud the far
lake verge, — long nebulous bands, such as you may
have seen in old Japanese picture-books, and must
have deemed only artistic whimsicalities unless you
had previously looked upon the real phenomena.
All the bases of the mountain are veiled by them,
and they stretch athwart the loftier peaks at different heights like immeasurable lengths of gauze . . .
so that the lake appears larger than it really is, and
not an actual lake, but a beautiful spectral sea of
the same tint as the dawn-sky and mixing with it,
while peak tips rise like islands from the brume . . .

an exquisite chaos, ever changing aspect as the delicate fogs rise, slowly, very slowly.

"As the sun's yellow rim comes into sight, fine thin lines of a warmer tone — spectral violets and opalines — shoot across the flood, treetops take tender fire, and the unpainted façades of high edifices across the water change their wood colour to vapoury gold through the delicious haze.

"Looking sunward up the long Ohashigawa, beyond the many-pillared wooden bridge, one high pooped junk, just hoisting sail, seems to me the most fantastically beautiful craft I ever saw, — a dream of Orient seas, so idealized by the vapour is it; the ghost of a junk, but a ghost that catches the light as clouds do; a shape of gold mist, seemingly semi-diaphanous, and suspended in pale blue light."

But not by vision alone did he receive his multitudinous impressions. His writings are full of an almost equally surprising sensibility to sounds — to voices of frogs, of birds, of insects, of animals, of human beings, of winds, and more than all of bells. In many places he speaks of these, and in "Kwaidan" he says: —

" . . . In the boom of the big bell there is a tone which wakens feelings so strangely far away from all the nineteenth-century part of me, that the faint blind stirrings of them make me afraid. Never do I hear the billowing peal but I become aware of a stirring and a fluttering in the abyssal part of my ghost, — a sensation as of memories struggling to reach the light beyond the obscuration of a million deaths and births. . . ."

There are constant records in his writings of odours and perfumes. Of smells of flowers and herbs, smells of fruits, smells of flesh, of races, of incense, of old books, of all the thousand intimations seized upon by keen and delicate olfactories. And he possessed an equal tactile susceptibility to the touch of waters, of leaves, of air, of stuffs, even of bodies; — he remarks upon the coldness of the skins of negroes and other tropic peoples as compared with those of races of the temperate zone, though the blood of the former has a permanently higher temperature.

This extraordinary percipiency of all the senses means, of course, that the mind behind them is of such activity as to constantly demand of them their highest efforts, and by their help "such a brain can daily receive billions of impressions that common minds cannot receive in a whole life-time." . . .

Every quality must have its defects, and the penalty of high mental and nervous organization is a greater capacity for pain, as for pleasure. Every door of sense and perception being so wide open it was inevitable that the dweller within should be peculiarly defenceless against the harsh or inimical elements of existence. The natural, inevitable result was an exaggerated timidity and shyness, a tendency to suspect evil intention where there was merely rough good-nature, or, at the worst, carelessness. And being without claws and talons himself he fled in horror from those so armed, or became the helpless prey of the fanged members of human society. This was the reason he so dreaded and distrusted the Western world with its stern ruthless

mêlée of competitive democracy. This was why he
found such peace and safety, and a new power of
expansion in that last survival of the old feudal life
of Japan at Izumo, with its protected and ordered
social organization from which the struggle for life
was in so large a measure eliminated, and the fine
amenities of daily intercourse were raised to a lovely
art.

Had Hearn's life been happy and fortunate no
doubt this extreme of sensitiveness would have
gradually adapted itself better to its environment.
But the cruel experiences of his youth only exacer-
bated it, until he found himself driven to seek peace
and safety in solitude; driven to evading even his
friends. Those who really loved him understood the
necessity of his being what he was, and realized that
the very qualities that made him rare and valuable
required on their part a special patience and delicate tenderness. They remembered that the bubble
which mirrors with magic veracity and prismatic
beauty a whole landscape is destroyed by a rude
or careless touch. . . .

Much of the unhappiness of his life was caused by
his own comprehension of his lack of capacity to fit
easily into the social organization, for his affections
were as ardent and keen as his perceptions, and he
cries with poignant regret and yearning in one of his
letters: —

. . . "No one ever lived who seemed more a
creature of circumstance than I; I drift with various
forces in the line of least resistance, resolve to love
nothing, and love always too much for my own

peace of mind, — places, things, and persons, — and lo! presto! everything is swept away, and becomes a dream, like life itself. Perhaps there will be a great awakening; and each will cease to be an Ego: become an All, and will know the divinity of man by seeing, as the veil falls, himself in each and all."

And again he says: —

"Perhaps the destiny of all is to be molten by that mighty Image-maker, Death, into some great, sweet, passionless unity."

But hopeless of any happy union with the hurrying, indifferent, rough-fibred world, in which he was constantly at fault, constantly stumbling and being wounded, he hid himself more and more from it, and built himself a castle of silence and solitude where no one was admitted.

Yone Noguchi, the Japanese poet, in his "Appreciation" of Hearn has understood and explained. He says: —

"He threw the world and people out, and shut himself in his own sanctum, as you have to close the *shojis* after you have burned incense to keep its odour . . . his only desire was to be left alone with his dreams, and the dreams themselves were ghosts, under whose spell he wove the silvery threads of the ideal, and wrote the books with the strange thrill which no one else could ever feel."

Comparing him to Akinari Uyeda, the Japanese, who also sought a shrine of solitude, Noguchi says: —

"I say that the grey-coloured region of solitude was a triumph for them, not a defeat by any means; they found life in silence, and a ghost's virtue in

shadow and whisper. They slowly walked following
after a beckoning hand of the oldest incense, half a
vision and half a reality; they placed their single-
minded confidence on the dream-breast of the
spirit, and sought their own emancipation."

It is because the personality of Lafcadio Hearn
was pitched upon this keen, sustained, and penetrating note that it cannot be considered with indifference. As every object is said to have a musical
key, to which it will vibrate when that key is struck,
so every nature has its essential *timbre*, and can only
answer to its own fundamental. If a nature be out
of harmony with such an individuality as Hearn's
no explanation will bring the two into scale.

To answer the inquiry as to what the writer gave
to the world of ideas, as apart from his artistry in
style, what he has done to give him a claim to the
serious respect of thinkers, is an easier task than to
analyze his personality.

First of all may be offered his eighteen volumes as
sufficient reply. But eighteen volumes of any man's
work must contain portions properly negligible, and
comparatively few have time to sift and weigh it,
and draw a broad conclusion as to the value and
permanence of so large a body of achievement.

The first and perhaps always most dominant
quality of his work is its innate beauty, its sensuous
imagery. Though not an American, Hearn ranked
as an American writer, and formed his style and
learned his art in this country. And it is precisely in
those two elements that American literature most

lacks — in innate beauty and sensuous imagery.
Poe alone, of all our native writers, has had that
passion for assonance, for melodious words for their
own sake, for velvety undertones, for plangent
phrases, for canorous orismology. American writers
have almost never been masters in the technique of
their art. And their audience has scarcely missed it,
being more interested in life than in literature. Stevenson says that "A taste for the precise, the adroit,
or the comely in the use of words comes late." But
Hearn had always a passion for it. He sought un-
weariedly not only for *le mot juste*, but also for *le
mot et la pensée belle;* loved an alliteration; delighted
in onomatopœic phrases — such as in "Chita:" —
. . . "And interweaving with it all, one continu-
ous shrilling — keen as the steel speech of a saw —
the stridulous telegraphy of crickets."

He wrought with an artist's amorous patience to
find expression for the splendours of the pageants
of tropic skies — "the toppling and smouldering
of cloud-worlds after the enormous conflagrations
of sunsets, — incandescence ruining into darkness;
and after it a moving and climbing of stars among
the blacknesses, — like searching lamps." —

He sought for a vocal echo of the prodigious
Voices of the winds and the waters — "the witch-
call of Storms." "Chita" is but a long sonorous
sea-hymn. —

He endeavoured to reproduce in words the fire
of jewels, the clang of swords, the beauty of women,
the agonies of love and of death; bringing to our
literature, always rather dry and thin, the element

it lacked of passion, of ardour, of prodigality of music and loveliness.

American literature has always been afraid of the sensuous; has suffered nervous discomfort in the presence of passion. Its Puritan element has never been quite able to disassociate sensuousness from sensuality, passion from sexual license, and there is a tendency among some of Hearn's critics to pinch their lips, shake their heads, and hint at the connection between the two; to talk of abnormality and "decadence," or "sexual preoccupation." No charge could be more monstrously unjust. He has written ardently of the beauty of women — as in "The Making of Tilottama," (— it may be submitted that there is nothing innately immoral in woman's beauty —) but his preoccupation with all visible fairness is the most salient character of his genius, and a careful study of his books and of his great mass of letters will show that he is singularly free from all grossness — not once in any word of his, written or printed, is found the leer of the ape, the repulsive grin of the satyr. He wrote of women with even less passion than of light, of sound, of colour, of perfume. And he always wrote of them with tenderness. In a letter to Osman Edwards he says, apropos of Loti's "Madame Chrysanthème:" —

"There is not much heart in Loti; but there is a fine brain; and there is a nervous system so extraordinary that it forces imagination back to the conditions of old Greek life, when men had senses more perfect than now. Very possibly this Julian Viaud

has in his veins old blood of Magna Græcia. No
other literary man living sees and hears and smells
and thrills so finely as he; we are in presence of a
being of immeasurably superior organization —
therefore exceedingly unhappy in this world of the
nineteenth century. I doubt whether he has ever
loved, or could love — in our sense. But I think we
must study him as a creature apart.

"As for what he says of Japanese women, it is
perfectly, impeccably accurate so far as it consists
of observations of sense. Loti's senses can never err
any more than a film on a photographic plate with
a sensibility of one hundred. But he keeps to the
surfaces; his life is of surfaces. Almost in the way
that some creatures have their skeletons outside of
themselves instead of inside, so his plexuses of feeling are. — What the finer nature of the Japanese
woman is, no man has told. Those who know cannot tell: it would be too much like writing of the
sweetness of one's own sister or mother. One must
leave it in sacred silence — with a prayer to all the
gods."

In another letter to Professor Edwards he says: —

"This reminds me of Pierre Louys — have you
not noticed the tendency to *cruelty* in his work? I
delight in normal healthy sensualism — or sensuousness, at least, but that is always ideal in its emotional life — therefore tender, and therefore partly
unselfish. The other tendency seems (in modern times
at least) toward necrophily — Altruism is perhaps a
test of the question whether anything is artistic in
the true sense — Does a book, or a picture, or a

statue, or music fill you with a generous desire to
sacrifice self for the sake of an ideal, a principle or
a person? The first recognition of a girl's beauty
does this for the average healthy young man. A
work of art ought to do the same thing — help to
make us unselfish. The youth wants the girl of
course, but he is willing to die for her — to cut off
his hand for her sake. Well, a work of art ought to
stir the sensuous life in us, the life of desire in a
healthy way, but ought it not also at the same time
to make us feel that there are things which it were
beautiful to die for?'"

It is not in this manner — and a hundred passages
of like tone might be quoted — that the sensualist
writes of woman.

As always, the best statement about his own attitude toward the tendency of the school of decadence has been made by himself — also in letters to
Professor Edwards: —

"I fear I am a hopelessly insensible man to the
decadent movement. I believe that Hugo and Baudelaire and the matchless Gautier exhausted the
real capacities of language in French poetry — just
as Rossetti and Swinburne have done in English
romantic poetry, and that no amount of ingenious
effort will produce really new effects until the language itself becomes vastly enriched. And I must
confess that I love lucidity, sharpness, firm, hard
outline — the style of the 'Emaux et Camées.'"

But vagueness was the least heinous of the qualities which aroused his antipathy. He expressed
himself as "angry and disheartened" with "Poètes
d'Aujourd'hui," and thus pronounced anathema: —

"The new poetry is simply rotten! — morally and otherwise. I am not prudish: I still think Gautier's 'Musée Secret' (in the 'Souvenirs' of Émile Bergerat) the finest poem of an artistic kind in the French or in any other language. But there is in it a splendid something entirely absent from the new poetry — the joy of life. There is no joy in this new world — and scarcely any tenderness: the language is the language of art, but the spirit is of Holbein and Gothic ages of religious madness. I do not know that poetry ought to be joyous, in a general way; there is beauty in pain and sorrow. Only, — is ugliness or pain, without beauty, a subject worthy of poetry? (I am not including subjects of cosmic emotion in the question.) 'Ionica' — a rare English example of exquisite grace and loveliness in melancholy — contains a dozen little pieces, any one of which is worth all the pieces in 'Poètes d'Aujourd'hui:' I think it illustrates what I mean. What has neither joy nor beauty, nor the power of bestirring any great quality or volume of emotion, any cosmic feeling or generous feeling, ought not such a matter to be excluded from poetry proper? . . .

"I re-read every year the best of Anatole France. His 'Thais' I have had but a short time; yet I am never tired of reading it over and over by fits and starts. So, too, with the 'Rôtisserie de la Reine Pédauque' — and the priceless volumes of short stories and sketches — I now never buy a book that I cannot feel sure of wanting to re-read. That is a test of which the value must be relative — must depend upon temperament; but I doubt if there be a better.

There are dangers, I suppose, in the freedom enjoyed by French letters. But, after all, I imagine that English and American training suppress too successfully the life of the senses. Are we not really more barbarous than the Latins — at least than Italians and French? Surely our language is less perfect than theirs — though perhaps stronger to express all that relates to force and profundity. What Englishman or American could write a book like 'Thais' or the 'Rôtisserie de la Reine Pédauque'? And yet — happily be it said — no Englishman or American could or would write such a thing as 'Aphrodite' or the 'Bilitis' of Louys. 'Thais' is an immortal book — an ironical psychological study beyond all parallel. 'Aphrodite' and 'Bilitis' are crimes. I feel they are. (Why? I think it is because they are totally unsuggestive, and written by will.) And the same freedom that permits, and ought to permit, 'Thais,' when unrestrained by the real sense of higher art, produces necessarily 'Bilitis' or 'Aphrodite.' There is the ethical difficulty. Taine says that the powerful Northern temperament renders it impossible for Englishmen to dare what the Latin can do with ease, safety, and grace. Probably he was right. But what would he have said to the publication of 'Bilitis'?"

In one of the letters in this volume he says, — and a recent episode makes it curiously apposite, —

"Why do we feel that a poet like William Watson has no right to be a mocker, to say cruel things to his fellow man? We feel the same in reading Tennyson's terrible satire on Bulwer-Lytton, and Browning's brutal anger at FitzGerald. I think we regard it as we regard an obscene poem by a priest, or in other words, a sort of sacrilege to self. We have not learned — (as I think we shall some day) — to confess aloud that the highest poetry is a religion, and its world priests the true prophets and teachers. But we feel it. Therefore we are shocked and pained when these betray any sign of those paltry and mean passions above which their art at other times lifts us."

And to another friend he wrote, — speaking of the artist, —

"What is his duty in the external order of things to art and to ethics? Is it not to extract the gold from the ore, — the rubies and emeralds from the rubble? I think it is. What I would pray you to do is to put a lily in the mouth of Hell. Then the petals of the lily will change into pure light, like those of the lotus of Amida Buddha."

Osman Edwards says of him: —

"The absence of tenderness could not be atoned for by any verbal dexterities in the judgement of Lafcadio Hearn. Throughout his own books, like inextricable golden threads, the twin emotions of joy and tenderness lend meaning and unity to the vaguest and driest of themes. There is always a hinted kindness, a suggested sympathy in explanation or allusion, which links his study of impersonal facts with warm humanity."

As his character cleared and crystallized with years his love of beauty deepened through the vis-

ible to the invisible. Behind the outward veil he
perceived "the inward and spiritual grace," of
which the envelope was but the radiant simulacrum.
He perceived moral as vividly as he did sensuous
beauty, and his works are in large part tender chronicles of sympathy with humble virtues; chronicles of
pity, of courage, of loyalty, simplicity and kindness.
Such as "A Street Singer," "The Nun of the Temple of Amida," "Les Porteuses," and many, many
more. And woven all about these compassionate
tales of the pains and sorrows, of the goodness and
bravery of life are endless limnings of bees and ants,
of frogs and birds, of butterflies and flowers, of lights
and shadows, of music and dreams — as the early
Italian painters wound around their pictures, in
mere exuberance of creation, those lovely garlands
of green and purple grapes, of sun-burnt pomegran-
ates, of roses and laurels, of lizards and peacocks.

Because of all these loving reproductions of little
humble beauties, and because of the delicacy of his
method in treating of them there is a frequently expressed impression that the scope of his interest was
limited generally to small, half-negligible things. That

> Lips that blow through bronze can breathe through silver

is always hard to believe, and because he would rewrite seventeen times an impression of the jewelled
play of colour on a dragon-fly's wing one may deduce
the conclusion that he was therefore incompetent
to deal with the larger, sterner matters. Out of so
much that might be quoted to the contrary is chosen
this extract from the essay on "Dust:"

. . . "Remember, man, thou art but dust — Ah! but dust remember thou hast been Sun, and Sun thou shalt become again — Thou hast been Light, Life, Love; — and into all these by ceaseless cosmic magic thou shalt many times be turned again! For this Cosmic Apparition is more than evolution alternating with dissolution: it is infinite metempsychosis; it is perpetual palingenesis.

"Suns yield up their ghosts of flame; but out of their graves new suns rush into being. Corpses of worlds pass all to some solar funeral pyre; but out of their own ashes they are born again.

"This earth must die: her seas shall be Saharas. But those seas once existed in the Sun; and their dead tides, revived by fire, shall pour their thunders upon the coasts of another world. Transmigration — transmutation: these are not fables. What is impossible? Not the dreams of alchemists and poets, dross indeed may be changed to gold, the jewel to the living eye, the flower into flesh.

"What is impossible? If seas can pass from sun to world, from world to sun again, what of the dust of dead selves — dust of memory and thought. Resurrection there is — resurrection more stupendous than any dreamed of by Western creeds — Dead hearts will live again as surely as dead suns and moons —"

Which demonstrates that his lips could blow through bronze too.

But all this, — his delicate fashionings in the jewels and ductile gold of words, his passion and sensuous

imagery, his discernment of humble goodness, of
the pathos and beauty of so many unconsidered
persons and things, his dreams of the great cosmic
flux of the universe, — are not his only claims upon
the consideration of thinkers.

Much has been written about Japan, varying in
value and point of view. Loti's "Madame Chrysanthème" was one of the first attempts to interpret to
the West the qualities and characteristics of an almost unknown people which aroused any general
interest and attention. It was however a record of
more or less superficial impressions, important because of being the work of an artist and a subtle
impressionist. Professor Percival Lowell's "The
Soul of the Far East" struck a deeper note because
the author was a scientist, who was also a man of
imagination. Despite some assertions to the contrary it was these two books — for the second of
which Hearn conceived a passionate admiration —
and some conversations with a friend recently returned from Japan, which decided his removal to
that country. At first a mere expedition in search
of literary material was planned. He had no glim-
mering of the great work fate had set him to do. In
fact it is doubtful whether he ever fully realized the
importance of what he had done; how serious was
his task, and how adequately he accomplished it.

It has been many times rather cynically pointed
out that his first delight and enthusiasm was later
cooled, and occasionally was subject to violent reactions, — and this it is hinted is a sign of want of
stability and judgement. One might as reasonably

demand that a lover should remain always at the pitch of fervour of the bridal morn. His first book — "Glimpses of Unfamiliar Japan" — is a record of this first intoxication, and though he grew sometimes to doubt if it was wholly justified, yet he always differentiated between the spirit of the old feudal Japan which still lingered in Izumo, and which he never ceased to love, and Japan playing at jiujutsu with the Occident, grasping at the weapons of the West to defend herself from its encroachments, and conquering her enemy by yielding to those Western tendencies which he so heartily detested. Yone Noguchi says of this early work: — "It spoke in perfect accord with the sweet glamour of old Japan, where the sea of reality and the sky of vision melted into one blue eternity," — and in speaking of the vanishing in Hearn of that first "Horai" (Vision of the Intangible) Noguchi says, — with a quaint foreignness, — "His Horai, where the shadows of splendour strange and old deepened under the sunlight, sad like memory, and the milky vision hung like an immense spider-web, and shivered like a ghost, and the sadness and joy of the soul of thousands on thousands of years blended into an infinite waste of song, vanished at once when he left old Japan in Izumo — the place of his love first and last."

Had this early passion of enthusiasm been all, we should have had a beautiful vision poetically recorded, and no more.

It is difficult now to recall — in the greater diffusion of knowledge of that so long Hidden Kingdom

— how entirely ignorant of everything concerning Japan were even well-educated Westerners in 1890. Nine out of every ten vaguely thought of it as a sort of an outlying province of China, and if they reflected upon the matter at all, wondered why Commodore Perry had taken the trouble to force a lot of little half-savage "yellow monkeys" to open their ports to trade. Gilbert and Sullivan's comic opera "The Mikado" was about the only "document" with which the multitude was at all familiar. Loti's and Lowell's books had been studied only by those avid of the exotic. Miss Bird's travels and Professor Chamberlain's Japanese studies had appealed mainly to the explorer, the ethnologist, and the student of Oriental art. The missionaries had disseminated the impression that these were a people almost entirely without a religion, and the merchants trading in their ports declared them without exception liars and thieves. There were some more instructed, of course. The artists had begun to study their drawings, ceramics, and carvings with the keenest delight and interest, and travellers reported the country full of enchantment, but the impression of the general was as vague and mistaken as has been indicated.

"Glimpses of Unfamiliar Japan" was the first book concerning Japan written with a sympathetic endeavour to interpret, from their own point of view, those unknown people to the Western world; was the first book which attempted to picture with intimate tenderness the remains of the feudal civilization so recently superseded, without understanding

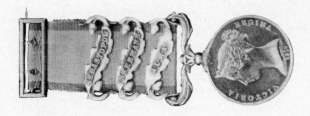

CRIMEAN WAR MEDALS

Received for gallantry by Surgeon Major Charles B. Hearn

of which there can be no comprehension of the race, and the forces which had moulded it. The book had no sensational popularity, but its sufficiently numerous readers laid it down with an entirely new idea of Japan and the Japanese.

The "Glimpses" was printed in 1895, and every year of the following ten saw issued one or more volumes — twelve in all — devoted in the main to the interpretation of Japan to the West.

Had this work been undertaken with a definite design its character would have probably been very unlike the form it instinctively assumed, but whether it would have been more valuable, have been so great an achievement, may be open to doubt.

It was built up almost unconsciously; bit by bit — an excursion here, a study there; a passing impression recorded, investigations as apparently unrelated as "The Eternal Feminine" — as seen by the Japanese — and a study of the poems on frogs. It was made up of apparently disconnected pictures of the life of the people, their superstitions, their witchcraft, their dogs, the children's games, the education of the young, their manners, their crimes, their agriculture, — seemingly a mass of uncorrelated fragments having no plan or purpose until the whole was at last summed up in "Japan: An Attempt at an Interpretation." Then it was to be seen that these results of fourteen years of seemingly desultory labour had become perhaps the completest record ever made by one man alone of the life of a race and a people. The whole stood out a rounded

and complete figure; became a reproduction of a
civilization as remote from us as the life of the
Greeks three thousand years ago. It is, no doubt,
hardly yet understood how important so complete
a presentation of this race is to the sum of our knowledge. What Japan may portend is as yet but dimly
adumbrated. For this civilization, unlike all others,
has voluntarily grafted upon its main trunk the
knowledge and power worked out through ages of
blood and struggle by other peoples. And the graft
has flourished beyond credibility, nourished by the
strong sap of a folk who had stored up an enormous
vitality in peaceful seclusion, while the evolution of
that borrowed mechanical and scientific knowledge
was being achieved at tremendous cost by the races
from which it was adopted.

To analyze the completeness and profundity of
Lafcadio Hearn's study of Japan would require
more space than is here available. He was the first
to divine the granitic quality at the core of the Japanese people, while as yet the outside world saw
only the silken envelope of their manners. In the
paper on "Japanese Civilization" in "Kokoro"
(written fifteen years since) he discerned what he
described as the *fluidity* of that civilization, and its
consequent ability to achieve great results with
small expenditure for tools and means. An acumen
since abundantly demonstrated. And of these people, whom ignorant missionaries had described as
practically without religion, he showed that they,
more than any of the Occidental peoples, had been
moulded and shaped almost wholly by their creeds.

The strange contradictions to be found in the Western civilization have been largely the result of the fact that its religion for the last two thousand years has been an imported, an adopted creed; not sprung from the genius of the European race, and therefore always a garment in which the wearers have moved not entirely at their ease. A people's religion being that people's attempt to explain to themselves the phenomena of the world in which they find themselves, and a code of moral laws suited to the needs of their special existence, Hearn set himself ardently against all attempts to impose foreign creeds upon Japan, which he perceived had worked out for herself a cult peculiarly adapted to the character of her consciousness.

Few Europeans have been so fitted to comprehend the fundamental meaning of the Japanese cult as Hearn.

Every thinker appears to have some one master thought; some dominant prepossession that for him colours all life, which is the key word of the language of his mind. Professor Chamberlain says that no one could understand Lafcadio Hearn who did not take into account his belief in Ghosts. Naturally Professor Chamberlain does not mean the gibbering, clanking spooks of Anne Radcliffe, nor the banjo-playing, squeaking, clammy-handed materializations of the spiritualists' cabinet. But the word "ghosts" appears a thousand times in Hearn's books, in endless association with all his thoughts. Already, when hardly more than a boy, he begins to talk of heredity, — of "the Race-Ghost." Be-

gins puzzling over those blind instincts and tendencies, those strange impulses, desires, and memories
that well up from the unknown deeps within us and
startle by their lack of relation with our outward
consciousness. Already he begins to ponder over
what the psychologists now attempt to define as the
"subliminal self."

As long ago as 1882 we find him saying: —

"Why these longings for lands in which we shall
never be? — why this desire for that azure in which
we cannot soar? — Whence our mysterious love for
the tumultuous deep into whose emerald secrets we
may never peer? . . . Can it be that through countless epochs of the immemorial phylogenesis of man,
— through all those myriad changes suggested
by the prenatal evolution of the human heart, —
through all the slow marvellous transitions from fish
to mammal, — there have actually persisted impulses, desires, sensations, whereof the enigma may
be fully interpreted by some new science only, a
future science of psychical dysteleology? . . ."

Because of this prepossession — at that time far
less common to the Occidental mind than it is to-day
— he found himself at once in sympathy with the
dreams of Buddha, with the ancestral worship of
the Shinto faith. To understand him at all it must
be understood that Lafcadio Hearn was a mystic —
not a mystic in the ordinary pietistic acceptance,
but one seeking forever to discern the permanent
behind the impermanent; the noumena behind the
phenomena. Straining to touch the ultimate significance of the visible; to know the essence of that

phantasm of beauty by which his soul was so bewitched; to lay hold upon the secret cord upon
which all being is strung.

Perhaps all mysticism has its origin in just such
acute hypersensitiveness of the perceptions as was
his. Phenomena impact upon such senses so acutely
as to suggest more than the merely obvious; it hints
to them of forces more tremendous than the form
and demonstration of the phenomena.

In the prescientific period such Sensitives shrank
from this impact into the protection of asceticism —
the natural armour against too vivid feeling — and
sought intellectual satisfaction in conceptions of that
prodigious force as the emanations of some divine
super-man whose personality absorbed and blotted
out their own. A deity to whose will and whose
dominance they yielded their minds and hearts
with a passionate loyalty of self-abandonment.

Hearn came too late for this anthropomorphic
vision to satisfy his intelligence. Scientific knowledge of the real size of the universe had made it impossible for his imagination to cast upon the deeps
of space any enlarged shadow of humanity as the
source of nature; any vast eidolon of man as the
fount from which the universe had sprung. His
imagination was too bold to need a personification
as a necessary form for this force. He could think of
it as without individuality. The child can hardly
conceive of thunder other than as the voice or movement of a mighty being, but the man recognizes it as
merely enormous vibrations following inevitable
laws of diacoustics. So this modern mystic sought

for his noumenon in a conception of evolution, in a dream of a prodigious systole and diastole of the universe through infinite metempsychosis.

Because of this character of his mind he found in Herbert Spencer — who was in this sense the Arch-Mystic of science — the terminology of his imaginings. Because of this Spencer's theories remained always to him the ultimate revelation of truth, and he resented any doubts of the philosopher's postulates.

Hearn's attitude to women, so misinterpreted by vulgar minds, had its origin in this mystic sense of her being the channel of heredity. In a sense of the tenderness of eternal motherhood in her smile, of the transmission of a million caresses in her fairness — a fairness which had blossomed through the nurturing warmth of endless aspiration toward beauty and love.

It may be suggested, too, that his delight in all the little humble forms of life was a part of this quality, shared by other mystics, such as he of Assisi, who found his universal intimations of divinity in even his "Little Brothers," the birds; in even the stones to whom he preached salvation.

Because of this trend of his thinking the genius of the Oriental faiths was sympathetic to Hearn. His belief in the eternal flux of life, the ever reincarnated spirit, which to his Western contemporaries had seemed the merest fantasy of a dreamer, was in the East a matter of course, a conviction self-evident and needing no defence. The Orient's cosmic intuitions, evolved through a hundred centuries of

infinite spiritual travail — those prodigious intuitions of the essential oneness of the universe, of the
enormous circle and unbroken continuity of life —
which we are vaguely beginning to perceive, and
stumblingly endeavouring to find terminology for,
his mind leaped forward to grasp and define.

He says: —

"Merely by reason of illusion and folly do we
shrink from the notion of self-instability. For what
is our individuality? Most certainly it is not individuality at all: it is multiplicity incalculable.
What is the human body? A form built up out of
billions of living entities, an impermanent agglom-
eration of individuals called cells. And the human
soul? — a composite of quintillions of souls — we
are each and all infinite compounds of fragments of
anterior lives — and the universal process that continually dissolves and continually constructs personality has always been going on, and is even at
this moment going on in every one of us. What
being ever had a totally new feeling, an absolutely
new idea? All our emotions and thoughts and
wishes, however changing and growing through the
varying seasons of life, are only compositions and
recompositions of the sensations and ideas and desires of other folk, mostly of dead people, — millions
and billions of dead people — *I* an individual, — an
individual soul! Nay, I am a population — a population unthinkable for multitude, even by groups of
a thousand millions! Generations of generations I
am, æons of æons! Countless times the concourse
now making me has been scattered, and mixed with

other scatterings. Of what concern then the next
disintegration?

"Perhaps after trillions of ages of burning in
different dynasties of suns, the best of me may come
together again." . . .

We shall wait long, I fear, before the sidereal
winds, blowing the dust of worlds round and round
the long roads of the universe, shall bring together
again the atoms that made this man. This shy,
wild, beautiful spirit that was Lafcadio Hearn; with
the race-ghost of the Greek in him urging him always toward the quest of beauty and truth — min-
gled with the strain of those mysterious nomads,
the gypsies, that made of him a wanderer and an
exile, forever seeking some vague goal, some dream,
some longing never to be attained.

Remembering what his restless, passionate, unhappy life was, rather than to accept this doctrine
of eternal flux and change, this endless wheel of
being, one would be wishful for him of that desire
of his countryman, Cleon, the Greek, —

> Wishing thee wholly where Zeus lives the most
> Within the eventual element of calm.

LETTERS TO
BASIL HALL CHAMBERLAIN

THE JAPANESE LETTERS OF LAFCADIO HEARN

I

LETTERS TO BASIL HALL CHAMBERLAIN

YOKOHAMA, April 4, 1890.

DEAR PROFESSOR,—I know that you are a very busy man; and deem it best to send my personal letter of introduction by mail, and to ask that you will kindly let me hear from you in regard to the time most convenient to you for my visit.

I am more anxious than I could tell you to make a good book upon Japan; and the Messrs. Harper are very desirous to publish such material as I may be able to give them. But otherwise they are not aiding the venture; and the risks are all my own.

If it be possible for me to obtain some employment in Japan, — such as English tutor in a private family, or any position I might prove capable of filling satisfactorily, — I will have no fear of failing in my undertaking. I think that until one can learn at least the spoken language of a people, and something of their emotional nature, one cannot write truthfully concerning them. In the West Indies, I was able to give two years' study to the dialects and folk-lore of the French Colonies, — and so could produce a book which I think would interest you. But I have been already long familiar with the general character of the old colonial life. In Japan I could not hope to do justice to those phases of life I wish to study, without several years' sojourn.

I believe you have read and spoken kindly of my little volume, "Some Chinese Ghosts." To one long familiar with the life of the Orient, probably the book will seem full of misconceptions; but I think you will understand from its workmanship that I labour sincerely, in the artistic sense, and may be capable of better things when I can obtain larger knowledge of those topics on which I have hitherto only been able to write as an amateur.

If you can possibly help me in this regard, my dear Professor, I think I will be able to more than realize any expectations of the Messrs. Harper & Brothers. Only those who belong to literature as you do, know the weight of the obstacles to sincere work that an artist without ample means must struggle with, or the gratitude earned by those who aid him with opportunities.

I believe Mr. Ichizo Hattori belongs to the University. I met him at New Orleans, where he had charge of a very interesting Educational Exhibit at the Exposition, about which I wrote several articles for Harper's periodicals. I think he will have a kindly remembrance of me.

With best regards, believe me,

Very sincerely,

LAFCADIO HEARN.

YOKOHAMA, April 6, 1890.

DEAR MR. CHAMBERLAIN,—Your kindest letter brought me a good deal of encouragement and pleasure. I am sorry to be obliged to tell you, however, that (although the British Consul of New York refused to believe it until he could obtain the personal affirmation of the Editor of *Harper's Magazine*) I am *not* an American citizen; and my passport, issued at New York, establishes my English citizenship in Japan.

However, I trust this will not prove an insurmountable obstacle. I would be more than glad of being able, in exchange for any service I could render in a Japanese family, for example, to have a small room in which I could write, and such board as they might choose to give — without salary. I shall be able to earn a fair income from *Harper's Magazine*, if I can simply assure living expenses.

I have a copy of my last book, just published, which I will bring you when I have the pleasure of an interview. It will give a better idea than I can otherwise express of what I should like to attempt in Japan.

The little I have already seen of this marvellous country so far surpasses anticipation that I am almost afraid to see more for the moment: impressions so multitudinous and so sharply novel come to me every day that the mind refuses to digest them. Everything seems enchanted now. . . .

Believe me,

Very gratefully yours,

LAFCADIO HEARN.

TOKYO, April 9, 1890.

DEAR PROFESSOR CHAMBERLAIN, — I am writing again, not with the idea of causing you any additional trouble, but rather with the hope of facilitating matters. An English teacher whom I met here, has given me some information about Japanese schools; and from what I could learn through him, I think I should be very glad to serve as English teacher in a public school for several years, if desirable. I should not be at all particular as to what part of Japan I might be sent, nor for how long a period my services might be required.

I think it best to state my position even before hearing from you, — in case of there being any vacancies which I could occupy in the country. If I have the chance, I think I shall be able to make myself valuable. The opportunity to teach means the opportunity to learn and observe; and this seems more important to me every day, as I am beginning to understand the difficulty of comprehending Japanese life, even in any number of years, without some knowledge of their language. Your "Handbook of Colloquial Japanese" has not encouraged me: I had no idea before seeing it what a task I had undertaken.

Sincerely,

With best regards,

LAFCADIO HEARN.

April 11, 1890.

DEAR PROFESSOR CHAMBERLAIN, — . . . The school in Kyūshū seems a pleasant prospect, —

being, I suppose, in a remote place; and if the salary be sufficient to exist upon, I would prefer it to anything in Tokyo but for the necessity of waiting so many months. This I fear I could not afford to do. I have heard of an immediate opening in a private school in Tokyo; but the salary is only 50 yen. So I am not sure yet which way I shall move; but I am quite sure that I shall soon be able to settle down to work, and study Japanese — thanks to your sympathetic kindly efforts.

I enclose to you the Creole Grammar you wished to see. It is the best of the Martinique grammars of its kind; but, nevertheless, far from perfect. The Grammar of the Mauritian Creole, by Baissac, is better arranged; that of the Guyane Creole, by Saint Quentin, is also very satisfactory. There is a grammar of the Trinidad patois by a coloured man named Thomas, full of errors in etymology, but otherwise very curious and not without value. The Louisiana patois has been written of in a less elaborate way by Alfred Mercier. I can obtain his study for you, should you care to look at it. There are many books — catechisms, etc., in various Creole dialects. The "Kreolische Studies" of Dr. —— (I cannot for the moment remember the name) of Vienna, is an immense series of studies on a great variety of colonial dialects, including, I believe, the Batavian and the Boer "Creoles"; but these would not, I think, come under a Creole's definition of Creole.

If I can tell you anything you would like to know about the Martinique patois, — the only one I am able to speak a little, — I will be glad of being so able to interest you.

Very truly and gratefully,

LAFCADIO HEARN.

October 6, 1890.

DEAR MR. CHAMBERLAIN, — I was extremely pleased this morning to hear from you that you had received the books all right, and that they were new to you. I was terribly afraid I had sent you something you would not care about. I am also pleased to hear you received the copy of "Youma" for Mrs. Napier, whose kind words about my work I am very grateful for. . . .

I have discovered that at Rakuzan, which is about one ri north of here, there is a pottery called Rakuzan-yaki, where some remarkable work is turned out. I saw the Three Apes of Koshin, Lord of Highroads, for example, exquisitely modelled in a clay about the colour of this paper. The designs of artistic objects made there impressed me very much. The Governor of Izumo, Mr. Koteda, who invited me to his house, showed me many beautiful things which had been made in Izumo of old, delicious laquer-work. This is no longer made so wonderfully, but there are artists in Izumo. I found out one in quite a curious way. In a temple-court, among several statues of Jizo, I saw one in which the God was represented, as he ought to be always, like a beautiful Japanese boy, and I enquired of the priest who had made it. He gave the address of a carpenter. I found the carpenter was a famous woodcarver, Arakawa Jinosuke. We have become great friends.

I almost forgot to tell you that another celebrated place near Matsue is Oba, about 2 ri south from the city south, where Nominosukune, father of wrestling and wrestlers, has his tomb, — and, I think, a shrine. (The weather has been so frightful I could not go to see it.) Now Nominosukune is said to have been a native of Kizuki, and a member of that Senke family to which the "Ikigami" belongs.

. With best regards and kindest wishes for your health, believe me always,

Yours faithfully,

LAFCADIO HEARN.

MATSUE, May 22, 1891.

DEAR PROFESSOR CHAMBERLAIN, — . . . Just at this instant your letter enclosing Mr. Lowell's comes to me. As Mr. Lowell's letter touches some remarks in my own, I conclude he is in Japan, — which is very delightful, as I trust to see him one of these days. It gave me no small pleasure to hear a kindly word of praise from him. I am not quite sure whether the little song to which he refers ("Petits amoureux aux plumes," etc.) is Béranger's: I think it is, for it rings of the soul of the man; — it came into Martinique with Paul Bert's text-books, and the radical secularization of the schools.

What I try to say and think in opposition to the terrible inference of the Soul of the Far East, is, I know, contrary to my own philosophy (vide Herbert Spencer, "First Principles," Ch. "Dissolution,"

par. 178). The effect of European civilization has
been "a change from integrated motions to disintegrated motions." But the introduction of Chinese
civilization must have had a somewhat similar effect; — and if Japan can do with Western civilization what she did with Japanese, she would seem
to afford, not the example of a general law, but a
magnificent exception thereunto. To do it, would
require a prodigious vitality, of course, a vitality
incompatible with the highest intellectual condition
of a people, perhaps. I am constantly more and
more impressed with the unspeculative character of
the Japanese, — so far as I have been able to perceive their mental tendencies. They do not seem to
find pleasure in the suggestions of philosophy: —
they read Herbert Spencer without a suspicion of
the tremendous ghostly fact behind his whole system; and I have not yet met any one among them
who finds pleasure in the study of relations of things.
But, everything considered, there is a charm about
Japanese life and thought, about their way of taking life and enjoying it, so deliciously natural, that
only to be in its atmosphere a while is like a revelation of something we Westerners never suspected.
What is this? Mr. Lowell can perhaps tell very
charmingly. His observation in "Noto" that the
Japanese are the happiest people in the world, is
superlatively true. It is the old Greek soul again.
To escape out of Western civilization into Japanese
life is like escaping from a pressure of ten atmo-
spheres into a perfectly normal medium. I must also
confess that the very absence of the Individuality

essentially characteristic of the Occident is one of
the charms of Japanese social life for me: here the
individual does not strive to expand his own individuality at the expense of that of every one else.
According to a French thinker, that is the great law
of modern life abroad. Here each can live as quietly
in the circle of himself as upon a lotos-blossom in the
Gohuraku: the orbs of existence do not clash and
squeeze each other out of shape. Now would not
this be also the condition of life in a perfected humanity?

I travelled through Japan westward to Noto with
Mr. Lowell, step by step, — feeling all the pleasures, vexations, and dangers of the trip as acutely
as if I had been accompanying him in body; sym-
pathizing with every sensation, but finding the
greatest pleasure in those delightful little thoughts,
which sprinkle the whole work through, — snatches
of intimate conversation. They also, I thought,
made the particular and unrivalled charm of "Cho-
sön." Such books of travel could not have been
written by any one a generation ago; they reflect
the thought of another era, — men now think
thoughts they never dared to think before.

If Mr. Lowell comes to Izumo I will show him a
belt of glass let into my shojis, so as to give one the
idea, when sitting down, of "being strangely out-of-
doors;" and when standing up, of "being uncomfortably indoors." There is no canned milk here;
but there are also scarcely any articles of European
diet. I have even been wicked enough to discourage
the local manufacture of bread, by absolutely re-

fusing to buy it, to the extreme astonishment of the baker. But there is superb lake scenery, which would leave memories behind much better than the awful recollection of the Onigajo.

Well, I have written enough to strain your patience, for I know your time is more precious than mine.

For the moment, good-bye, with best regards to Mr. Lowell, and believe me,

Ever faithfully yours,
LAFCADIO HEARN.

MIONOSEKI, August 27, 1891.

DEAR PROFESSOR CHAMBERLAIN, — Mionoseki is about the very most Japanesey town I was ever in. The streets are so narrow that I could jump from the second story of my hotel into the second story of the opposite building. But the vistas are delightfully picturesque. The town curves along the verge of a semicircular bay, with a demi-line of curiously corrugated volcanic hills behind it, — so that the streets are squeezed between this semicircle of hills and the water, — which is deep close to shore, so that vessels can move close to the houses. I take a swim in the bay each morning, stepping out from the back-door of the hotel from a stone wharf into the sea. Sakai, however, is still better for swimming. The water at the door of the hotel in Sakai was sixteen feet deep and as clear as plateglass. At Sakai it was a sort of fjord between Izumo and Hoki, very long and narrow, like a river mouth, but very deep, so that large vessels can come in. At Mionoseki the bay is nearly the shape of a clamshell. The manufacture of pretty bamboo baskets of all conceivable designs, and other bamboo ware, is the meibutsu.

The Miojinja disappointed me. It looks nearly as fine as the exterior of the Hinomisaki shrines, but interiorly does not bear the shadow of a comparison with them. The grounds are however dignified, and in the centre of the main court I saw a bronze lavatory, — like the molten sea of Exodus, — which must have cost many thousands of dollars. The mamori were not interesting. However this is the great place for mamori. The Koto-shiro-nushi-no-kami of Mionoseki is the Great Deity of the hyakushō-no-jin. He protects their crops. Here are most of those charms made which feather those "arrows of prayers," I previously described to you, and which the country-folk buy myriads of to stick all over their fields. I am going to send you a specimen. Here also are sold magical rice-seeds. Whatever crop you wish to grow, this rice-seed will produce it. Only sow the rice and pray. There will arise barley, wheat, maize, watermelons, or cabbages, according to the heart's desire.

The picturesqueness of the place enchants me. But the popular bathing resort half a mile off — Kaisuiyoku — is abominable. Why do the Japanese deliberately pick out bathing resorts where the bottom is all jagged rocks and stones ? — as at Oiso ? And why, oh why do they prefer such damnable places to smooth velvety beaches of sand ? Is it only because of their rare artistic perception of the beauty of stones ? I have been a convert to this religion of stones; — but stones under water, unseen, sharp-edged, brutal, only remind one of the shores of the Lake of Blood in the Buddhist Kakemonos.

More and more watching the happy life of these people, I doubt whether our own civilization is morally all we believe it is. I cannot help thinking that what Kaempfer so long ago said about the Japanese holds good to-day, — that "they far outdo the Christians." And perhaps our moralists, with their Semitic ideas about original sin, are responsible for a very serious misrepresentation when they allege that because the Japanese ideas of sexual morals are different from our own, they are really much worse. Judging from what I have witnessed "behind the scenes" of city life abroad, they are much better on the whole in practice, though not perhaps in theory. Christianity while professing to be a religion of love, has always seemed to me in history and practice a religion of hate, with its jealous and revengeful deity, its long record of religious wars and inquisitions, and its mutual reproaches between sects of being under the curse of eternal perdition. No such feeling of religious hate seems to me possible to exist in Japan. As the Romans persecuted only religions which proved hostile to their government, so Japan seems to have never hated any faith which did not war upon national integrity and morals.

What is really the main object of life? or what should be one's main purpose in life? To succeed in money-making by imposing on others, or to waste one's existence to win empty praise when one gets old, or to simply cultivate one's self as far as possible for the better, and enjoy this existence all one can? The last seems to me much the more rational and moral, and it seems to be somewhat Japanese. Then what a very charming influence upon life has this creed of preëxistence and transmigration, — with its promises for future births, and its fearlessness about journeying to the Meido, whither one travels with just a little tear or two only, as if bound for a long trip abroad, simply a voyage to the West or South, somewhat longer than usual.

The effect of proselytism in Izumo appears to me very unfavourable. The converts are few; but they retrograde morally and mentally. Two boys converted here some years ago, became insane. Although I think such denunciations are cruel and useless in most cases, I could not feel sorry that the leading Shinto magazine spoke of these cases as visitations of the wrath of the Kami: — they will render it more difficult to attempt proselytism upon weak-minded or nervous boys.

But these are mere individual notions. Perhaps it is not intended in the eternal order of things that any people in the world shall continue to remain honest, and simple-hearted, and ingenuous, and happy. Perhaps the law of progress means increase of misery and wretched development of selfishnesses and jealousies and oppression of the many for the benefit of the few. Perhaps Schopenhauer is right, perhaps everything is irresistibly tending to that condition, supposed, I think, by Renan, when the universal apprehension of the variety of existence should beget the universal will to cease to exist, at a

time when the mere volition should suffice to produce instantaneously the desired result.

Ever faithfully yours,

LAFCADIO HEARN.

P. S. The God of Mionoseki is also the great God
of sailors here. They pray to him for fair weather.
There are no hens or chickens here, for the reasons
already given in a former letter; but there are
ducks, and *ducks' eggs*.

September 4, 1891.

DEAR PROFESSOR CHAMBERLAIN, — . . . I think
I wrote you before that the fox superstition in Izumo
has special peculiarities, and is strong enough to af-
fect the price of real estate to a very large amount.
You know the translation by James of the "Dis-
course upon Infinite Vision." Now the most telling
point of the whole thing to me was the priest's
appeal to his hearers' superstition about the fox to
prove his metaphysical argument, and the immediate success of that appeal. Even among the mod-
ernly educated here, the belief in the three kinds of
foxes prevails to a large extent. Just as a student
once wrote for me in an English comparison: — "It
is hard to say if these stories of foxes are true. *But it
is hard to say that they are not true.*"

What you say about Mr. Lowell's being probably
less intimate with the common people than I now
am, is, I think, true. Certainly so large a personality
as his would find it extremely difficult — probably
painful — to adopt Japanese life without reserves,
its costumes, its diet, its life upon the floor, its inter-

minable small etiquette, its everlasting round of
interviews with people who have nothing to say but
a few happy words, its Matsuri customs and household formalities. He has what the French would call
une envergure trop vaste pour ça; and for so penetrating and finely trained an intellect, the necessary
sacrifice of one's original self would be mere waste.
Still, I think it is only by this way, in the course of
years, that I can get at the Kokoro of the common
people, — which is my whole aim, — the religious
and emotional home life. What I have seen of the
educated modernized Japanese does not strike me as
worth studying for literary purposes. They seem to
me like a soft reflection of Latin types, without the
Latin force and brilliancy and passion — somewhat
as in dreams the memory of people we have known
become smilingly aërial and imponderable.

Your illustration about homeopathy is superb, —
a little severe, but I think it is impossible to state
the whole weak side of anything without some forci-
ble severity. But the ultimate tendency would thus
be toward a second Ryubu-Shinto, — would it not?
I must confess I would sacrifice much, if I had anything worth sacrificing, to see a pure strong revival
of Buddhism. But the Buddhists seem to have no
great men now, no forces: — no possibility of another Nichiren, is there? I fear it cannot come: this
hoped-for revival, through native sources alone; the
Buddhist scholars are lukewarm souls — mere book-
worms. But it might come through the influence of
the Western higher philosophy, indirectly. To make
the Japanese people simply irreligious, would de-

stroy everything beautiful in their life, and nothing
seems to me so admirably suited to that gentle life
as the faith of Buddhism. The sight of a superb
Japanese iron-clad at Mionoseki the other day, filled
me with regret. That splendid monster appeared as
an omen of some future so much more dismal and
artificial than the present. . . .

September 10, 1891.

DEAR PROFESSOR CHAMBERLAIN, — I have returned from Kakaura and the neighbouring caves
— one of which is (by reason of its legends largely)
the weirdest place I ever saw. . . .

Women boatmen took us to Kaka. After leaving
the tiny bay of Mitsu-ura, the boat follows the coast
to the right. An awful, black, iron-bound coast,
where the surf is never still, — eccentric, jagged,
ravined, upheaved, breached, turned upside down in
places; strata-lines at all conceivable angles from
╱ to ╲, and vice versa. After about two hours'
rowing, reached a pretty bay, quite large, in a
corner of which is Kaka. Passed the bay and made
for the caves. There are two, the old and the new.
The new is the further. We went there first. A
superb sea-cave, or caves; for there are three openings. The water is deep and clear. One of the women took a stone and rapped on the bow as we
entered. I wanted to take a swim, but was assured
the Kami would be displeased. It would be "certain
death." These caves, although sacred to the Kami,
contain a rock from which milk is said to drip for the
ghosts of Jizo's pets to drink. From here we made

our way back to the alleged "older cave." Here was the weirdness. This cave is doubled and has a floor of solid rock. Thousands upon thousands of stone-piles cover it, heaped up at night, 't is said, by the ghosts of little children coming to worship the statues of Jizo. I saw tiny footprints a few inches long in the sand, said to be the prints of the feet of the little ghosts. Shinto and Buddhism join hands here. There are several statues of Jizo, before each of which is a small torii and a pair of gohei.

Thence to Kakaura, a delicious sleepy little port. The prettiest, gentlest, sweetest population I ever saw. All the boys looked like Jizo and all the girls like Kwannon. I would like to buy Kakaura and put it in my toko.

I think Jizo is far the most interesting and popular deity in Japan. All the tenderest poetry of Buddhism is his aureole. Never have I travelled on a road or passed a hamlet where he was not. Even in Kitzuki he prevails. I have written hundreds of pages already about him. I imagine that he will be the last of the Buddhist divinities to pass into the Nirvana of oblivion, supposing that Buddhism itself must pass away.

But I am sorry that I cannot send you any mamori. There is no temple or *to* or anything near the caves, — only the awful goblin coast and the awful sea, Hotoke-no-umi. There are also plenty of sharks.

Just as in the West Indies, so in Japan I find that there are extraordinary physical differences between the populations of villages only a few miles apart.

Some physical type becomes dominant when the population is isolated by absence of good roads, by mountains, by those local conditions which determine the fate of communities.

Very truly,
- LAFCADIO HEARN.

February 12, 1892.

DEAR FRIEND CHAMBERLAIN,—What a delight it was to get your charming Manila letter; and how I envied you: — not only those things which you liked, but also even those things which you did not like; the rich, divine, moist, life-sapping and life-giving heat of the tropics, and the exquisite romance of rummaging in old monastic libraries; — and (but will you please forgive me for saying so?) the Spanish dance-music. There is an estudiantina serenade, played only upon mandolines and flutes, which I used to hear on tropical nights, but of which I never learned the name; and sometimes I dream of it, and wake up with such regret that I dare not sleep again; until I tire myself out reading or writing. I wonder why. Is it the melody only, — sweet as a cooing of doves, — or is it the vision of palms under the southern cross, and thoughts of purple sea, and odors of orange and lemon flowers? I can't quite decide; perhaps if you heard a Spanish melody in London, or (dare I say it?) a Japanese geisha-song, the memories evoked by it might seem so pleasant that you would forgive the notes. The reason I can't decide, however, is that the rhythm of an African drum-bamboula skilfully played, delights me in a kindred way; and of course that is not music, though it is certainly capable of expressing certain animal emotions;—excitements and frenzies that are contagious. And you will be horrified to hear that I cannot delight in Wagner and intellectual music, not having any cultivated musical sense. I am told it must be acquired slowly, by study and opportunity. As I have said so much, I want to say something more. I cannot like the professional music of the Japanese,—that is, vocal,—as I like the chants of the peasantry, the occasional queer bursts of quaverings and long weird plaintive tones breaking here and there into fractions of notes. Some of these seem to me very pretty, and savagely natural, like the chant of a semi, or a wild bird. . . .

From what you tell me about Manila, I conceive the social life must be much like that of the Latin West Indies; the same dining hours, the same amusements, the same incapacity for intellectual pursuits forced by the tropical climate. I could only work in such heat from 5 A. M. till 11; for the rest of the day, to work was to risk one's life. But that is not the worst. The worst is the development of morbid nervous sensibility to material impressions, and absolute loss of thinking power, accompanied by numbing or clouding of memory. (And yet — I love the tropics.) As for the half-breeds of Manila, if they made no impression, no strong physical impression of attractiveness, I would doubt if the race would compare with the West Indian half-breeds in physique. The ungainliness of the pure whites would, I think, be the result of the same convent training

which makes Creole women so clumsy at a certain
time of life. By the way, the use of the word "convent," you call attention to, is, I think, a very old
one in Latin countries, in the signification of monastery. I think you will find the word so used in
nearly all the old traditions of the Middle Ages,—
such as the legends of Francis of Assisi, and our
poets follow suit; — for instance, Longfellow in
"The Golden Legend," and the "Legend Beautiful,"
and Rossetti, Tennyson, etc. The distinction between "convent" as a nunnery, and "monastery"
is, I think, only a popular English one. The former
word signifies really the house of a religious order
of either sex.

·I have never read Valera, — indeed, until you
wrote about him, I had imagined the name to be a
French pseudonym for one who wanted to call attention to his stories of Spanish life. (You know he
is much read in the French version, — at least I
often saw notices of his books in French papers; but
I thought they were books by a Frenchman.) But,
speaking of books, if you have not read Rudyard
Kipling at his best, I think you will have a treat in
"Life's Handicap," especially. There is a prodigious
compressed force in the man's style that reminds me
at times of the style of the Norse writers, like Björnson. A great test of a book is, "Can you read it
twice?" Certainly one cannot read Zola twice, —
perhaps not even Maupassant, though so wondrous
a story-teller is Maupassant. But you can read the
short stories of "Life's Handicap" several times
over, always with the same charm. I can also recom-

mend "Wee Willie Winkie," "The Gadsbys," "Soldiers Three," " Under the Deodars," "Plain Tales from the Hills," "The Light that Failed." The Macmillan editions are much fuller and finer than the Indian prints.

Though it pleased me so much to hear that Japan seemed more beautiful as you recede further from it (— and, indeed, all that I love in the tropics is Nature and that in man which reflects tropical Nature's fine side), — still, did not Spanish politeness suggest to you with new sudden force the faint resemblance of the Japanese to the Latins? It will be, however, in England, I fancy, that you will enjoy Japan best from a distance. There the contrasts will focus most sharply.

My next Japanese volume (No. 2) must consist, if possible, of story-matter, or sketches constructively resembling stories. But I am in despair about conversational work. In a story, the foreign idiom, however queer, must remain the foreign idiom in English; otherwise one simply makes Japanese talk and think English. Even Mr. Dening, who ought to know artistically better, does this. Hepburn's Dictionary makes no attempt at etymology, — only an English rendering is given. What tremendous work, however, to give the morphology of Japanese words. Yet how essential to a clear comprehension of their artistic use by any one, not a scholar. . . .

With best regards and earnest wishes for a pleasant English summer, believe me,

Ever faithfully yours,

LAFCADIO HEARN.

December 9, 1892.

DEAR PROFESSOR, — How glad it made me to see your writing again! — and to find myself so kindly remembered.

How supremely we are at one on the subject of Gothic architecture. It is in his judgment of it that I think Taine's great artistic weakness lies. He follows Brunelleschi; — considers durability, architectural interproportion and balancing, — shows astonishing insensibility to meaning. Perhaps because he is no poet. It is the only architecture that is really alive. Victor Hugo perceived one phase of it; — not the beautiful, but the awful, — the sense it gives one of being in the skeleton of some tremendous animal. Certainly within it is all bone and tendon, jointings, articulations, ribbings, vertebræ, — processes fantastic and innumerable. Without it is a hymn whose strophes rise and burn to heaven as flame, — it is a conflagration of aspirement in stone. How I wish I could have seen Cologne. That is one of my hopes and dreams. The style is severe; but what must be the impression of a choir 160 feet high, and towers over 500. I am all pagan; but Greek architecture, I feel, is only stone. Gothic is soul, — or better Spirit, using the sharp-angled flame-word.

Your letter from Manila bewitched me. I shall hope and scheme to go there some day, — at least for a winter. How I should enjoy the native life, I don't know; the Malay, or Tagal, seems rather impenetrable; but as to the colonial life I think I could make some literary finds. . . .

I have been interested in the worship of Needles,

to which Mochi are offered, and in the discovery of
a curious Izumo household ceremony anciently practised before every Kamidama on a certain Matsuri
for the expulsion of foreigners from Japan, — and
in the history of the Goblin of the Snow, — and in
the discovery of a belief in 9 (nine) souls. Why nine?
And Mason will tell you about my notes on prayers
for the Souls of animals, and other matters.

Meanwhile I have read Batchelor's book on the
Ainu which suggested the following observations:
(1) I suspect a connection between the Japanese
gohei and the Ainu inao.

(2) I feel almost certain that Batchelor is wrong
and Miss Bird right about the religion of the Ainu.
The law of religious evolution, now clearly laid down,
seems to me to preclude the possibility of a natural
monotheistic conception on the part of a primitive
race. The Ainu may now profess a belief in one God,
"Creator of heaven and earth;" but is that belief
not a modern *imported* one? I feel sure almost that
it is.

About myself, I am all right for Kumamoto for
another year, I suppose, — perhaps as long as I like.
. . . I'll write more about my own affairs another
time.

Yours ever faithfully,

LAFCADIO HEARN.

KUMAMOTO, December 12, 1892.

DEAR PROFESSOR, — "In summer the heat is so
hot that we can accomplish nothing; and in winter
the cold is simply impossible to bear."

The above extract from a composition I have just corrected, expresses correctly the local opinion of this climate, — all of which is introductory to a confession. You may recollect my former confession about returning to the flesh-pots of Egypt. (And I have never been able to go back to Japanese diet, except while travelling.) But I did without fire for two winters; for a hibachi is not fire, you know; it is only a ghost, or a pipe-light, — and a Kotatsu requires a prolonged discipline of the spinal muscles, which I lack. And this winter, in spite of my love and enthusiasm for things Japanese, I find myself obliged to hire many carpenters to fix my study, — putting in glass shoji, and *erecting a stove*. Because the cold "is simply impossible to bear." And I have changed my residence to "Tsuboi, Nishihoribata 35," — obtaining a pretty house, with a pretty garden, — surrounded by cemeteries and images of Gods.

I wonder if you ever heard of a strange old superstition that a miko, or even the wife of a Kannushi, cannot rest in the grave, but is eaten by a goblin wolf after death. The goblin comes to the grave and howls, and the corpse then rises up to be devoured, just as Southey's Old Woman of Berkeley gets up when the devil calls. It is a superstition of the Izumo peasantry. Please don't mention my name in connection with it if you happen to speak of it to anybody else. I can't afford to write about many things in connection with rustic Shinto, which is a totally different thing from the majestic and dignified Izumo Taisha. The peasant's Kannushi does queer

things; — primitive things, — extraordinary things.
But why should the peasants have so ghastly a fancy
about a faith which they respect most profoundly
otherwise. The origin of such a hideous story cannot
be in Shinto itself, which has always respected woman. And it cannot be naturally in Buddhism which
vindicates the holiness of womanhood so magnificently in the Saddharma Pundarika, — a passage
finer by far than that of Christ and the adulteress,
not in its humanity, but in its spirituality. Perhaps
there survives an older belief than any form of
either religion we know of, attaching an idea of evil
to the assumption of any sacerdotal function by
women, — an idea going back to that remoter age
in which a priestess could exist only as a witch?
What do you think?

I hope Mason has preserved for you the pretty
lines of Rudyard Kipling about the Daibutsu at
Kamakura. I enjoy him, — not the poetry of the
effort, but the prose of it. It is delicious. Alas! I
had written my commonplace stuff about the Daibutsu long ago; — long before. Would I could atone
for it now! But then Kipling is a giant in all things
compared to me. Read the Queen's words on pp.
250–1–2 of the "Naulahka." I think they will bring
tears. Immense force without the least appearance
of an attempt or wish to effect. I despair when I
read that man's work.

"Calm as a deep still water," says an ancient
Sutra of the Teacher. And there at Kamakura He is
even so — deep, still, and luminous as the ether. . . .
To lie about the beautiful is to lie about the Infinite

Goodness and the heart of Life, — and there is for-
giveness never for that sin.

But I won't tire you any more now.

Good-bye.

Ever most truly,

LAFCADIO HEARN.

KUMAMOTO, December 21, 1892.

DEAR PROFESSOR, — "I take my pen in hand" to
write of my new home, and matters in connection
therewith. The house is pretty, and it has a landscape garden, — not so quaintly beautiful as that in
Matsue, but quite nice with artificial hills, pines
trimmed strata-fashion, and an amazing multitude
of stones. There are glass bells tinkling at the eaves;
and there are monkeys painted in the watercloset.
Fancy a real monkey in a watercloset. This alone
strikes me as an incongruous and unpleasantly suggestive decoration. The stove works well, and I
could make you comfortable in my glass-box of a
study.

But in order to go to Nishihoribata, we had to
move in a northerly direction, thereby offending
Kojin, who hates the north, and all who move that
way. (Oh, Kojin, — if you knew how far south
I should like to go, we would be wonderful friends.)
Kojin seems to have no image; in Izumo he is always
a tree. He is no relative to Koshin, and old girl's
dolls and boy's dolls are given to him instead of
being thrown out. But the origin of him I can't
make out. I thought he was Shinto, but he stands in
Buddhist courtyards. Well, in order to placate him

we had to have rites performed by a Buddhist priest. The prayers were not addressed to Kojin at all, but to Shoten. Who is Shoten, I can't make out, further than that 't is Shoten who is to preserve us from the wrath of Kojin. Mamori were given to us; and I ate some rice blessed by the Bonsan. This is, perhaps, to keep Kojin from disturbing my inwards. (May the Tathagata pardon me for speaking thus plainly about gods whom I cannot understand.) The line of demarcation between Shinto and Buddhist deities is as difficult to define as that between the vegetable and animal world, or between certain contested varieties of the human race; and the more I find out, the less sure I am of anything about them.

A paragraph in the mail about Daikoku reminds me of something I wanted to tell you long ago. That the Rat should figure as a retainer of Daikoku, and in the neighbourhood of his rice-bales, naturally seemed queer to many familiar with the picture on the bank-bills. But in Izumo where Daikoku is Oho-kumi-nushi-no-kami, the mystery is not. There the rat is the Mouse of the Kojiki (page 73) who whispered, — "The inside is hollow, hollow." In your note on the same page I find that the word might be translated either "rat" or "mouse." This story is among the people. I got it from no priestly authority, — and it seems to explain the relationship perfectly well.

And I wish you a merry Christmas, a happy New Year, and good health and good luck.

Ever most truly,

LAFCADIO HEARN.

P. S. Do you know what it is to be hungry for a sensation? I suppose not, because you are in the habit of receiving them daily. But I can't get any here, in winter especially. I can only grind, grind all the time. Perhaps I have exhausted capacity for sensation in a Japanese city. Things which used to seem to me wonderful now produce no effect at all. I must try to make occasional voyages to the tropics.

KUMAMOTO, January 14, 1893.

DEAR CHAMBERLAIN, — Your delightful lines came this morning, and I waited only till after class to have this chance of chatting about something very close to my heart. I have just sent away an article about it, — under the rather misleading title, "The Japanese Smile."

Your lines about Lowell almost put him into my room, and I think I can hear him talk. Now for some presumption. He is so much larger a man than I, that I would feel it presumption to differ with him on any point if I did not remember that in the psychological world a man may grow too tall to see anything near him clearly. Now first for my present position. Of course no thinker can ignore Lowell's book. The idea is too powerful, too scientific, and too well sustained not to demand the utmost respect and study. I have given both. The result is that I must *fully accept* his idea as a discovery. The point on which I struggled longest was Spencer's statement that the "highest individuation must coincide with the greatest mutual dependence," —

that evolutional progress is "at once toward the greatest separateness and the greatest union." This point was hard for me to accept because, in view of other studies I made, hard for me to understand. Now understanding it, taking it as a conviction into my mind, nothing remains but to accept Lowell's view.

But still we are not at one. This is because his standpoint of pure science is too high to allow of that intimacy which means soul sympathy. I have tried to study from the bottom what he has observed from the top. Now, to me, the most beautiful, the most significant, the most attractive point of Japanese character, is revealed by the very absence of that personality to which Mr. Lowell's book points as an Oriental phenomenon. I do not mean the fact *in itself*, but that which it signifies. What it signifies was very, very hard for me to understand. I could not understand some points until after a weary study of the Chinese classics. Others I understood, by guess, from passages in the Kojiki, — in old poems, — in Buddhist texts. Most of what I understand, however, I learned from mixing in the life of the people, observing, watching, questioning, wondering. Of course even now my knowledge is trifling. Still, it teaches me this: —

(1) That the lack of personality is to a great extent voluntary, and that this fact is confirmed by the appearance of personality, strongly and disagreeably marked, where the social and educational conditions are new, and encourage selfishness.

(2) That every action of Japanese life in the old

Japan, from prince to peasant, was religiously regulated by the spirit of self-repression for the sake of the family, the community, the nation, — and that the so-called impersonality signifies the ancient moral tendency to self-sacrifice for duty's sake.

And this, here badly expressed, confirms my often avowed belief that on the moral side the old Japanese civilization was as far in advance of the Western, as it was materially behind it. This advance was gained at some considerable sacrifice to character and mental evolution. But the loss does not signify that the moral policy was wrong. It signifies only that it was too much in the direction of mutual dependence. It was the highest possible morality from any high religious standpoint, — Christian or pagan, — the sacrifice of self for others. But it was in advance of the time. The indications are that the highly selfish and cunning, as well as the unselfish and frank qualities of man are necessary to the preservation of society and its development; and that in a civilization based upon the Occidental plan, the former qualities are still much more valuable to a community than the latter. But an ideally perfect state would be the Oriental form of Confucian government, with Japanese morals, unstiffened by ultra conservatism, stimulating the development of the higher emotions and repressing the ignoble self only. It is just to such a state that we hope to attain in the unknown future. I think we have thrown Japan morally backward a thousand years; she is going to adopt our vices (which are much too large for her). I agree with Percival Lowell, but I also agree with

Viscount Torio (a wonderful thinker), and I venture
the opinion that both views are reconcilable. It
does not follow because we have cultivated mental
and physical force to the highest pitch so far known,
that our methods of cultivation are natural and
right, or that we may not have ultimately to abandon all our present notions about the highest progress and the highest morality. Personally I think
we are dead wrong, but that's another matter.

And now, begging pardon for so long a howl about
abstracts, — let me talk about my book. I have
written to the firm *asking them to make it still larger.*
What insolence! But I offered to sacrifice all com-
missions, payments, and even remuneration for
articles. To me the all important point is to get out
a thoroughly sympathetic book, without morbidness, just enough fun to keep in tone with modern
thought. I hope I shall succeed. If not, I must try
another publisher, rather than cut down the book.
But I don't want another publisher. They are the
Macmillans of America, beautiful printers, and
essentially a *literature* firm. If I had Lowell's genius
and Lowell's independence, how happy I should be.
He can go where he likes, see what he likes, write
what he likes and make beautiful books. I am heavily handicapped even in competing with writers as
much below Lowell as he is above me.

I like a rainy day, too, with a purring stove in
the room, and some writing to do. My best wishes
ever.

LAFCADIO HEARN.

KUMAMOTO, January 15, 1893.

DEAR CHAMBERLAIN, — Heart's thanks for kindly words of sympathy just received. If the publishers prove intractable, any MS. you would like I will offer for use in the manner suggested. I had thought of some day becoming a member of the Society; but I wanted to wait until my book appeared, — which would give me a better claim than I have now. I may try during this year what I can do with English publishers for Japanese sketches. The American literary magazines pay too little; and the illustrated magazines cut a man's work up on the Procrustean system to hit the public with exactly a certain number of words. I'll never get rich with publishers, unless I become awfully old as well as famous in literature, and able to make my own terms.

We've had no snow here, — never any to speak of. But the weather is fitful enough. By the way, I forgot in my last to chat about Mr. Lowell's "impersonality" and "personality" as an abstract quantity. I think as a quality, personality cannot be said to exist at all in the transcendental sense. I don't believe in *that* sense of it. The impression certain men can produce upon others by their nerve presence is not, and cannot be proved to be, due to anything magnetic or hypermagnetic inside of them, — but to the recognition by others of force of aggressive will and other traits, uncommonly developed; — they cause, in other words, a certain sense of caution and danger. A blind man could not thus be impressed by a new advent to any extent, unless his hearing had developed a sensitiveness to voice-tones as subtle as sight itself. In other words the impression produced by character upon us, can be altogether explained by instinctive knowledge of our own potential relations to that organization through inherited memory, or, more scientifically, race experience. There's nothing else in it, psychic or odic. It is only the question of knowing by sight what dog will bite on slight provocation. Don't you think so? Individuality alone is a *real* fact.

Ever faithfully,

LAFCADIO HEARN.

January 17, 1893.

DEAR CHAMBERLAIN, — I'm writing just because I feel lonesome; is n't that selfish? However, if I can amuse you at all, you will forgive me. You have been away a whole year, — so perhaps you would like to hear some impressions of mine during that time. Here goes.

The illusions are forever over; but the memory of many pleasant things remains. I know much more about the Japanese than I did a year ago; and still I am far from understanding them well. Even my own little wife is somewhat mysterious still to me, though always in a lovable way. Of course a man and woman know each other's hearts; but outside of personal knowledge, there are race-tendencies difficult to understand. Let me tell one. In Oki we fell in love with a little Samurai boy, who was having a hard time of it, and we took him with us. He is now like an adopted son, — goes to school and all that. Well, I wished at first to pet him a little, but I found that was not in accordance with custom, and that even the boy did not understand it. At home, I therefore scarcely spoke to him at all; he remained under the control of the women of the house. They treated him kindly, — though I thought coldly. The relationship I could not quite understand. He was never praised, and rarely scolded. A perfect code of etiquette was established between him and all the other persons in the house, according to degree and rank. He seemed extremely cold-mannered, and perhaps not even grateful, that was, so far as I could see. Nothing seemed to move his young placidity, whether happy or unhappy his mien was exactly that of a stone Jizo. One day he let fall a little cup and broke it. According to custom, no one noticed the mistake, for fear of giving him pain. Suddenly I saw tears streaming down his face. The muscles of the face remained quite smilingly placid as usual, but even the will could not control tears. They came freely. Then everybody laughed, and said kind things to him, till he began to laugh too. Yet that delicate sensitiveness no one like me could have guessed the existence of.

But what followed surprised me more. As I said he had been (in my idea) distantly treated. One day he did not return from school for three hours after the usual time. Then to my great surprise the women began to cry, — to cry passionately. I had never been able to imagine alarm for the boy could have affected them so. And the servants ran over town in real, not pretended, anxiety to find him. He had been taken to a teacher's house for something relating to school matters. As soon as his voice was heard at the door, everything was quiet, cold, and amiably polite again. And I marvelled exceedingly.

Sensitiveness exists in the Japanese to an extent never supposed by the foreigners who treat them harshly at the open ports. In Izumo I knew a case of a maid servant who received a slight rebuke with a smile, and then quietly went out and hung herself. I have notes of many curious suicides of a similar sort. And yet the Japanese master is never brutal or cruel. How Japanese can serve a certain class of foreigners at all, I can't understand. Possibly they do not think of them (the foreigners) as being exactly human beings, — but rather Oni, or at best Tengu.

Well, here is another thing. My cook wears a smiling, healthy, rather pleasing face. He is a good-looking young man. Whenever I used to think of him I thought of the smile, I saw a mask before me merry as one of those little masks of Oho-kumi-nushi-no-kami they sell at Mionoseki. One day I looked through a little hole in the shoji, and saw him alone. The face was not the same face. It was thin and drawn and showed queer lines worn by old hardship. I thought, "He will look just like that when he is dead." I went in, and the man was all changed, — young and happy again, — nor have I ever seen that look of trouble in his face since. But I know when he is alone he wears it. He never shows his *real* face to me; he wears the mask of happiness as an etiquette.

Do you remember that awful Parisian statue, a statue of which I forget the name, though the name might be, Society? A beautiful white woman bends smiling above you in stone. A witchery is that smile of hers. After admiring her a while face to face, you turn about her, to see more of the artist's work. And then, lo and behold! the face you looked upon turns out not to be a face at all; it was a Masque; you now see the real head thrown back,' in a distortion of unutterable pain. I think such an Oriental statue might also be made. This Orient knows not our deeper pains, nor can it even rise to our larger joys; but it has its pains. Its life is not so sunny as might be fancied from its happy aspect. Under the smile of its toiling millions there is suffering bravely hidden and unselfishly borne; and a lower intellectual range is counterbalanced by a childish sensitiveness to make the suffering balance evenly in the eternal order of things.

Therefore I love the people very much, more and more the more I know them.

Conversely I detest with unspeakable detestation the frank selfishness, the apathetic vanity, the shallow vulgar scepticism of the New Japan, the New Japan that prates its contempt about Tempo times, and ridicules the dear old men of the pre-meiji era, and that never smiles, having a heart as hollow and bitter as a dried lemon.

And with this, I say good-night.

Ever most truly,

LAFCADIO HEARN.

January 19, 1893.

DEAR CHAMBERLAIN, — . . . I know your own sentiments about free opinion, but there are social questions. In my preface I have taken the ground that Japan has nothing to gain by Christianity. If you think that is all right as a private opinion, I'll let it stand. If you think my heterodoxy could reflect in any way unfavourably upon the mention of yourself in the work, I'll strike out, or modify the preface. Still, I really think just what I say; the Japanese are better than the Christians, and Christianity only seems to corrupt their morals. I have n't gone that far in the book; but I am quite sure my opinions, so far as present things go, are not much out of the truth.

Fiske and others cling to the name Christianity with the desperation of drowning men; it is only a name. Our Western faith is far higher than the thing called Christianity. Our ethics have outgrown it, and burst their clothing of dogma. Our social evils are unaffected by it, except for the worse. We had to give up the legends of Genesis, the various traditions of Scriptural authorship, the belief in miracles, the belief in inspiration, the belief in vicarious sacrifice, the belief in the divinity of Christ, the belief in hell and heaven, the belief in the Father, — the belief in everything but the Holy Ghost. That is advanced Unitarianism, I believe. I 'm afraid, like Ruskin, of the Holy Ghost; the Lord and Giver of Life, — that we don't know anything about, except as He "wells up in consciousness." But what is left of Christianity? Why, nothing whatever essentially of Christ. And just as surely as everything else has gone, so surely the very name must go at last. To the thinkers of a higher and more rational faith in the future, the very name — recalling so much that is horrible in human history — will be discarded because of its exclusiveness, its narrowness, and its memories of blood and fire. (There's heresy for you!)

I should find living away from all Europeans rather hard, if it were not for the little world I have made around me. Some of it lingers in Matsue; but there are nearly twelve here to whom I am Life and Food and other things. However intolerable anything else is, at home I enter into my little smiling world of old ways and thoughts and courtesies; — where all is soft and gentle as something seen in sleep. It is so soft, so intangibly gentle and lovable and artless, that sometimes it seems a dream only; and then a fear comes that it might vanish away. It has become Me. When I am pleased, it laughs; when I don't feel jolly, everything is silent. Thus, light and vapoury as its force seems, it is a moral force, perpetually appealing to conscience. I cannot imagine what I should do away from it. It is better to enter some old Buddhist cemetery here, than moulder anywhere else. For one may at least vaguely hope the realization of the old Buddhist saying: "The relation of father and child is but one life only; yet that of husband and wife is for two, and that of master and servant for three." You know the verse, of course.

Very faithfully,
LAFCADIO HEARN.

January 23, 1893.

DEAR CHAMBERLAIN, — With a penetration peculiarly your own, you have probed my weak point
(one which your criticism makes me feel aware of for
the first time strongly). Yes; I have got out of touch
with Europe altogether, and think of America when
I make comparisons. At nineteen years of age, after
my people had been reduced from riches to poverty
by an adventurer, — and before I had seen anything
of the world except in a year of London among the
common folk,— I was dropped moneyless on the pave-
ment of an American city to begin life. Had a rough
time. Often slept in the street, etc., worked as a servant, waiter, printer, proof-reader, hack-writer, gradually pulled myself up. I never gave up my English
citizenship. But I had eighteen years of American
life, — and so got out of touch with Europe. For the
same reason, I had to work at literature through
American vehicles. That is no matter, however, because it has only been within the last few years that I
learned to master my instrument a little, — language.
My first work was awfully florid. I have a novel,
"Chita," written in 1886, though not published for
two or three years later, which I am now ashamed
of. Self-control was the hardest thing to learn.
Now I have got on far enough not to be afraid to
offer work to an English publisher. Your offer of an
introduction is of the highest importance possible.
As for the book I think there is no doubt the publishers will yield. But I would like to try my next
luck with an English firm, very much. . . .

You tell me about your difficulty in literary composition, — perhaps I can make suggestion. I do not know your method, and everybody has his own. But I think I know your difficulty, — that it is also my own in Japan. Composition becomes difficult only when it becomes work, — that is literary labour without a strong inspirational impulse or an emotional feeling behind it. Now, in Japan, after the first experiences are over, — I can't imagine anybody having either an inspiration or a strong emotion. The atmosphere is soporific, grey, without electricity. Therefore work has to be forced. I never write without painfully forcing myself to do it.

Now there are two ways of forced work. The first is to force thought by concentration. This is fatiguing beyond all expression, — and I think injurious. I can't do it. The second way is to force the *work* only, and let the thought develop itself. This is much less fatiguing, and gives far better results, — sometimes surprising results that are mistaken for inspiration.

I go to work in this way. The subject is before me; I can't bother even thinking about it. That would tire me too much. I simply arrange the notes. and write down whatever part of the subject most pleases me first. I write hurriedly without care. Then I put the MS. aside for the day, and do something else more agreeable. Next day I read over the pages written, correct, and write them all over again. In the course of doing this, quite mechanically new thoughts come up, errors make themselves felt, improvements are suggested. I stop. Next day, I re-write the third time. This is the test time. The result is a great improvement usually,—but not perfection. I then take clean paper, and begin to make the final copy. Usually this has to be done twice. In the course of four to five rewritings, the whole thought reshapes itself, and the whole style is changed and fixed. The work has done itself, developed, grown; it would have been very different had I trusted to the first thought. But I let the thought define and crystallize itself.

Perhaps you will say this is too much trouble. I used to think so. But the result is amazing. The average is five perfect pages a day, with about two or three hours work. By the other method one or two pages a day are extremely difficult to write. Indeed I do not think I could write one perfect page a day, by thinking out everything as I write. The mental strain is too much. The fancy is like a horse that goes well without whip or spur, and refuses duty if either are used. By petting it and leaving it free, it surpasses desire. I know when the page is fixed by a sort of focussing it takes, — when the first impression has returned after all corrections more forcibly than at first felt, and in half the space first occupied. Perhaps you have done all this in prose, as you must have done it in other work; but if you have not, you will be astonished at the relief it gives. My whole book was written thus. Of course it looks like big labour to rewrite every page half a dozen times. But in reality it is the least possible labour. To those with whom writing is almost an automatic exertion, the absolute fatigue is no more than that of writing a letter. The rest of the work *does itself*, without your effort. It is like spiritualism. Just move the pen, and the ghosts do the wording, etc. I am writing this only as a letter to you. It makes so many pages. If I were writing it for print, I would rewrite at least five times, — with the result of putting the same thoughts much more forcibly in half the space. Then again, I keep the thing going like a conjurer's balls. The first day's five pp. are recopied the second, and another five written; — the third day the first five are again recopied, and another five written. There is always matter ahead, though, I never recopy more than the first five, at one time. When these are finished, then I begin the second five. The average is five per day, 150 pp. per month. Another important thing is to take the most agreeable part of the subject first. Order is of no earthly consequence, but a great hindrance. The success of this part gives encouragement, and curiously develops the idea of the relative parts.

Well, perhaps, I have been telling you something you know more about than I; but comparing notes is always good, and often a help. And now for another subject.

There is a queer custom in Izumo which may interest you. When a wedding takes place in the house of an unpopular man in the country, the young men of the village carry a roadside statue of Jizo into the Zashiki, and announce the coming of the God. (This is especially done with an avaricious farmer, or a stingy family.) Food and wine are demanded for the God. The members of the family must come in, salute the Deity, and give all the Sake and food demanded while any remains in the house. It is dangerous to refuse; the young peasants would probably wreck the house. ´After this, the statue is carried back again to its place. The visit of Jizo is much dreaded. It is never made to persons who are liked. In the cities this is not done, but stones are thrown into the house in heaps. Such an action is an expression of public opinion almost as strong as that of our Western charivari.

Ever faithfully,
LAFCADIO HEARN.

. . . English self-suppression is certainly a marvellous quality. Yet it is something so different from this Eastern self-control. Its pent-up vital force moreover finds vent in many ways unknown to the Orient, and foreign to its character. And lastly; is it not considerably one-sided? Is it not confined to the outer repression of everything suggesting weakness or affection, — not to the masking of other feelings? Think of Heine's Englishman, with a black halo of spleen cutting against the sunny Italian sky! But, jest aside, see the Faces of London (I remember them still) or the Faces of any English crowd. There is such pain and passion there. Again, the extraordinary mobility and development of the facial muscles, shows something totally different to the Buddhist jihi-calm of these Japanese masks. If we could draw a line at all I would say it lies here: — We suppress the amiable facial expression, and expose the aggressive and the sorrowful and the painful feelings; — while the Japanese cultivate the

former, even as a mask, and suppress, in physiognomical play, everything representing the latter.
Of course the peculiar nakedness of the American
face greatly exaggerates the harder side of physiognomy, as we know it in Europe. America is the
country of terrible faces: Fourier ought to have lived
in it before writing his chapter on the physiognomy
of the civilizés. One other thing in the way of op-
posites, I think, is that we suppress certain forms of
action more than their expression by physiognomy;
while the Japanese repress the facial exhibition
more than the action which would be the ultimate
possible result of the feeling in question. A Western
man would (unless belonging to a very artificial class
of society) be apt to look serious before killing himself. But even the average Japanese would smile
more pleasantly, and act more kindly than usual,
just before cutting his throat or lying down in front
of a railway train. Hard and fast lines, however, are
difficult to draw. Nothing is so hazardous as to attempt to make any general statement,—and yet
no temptation is stronger.

Ever with best wishes,

LAFCADIO HEARN.

February 4, 1893.

DEAR CHAMBERLAIN, — . . . It is the Setsubun;
and we have cast out the devils. I have had various
little ceremonies performed upon me to keep me well
and happy under the protection of the Gods for the
year. The other day we presented a lantern to Fudo-
San. When I get ever so little sick, all sorts of pretty

prayers are offered up to the Gods for me; and little vows of self-denial are made. I protested a year ago against some of the vows. I had been really sick, and my father-in-law (he is a charming old man) vowed to live upon some totally unsubstantial diet for a year, if I got well. I made such a pretence of anger about that, that the vow was changed for a more rational one, — a present to the Gods; but in all ordinary matters, I like these simple little acts of faith and piety and encourage them, and reverence the Gods. So that my foreign names appear upon many wooden tablets at various queer old shrines.

You ask about Matsue foreigners. If it is nothing very special I think I can get you whatever information you want. . . .

. . . Just now I can't remember the names of the beasts who were there before B—, — but the story is not spoiled for that. They aimed especially at converting Samurai girls,— because these were educated, and supposed to still possess some small influence. They were also very poverty-stricken, — desperate, starving; struggling between death and dishonour, — for Samurai girls had high notions of chastity. What the missionaries wanted were native local proselytizers. They induced one girl by promises of employment to become a preacher for them. They paid her three yen a month. Of course in becoming a convert, she became a social pariah. Her people cast her off; common folk despised her. She was an innocent sort of a girl, — talked simply and feebly, — betrayed in her very manner the necessity and the compulsion. The people paid no attention to her. The missionaries dropped her as a useless instrument. Then no one would give her work or help. She became a prostitute. But even as a prostitute, her connection with proselytism had rendered her disreputable. So she was sold to an Osaka brothel.

After what you say about your own latitudinarianism, I am not afraid of my preface; it will not be offensive to you in the least. I hold with Lecky on the church in the Middle Ages, — socially it was a cementing force, — intellectually a curse to humanity, perhaps, but even this may yet prove to have been a necessary evil. The intrinsic merits claimed for it, I can't help thinking really to have been outside of it, — older than it, — superior to it. The germ of the eternal truth is the same in all faiths, — the same flame dimly burning within receptacles of forms beyond memory for multitude. To abuse the receptacles, the wrappings, the coverings, of one light more than of another would perhaps be irrational in itself, — if one did not feel that, as dissolution is as necessary to advance as integration, there are ripe times and green times. When one sees dogmas used for wickedness of all sorts, and all the good men outside of them, one thinks it time to say even outrageous things.

By the way, what you say about Rome awakes a chord. You know, I suppose, that my relatives tried once to make a priest of me. My father was an Episcopalian; but after his death in India, I fell into the hands of relatives who sent me to a Jesuit College. By the Jesuit standard, I was a fiend incarnate, and treated accordingly. How I hated them. My impotent resentment used to relieve itself in the imagination of massacres and horrible tortures. I hate them and have nightmares about them still. And yet at times, there comes to me a half wish to be a monk. This is all a romance, — the romance of the ideal monastery, with gothic ogives, libraries of vellums illumined by the stained-glass windows, etc., and rest from struggle. But the reality is Browning's "Soliloquy of the Spanish Cloister." Still, there is a world of romance in old Romanism.

Don't you think the Greek church (my mother's) has a better chance of life? Russia seems to me the Coming Race. I think there will be some day a Russian Mass sung in Saint Peter's. And that Cossack soldiers will wait, at Stamboul, in the reconsecrated basilica of Justinian, for the apparition of that phantom priest destined to finish the mass interrupted by the swords of the Janizaries of Mahomet 2nd.

(Next time, I'll say something about Spencer. To-night I must say good-bye.)

Ever most truly,

LAFCADIO HEARN.

KUMAMOTO, February 5, 1893.

DEAR CHAMBERLAIN, — Well, I have read "Le Disciple." My first impression of the book was an unfair one; — I was annoyed by the writer's posing as a philosopher and moralist, and by his superficialism in the former rôle, — as well as by the extraordinary morbidness of the book. Even now I strongly suspect Bourget has not studied modern philosophy, but rather morbid pathology, — neurological experiments, obscene and otherwise, at the Salpêtrière, — something also perhaps of hypnotism. But after thinking over the matter, I must confess art in the book, must recognize the possibility of the types, and must acknowledge discovering in it the same purpose characterizing "Cruelle Énigme," and "Un Crime d'Amour;" revelation of faith and truth through consequences of inflicting suffering, — or, perhaps better, Nature enforcing recognition through the results of attempts to outrage and blaspheme her. Besides I have met and known M. Greslon, — a young professor of philosophy at a Colonial College, who used to analyze his own sensations for my benefit, dissect the feelings of the poor half-breed girl he lived with and whom he assured me he hated, and set down in a secret journal all her words, thoughts, etc. (as well as those of his unsuspecting male friends). He died of yellow fever; — we examined his papers, read a part, stared foolishly at each other, and burned the whole. I think he is better dead, — but having known him, I can't deny the possibility of Robert Greslon. He has lived; therefore he lives. He is a peculiarly modern French product.

There are certainly, however, weak points in the book from a philosophical point of view, — which cannot be said, perhaps, of "Crime d'Amour," or "Cruelle Énigme." The author's imagination about the old materialist doing for the evolution of sentiment what Darwin did for the evolution of species, is weak. (The comparison cannot hold; for Darwin did not discover the evolution of species at all, — but only certain natural laws relating to it.) The fact is that the evolution of sentiments has been very elaborately traced out by modern psychology, and that so far from narrowing our comprehension of the value of what is beautiful in human nature, has enormously expanded it. I am not prepared to deny that a mere study of the conclusions of scientific investigation in this line (without a profound knowledge of the tremendous and eternal facts behind them), may not lead to very evil shallow notions. A study of ultimate facts is absolutely necessary, and there is a vast class of persons which never attempt that study. (Bourget certainly seems to be one.) The question of animal origins of sentiment can appear materialistic and shocking only to an ignorant mind. When we learn that the origin of our pleasure in the sense of colour (now transformed into pure æstheticism), may be sought for in the first development and utilization of the sense for the discovery of food; — or when we are told that our pleasure in odours has a like origin; — or when we find that the history of maternal love begins with the apparition of milk-secretion in the mammalia, etc., etc., — how much nearer to the great mystery of things does that bring us? On the contrary the horizon recedes. What is Life, Feeling, Will —? No man not insane can pretend to say. But the more we learn the more the awe of the mystery. And taking for example the sweetest thing in the world, — a perfect woman-soul, — how infinitely more pre-

cious it seems to us as the sum of all the goodness of
a chain of lives reaching back through a million
years into "God" or "The Unknowable," than as
the spontaneous creation of a theological deity.

Then, again, there is the suggestion in Bourget
that education can transform character, — in the
individual. This seems to me the weak point of the
book. It is opposed to modern philosophy altogether; it would be ridiculed by any country school-
master in New England. A character like the Greslon of Bourget, or the Greslon I knew, is not made
by education, but simply defined. As truly as "a
silk purse cannot be made out of a sow's ear," just
so truly the converse. As surely as there are inherited forms of vice, just so surely are there ancestral moralities. Nay, the latter is the rule, the
former the exception. The poor people, *en masse*,
are moral; — the goodness of ten thousand years is
in the marrow of their bones. No system of education possible in modern society can make a naturally
good man into a real scoundrel. Education can only
give definition to preëxisting tendencies.

To this it may be answered that there are characters in which the tendencies to good and the tendencies to evil are so nicely balanced, that an error in
education might throw them out of equipoise. This
supposition is, in nine cases out of ten, based on a
theological superstition, — unconsciously. As a fact
there is no such delicate equipoise possible in nature.
Each being represents a sum of tendencies inherited
out of the unknown, — the course of a stream of
life whose flow must be decided partly indeed by

conditions, but even more so by its own intrinsic volume and power. As well talk of turning a river with a pebble as of transmuting a character by education. If character is psychically a sum of inherited tendencies, it is physiologically a plexus of nerve tissue. In both its phases it may be changed, or at least modified, in the course of generations, by additions and subtractions and influences of infinite complexity; but never in a single life. "Can the Ethiopian change?" etc. Who so well aware of this fact as the Jesuits? Out of ten thousand students they choose, finding perhaps ten fit for their work.

And what an unnatural presentation is that of a veteran philosopher resting upon the assumption that right and wrong have no abstract existence. That might do for an uneducated scepticism ("workingman's atheism"), — scarcely for anybody with capacity to read and think. Certainly vice and virtue exist only relatively to human society (and animal societies also); but their concrete importance is nowise lessened by the knowledge of their limitation as social facts. One may hold vice beneficial, like Mandeville, or the reverse; but a simple denial of good and evil as facts would be exactly similar to a denial of pleasure and pain as real sensations. Indeed I think that to modern philosophy vice has taken a new and terrible magnitude, and virtue an awful beauty. As sums of human experience with good and evil, or with pain and pleasure, how incomparably vast they seem. What is a crime, declared crime only by a local code or a sectarian dogma, compared with crime recognized as crime

against the whole consensus of all human moral
experience!

Here I may say something Bourget has defined in
my head, — I doubt the spirituality of the Latin
races. They seem to me essentially materialistic.
The emotional life of them seems to be in the nerves,
even their most exquisite sensations. Taine has
well shown how debauchery and vice are contrary
to the Northern nature in a sort, — how the English
instinctively recognize they can't be immoral without becoming brutal. On the other hand the French
seem unable to become philosophical without becoming grossly materialistic. They talk forever of
"abîmes;" yet which of them dive to the profundi-
ties or soar to the heights reached by the Genius of
the North? Imagine a French Goethe: or a Spanish
Richter: or an Italian Emerson or Carlyle. Compare even their realism with Northern realism, —
say Kipling with Maupassant. Find anything resembling what Clifford calls a "cosmic emotion" in
their positivism. Even Renan is a Breton, — not a
Latin. Fancy a Frenchman writing anything with a
sustained ghostly charm of intellect in it like "The
Soul of the far East." The nearest approach to soul
in French books is an extreme sensual refinement, —
a vibrant sense of nature in relation to the body;
and this quality, — (easily mistaken for something
higher) vanishes with youth, and the dulling of the
nerves, — and there remains the ashes of the commonplace.

Then what force in a Scandinavian or Russian
novel, compared with a Latin one. For morbid pa-

thology Bourget is a child to Dostoievsky; — for
another sort of story, compare Tolstoi's "Cossacks"
with the best work of Mérimée, — say "Carmen"
or "Colomba." I rather think it desirable that Europe should "become Cossack." We are growing too
nervous and tired and enervated in the West; — a
general infusion of barbarian blood would greatly
assist, and improve literature. Our morbid Englishman is Mallock. I read and detest him; his work is
symptomatic. If you have no liking for him, give
the book to some friend who may. By the way, do
you know Sacher-Masoch? I have sent for his novels. If you have not read "La Mère de Dieu," you
will have a treat. I think he is a Jew; and I am very
fond of the Jewish novelists. The best are Slavs, —
or at least from the Slavic side of Austria. . . .

I am charmed by your delightful suggestion of
faith in future possibilities beyond scientific recognition, — though too much of a Spencer lover to
think of Spencer as dogmatic. We know that memory is inherited, — only in the process of transmission it now becomes transmitted into instinct and
impulse, — into vague unaccountable shrinkings
and aspirations, loves and fears. But why should we
hold it must always be so. As the spectroscope reveals the existence of colour-scales invisible to our
imperfect vision, there may well be psychic facts
undreamed of yet awaiting discovery. The time
may come when the fable of the Bodhisattva's memory will prove a common truth, — when with each
advance in development there will lighten up recollections of past existence, and one can say, — "What

a fool I was to do that thing five thousand years ago." Remembrance of all the past in all its details might be horribly unpleasant, but also incalculably useful. And I can imagine (illegitimately, perhaps, but still imagine) a condition of developmental activity in which time and space would have no relative existence, — and a thousand years be as a day. There is one grim fact about our new philosophy. We know that we are approaching slowly a degree of equilibration which means happiness; but we also know that the dissolution of a solar system is as certain as its integration. Everything evolves only to dissolve, — so far as known facts teach us. After all, we have reached no further than the unscientific but strangely inspired thinkers of India, with their ancient theory of cycles. Buddhism and Spencer, before the Ultimate, stand upon the same ground. And I think of your wise saying about taking one's faith ready made. Assuredly it seems the most rational, and beyond doubt it is the prudent course for those who can devote their minds to more momentous and useful things. Then I would say for me Buddhism.

Mason said a delightful thing in his last letter to me, about the effect of Japanese art in teaching him to see and feel the beauty of snow. I have had the same experience. European art does not seem to me to have ever caught the Soul of Snow as the Japanese art has, — with its fantasticalities, its wizardisms. And the Japanese fancy has its "Snow-women" too — its white spectres and goblins, which do no harm and say nothing, only frighten and make one feel cold. I can see the beauty of snow now, but still it makes me shiver. I think the Yukionna sometimes when I am asleep, passes her white arm through a crack of the amado into my sleeping room, and in spite of the fire, touches my heart and laughs. Then I wake up, and pull the futons closer, and think of palm trees, and parrots, and mangoes, and the blue of the tropical water. What a delight it would be to follow the birds south every autumn. — But I forgot, you dislike heat, and blazing sun, and perspiration.   Ever most truly,

LAFCADIO HEARN.

P. S. What you said about railroads and Christ is admirable. I am beginning to doubt very strongly the ultimate value of our boasted material progress, — to doubt "civilization" as a human benefit.

I promise not to write so long a letter again. Really, I am ashamed of thus intruding on your time, you *must* be bored if you read all this.

February 6, 1893.

Dear Chamberlain, — Your letter about the method of composition has come, — far more lucid than my rather vague epistle on the same subject, which I now find requires some further explanation. Of course I did not mean printed pages, — only MS. pp. like this: I could not make 150 good printed 12mo pages in less than four months under very favourable circumstances and with the hardest work. Besides, I was speaking of forced composition. Inspirational work, emotional work, is just twenty times harder, if it can be measured at all. Too much importance cannot be attached to the value of an emotion, — the "kernel," as you so aptly term it. But this comes only as a feeling. To perfectly disengage it (*le dégager*), develop it, discover its whole meaning, focus it, is killing work. There is delight in looking at the result; but that is obtained only by actually giving one's blood for it. I am talking now, perhaps, as if I were a big instead of a very small writer; but the truth is that the cost is greater in proportion to the smallness of original power. I have had to rewrite pages fifty times. It is like a groping for something you know is inside the stuff, but the exact shape of which you don't know. That is, I think, also the explanation of the sculptor's saying that the figure was already in the marble; the art was only to "disengage it."

Didactic work is one of the hardest, of course. Nothing is harder to write than a primer. Simplicity combined with force is required; and that combination requires immense power. (There I reverence Huxley, for example.) And as you excellently observe, the effect of the work is in direct ratio to the pains taken to produce it by a master hand. This takes no small time to learn. What apparent ease in writing really means I regret to say that I only learned a few years ago; if I had learned sooner, it would have done me much good.

Otherwise your method is in all points like mine. I have to do much excision of "verys," "thats" and "whiches," — to murder adjectives and adverbs, — to modify verbs. Every important word seems to me to have three qualities: form, sound, and colour. After the first and last have been considered, follows the question of the rhythm of the sentence. This I think may approach blank verse, at the termination of paragraphs, if a strong emotion be expressed. It may be smooth as oil if the effect to be produced is smooth, — or rough, — or violent as may be. But all this is never done by rule, — only by instinctive feeling, half unconsciously. In the body of a paragraph too much flow and rhythm seems to hurt the effect. Full force is best reserved for the casting-throw of the whole thought or emotion. I should like now to go through many paragraphs written years ago, and sober them down.

Print, of course, is the great test. Colour only comes out in proof, — never in MS. I can't get anything perfect in MS. A friend is invaluable. You are very lucky to have Mason. I have nobody in Japan to read to, or to ask advice of; and I feel the void very much. Why a man of such delicate taste as Mason does not himself write charming books, I don't know. Perhaps you could make him try.

Then I keep note-books. I have no memory to speak of, since my experiences with tropical fevers and other sickness. I note down every sensation or idea, as you say *au vol*. And I have classified note-books, — with indexes; must show you some one of these days.

Now I am just going to "lie fallow" for six months. Indeed I can do nothing else; for there is nothing to see, hear, or feel in Kyūshū, I think. And I want to learn something thoroughly, so as to try to write stories or sketches of a better sort. I want sensations too. But out of Japanese life I fear no strong sensation will ever again come to me. I feel fizzed out. *"Mon âme a perdu ses ailes."*

Faithfully ever,

LAFCADIO HEARN.

Wonder if you will have patience to read the long scrawling scraggy letter I sent yesterday. You must not think I mean to be so verbose often.

February 18, 1893.

Dear Chamberlain, — . . . Let me pray and beg and entreat and supplicate you to read Loti's "Roman d'un Spahi." It will give you a better opinion of him. I regret I have no copy to send you. Otherwise I feel inclined to agree with you about his later books, his " Fantôme d'Orient," etc. However, I am sure you must have liked "Rêve;" if you did not, I can only explain the fact by the supposition that its tropical charm appeals to nothing in your personal experience as it does, almost poignantly, to something in mine. I know the strange equatorial twilight, — the *petite rue triste, triste,* — the planter's interior with the banana shadow trembling in a square of sunlight on the bare floor, — the furniture, — the hat, — the young woman with the great sad eyes. Nay, I know the cemetery. And when I read that story first, it made me very thoughtful for a long time, so that for a week I did not like to talk; I wanted to enjoy the pleasure of the ghostly pain.

Then don't you think there was a touch of weird

pathos in Viande de Boucherie? it affected me very
much. The Japanese tale is made unnecessarily repulsive; — still, I liked that trembling in the leaves;
when the spirits of the ancestors come to take the
poor soul unto themselves, — and the suggestion
that the miserable little corpse will live again in the
blossoming of the azaleas and marvellous flowers;
purified by the all-tender soul of Nature, and re-
stored into her eternal youth.

But I fear Loti's nerves are played out. His work
has become morbid of late. Only in exotic subjects
he excels all others living, I think. His pictures of
the Pacific, of Senegal, of South America and the
Mediterranean bewitch me beyond all utterance. I
don't agree with James, that his great work is in
"Mon Frère Yves," and in "Pêcheur d'Islande."
Indeed I don't think James really read those other
works. To me Loti seems for a space to have looked
into Nature's whole splendid burning fulgurant soul,
and to have written under her very deepest and
strongest inspiration. He was young. Then the
colour and the light faded, and only the worn-out
blasé nerves remained; and the poet became, — a
little morbid modern affected Frenchman.

Loti used to write to me a little, — not very
familiarly, and I have his photograph. It is rather
disappointing in some respects, he looks more like a
fop than a great poet. But since he became a member of the Academy, he answers letters only through
his Secretary, —

"*Monsieur,*

   M. Pierre Loti vous remercie," etc., —

which is simply disgusting. Again the translation of his worst books must accentuate his error in departing from the path in which Nature herself taught him to excel. Perhaps she is punishing him for not loving her enough, — with his heart instead of his nerves.

Never mind, I'll have a treat for you in Sacher-Masoch.

"Returning to Sir Walter," etc., reminds me of my own recent experience. I used to adore Tennyson's "Idyls of the King." But to-day what artificial, strained, over-delicate conservatory work they seem, after a fresh perusal of naïf Sir Malory's "Morte d'Arthur," which is all pure human nature. After for years studying poetical prose, I am forced now to study simplicity. After attempting my utmost at ornamentation, I am converted by my own mistakes. The great point is to touch with simple words. And I feel my style is not yet fixed, — too artificial. By another year of study or two, I think I shall be able to do better.

The winter here has been snowless and beautifully clear for the majority of days. Wherefore I ought to be happy, and would be if I had a friend like Nishida here. Also I find I am morally better by reason of the stove and a warm room. My folks say I have never said a cross word since I had a warm room. Heat thus appears as a moral force. Just think how holy I should be could I live forever under the equator.

Ever most faithfully,

LAFCADIO HEARN.

Nishida and others *admire* your Japanese writing,
not as *yours* merely, but in itself. I won't tell you
the prettiest things he said about it; but I can't see
the fine differences between your Japanese writing
and that of others, except the differences caused by
the use of a pen of a peculiar kind. But Nishida said
if I studied Japanese writing *for ten years*, — even
then I would not know good writing if I saw it.
Heigho!

My chat about Loti has defined something else in
my mind. (I feel more and more convinced that
Frenchmen think only with their nerves, — and too
much with the pudic nerve especially.) There was
Gautier, — wondrous artist (I translated and published his Contes and Nouvelles when I was too
young to do the work well); and that magician of
language never appealed to anything behind the
senses. His most perfect poem — "Musée Secret,"
perhaps the most perfect poem in the French language — was marvellous; — a Greek god could not
have done better; the thoughts, the words, the comparisons, the allusions, the melody are simply *divine*.
But . . . the subject? (It is published in Bergerat's
"Souvenirs de Théophile Gautier.") Such work daz-
zles and makes the senses reel with its sensuous splendour, — yet when I turn to the simple little poem containing the verse (I know not the author's name), —

> Nos clairons sonnaient "En avant,"
> Elle a pleuré, pleuré, pleuré; —
> J'ai marché, — et je marche toujours, —
> Et jamais je ne reviendrai, —

there I feel the Eternal Heart beating, which lives

beyond space and time. Or take again a comparison of North and South: —

> Nombril, je t'aime, astre du ventre,
> Oeil blanc dans le marbre sculpté,
> Et que l'Amour a mis au centre
> Du sanctuaire ou seul il entre,
> Comme un cachet de volupté.
>
> (GAUTIER.)

This is very, very fine use of language of course, but the simple —

> She is more beautiful than Day —

of Tennyson is worth a million of it. Of course these comparisons are absurdly extreme; but I think they are characteristic. Put the best poem by the *rather* spiritual Hugo beside Heine's " Pilgrimage to Kevlaar." We have French-English poets, however. Swinburne's music is indeed wonderful, but I 'd rather read the old ballad about the harper who

> Could harp the fish out of the sea
> Or bluid out of a stane,
> Or milk out of a maiden's breast
> That never bairns had nane.

I hope for the Russian invasion of the West. When the Russians have, after the conquest, reached the point of writing poems like Gautier's "Nombril," and the other, it will then be time for the Chinese to conquer the world.

L. H.

February 24, 1893.

DEAR CHAMBERLAIN, — "Doña Luz," which I have nearly finished, has been producing a curious phenomenon in my mind. I told you I had forgotten

most of my Spanish, after ten years out of touch
with everything Spanish. Beginning "Doña Luz," I
was surprised to find how obscure everything
seemed; but as a portion of each sentence remained
clear, I determined to go on and see what the effect
would be. On the third day I was astonished, —
because nearly everything came back to me again;
and even the parts at first obscure lighted up suddenly as with a flash. And now I find myself able
even to think a little in Spanish again. But that
was only one side of the experience.

With this resurrection of the memory of Spanish,
recurred to me, with vividness extraordinary, two
episodes of my early Spanish studies, — long forgotten, — especially the memory of a certain blue-
washed balconied room in an old Creole house over-
looking bananas, and one enormous fig tree. The
two episodes may perhaps amuse you, — since you
say you can really sometimes find recreation in my
scribbling.

My first teacher was an old man with a long face,
like Alva, and a long beard. He had two gypsy-
looking daughters, — really attractive señoritas,
and two swarthy sinister-looking sons. A peculiarity of the whole family was that I never saw any of
them smile. One day the old man and I had some
sharp words. He had borrowed from me a considerable sum of money, which he failed to return. On
my using some indignant language, he threatened
me with his sons. Now I had seen his sons, — so I
put a revolver in each pocket whenever I went out.
But I learned a few days later that my revolvers

would have been of no service. For one of the sons, having a slight difference of opinion with a planter, blew out the man's brains with a double-barrelled shot-gun near my house. A revolver is useless against buckshot. I thought myself lucky, and resigned myself to the loss.

Then I obtained a milder teacher, — a Mexican youth, with a very curious Indian face. He spoke only the tropical Spanish, — which has no thay or difficult erray; but that was just what I wanted. We became companeros. But somebody found out his name, and translated it. This proved disastrous. For his name was *José de Jesus y Preciado*. It was translated into "precious Jesus" by some rascally young Americans; and poor José was accused of being a peripatetic blasphemy. Wherefore he was obliged to return to the land of Ixtacihuatl, — where such names are in the odour of sanctity, and I saw him no more. So much for the Episodes. As for "Doña Luz," I don't know what to compare the art of it to. It has a sort of quiet, intimate, yet unforgettable charm. I thought of Goldsmith, and I thought of Sandeau, — but Valera is essentially and inimitably Spanish. I am going to read all the Spanish I can for the next year or so; — especially as I hope to spend a winter one of these days in Manila, or some little city of the Philippines. For my purpose I fancy the smaller and more remote the town the better.

I have little news, except a discovery about Inari. After all there are stone foxes, — if not in Kumamoto, at least very near to it, at the little village

of Takahashi-machi, 2 ri from Kumamoto. But
these foxes are mythological hybrids; they are half
Karashishi and half foxes, — and the Karashishi
element predominates strongly. Even their attitude is rampant. Well, what is most curious is that
they are not Shinto, but *Namu-miyo-ho-renge-kyo*,
and incense is burnt, and Buddhist prayers said before them. In Izumo it is not uncommon to find
a Jizo or other Buddhist deity captured by Shinto;
but a fox-deity captured by the Nichiren-shu is
certainly new to me.

Faithfully ever,
LAFCADIO HEARN.

April 5, 1893.

DEAR CHAMBERLAIN, — I suppose it is no use to
tell you that I felt lonesome after your visit, and
selfishly vexed that you could stay only for those
few hours. Well, you see! — in spite of our agreement upon the futility of hurry-scurry and frantic
effort as means to happiness, you committed hurry-
scurry; — we can't help ourselves always. And,
Thackeray-wise, I thought of all the fine things I
wanted to say after you were gone. I wanted to
show you a doll, that was the philosophical toy of
an Emperor, — and two ink stones of Bateiseki, —
and an extraordinary text, — and. . . . But I was
so inwardly worried by the mere thought of your
going away so soon, that I forgot them. It is really
immoral only to stay such a short time; it is a para-
lyzing of wishes and intentions. Still, I would not
have missed it for anything. It knitted closer, or

rather re-knitted my old tie of gratitude and friendship; and in spite of our best endeavours such ties
will slacken a little if friends never see each other.
For we cannot be altogether ourselves on paper.

I sent the bulk of the ofuda and mamori by express, the package was too large for parcel-post. But
I kept back many things I knew you had. Also I
kept back two mamori you have not, — two that I
don't like to surrender altogether on account of
associations, but which I can send you for use whenever you want them. Or, to speak more frankly, my
folks begged me not to send away those two, which
we got under peculiar circumstances while travelling.

. . . The day after you left it . . . snowed! I
thought of you, and felt uneasy; for you had a cold,
and the change must have been terrible a few hundred miles north. What an unmerciful winter.

To return to older topics, an idea is growing upon
me about the utility of superstition as compared
with the utility of religion. Indeed the latter is but
an elaboration of the former, and both have truth
at the bottom of them. Superstition in Japan has a
sort of shorthand value in explaining eternal and
valuable things. To preach to people (who know
nothing) about sociological morality, — or the relation of cleanliness to health, — or other things of
that kind, — would certainly be waste of breath.
A superstition serves the purpose infinitely better.
But I think the superstition is in many cases developed after the practice begins. Some practices
must have originated simply in the will of political
or religious rulers. After the force of their com-

mand had spent itself, it was continued and revived
by new beliefs. The beliefs that to drop nail parings
in a hibachi will cause madness; that not to shave
the hair and eyebrows of Samurai children will
cause them to have misfortune in war; that to lay
futon unevenly will cause a quarrel between husband and wife; that to make the Shoji of a room over-
lap to the left instead of to the right is to invite
misfortune; that to leave a room unswept is an in-
vitation to Bimbogami; that to touch a pillow
with the foot is displeasing to the gods; that to tread
upon or crumple either written or printed paper, or
writing of any kind, is wickedness, — all these and
a hundred others are so closely related to practical
truths of a much larger character than themselves,
that one feels a new respect for superstition in
analyzing them. Is n't it the same with much of our
Western religion? Why, it was only the other day
that the proposition for the teaching of sociological
morality was made for the first time in America; in
other words, it is only at the present day that we are
able, in our very highest educational institutions, to
rationalize morals and scientifically illustrate the
relation of actions to consequences. Hell and damnation, angels and devils and myths, have certainly
had incomparable value as shorthand religious
moral teachings. Fancy trying to get into a peasant's head the whole reason why adultery, incest,
or murder are punished as crimes.

I hope if we are to have another winter like this,
that you will be able to spend it in a warm country,
— a tropical country. Dr. Haga has nearly cured me,

but the climate helps him. Tokyo is so changeable.
How you would enjoy a West Indian winter! For
six months it is heaven; after that you begin to feel
the drain on the system. But six months is a wonderful tonic. If ever I get rich enough I have three
ambitions to fulfil: — (1) A winter in Manila;
(2) A winter in Pondicherry; (3) A winter in Java.
These will perhaps be the luxuries of my old age,
if I have any.

Ever with sincerest regards,
Lafcadio Hearn.

April 10, 1893.

Dear Chamberlain, — Your kindest letter from
Moji made me very glad; — also took away some
uneasiness, for it hinted your intention of shortly
getting home, which I really think is best. I have
not been feeling comfortable about that cold of
yours; and prolonged further travelling, in fitful
weather, might I think make it worse, — especially if you are out of the reach of recuperative
solid food. Sometimes I have been quite miserable
while travelling for want of even good Japanese food,
which I had to make up for by sake. I hope this
will find you already at home, before a big pink
fragrant roast of beef, with a bottle of claret beside
you, and your cold quite well. Since I wrote last the
Spring has really come; my trees are turning pink
under the green. And to-morrow or next day I expect to hear my fate from Boston; the only doubt
now seems to be the question of quantity, for which
I made a stout fight.

My little wife was more than pleased by your kind words of thanks. You surprised my house, by the way. To hear an Englishman speak English was not a new experience, of course; but to hear an Englishman "speak better Japanese than a Japanese" and so as "to make Japanese blush for their Japanese" was an astonishment. I translate these little compliments verbatim, because they were straight from the heart, and cannot seem to you to have been uttered with any idea of flattery,—for they were too innocent to think of that.

I sent you the "Naulahka" to amuse you the next wet day, and my Gougaristic first-novel. The ofuda went by express. I have been thinking over things. I have some curious legends about many of the ofuda which might come in useful some day. For instance there is a family in Matsue which has for its *mon* an ofuda of Ise. Why? The story is that once a servant of the family went to Ise in despite of the master's order to remain in the house. When he came back the Samurai flew into a rage and killed him. Then the murderer felt sorry, and buried the body in the garden, — or bamboo-patch. The day after the servant came back again, and apologized for his absence at Ise. You can guess the rest of the legend. When the grave was opened there was no dead body there, — only an ofuda cut in two as if by a sword-slash.

Well, I have various legends of this kind. I think I can get from Matsue ofuda relating to other traditions. I don't believe in "writing up" to illustrations in most cases; but in this particular sort of study it is well worth while. There are the beautiful or curious legends of Hinomisaki, of the Matsudaira Inari, of the Tenjin ofuda, of weird Zenkoji (where I want to go next summer); and there are songs, and there are proverbs. To use all will be impossible. But to use the strangest and most imaginative by selection would have a startling effect. A specially interesting department would be related to the ofuda and mamori of children or of Children's Gods, — with Jizo in a hundred forms at the head. All this for future pleasant lazy days. I won't impose on your eyes any more this time, but will say good-bye (till next American mail comes).

With best regards, and kindliest remembrances from us all here,

Ever most faithfully,
LAFCADIO HEARN.

April 13, 1893.

DEAR CHAMBERLAIN, — Talk of the "pendulum!" How my letters must amuse you between times! (I say amuse, knowing your patience.) They reflect my own perturbations of spirit. But they are certainly a record of illusion and disillusion. Now only is it time, according to Amiel, whom you quoted in your book, that I ought to be able to treat the subject of Japan at all sensibly. But Amiel, like our friend Mason, did not write at all; he only made notes. He waited, like Mason, till the illusion passed. And had I so waited, I believe I could never have written at all. Happily I will have at least two indulgent readers.

To-day there was a ceremony which partly reconciled me to these people. There is a dear old Tempo man in the school, — famous in the history of the Revolution. His name is Akizuki. To-day was his seventieth birthday. He teaches Chinese to the boys. Well, all the students and all the teachers subscribed to a feast in his honour, and made speeches and did very pretty things. The boys got an oil-portrait of him painted, and took it with them to the banqueting hall. All this was nice. But soon there will be no more of these lovable old men, — nothing but addle-pated young sports with billy-cocks and cigarettes and billiards on the brain. That they can honour beautiful old age at least shows that they are not quite dead yet to themselves; but I fear the process of ossification is very rapid. There will be no hearts after a time (among the men); Waterbury watches will be substituted instead. These will be cheap and cold, but will keep up a tolerably regular ticking.

I was looking at your article on fans in "Things Japanese" yesterday, and noticed that you say all subjects are treated on fans, "except perhaps religion." The "perhaps" saves the statement; but last summer I saw many religious subjects on fans, — torii, miya, matsuri, etc., and quite a number of fans decorated with the chubby figure of Fukusuke. But the important point I would suggest is that religious fans actually form a very striking class by themselves. Nearly all the temples give away fans decorated with pictures of the holy place. These, I think, would be worth a special

mention in any work on ofuda and other sacred
curiosities.

We were talking about education the other day.
I have been thinking that the deficiencies of educational systems will have in the future to be met
with by means which it is now impossible even to
imagine. Perhaps one would be the abolition of
schools, — as too mechanical and wasteful of time.
(Herbert Spencer, I believe, never went to school
at all.) But here is the difficulty, — always growing, — which the future must face. According to
the present system, one-fourth of life at least must
be devoted simply to preparation. Another fourth
must be given to the struggle to live and maintain
a family. At least half of life must go to the mere
effort of preparing for life. This, I know, is commonplace. But all the sciences, enormously expand-
ing and subdividing into branches, are outgrowing
the institutions established to teach them, and must
continue to outgrow them with ever-increasing rapidity. (Who, for example, can now pretend to be
a good general physician? one must take a branch,
and make it a life study.) The enforcement of spe-
cialization into even rudimentary educational systems could only meet the difficulty for a certain
time;—it is one that never can be buried. And already the result of much high education is only a
smattering of much with a knowledge of nothing, —
for the average student. Our brains eat up our lives
and the life of the world, — and yet are starved or
fed with ornamental bric-à-brac. Progress is leading
us to a future in which it will require half a century

to merely prepare a brain for work; and unless the Elixir of Life be discovered, what is the use? "Inkyo" would scarcely be possible in the West. The parents (except among the really wealthy) die long before their children are able to do anything. I can't escape the conviction that an enormous part of what we now imagine to be education must be pitched overboard to lighten the ship. And we shall never, never have any more time to enjoy the world.

Ever faithfully,

LAFCADIO HEARN.

P. S. —"Ah!"

(1) Statistically it has been admirably shown that education does not decrease criminality. The superstition of the West has been that the lower classes should be educated to keep them from being dangerous. But education has made them much more dangerous than they ever were before.

(2) Buckle pointed out years ago that on the other hand, the extremely high culture of a superior class, so far from enabling it to elevate the class beneath it, actually exiles it from all other classes, — as in Germany where even the language of the scientific classes had become totally unintelligible to all others. Since Buckle's time, the same might be said of the highly cultivated classes of other countries, — their thoughts, their words, their books are hieroglyphics to the multitude.

(3) A world of extraordinary possible results can be imagined from the future aggravation of both states of things.

(4) The government of the ancient Orient,

"founded upon benevolence," resolved the difficulty unconsciously in a much better way. The education of the people shall be moral only, — shall be the teaching of eternal truths, — the relations of the family, the duties of children and subjects. And he who says anything new shall be put to death. Also he who invents inventions shall be killed. Both laws I find in the sacred books of China. They are good laws, from one point of view. And after all the matter is brought back to a celebrated maxim of Spencer's —

That the object of all education should be simply to make good fathers and mothers.

Here the ancient Orient agrees with Mr. Herbert Spencer.

But how can people be educated to become good fathers and mothers, if the largest part of life must be devoted merely to learning that which is of no practical use, — and if for the really learned marriage becomes more difficult with every generation.

The imposition of Chinese laws upon the West for a time might not be so very bad.

"Let him who says anything new, or him who shall invent anything new, be put to death."

I send a couple of Masoch's volumes of stories for you and Mason to while away dull moments with.

April 17, 1893.

DEAR CHAMBERLAIN, —. . . I find out it is not the custom here to call on the Director. And I have never spoken to him yet. But he is evidently a disciplinarian. Since he came, things have become more exact. The clock that used always to strike twelve when it was only eleven, has been corrected; tablets covered with Chinese characters proclaim rigid enactments and boundaries; and the students who assembled to hear long speeches were dismissed with a few words of Lacedemonian brevity and conciseness, almost as soon as they formed ranks. The new Director is a fine man, — looks like a handsome Jew, — walks with a long stride like an ostrich. I should like to know the mystery of him.

Why am I writing this letter? Well, just because a new idea came to me somewhat definitely. The Japanese problem is such a huge one, that I am venturesome enough to believe you have time to listen to any ideas about it not already worn out. The idea I refer to was given me by the sight of the American newspaper of which I used to be literary editor. It comes to me filled with columns headed "Feminine Gossip," "New Fashions," "Woman in Art," "Clara Belle's Letter about Small Feet," etc., all accompanied by small outline woodcuts, representing wonderful women in wonderful dresses. The original poetry is all about love and despair. The stories are tales about enamoured swains and cruel beauties. The whole thing is now nauseating to me, — yet I used to think it rather refined compared with other papers. At all events it is a type of several hundred. As a type it is suggestive.

"Teacher," cry my students, "why are English novels all about love and marriage? That seems to us very strange." They say "strange." They think "indecent." Then I try to explain:—"My dear lads, the world of the West is not as the world of the East. In the West, Society is not, as you know, constituted upon the same plan. A man must make his own family; the family does not make him. What you do not know, is that for the average educated man without money, life is a bitter and terrible fight, — a battle in which no quarter is given. And what is the simplest and most natural thing of all in Japan, — to get married, — is in the West extremely difficult and dangerous. Yet all a man's life turns upon that effort. Without a wife he has no home. He seeks success, in order to be rich enough to get married. Success in life means success in marriage. And the obstacles are many and wonderful." . . . (I explain.) "Therefore English novels treat of love and marriage above all things; because these mean everything in life for the English middle classes at least; and the middle classes like these books, and make the men rich who write them well, because they sympathize with the imaginary sufferings of the lovers. Which you don't, — because you can't, — and I guess you're just about right on that score."

But I know my explanation is very partial. Still, without endangering my reputation, I can't go into further particulars. The further particulars might be furnished by the American newspaper already referred to, — as a type of newspaper. England has countless kindred papers. But the supreme art of the business is French, — the *Charivari*, the *Figaro*, the *Petit Journal pour Rire*, etc.

What do they tell us? I think it is this: That the

Western Civilization is steeped in an atmosphere of artificially created . . . passionalism. That all art and all literature open to common comprehension are directed to the Eternal Feminine. That our pleasures, the theatre, the opera, the marvels of sculpture and painting, the new musical faculty, — all are shapen with a view to the stimulation of sexual idealism. Nay, the luxury of it, — the voluptuousness, — betrays itself in the smallest details of business or invention, — from the portrait of an actress or ballet-dancer on a package of cigarettes, to the frescoes of a Government building; from a child's toy, to the bronze lamp upheld by a splendid nude at the foot of a palace stairway. If the God of the West is Money, it is only because money is the Pandarus that holds Cressida's key. In education, indeed, our object is to delay puberty and its emotions as long as possible, — so as to store up force in the individual. We lie, dupe, conceal, play hypocrite for a good purpose. But when the children become men and women, they are suddenly plunged into an atmosphere full of the Eternal Feminine, and for the rest of life they can escape it only by fleeing to some less civilized country. Of the evils thus produced, nothing need be here said. They are only the accidents; — they don't explain matters.

Now your Japanese thinks it indecent even to talk about his wife, and at least impolite to talk about his children. This does n't mean he is without affection at all. The affection is all right, — but the mere mention of it, he thinks, suggests other matters, — unfortunate necessities of existence. He introduces his wife to a European, simply because he has heard it is the strange and barbarous Western custom to do such things; but otherwise his women live in shadow, by themselves. They are used to it, — would be unhappy or awkward if pulled out of it. He does not mention his marriage, except to a few intimates invited to the wedding; and still more rarely the birth of his child, — for obvious reasons. An English novel (of the Trollope sort) would seem to him a monstrous morbid piece of nonsense. A Parisian ballet would seem to him worse than ever any Methodist minister deemed it. And he would hold at sight any Japanese Joro more modest than the Society belle who shows her shoulders above the lace-fringe of an evening dress. His atmosphere is cool and without illusion. His artists succeed best with nature and least with man. We are all opposite. Which is the best condition for future intellectual expansion?

(I am only hazarding all this.) At present the condition of passional thought in the West does seem to me morbid, exasperating. But I think it does more than evil. It is a creative force in the highest sense. I think so. The process is slow, and accompanied with ugly accidents. But the results will perhaps be vast. All this woman-worship and sex-worship is tending to develop to a high degree certain moral qualities. As the pleasure of colour has been developed out of perceptions created by appetite, so out of vague sense of physical charm a sense of spiritual charm is being evolved. The result must be rather elevating and refining at last, than gross and selfish. It seems the latter to one who looks, — say at that American newspaper. But just as uncultivated minds like the force of raw bright colors, and care nothing for delicate tints, — so imperfectly cultivated minds need strong coarse impulses to bestir them in emotional directions. I think the general direction is one of gentleness, nervous sympathy, generosity. There is surely a vast reserve of tenderness in even our roughest Western natures, that comes out only in the shocks of life, as fire from flint. By tenderness I don't mean simple woman-loving, sexual inclination, but something higher developed out of that more primitive loving, etc., — sensibility, comprehension, readiness to do for the weak on impulse. I can't see this in the Orient, — except among the women. Did you not say that the Japanese woman preserved the purity and grace of the native tongue? Well, I think she has preserved also the whole capacity of the race for goodness, — all locked up within her. . . .

And here my pessimistic epistle shall close.

Ever,

LAFCADIO HEARN.

P. S. — The main point I wish to suggest is this, — that in order to understand Japan, the sexual question must be very carefully considered, as a factor in forming psychological differences. This subject is too large for me; but a man like Lowell might do much with it. I am afraid to try. Lowell has once alluded to it; but I don't think it is a mere side issue.

April 17, 1893.

DEAR CHAMBERLAIN, — I am beginning to think I was a great fool to write a book about Japan at all. My best consolation is that every year other people write books about Japan on the strength of a trip only; — and that excuse is very bad. A friend, who never minces matters, speaks to me thus: —

"You think you were very kindly treated in Izumo?"

"Oh, yes!"

"And that you have not been kindly treated in Kumamoto. Very well, — that is natural. But do you know why you were kindly treated in Izumo?"

"Well, I should like to get your opinion."

"Simply because you were a new thing, — therefore a wonderful and a strange thing. Everybody wanted to see you; you were a curiosity; — so they invited you everywhere, tried to please you, showed you everything. That was their way of gratifying their curiosity. They did it as politely as they could, so as to leave a pleasant impression. Also, they are very simple people there, and thought you much wiser and greater than you really are. So they asked your opinion about things, and published your opinions in the paper, — did n't they?"

"Yes."

"Well, that was all simply because you seemed to them a wonderful and curious person. But in Kumamoto you are not a wonderful or curious person. The public are accustomed to foreigners of various kinds, and the Kumamoto folk live in the routes of travel. As for the teachers, all are Tokyo men, —

perfectly familiar with foreigners. You cannot appear to them in any new rôle that would interest them. You are not interesting to them at all; and they are not simple, foolish people, like the Izumo folk. Also they are not agonizingly polite. It is an old Kyūshū tradition not to be; it is thought to be weak, flabby, unmanly. You won't find these people bowing and scraping to you."

"That is true."

"They don't even do it to each other. They stand off from each other. They don't think foreigners any better than themselves. And you will find it the same if you go to any other civilized part of Japan. In a place like Izumo, out of the line of railroads, you are interesting to the ignorant folk because you are a foreigner."

"Hm."

"Yes; but in other parts of Japan you are uninteresting for the very same reason. To educated Japanese you cannot be interesting. You cannot talk to them; you don't understand their ways, — don't belong to their life. You are not a show, or a novelty; you are only a teacher, — with nothing remarkable to recommend you to strangers. But you are not less well treated, — perhaps much better treated, than you would be elsewhere in civilized Japan."

"But why did n't you tell me all this before?"

"Simply because I did not want to spoil your pleasure. You were very happy, were n't you? But you would not have been so happy if I had told you before. I tell you so now simply as a sort of consolation. It was better for you not to know in Izumo. It is better for you to know in Kumamoto."

"Yes, but my book is all wrong."

"Why all wrong? Does n't it express a real effect; — the effect of the efforts of people to please you? And they were really sincere in that, — though not exactly because they thought you all that you imagined they thought you. If you described your own feelings, the book will be in that sense true. But if you write about Japanese character, of course you will be mistaken. You do not know it. Indeed I do not believe you could ever learn it. It seems to me natural that you should not. It would seem to me a miracle that you should."

This is the sum and substance of information that takes the starch out of me, but is really very consoling. It is always consoling to stand upon solid ground, even if the prospect is not delightful, after a voyage in seas of delusions and mysteries.

The educational question is growing upon me. The other day a young man, — the cleverest in his class, wrote me these words: —

"When I think of my child-studies, my first days at school, I can hardly avoid despair. Embarrassments have come; — I feel my bodily energy slipping away; my diligent spirit is gone; my brain seems dull, feeble, and unrenewable. [He means worn out, but there is a pathetic force of expression in the mistake.] And the more I am dismayed, the worse I become in all things. I feel a destruction gathering over me. But who made all this so? I think it was my negligence; — that I have no one to blame but myself."

All this seems to be very pathetic. A young brain is wearing out from overwork; and the student accuses himself of not studying hard enough, — totally ignorant of the fact that he is quietly killing himself. Some day I expect to call his name, and get no answer. It is not the first call, nor the tenth. But it is the first time I have seen the feelings of the struggle so simply expressed, with such amazing artlessness.

The delicate souls pass away; the rough stay on and triumph. As Spencer says, "the first requisite to any success, is to be a good animal." Students have the superstition that strong will is enough. They ought to be taught better, for simple humanity's sake.

Ever faithfully,
LAFCADIO HEARN.

April 19, 1893.

DEAR CHAMBERLAIN, — Really I never want any better consolation for blues than a letter from you, and the occasional indulgence of my own feelings in a letter. This latter indulgence I think excusable only because truly reactions are an inevitable part of life in the Orient, and have therefore something more than a purely personal meaning.

But the mental blues are gone, and instead of them comes a blaze of blue light, true summer color, into the room where the stove was. For the winter partition and the stove itself have been removed, and the room is open to the sky and to a burst of blossom-splendor from the garden. I had no idea

what wealth of flowers I had, there are fully forty
kinds. Also the grass of my garden has changed
from yellow to soft green. — Oh! do you remember
the awful dead-yellow of those stagey, humpy, pokey
hills in Luizenji garden, — that looked just as if
they had been sheered out of dead wood, and painted
with yellow ochre?? I suppose even they are green
now; but I am much too afraid of them to go and
see.

I fear I can't get so far away from Kumamoto as
you kindly suggest. There will be batches of proofs
coming every ten days, and such a trip, to be enjoyed at all, would take much more time. The ten
days would barely give me one half hour's chat with
you at Miyanoshita; and that would only make me
hungry for more. The most I expect to attempt will
be a short run to Nagasaki. Of all this I am not
indeed quite sure; but the mail will soon enlighten
me.

I am sending another batch of novels to Mason;
you will have time to read them at Miyanoshita
anyhow, later on. Tell him to read "La Pêcheuse
d'Âmes" last. I fear you will not like it for two reasons:—it is bloody, and the incidents seem improbable. Bloody it certainly is, and in places too theatrical;—yet in a country which produced such a sect
as the Skopsi (is n't that the name?) what might
not be possible?

I read Anstey's "Giant's Robe," the other day,
having bought the book because of a reference to it
in one of Kipling's tales. It is clever, in a way; but
it is not real art, I think. Seems to me the English

public are easily satisfied; give them a new plot, and the rest does n't matter. The success of "Called Back" seems to be a disgrace to public taste.

Another thing I read was Dickens's "Loyal League." I was perfectly astounded by some of his notes. He calls Kwannon "the Buddic (!) Venus." Is n't that enough to make one shriek? The impression of the whole story is very unpleasant as he tells it; for that reason, I prefer Mitford's version. But whether the Japanese original is also so emotionally hard and coarse as Dickens makes it, I am in doubt.

After having been for three years shaved in religious silence by a being with a face like Buddha, I felt (the other day) a sort of regret for the American barber who parts his hair in the middle, and insists on telling you all about his girl. I used to think him a frightful plague. But now the memory of him becomes almost . . . no, positively grateful.

I have been trying to think exactly what I was doing just at the time you came to Japan; and I remember now that I was writing a story for a weekly family paper which never paid anybody. The story was a serial. The idea was about a man manufactured by chemistry, — an indestructible man, who ate nothing but diamond dust and steel filings. I carried that man through various chapters of modern life, — made him sit down with impunity upon circular saws, and pass through all sorts of conflagrations, battles, and dynamite explosions. After which I was puzzled what to do with him. He could not be killed; yet it was necessary to make him disappear. Wherefore, I had him swallowed up by an earthquake. Little did I know at that time what an earthquake was. I wanted to know. But now I have a really disgusting fear of earthquakes.

Yes, work is the greatest happiness, voluntary pleasant work, with the certainty of creating sympathy. I wonder if I shall ever be able to do any more of it. I have begun many things, but can't finish them; the question always comes up, — "But would he, or she, have such sensations or thoughts?" And the answer is generally "No." Therefore my hope of "effects" is always withered up. An editor of a magazine offered me some time ago almost any terms for "A Japanese novel of three hundred pages or so." A Japanese novel? ? ? If I could only write one little baby sketch, and write the truth about the inside of an Oriental brain. But I can't. I wonder if Lowell could. His intuition is infinitely finer. This thing, however, seems to me something that intuition cannot give. A general theory will not do here. If there were absolute fatalism, stolidity, insensibility, — one could do — anything. But everything I first suspect the absence of, always turns out at a later day to exist, only in a peculiar way, like a blue moon, or a tree with scarlet leaves. So I don't know what to do. I am in literary despair. Perhaps I had better resign myself to write of dead suns, — old memories of queer places where the rule of thinking was at least Aryan.

The old man's festival the other day was rather a nice affair. Many Chinese poems were composed in his honour. Then a poem which he himself composed was solemnly sung. Next day a servant brought to me a porcelain wine-cup, in which was lined in golden text the old man's Chinese poem. (I had sent a gift of wine to the feast.) But I know not at all the emotions of the occasion, — nor will I even know in heaven, since my soul or souls must wander back to its or their own kindred. Buddha would never let me into his Paradise, because I can't understand.

I wish you and I together could travel to Izumo some day. It rejoices me much to hear you are getting strong. But you can't take too much care of your throat, in this horrid weather. It may be perfectly frank in the Tōkaido region; but I can swear it is almost as treacherous as Atlantic weather here. One hour the hills are sharp as amethyst crystals in a cloudless sky, — the next, they are invisible; and there is furious wind and rain.

Ever faithfully,
LAFCADIO HEARN.

April 28, 1893.

DEAR CHAMBERLAIN, — . . . I had a treat for you, but as you have no time to read, I'll send it to Mason instead. "Le Roman d'un Enfant." It seems to me very nearly the best thing Loti has written, and will give you a better opinion of him. Indeed I think it is a sacred book in its way.

Your criticism on my letter is penetrating. But in the interval an audacious idea has been taking visible shape in my mind, — definitely, strongly, — upsetting all my other ideas about the future of

West and East. Perhaps I may venture to bring it
out some day. But it will be a hard piece of work, —
as I must give scientific records for every point taken.
It is this: — That the larger brained and nervously
more complex races of the West must give way at
last to the races of the East, — and that Buddhism
in some form will exist after Christianity and Christian civilizations have vanished. The argument
must be based first of all upon the enormous cost
of individuation to the West, compared with the
future cost of equally efficient (for sociological purposes) individuation to — say the Chinese. Vast
races of highly complex creatures have already disappeared from the world simply because of the enormous costliness of their structures. The evolution
of machinery furnishes certain parallels for study in
the question of economy of force and economy of
expenditure. Then there will be artificial conditions to consider, as set in antagonism to purely natural but equally efficient conditions. Of course the
question of the survival of races is that of the survival of the fittest. But are we, as you suggest ask-
ingly, are we the fittest? The fittest life is that
capable of meeting all exterior influences inimical
to it by interior adjustments of its own powers. Are
we most able to do that? I think we are now, —
but *only because we avail ourselves of artificial means
to oppose to natural forces.* We do this by intellectual cunning. But that intellectual power is obtained
by us only at so vast a cost, that it can only belong
to a very few. Given the same powers to the select
of a race to whom the cost of being and thinking

has been made by nature and habit infinitely less, — and what will we be in the competition? Less than nothing. The forces of national expansion are aggressive forces and very costly ones. But they do not represent the highest of our powers. The highest of our powers are of no use or meaning in self preservation and race contest. And the aggressive powers in our races are the most easily imitated and acquired by those nations we call inferior and barbarous. But that's enough to bore you with. I only suggest an outline of what I mean. In that case Japan ought to tie her future to China, when circumstances render that possible. Buddha will be safe anyhow.

Good-bye, with sincerest wishes that you take the best possible care of yourself for a while,

Ever,

LAFCADIO HEARN.

May 2, 1893.

DEAR CHAMBERLAIN, — First let me thank you and Mason for that delightful telegram, — a shake-hands over a thousand miles; it was extremely kind and pretty of you.

I have just got your letter about the globe trotter. I know the horrid person only too well; — I sympathize with you. There is only one way to do with such animals when one is obliged to be with them. Each and all know something, of course, which enables them to travel; — you can make them talk about themselves, about "grub," about. . . . But I beg pardon, really *that* would not do for a respectable gentleman to talk about. What I meant to say was the way I have to do with them. I know the animal; I know its machinery; I hint to it of things unholy, — and at once it gets wound up, unrolls, and utters its heart's music. I do this because I can't talk to it. I make it talk to itself until it gets tired and goes away. And sometimes, though not always, there is literary material to be extracted from its artless vulgarity and its sense of greatness.

What you say about letters that *coulent de source* I feel strong sympathy with for two reasons. In the first place letters not spontaneous give one the notion that the writer feels a certain distrust in abandoning his thoughts to paper, and consequently has not towards his friend that perfect feeling which casts out fear. The second is that the receiver is also forced into a certain constraint and artificialness in his replies; — then the matter becomes a mere drudgery. Of course there are other cases, — such as the very curious one you suggest, which I take to be ruled by a sort of æsthetic formality, — the reluctance of the artist to be for a moment inartistic, like Théophile Gautier answering a reproach about not writing by the phrase: "Ask a carpenter to plane a few planks for fun." (I have not heard of Lowell at all as yet, except through the reference you make to a visit from him; consequently I suppose he changed his mind about Kumamoto.)

I said in my last that your criticism about one of my suggestions was penetrating. It proves so more than I fancied. The disintegration of the family must continually increase, must it not? under the continual stimulus of this universal Western passion. Then there must ensue a continually augmenting contempt for old age and its wisdom in the things of life, — and a universal irreverence for all things truly worthy of reverence. The ultimate results seem to point to social disintegration. But I am not a trained thinker, and not a scientist. I fear one needs to be both in order to treat this extraordinary sexual and social question. I can only dare to attempt suggestions; it requires a power like Lowell's to synthetize all the huge mass of facts, and dash a cosmic idea out of them.

I cannot help thinking this idea of throwing open Japan to mixed residence is sheer wickedness. To do so would be, I sincerely believe, a monstrous crime. Pride and conceit are steering the Japanese that way. They over-estimate their force. They are enormously strong while they remain conservative. But to introduce into the vitals of their nationality the most active possible elements of dissolution seems to me suicidal. I trust the race instinct will prevent it. Otherwise Lowell's prediction will prove, perhaps, true, — that the race will vanish from the earth. Of what importance to refuse the sale of land to foreigners, and yet leave them free to make other investments large enough to involve a possibility of international quarrel. The admission of foreigners to Japan is only the other side of the question of the admission of Chinese to America. The Chinaman is dreaded because of his power to under-live the white; — the white is equally to be dreaded because of his ability to over-live the Oriental. One race can squeeze out the other; the other crushes and absorbs. But what can prevent the danger? certainly not the howl of one small writer like me.

Those wonderful Russo-Jewish novels I hoped to make you read have come. I am enraged to think you have no time to read. Of course it's no use to send them now. Only tell me when you get hungry for something strange, powerful, and unexpected.

Ever with best wishes,

LAFCADIO HEARN.

May 12, 1893.

DEAR CHAMBERLAIN, — In the dead vast and middle of last night there came a telegram from Lowell, saying that he had sent a letter sixteen days ago, and to enquire therefor. I enquired as soon as possible, sending my little boy to the P. O. When he had delivered his message, instead of replying, the P. O. asked: —

"What is your name?"

"Kumagae Nasayoshi."

"Naruhodo! And you are in the house of the Sensei?"

"Yes."

"Naruhodo! And of course you speak much English?"

"No."

"Naruhodo! But you are not of Kumamoto?"

"No."

"Naruhodo! You are from the West?"

"Izumo."

"Ya! The people of Shimane are curious people. There is one in our P. O.; you know him."

"No, I do not."

"Naruhodo! The people of Shimane say 'fu-bachi, futatsu, fugashi'; they say 'jiji; ji-roku'; — they say 'sanji' for 'sanjui.' Ah yes!"

"But the letter?"

"The Sensei received a telegram."

"Yes."

"The letter was sent — when?"

"Sixteen days ago."

"Naruhodo! Then it could not possibly have come to Kumamoto. To come to Kumamoto and not be quickly delivered is, for a letter, exceedingly difficult. We know all about the letters of the Sensei; we count them. Exceedingly very many there are. He gets letters daily. To-day, as you know, he got one?"

"Yes."

"Then the reason of the not seeing of the letter the Sensei desires is not difficult to understand."

"It is difficult."

"Oh, not. It is not difficult. The reason is simply that the letter never came to Kumamoto."

"Ah!"

"For having once come to Kumamoto it should have immediately been delivered."

"Ah!"

"But since it did not come, it could not have been delivered."

"Thanks."

"And therefore, not having been delivered, the Sensei did not receive it."

"Thanks."

"What have I done, etc."

To dispute the premises would have been quite useless, — so accepting the conclusion I prepared an elaborate telegram. The address upon Mr. Lowell's telegram was simply "Kokumeikwan." Masa trotted off again to the heart of the town. The telegraph man disputed the address. Such an address would not suffice, — would give at the other end of the line enormous tribulation. For to send a telegram to Kokumeikwan was like unto sending a telegram to Tokyo, — to Japan, — to the whole Orient, — to the whole of this vale of tears. And I suppose it best to address you on the subject, as you have an address of a sharply defined character. I think you told me that Lowell, like many another literary man, dislikes writing letters. I am especially sorry therefore for the mystery of the letter in question; it is discouraging and demoralizing, and would justify him in swearing by the eight hundred myriads of the Gods never to write another letter again for the rest of his life.

I have your kind letter about "Chita," etc. That you could read the book at all, is some encouragement, — that is, persuades me that at some far-distant time, by toning down the thing, some of it might be preserved in a new edition. But I feel it is terribly overdone. You are right, too, about Miss Bacon's severe and rather dry style. It has power, and it never tires, if the subject be of interest. A poetical style is only justifiable in the treatment of rare, exotic subjects. Those are the subjects I most love, however; — how I envy my cousins in India, who will never write a line in their lives. I would give ten years of life for one year in India; — I can't ever hope to get it. But a host of small relations, to whom it is a mere source of living, cannot only get any number of years in India, but can blaspheme the Gods at being obliged to live in such a blasted country.

What an education the Orient is! How it opens a man's eyes and mind about his own country, about conventionalisms of a hundred sorts, — about false ideals and idealisms, — about ethical questions. But it is a bitter life. I am ashamed to say, I feel worn out. Ancestral habit and impulse are too strong in me. I never understood how profoundly a man can be isolated even in the midst of an amiable population. I get letters from relations in England that make my soul turn, not sky-blue, but indigo. I must be able to travel again some day, — to alternate Oriental life with something else. ˙And I am not without hope that will prove some day possible.

I wonder if I am right in thinking the Tempo men larger brained than the present University men. Somehow or other, the most highly educated Japanese strike me as pitiably small when it comes to thinking about any subject whatever; — they talk like boys of fourteen or fifteen years of age. They have no grasp of questions; — no conception of relations. It is impossible to talk with them at all. Now the old men whom I have met were of a larger breed. They thought in a narrow circle, — but fully, and originally, and well, so far as I could divine from interpretation. They gave me ideas. The class I am now in contact with have no ideas. Under such studies as they have made, their brains seemed to have shrivelled up like kernels in roasted nuts. When they try to talk there is only a dry rattle. Perpetual questions about things that a new-born babe ought to know; and withal a conceit as high as the moon; — an ineradicable belief that they have mastered all the knowledge of the nineteenth century, — and that a foreigner is a sort of stupid servant to be used, but never to be treated as a real human being.

The other day I wrote a long article about Japanese students, intending to send it to the *Mail*, a plea for them; but reading it over I came to the conclusion I did not know enough about the subject of educational organization. Everything is kept concealed as much as possible from a foreign teacher. Some day when I get more information, I may try to develop the theme in another way. I think the present system is dead wrong; — I think so by its results. The boys are overworked. The standard is low; the years are wasted. But who would thank me for proving it?

We had a curious contradiction in official theories the other day. One minister tells the Governors if there be trouble in their provinces they are responsible. The other minister tells students if they are dissatisfied the fault is their own. That the perpetual change of governors and teachers and directors, — the general flux of national disintegration, — must lead to large troubles, never seems to occur to these great statesmen. They are pitiably small; to judge by their idea of applying law to results instead of remedies to deeply seated and ever-increasing causes. For the first time I feel like saying, "D—n Japan!" After all, the loss of her nationality might not be the worst fate for her. What a blue letter. I am ashamed.

LAFCADIO HEARN.

May 30, 1893.

DEAR CHAMBERLAIN,—Your criticism about my idea of a volume of stories delights me.

But I am not insensible to the comic side. I want the best of anything I can get in that direction. I want it, however, under reservations.

In the "Glimpses of Unfamiliar Japan," I think you will find something more than pathos. I think you may have found something more than the minor key even in the West Indian Sketches. But — besides the fact that I know the narrow limitations of my own power, I have an artistic theory about comedy.

For sincere work I think comedy should always be very close to tears, — as it is in real life. Shadow and sun make the picture. The strongest possible pathos is created by the use of comedy in the proper time and place.

But it is very hard to do this. Those who have been able to do it well are the giants. Take Heine's work; what is the nervous power of it; surely, aside from mere verbal art and fancy, it is in this very thing. He amuses, caresses, brings tears; then with a lightning flash of sarcasm he illuminates the bitter gulfs. Or the mockery first, and then the pathos. I don't think the Elizabethan writers knew this art; they had to introduce fools and mad people to offset tragedy. It seems to me an art yet undeveloped. Most men can work safely only in one direction, — having but one faculty powerfully developed. Heine had two; — but he was only half alive in his best years. I think myself a book all in one key is weak. I should like to venture at work in two. But I am small. I am groping and don't know. All I can say is, — Any and every suggestion I can get during the next two years will be gold and diamonds.

The little follies, the childish errors, the blunders and mistakes of life, do not however make me laugh. I cannot laugh at the real, — unless it's offensive. Rather all these things seem to me infinitely pathetic; the comedy of them is the tragedy played by human children before the Unknown. In an artistic sketch, I think the comedy ought not to provoke more than a smile. But hard and fast rules are out of the question. And what would the Japanese say? They don't understand. I once ventured a jest in Izumo about the ancient Gods, — in the presence of one who did not believe. It was an innocent jest, too, — not derogatory to the Gods. But, — well, I never tried it again; not even when I heard much racier jests made by the same person.

I am not good, I fear, like you. I do not always give gentle answers, which is a sign of strength, but nasty ones, which is a sign of weakness. However,

I have lately effected a compromise with myself. I think this way: — "Assuredly, the people who ask you so impertinently to do things for money, conceive that money is an all-fired great consideration with you, — because it is with them. To undeceive them would injure their feelings, — stab them in the only place where they have any feelings. Wherefore it were more Christian to answer them according to their kind. An answer of this sort cannot satisfy them altogether, but it will teach them respect for you."

Therefore when I am asked, for example, to write letters for a particular sort of patronizing newspaper, "I am very grateful, dear Sir, for your kindly appreciation of my work, and for your courteous offer. In answer to your question about terms, I may say, that, although now unusually occupied, I hope to find time to write you a few letters on the following conditions: One thousand dollars in gold per letter, — to be paid in each case in advance, — by draft on London, — and copyright of letters to be secured in the name of my publishers, at your expense, — which, of course, will be trifling. Trusting, my dear sir, etc."

Now, if they really agree to the terms, they would be worth the while. If they don't, it is all the same, — except that they will see even an author loves money, and esteems himself at the right value. Of course, that is only me. You ought to charge enormous rates, and you might get them. Some years ago in New York, when there was no Russian Secretary, a Russian document had to be translated

in a hurry. There was only one man in New York
then who could do the work, and the man knew it.
The legend is that he charged $10,000 and got it.
If you write a perfumery ad. in Chinese for those
people you ought to charge enough to elevate the
price of the perfume bottles 150 p. c. ? ? ? The fun
of all this is that I, who write it, can't get any big
prices for anything yet. By dint of pretended scorn,
perhaps some day I shall get a gold mine all to myself.

Best wishes ever and thanks,

LAFCADIO HEARN.

June 1, 1893.

DEAR CHAMBERLAIN, — An idea has been growing
upon me, which you will perhaps think crazy, — but
it may be at least worth mentioning. It is this: —

Does it follow that because the Japanese mind —
(shaped by ancestral habits of imagination and
thought totally different from our own) — remains
insensible to much we esteem, that it is in this respect altogether undeveloped?

Of course I grant the musical question, and all
that. But — may not our sensibility to certain
classes of impressions be morbid? Might not morbid sensibility be a racial as well as an individual
outcome of high pressure civilization?

For instance, much we deem heroic, they consider merely a matter of course. I am not prepared
now to illustrate the matter much further: — it is
only a suggestion.

Funny things have been happening here. Two natives sold some ground to a Romish missionary. He obtained it only after great difficulty, and after having been roughly refused by many very poor citizens, although the price offered was quite big. The papers published with high praise the names of those who refused, among others, that of my former landlord who ironically offered his ground at ten thousand yen per square foot. Then the papers turned their attention to the sellers. The one was a doctor, the other a photographer. They were put into print as worse than beasts. The papers traced up their private history. The doctor had been a fraud, — married a widow for money and swindled her. With the money he had started practice. But he was a charlatan; and only dogs entered his house. Dogs slept in his office; and no patients went thither. Daily other revelations about him are being published. To-day is the fifth day. There were nearly eight columns of the matter in one of the dailies. But four dailies are at the work.

As for the photographer, he is declared to be poor shakes. In his gallery there is always dust and silence; and the place is festooned with the webs of spiders immemorially old. He is also tasting the bitterness of life.

The missionary started in, of course, by giving money to children. Some children refused it with scorn. The papers published their names. And a merchant, reading the same in some distant city, sent to one of the children, — a little girl, — a pretty silk handkerchief, and a letter full of commendations and of good advice.

And I rather like all this. The men who sell their ground to missionaries or sell their religion, *are* usually bad or weak and worthless characters. That is evident enough, — as they are acting against the Japanese conscience and against what they know to be national opinion. But why all this rage against the Bateren? Is he any worse than the other foreigners? What is the distinction made by the Japanese mind? And why do the papers elsewhere say nothing about sales of land to Protestant missionaries? Of course the thing is, strictly speaking, illegal; besides which it is, from the Japanese point, morally wrong. But why strain at the gnat and swallow the camel?

A queer Buddhist idea was given to me the other day. (I would like to find out more about it; but I must wait to get out of Kyūshū in order to attempt Buddhist work.) The idea is this: — Do not be angry or indulge secretly any wicked thought! Why? because the anger or the wicked thought, though secret and followed by no action, *may go out into the universe as an unseen influence and therein cause evil.* In other words, a man might be responsible for a murder committed at a great distance by one whom he does not even know. Weak, unbalanced minds, trembling between crime and conscience, may be decided suddenly to evil by the straw weight of an unseen influence.

I never heard this before. It is certainly worth following up. I don't wish to give it away, — except to you. Now the fact is, that the more I think about it, the more it seems to me that — it may be true. Don't think me quite mad, but believe me,

Ever faithfully yours,

LAFCADIO HEARN.

June 5, 1893.

DEAR CHAMBERLAIN, — Thanks for strictures and suggestions. I changed the text as you desired, except in the case of the word Kuruma. That has been fully explained in preceding articles. (By the way, I never heard a Japanese use the word jin-rikisha.) My observations about the sailors were based upon police reports in the Japan *Mail*. I killed the word gwaikokujin; as you said, it is an ugly word. I revised, indeed, the whole paper.

Recognizing the ugliness of words, however, you must also recognize their physiognomical beauty. I see you and the Editor of the *Atlantic* are at one, however, in condemning my use of Japanese words. Now, I can't entirely agree with either of you. As to the practical side of the question, I do. But as to the artistic, the romantic side, I don't. For me words have colour, form, character; they have faces, ports, manners, gesticulations; they have moods, humours, eccentricities; — they have tints, tones, personalities. That they are unintelligible makes no difference at all. Whether you are able to speak to a stranger or not, you can't help being impressed by his appearance sometimes, — by his dress, — by his air, — by his exotic look. He is also unintelligible, but not a whit less interesting. Nay! he is interesting BECAUSE he is unintelligible. I won't cite other writers who have felt the same way about African, Chinese, Arabian, Hebrew, Tartar, Indian, and Basque words, — I mean novelists and sketch writers.

To such it has been justly observed:— "The readers do not feel as you do about words. They can't be supposed to know that you think the letter A is blush-crimson, and the letter E pale sky-blue. They can't be supposed to know that you think KH wears a beard and a turban; that initial X is a mature Greek with wrinkles; — or that ' — no —' has an innocent, lovable, and childlike aspect." All this is true from the critic's standpoint.

But from ours, the standpoint of —

> The dreamer of dreams
> To whom what is and what seems
> Is often one and the same, —

To us the idea is thus: —

"Because people cannot see the colour of words, the tints of words, the secret ghostly motions of words: —

"Because they cannot hear the whispering of words, the rustling of the procession of letters, the dream-flutes and dream-drums which are thinly and weirdly played by words: —

"Because they cannot perceive the pouting of words, the frowning and fuming of words, the weeping, the raging and racketing and rioting of words:—

"Because they are insensible to the phosphorescing of words, the fragrance of words, the noisomeness of words, the tenderness or hardness, the dryness or juiciness of words, — the interchange of values in the gold, the silver, the brass and the copper of words: —

"Is that any reason why we should not try to make them hear, to make them see, to make them feel? Surely one who has never heard Wagner, cannot appreciate Wagner without study! Why should the people not be forcibly introduced to foreign words, as they were introduced to tea and coffee and tobacco?"

Unto which, the friendly reply is, — "Because they won't buy your book, and you won't make any money."

And I say: — "Surely I have never yet made, and never expect to make any money. Neither do I expect to write ever for the multitude. I write for beloved friends who can see colour in words, can smell the perfume of syllables in blossom, can be shocked with the fine elfish electricity of words. And in the eternal order of things, words will eventually have their rights recognized by the people."

All this is heresy. But a bad reason, you will grant, is better than — etc.

Faithfully,

LAFCADIO HEARN.

DEAR CHAMBERLAIN, — You have heard of Composite Photographs, and know their value. Here is a composite composition, — the closing examination theme. I have made no changes, — only taken sentences from various compositions.

The Story of Tithonus.

"Tithonus was a youth very handsome and polite.

"Aurora was the rosy-fingered Goddess of the Dawn, — a very fine young lady with rosy fingers.

"She was used to got up in the earlier morning every day, and she was very studious.

"She follen in love to Tithonus, and by her chariot taked him up to the sky.

"One day she ask to him that, — 'Sir, I can give you all thing you want.' Then he ask to her that, — 'Please give me the eternal life.'

"Hoping to enjoy the eternal life of her husband, Aurora ask to Zeus, Father of all the Gods;

"And soon the eternal life was bestow on Tithonus.

"But Aurora forget to request for the eternal youth; therefore Tithonus have the only eternal life.

"Gods have the eternality of youth as well as life.

"Tithonus came to become thirty of fourty years of age.

"He became every day more old.

"He become TOTALLY old.

"And felt the miseration of his life.

"He became grieving and very confusing for weakness of the old.

"Whenever he saw down from the seat of the sky a burial in mankind, he desire to die.

"He became old till only the bones and skins had remained, — like a wet paper was put over the wood.

"Aurora asked to Zeus to give her husband only one escapement of his torment by to die, — but in vain.

"Now Tithonus begged to the God to make him enable to die; but he was repulsed, — on that the God could not ever change his words.

"To the last desire he begged the God to make him a glasshopper and to hop on the ground.

"So for pity the God changed him into a glasshopper, which could hop about our world.

"And he is hop about the ground even now, and bears the dry looking.

"O from a man becomed the husband of the Goddess, and then to be changed into a vile worm!

"This should teach us well to ask never the inconsistent things."

June 10, 1893.

DEAR CHAMBERLAIN, — Certainly the nasty article of C. S. is discouraging, — not in itself, but as a type of much that is both written and unwritten. The supremely difficult task of the higher literature is to teach the public that idealism is *not* mere distorted fancy, imagination, rose-coloured spectacles, — but that it is penetrative, perceptive, reflective of eternal things. To educate public sensibility up to the point of comprehending great work, requires the time of at least a generation, — so that the true artist is but half understood in his life, unless he be quite small. The enemies of the human race are those who cry out that the work of the artist is a lie, and who clamour for ugliness, brutality, stench, — all that is capable of appealing to their own coarse nerves and vulgar brains. They can do more mischief in one hour, than an artist can do good in a lifetime. And the railroads, the steamers, the monstrous industrial and commercial expansion of our time, has placed every fair thing on earth within the reach of the vulgarian, the snob, the blackguard. The artistic future seems to me very dark. Should there be no thorough change or transformation of social conditions, — surely the feet must continue forever above the head.

Much has been said against the over-sugared work of Arnold; and quite as much, I think, might be said against Loti's tremendous pictures of Kyoto. Yet, although such work, from its want of the supreme artistic quality, self-restraint, rather assists than combats the mere brutality of such scrawlers as C. S., — still those men see below the surface, touch truth, discern eternal beauty where it really lives, and are in harmony with the sympathies and purposes of art's Religion. It does not matter, in one sense, that they would offer to persuade us that their ore is pure metal; their error is on the side of the highest truth. Kipling's little sketch of Kamakura is truer art; perfectly controlled, subtle, didactic. But I wonder if the mass of his readers can feel the delicacy of him. I fear they mostly seek the story only. And for one who can feel the beauty of that sketch of the Daibutsu, there will be a thousand to clap C. S. on the back as "a Christian and an Englishman." Surely it is uphill work now more than ever before to try to teach people to see truth and to feel beauty.

You were a true artist in your last letter. Those musical terms describing colour — ("the deep bass" of a certain green, etc.) greatly delighted me. You are often thus artistic in your letters. In your books you are severe. I suppose a scholar must refuse to indulge himself in colour and melody; his work is so much a work of compression, systematization, and solidity. Symonds — though so great a scholar — used to be pitched into in the most absurd way, because he wrote like a poet. The critics seem to have an idea that a philologist, an Orientalist, a historian, etc., has no right to indulge in a lighter vein. If he does, they suspect his real work, — like that of Michelet, — like that of Taine. All of which is a sort of instinctive selfishness, perhaps, — the world crying to its teachers: "We only want to learn; if you study ornament, you won't have time to teach us enough." But I often think what charming light things you could write, if you tried.

I am still doing nothing in the writing line. I am reading all I can. Have just finished Boswell, again; read Tennyson again, Byron, Scott, bits of Wordsworth, Milton, Shelley, — all of Molière, — with lighter stuff sandwiched in. When I am ready to do something, my style will be more flexible, I hope. By the way, have you read "La Cité Antique," by Fustel de Coulanges? I suppose you have. I am reading it for the second time, studying the curious parallels between the ancient Indo-Aryan family, home-worship, and beliefs, and those of Japan. In some matters the parallel is wonderful.

Faithfully,

LAFCADIO HEARN.

P. S. — If ever I get into a good place for it, I must begin Buddhist studies. I have a splendid idea for a popular book on the subject.

June 14, 1893.

DEAR CHAMBERLAIN, — Your letters of the 10th and 11th are before me, — two of the most delightful letters I ever received. I shall always treasure them up. You will have found in a letter already sent you that your idea about the value of musical terms to describe colour "enthused" me at once. And nevertheless you were not the first to hint of it. Some four months ago I bought, with great expectations aroused by the title, — Symonds's "In the Key of Blue." I was utterly disappointed. The essay which gives its name to the book, and several other essays in which attempts are made to describe by colour words and musical words, are dead unintelligible failures. Though I reverence almost religiously the man who could have written that blazing splendid chapter on Sappho in the "Studies of the Greek Poets," I felt that I could name at least twenty writers, — small ones, — who could double-discount his effort in the Key of Blue. But *you* immediately illustrated the values for me. When you wrote of "the deep bass" of that green I could see, feel, smell, taste, and chew the leaf; it was rather bitter in taste, and dense, and faintly odorous with an odour. But I must not attempt to write about odours. I have been thinking of soprano, alto, contralto, tenor, and baritone colours. There is one trouble; that either to apply or to appreciate a more elaborate musical terminology to colour, both writer and reader should have musical knowledge. I think Symonds's failure is largely, though not entirely, due to his attempt to use "Symphonies" or I might say "symphonic musical terms." One not even possessing a musical ear can feel such a piece as Gautier's "Symphonie en Blanc Majeur," but in Symonds's "Symphonies of Gray and Blue," etc., no one can discover any united effect. You can't see the thing as a whole; and just as soon as you have defined one of the images, all the rest blurs immediately, like a photograph fading out.

Long ago I said that words are like lizards in their power of changing colour with position. But they change much more than colour,—tonic value and force and psychology as well. Take, for instance, this one line from Andrew Lang's glorious prose translation of Homer, describing the wrath of Apollo when he drew the loud-clanging bow, — "*And the* PYRES *of the dead burnt continually in multitude.*" Here with the solitary exceptions of the curious word "pyre," every word in the sentence is in itself absolutely commonplace. (Of course "dead" is eyeless and cold; but only in one of its meanings.) But as Lang distributes them, Homer himself could not have been more strong, musical, mighty. One can see the vast bickering, and the fire-tongues lapping the night.

And yet, — and yet, — and yet (oh, what a heretic I am!) I can't agree with you that the question of the use of foreign words is a simple one. I don't think it can be decided for or against by the reader's knowledge of the language used. I am, indeed, convinced that the question does NOT end there. It goes a little further, overlaps the boundary, — flows over into indefinable lands of yet unknown extent.

In short, I think you forget Lewis Carroll. Now so long as we can enjoy "The Hunting of the Snark," or the tale of "The Jabberwock with Eye of Flame," — burbling as he comes, — we cannot, I feel sure, stop at the line you would lay down. To be sure these books of Carroll's have been offered to the world as nonsense books, — just like the nonsense rhymes about the "teary, scary bear," and "wicey, nicey apple pies." But they are NOT nonsense books. They contain a profound psychological teaching. Better nonsense has been, is being written every year by the ton. It is not nonsense that has made the supreme excellence and success of these books, with their infinitely subtle charm; it is superlative truth. The effect of words (among other things) upon the mind, — quite irrespective of meaning, — is shown. As for other matters, — did you ever jump out of bed, and try to write down at once, a wonderful poem or sentence composed during sleep? I have, not once, but many times. The result is very strange. There are words there which never existed in any language. The poem is really very fine; — but it won't do to publish just now (except in a nonsense book), because no publisher would consider it anything but the production of a raging lunatic.

The extracts from Erse or Gaelic, and other strange tongues which you cite against this view, did at first hit me hard. But on reflection, I recovered my first position again. The weak point of that argument to me is this, — that the texts are not fair representations of possibilities. The un-

known words are sinister, ugly, or absolutely colourless. (Indeed I can't even guess what language
one extract was made from; it looked like Peruvian?)
In other words, you have selected only the harsh,
grim, unsightly words which appeal to nothing already existing in the æsthetic or musical sense. But
suppose you had selected many vowelled liquid
Polynesian words, — or certain windy words from
the Finnish, — would the effect be equally dead?
I don't think it would. I know absolutely nothing of philology. I am a supreme ignoramus on
that science. But let me try to appeal to you with
an example. In Loti's "Roman d'un Spahi," in that
wonderful, magical chapter describing the mighty
burst of the African spring, and all nature in riot of
desire, and the savage dances under the great moon,
— there occur these words, perpetually recurring
like a refrain: — *"Anabilis Fobil; — faramata hi."*
What do they mean? I don't know; — perhaps you
do, because you know philology and many tongues.
But it is safe to say the general reader does not
know. Loti says he cannot tell; the words "would
burn the paper." Yet read that marvellous chapter;
and then I will defy you to say those words have no
effect upon you. They will have a strong one, —
partly musical, partly savage.

Besides, in our own songs, there are many re-
frains having no sense, — not even the sense of
onomatopœia. But they are always sung, for the
sound, the rhyme. Surely a word may appeal to
the imagination, must do so, if it appeals to the ear.
Now the trouble with the examples you cited is also

a musical trouble. They don't (except in the case of the Gaelic) appeal to my ear at all; if they did, they would have some effect. The effect of the Gaelic is rough and thick only, — because I don't know the meaning. But I know the accent, and I can hear the voices, as I heard them in my childhood.

I would suggest this amendment to your resolution: — That no words of an unknown foreign language should be introduced into artistic work, *except such as may, because of their sound, etc., have a striking effect on the imagination.* This would, however, exclude most Japanese words and words of many other languages, would n't it? because the sound cannot even be imagined by the reader in most cases.

You recommend me to write an article on words some day. I would like to, — from my own limited point of knowledge only; ignorance of philology would here be a great drawback. But it would be infinitely painful, laborious work. Because really the art of placing words is with most of us instinctive. It would be analyzing one's own sensations and tendencies of imagination; it would be nearly as hard as to write another "Alice in Wonderland."

Ever faithfully,
LAFCADIO HEARN.

June 15, 1893.

DEAR CHAMBERLAIN, — Do you remember Kingsley's impressive description in "Hereward" — of the coming of the Vikings: —

"And nearer and nearer came the OAR-ROLL. like thunder working up from the northeast," etc.?

In that description he gives the chorus of their chant, expressing "the revelry of slaughter:" "*Yuch-hey-saa-saa-saa.*" Introduced as he introduces it, it produces a great effect, — though nobody seems to know what it means. (I asked a delightful friend of mine, — a sort of gypsified painter who spoke half the dialects of Europe; and he assured me that in a part of North Germany, that old Viking chorus is still sung, as a refrain, I believe he said, of drinking-songs. But he did not know what it meant.) Perhaps it means nothing. But it sounds like sword-work.

One more: —

It was at Mionoseki that I went out in an ancient boat, moved with oars of extraordinary shape, to visit a man-of-war. As the men rowed, — all standing, — they sung, weirdly, — the boat song of that old coast. (I afterwards heard it in Oki.)

> Ara-ho, uo san osa-a,
> Ira-ho, en-ya-a-a.
> *Ghi! Ghi!*

At each Ghi, the stroke is given. The song is very weird, — beginning with a high wail, and sinking down almost to a whisper, — after which the ghi is hissed through the teeth. That day we rowed out of the Past into the latest mechanical Present and back again, — through a thousand years each time. Always the same weird song. I asked everywhere for a meaning to it. There is none. Now why cannot I put it into the book, — with its "Ghi! ghi!"?

Happy, happy, thrice happy the traveller who is able to write music by ear. Oh, if I could only give you musical copies of the extraordinary peasant songs I have heard, — strange, melancholy, penetrating things, that seemed to be of the earth, of the land, — the cry of the ancient soil itself, or of its ancient soul!

Yes; I read the Mayet case. A reaction against the missionaries I should be glad of; — but I fear it would be carried to other and less rational extremes. By the way, I am told the bateren here was a Russian. I think that had something to do with the violence of hate. Japan is instinctively afraid of Russia. She ought to see that her natural friend and ally is China. From China — in China — she has much to gain, nothing to fear; from Russia nothing to gain and much to fear, under certain possible conditions. The cost of the reaction against us is cheap, however, if it has revived Japanese art. And I have an idea about some of the modern Japanese art I have seen. I am not of those who can persuade themselves anything is more intrinsically valuable because it is old. I think that I have seen Japanese drawing just as fine as that of Hokusai, Kunisada, etc., made only a couple of years ago, and merely by way of cheap popular illustration. Nay, I even think much of the drawing now being done is better than the average of the old drawing. Of course we miss two things, — the ancient fancy and the ancient colour. But these may be revived and transformed. I have some very old pictures, and some quite new ones; and I like the new ones in some respects even better. Japanese art means to Japan much more than she yet understands; it means wealth, prosperity, beauty, everything. I don't think we can judge what she is doing so much by the work of her great men, as by the work of her common, cheap draughtsmen and decorators. And it is good, —very good.

. . . I shall not die happy unless I can spend some time again in a French, and much time in a Spanish colony. I think Manila is possible for me. I could take a six months' rest there from work. I suppose it cannot be so expensive as Havana. After all, it is only among the Latins that the charm of life still lingers in our Western civilization. Our industrial covetousness and restlessness, building cities up to heaven, blackening the face of the world with factory ashes, and the face of the sky with pea-soup fogs, is killing everything of sweetness and light. If Daikoku-San would only make me rich enough, I will promise never to go further than Java or some such place, — and will build him a torii of bronze. By the way, did I not tell you the story of the man who cheated the Gods? For he promised them a torii of good metal, and gave them a torii constructed of three needles.

·Ever,
Lafcadio Hearn.

P. S. Two important subjects I had forgotten:— Speaking of reaction, I have found it a good deal reflected even in the compositions of my students (this, of course *entre nous*). I have always had their confidence, even when I could get nothing else; and they write their thoughts. They frankly express their dislike of foreigners;—they wish to see them swept from the country, driven from the country. In Izumo (where I got some of the ancient charm-songs for driving foreigners away), the feeling was not so strong, perhaps. To-day it seems very strong. Many compositions express a desire for war. Many others lament the slavery of the country to foreigners. Many recall the case of Hawaii, which the Japanese were quick to notice; others cite the case of India, — "subject to brutal foreigners." All this is boys' work. Yes, but boys like these, mostly in the neighbourhood of twenty — form their opinions from general opinions. Individual, spontaneous opinions are rare among them. I can never even get them to express an original opinion, to suggest a subject for conversation. I have to help them to think. Assuredly their thoughts are made for them; — and mean something. Japan is going to retaliate for all the supercilious consideration she has received. I think we are secretly despised or hated, or both. Certainly despised as hirelings, and hated as superiors. This by the new Japan, of course. The politeness which is "benevolence in small things" is yet among the people. I have seen none of it among the educated here. As for myself, I am trusted and tolerated, — nothing more. If I speak, I am saluted. If I ask a question, I am politely snubbed or evaded. I have been made to understand, without being actually told as much, not to ask any questions. Of course with the students I am like an elder brother; there is no trouble there. And I do not try to check their feeling about foreigners. I rather encourage it. I encourage it

because it is patriotic, because it is just, because
it indicates national recuperation. What I always
discourage are such remarks as "Japan is only a
little country," etc., "ignorant people worship idols."
All such notions I combat, and strongly criticise.
I teach them respect for their own faiths, for the
beliefs of the common people, and for their own
country. I am practically a traitor to England
(eh?) and a renegade. But in the eternal order of
things, I know I am right.

The other subject is about Buddhism. It seems
to me the Japanese are awaking to the knowledge
of a fact which ought to have long ago been as plain
to them as the nose on the face of a Tengu, — namely
that the contemptuous attitude of the government
toward Buddhism has produced infinite moral
harm; and that with education and a corrupt priest-
hood, Japan must soon have no religion at all. If
I am not mistaken, there are signs that an effort will
be made to aid Buddhism educationally. The re-
generation of Buddhism would be, I think, the sav-
ing of much that is Japanese. Do you know Torio?
How I wish you and he could talk about what is
and what ought to be.

Well, I ought to apologize for writing so much.
But I think you may be interested in all things.

June 19, 1893.

DEAR CHAMBERLAIN, — . . . About the books.
Yes, I will make out a list later on, and send at the
same time what will cover the cost. In this perhaps I will not include Carlyle at all; for since I

wrote last I have been thinking that I need other
books much more, — possibly fewer, too, in number.
But I won't send any list till you are feeling quite
well, and settled again in Tokyo for a few months.
In the meantime I will be grateful for a loan of
Oliver Cromwell.

Assuredly Carlyle is no sweet pill to swallow;
and he never guides you anywhere. He is hard reading; one feels as if travelling over broken rocks and
boulders hidden by scrub. But there are lightning
flashes in that apocalyptic style of his which reveal
infinite things. I read only for the flashes. Even
then, only a little at a time, every day. Did you
ever know the agony of trying to read *Sartor Resartus
for pleasure?*

. . . And here is something else *entre nous.* I am
going, in spite of considerable self-mistrust, to attempt a philosophical article on L'éternel féminin —
in the West, as elucidated by the East. *Ex Oriente
Lux!* This idea has encouraged me to the attempt;
and I am therefore very careful of the idea, — like
one having made a discovery. While cogitating it
occurred to me that certain peculiarities of the art
of both hemispheres can only be explained by the
absence or presence of the dominant sexual idea.
Not only must the Japanese remain quite blind to
all in our literature, art, etc., created by that idea;
but we ourselves must suffer æsthetically by the
necessarily one-sided character of our own art, —
or æsthetic development. I shall have to work it
out before August, if possible.

I am also writing out a few extraordinary child

stories, which I think I might get Japanese illustrations for some day.

Is the tale of the old woman who drank so much of the Fountain of Youth that she drank herself back into babyhood, unwritten? Or is it Japanese? It has a savour to me of Western fancy; but I am not sure.

A funny story for you. At Kumamoto, they are vulgar folk — all the women play the samisen. Instead of calling in geisha, the poorer folk make their own music. Near us a family yesterday proceeded, after necessary delays, to celebrate the birth of a child. The wife played the samisen, the mother-in-law the drum, and the father danced to please the guests.

As all this was quite extraordinary to Izumo people, my folks went to look at it. It was night, and the gates were closed. A new servant alone was left to guard the front part of the house, while I guarded the rear. But the man thought he might also go to see just for a moment. He went to what he believed to be the gate of the street, opened it, and found himself in absolute darkness. There was neither moon nor stars. He returned, said a prayer to the Gods, and tried the gate again. Black as a coal! Then he came back and waited.

When the family returned he naïvely asked, "Was there any light in the street when you went?" "Plenty of light!" all said; "lamps and a big moon." "So!" exclaimed the servant triumphantly, "I *knew it was a fox!*"

Now the truth of the matter was that he had

opened the gate of the wood house, mistaking it for the smaller street gate, which it very much resembles, — and finding himself in the dark he was convinced that a fox was trying to deceive him. We all laughed; but he said: "It would not have been the first time that a fox put his hand before my eyes."

My old kurumaya has fox stories enough, but none of his own experience. He brought to the house, however, a young kurumaya who told us that one evening a military officer engaged him to take him to a house near the Hanaokayama. He took him there. The officer went into the house, — a superb residence, — bidding him wait. He waited until 3 A. M. Then he suddenly saw there was no house, and that his kuruma was gone. He got no money, and only found his kuruma two days later, — in a gorge.

Ever,

LAFCADIO HEARN.

June 25, 1893.

DEAR CHAMBERLAIN, —. . . You have smashed me, I confess, on the question of quoting foreign words of unknown meaning. Certainly I have no further argument to offer. I only venture to faintly suggest that sometimes, — sometimes, — in extraordinary cases, I still think there might be an artistic use of such words. Kipling ventures it in his ballads (I don't mean the Ditties, — they are, of course, only for the Anglo-Indian).

With 'er arm upon my shoulder, an' er cheek agin my cheek,
We useter watch the steamers an' the HATHIS pilin' teak, —

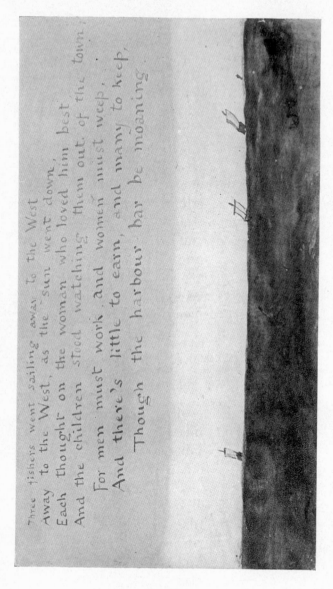

Three fishers went sailing away to the West
Away to the West, as the sun went down,
Each thought on the woman who loved him best
And the children stood watching them out of the town,
    For men must work, and women must weep, .
And there's little to earn, and many to keep,
    Though the harbour bar be moaning.

ILLUSTRATION FOR " THE THREE FISHERS "

From a sketch by Hearn for use with his Japanese students

Elephints a-pilin' teak
  In the sludgy, squdgy creek,
Where the silence 'ung that 'eavy you was 'arf afraid to speak!
  On the road to Mandalay.

But I won't say any more now. I fear I could not make many changes in the text of the book; but I will be more careful in future, and if I write any more Japanese stories I shall keep Japanese words out of them as much as I can.

For me, all is dead blank again. I'm paralyzed for lack of certainties. After writing one hundred pages of MS. (about) on the Eternal Feminine, I suddenly find myself checked by doubts of a very serious kind. I read your "Classical Poetry" over again to-day; and I find so many sweet thoughts in those poems that I fear my argument about the absence of the love-element from Japanese romance (except as the love of dancing girls, etc.) must be all wrong. But if I am all wrong, why do the Japanese hate our English society novel as indecent? Why are they utterly disgusted with our raving about kisses and embraces? You see my argument was going to be a glorious one. I had reasoned out that we can only see Nature as Masculine and Feminine (chiefly feminine) while the Japanese see Nature as Neuter, which we can't do at all. And the influence of all this on art and thought. But I can't work out my ideas half so soon as I hoped. I must take up something else in the meantime. . . .

I am sorry you did not like Sacher-Masoch; for I love him. But I must respect the combined criticism of yourself and Mason, as having weight. It is possible I may have placed too much value on the

books. But if you like Tolstoi (especially "The Cossacks"); Tourgueneff's short stories; Dostoievsky;
Gogol, — I don't see why you don't like my Austro-
Hungarian Jew. Mason does n't like these stories
either. But why? I don't like Howell's books because I detest the kind of people he writes about.
Perhaps you and Mason don't like S. Masoch's
people. But I can't understand how you don't like
"The Mother of God." Perhaps you will like Loti's
book better. You remember what I wrote you long
ago about my belief that his genius must expire with
that natural blunting of the nerves which comes
with the passing of youth. He says so himself touch-
ingly in his little preface — "*déjà autour de moi,
tombe une sorte de nuit.*"

Faithfully ever,
LAFCADIO HEARN.

June 27, 1893.

DEAR CHAMBERLAIN, — . . . I trust your
thoughts about yourself, as a worker, are only temporary, — the result of a lassitude quite natural
after travelling eighty or ninety thousand miles. I
do not believe you will continue to feel so. But I do
believe that it will be best for you to take all the
rest, and pleasure, and indulgence you can for at
least six months. Such, indeed, is the natural law
after long travelling. And the work gains by it after.
In the West Indian heat, memory and everything
failed me sometimes; and I said to my friend: — "I
can't write; I almost wish I was dead." For I felt
very blue. He (a physician and author) said: —

"Don't try to. Go to the country and read novels and bathe. We all feel that way here; it is only Nature's warning in the tropics to take rest, — to have some fun." I found he was right, and I never strained again. Of course it follows to reason that when the physical vitality runs low, the mental power for consecutive effort must become feeble; the reserve of both forces is the same. The nerve batteries must be left to fill themselves slowly; and the filling often takes a long time. Once, in my case, it took years to recharge. But I don't think age has anything to do with it. I am certainly much stronger now than I was at thirty. The only difference is that it takes us longer to recuperate at every successive decade. By the way, to-day I am forty-three. How many more years for literary work? I hope at least twenty; — I want only the material. And you will certainly feel the same way, if you take this small gadabout's advice to forget all work for six months, or at least three. Besides I would indulge myself if I were you. A good digestion means that everything is possible. "*Avec ça, on se refait toujours,*" said a French adviser once. If I were you I would give that digestion plenty of work with claret and beef and puddings and pies and liqueurs. And I would smoke cigars; and I would drink brandy. And I would not allow myself even to think of work till the surplus of returning strength — and nothing else — made work absolutely necessary to happiness. Of course, all this is mere repetition of my own experience, — and perhaps to you, mere verbiage. But I can't help suspecting that you do not allow yourself all the mere bodily gratification that you might allow yourself with good results. I think so because you told me that, although when I dined with you, you lived superbly, that when alone it is your habit to eat very little. So with all scholars, perhaps. But I wish you would cultivate the physical only, for a time. Perhaps no doctor ever told you this; but it is a curious fact in my own experience, — a man can scientifically triple the assimilating capacity of his stomach. And that means tripling the storage of physical force within himself. I could tell you extraordinary things but I fear to bore you; and indeed I would not have said all this but for my anxiety at hearing that you feel vitally low. Wherefore I talked of Nature, the greatest nurse, who brought me back to strength twice after the doctors declared me doomed, and I was able to eat only one raw egg a day.

I read part of your last letter with remorse. I am now all at one with you on the subject of Buddhism; and my first enthusiasm for Shinto, I fear, was wrong. I thought I saw in Shinto, the soul of Japanese Loyalty, — self-sacrifice, etc. I wrote enthusiastically about it; — I fear you will justly condemn my views. Perhaps I shall be able to modify some of them in proof. Yes, Buddhism makes an appeal to the human heart, and Shinto only to tradition and race feeling.

There is, however, a power, — a mighty power, in that, too. I can't remember now where I read a wonderful story about a Polish brigade under fire during the Franco-Prussian War. The French batteries are directed upon it; the fire of the mitrailleuses is atrocious. The Polish brigade stands still under the infernal hail, cursed by its German officers for the least murmur, — "Silence! you Polish hogs!" — while the ground is being strewn with blood and brains and entrails. Hundreds fall; thousands! and the order is always, "Close up, you Polish hogs!" Just one instant with the bayonet, — one chance to retaliate, to die like men! But the iron order is to wait. Men sob with rage. "Silence, you Polish beasts!" And then, at last, old Steinmetz, smoking his pipe in the carnage, gives a signal, — *the* signal. The bugles ring out with the force of Roland's last blast at Roncesvalles, the air forbidden ever to be sung or heard at other times — the national air (you know it) — "*No! Poland is not dead!*" And with that crash of brass all that lives of the brigade is hurled at the French batteries. Mechanical power, if absolutely irresistible, might fling back such a charge, but no human power. For old Steinmetz, smoking his pipe, had made Schopenhauer-esquely, the mightiest appeal to those "Polish brutes" that man, God, or devil could make, the appeal to the ghost of the Race. The dead heard it; and they came back that day, — the dead of a thousand years.

And then you know the tremendous story of the Cuirassiers at Reichshoffen, — dying to a man to cover the retreat; each regiment charging in turn over the torn bodies of those who had formed the first regiment. That was a grand failure and a grand sacrifice. But what is not a failure is the annual

ceremony, when, in the great camp, the roll-call of
the dead is called, and every buried Cuirassier answers "Present!" — through the mouth of the living, because the grand dead never die.

Now old Steinmetz smoking his pipe, waiting for
the right moment; the French people, keeping alive
the memory of the heroism of Reichshoffen, — both
have the same thought, — the thought that moved
Carlyle to say that not pleasure and happiness, but
pain and misery and death are the greatest attrac-
tions to men's souls, — that which they seek in preference to all else. (Carlyle puts it crookedly; but
there is a thought there.) The race feeling is the
most powerful of all impulses; stir it deeply, — and
to the living the value of life and fame and love
and all else disappear like smoke; and the dead become the masters; and the living only the instruments. Now, do you not think something of the
magic by which that feeling can be stirred, is possessed by Shinto? If it is, then Shinto is mighty.
If not, then Shinto is like a sacred awabi-shell,
empty and full of holes.

But my letter is too long. To-morrow I will write
you about the o-fuda book, and other things.

LAFCADIO HEARN.

July 7, 1893.

DEAR CHAMBERLAIN, — I suppose my letter
about eating must have seemed very simple to you;
but it was prompted by ideas which your answer
confirms. I had a very charming friend, Charles
Gayarre, the Louisiana historian, — a scholar of the

old Régime, who wrote French in the style of Cha-
teaubriand; he used to eat so carefully that everything was weighed for him. But his trouble was in
regard to digestion. When you told me you had no
trouble of that sort, I at once suggested the opposite policy, — because it succeeded twice in my own
case, and for another reason. It seems to me that we
conquer anything which takes a chronic form only
by a surplus of physical force in ourselves; and how
a man can get such a surplus while he eats like a
butterfly, I can't imagine. I mean I can't understand the scientific principle behind the treatment
you follow. So, being anxious, perhaps I said some
"simple" things.

The examinations are upon me; — the heat alone
is pleasing, — it has become almost West Indian; —
the outlook is very dull and discomforting. I want
to be working, and I have no material; for I never
got anything in Kumamoto, and I have done all I
could with my Izumo notes. I read; but reading is
tiresome, — seems to me almost wicked; — I think
of Kipling's lines, —

> One minute's work to thee denied
> Stands all Eternity's offence.

Yet I shall certainly never get any material here;
though my interests are here. Interest and literary
duty have become antagonistic. What shall I do?
is my perpetual plaint. A thought that eats into my
brain like an acid. Have I come to a standstill? I
would gladly pay a salary to somebody to teach me
Buddhism, — the living Buddhism. Then I could

write something. But to have no impressions, no pleasures, is certainly hell, — the Kwakto Jigoku variety. There is no religion here, — no poetry, — no courtesy, — no myths, — no traditions, — no superstitions. Beastly modernization!

The idea of which we spoke together is also growing upon me, — that thorough social disorganization is going to beget revolution. The spirit of insubordination, hostility to foreigners, disrespect to traditions, contempt for religion, and national vanity, — grows with prodigious rapidity just in proportion as the modernization becomes more thorough. The educated Japanese complains at being obliged to conceal his scepticism about the divinity of the Emperor. But when the peasant becomes equally sceptical he won't pay his taxes. I can't see anything for Japan now but revolution or a military domination; the latter would, I think, be the best. No; the country is certainly going to lose all its charm, — all its Japanesiness; it is going to become all industrially vulgar and industrially commonplace. And I feel tired of it. In short, the pendulum has swung the wrong way recently.

But this is n't the sort of thing to amuse you. What I want to give you is a specimen of an examination composition on the Story of the Three Caskets ("Merchant of Venice"), which I gave for a subject to my third year class.

"Once upon a time there was in Italy a man who was a very rich and most venerable.

"He has a daughter, very beauty — the bride of the all village.

"She has this fate when her father has die, — then all his furniture was to fall on her.

"So every men wanted to marriage to her.

"The father become old and sicked into his bed, — and could n't get up once more, — and he foreseed that sick is the last sick on his life.

"So he called his remarkable girle to his bed, and said, — 'I cannot get off of death, and I want a successor to my house —'

(I skip the instruction about the three caskets, and the description of the princes of Morocco and of Arragon.)

"This Prince chosened the casket of gold, and find inside the skeleton of the old man, — which wondered him unfortunately.

"The other Prince choosened the casket of silver, and find a Fool-Man inside, and in sollow runned away." . . .

Having much more of this sort of thing to correct, I must close. No news from America yet. I want to get to Nagasaki next week if I can. Perhaps I shall be able to get some impressions there, and to write you some letters, pleasant letters.

LAFCADIO HEARN.

July 14, 1893.

DEAR CHAMBERLAIN, — Your analysis of Loti is quite delightful; and what was more so was the announcement that parts of the book had pleased you, — as I thought they would. Loti's style is, of course, eccentric; but I am not sufficiently versed in the rules to answer the question about his curious

phrases. He is not, of course, classic; and in his best
work, which you have not yet seen, he violates all
classic traditions. I must try to find you "Le Roman
d'un Spahi;" "Fleurs d'Ennui;" and "Le Mariage
de Loti;" these were written before his nerves became dull. There is also in the "Propos d'Éxil"
some sketches of East Africa that are not less artistic
than the pictures of West Africa in the Spahi-book.
As for his moral side, you will find him much worse
than in "Madame Chrysanthème." Yet there is
wonderful beauty in his account of a night spent
with an Arabian fille, — "*Une sauterelle du désert.*"
The melancholy element is also much stronger in
these earlier books; but it there seems natural, —
as the splendour and pitilessness of tropic Nature,
ignoring man, naturally causes melancholy. Vast-
ness of plain and cloudless sky; mountains and
Amazonian floods, of course, make us feel our own
impermanency, and the awful youth of the world.

I am glad you have not read much of Gautier's
verse; because there will be a glorious revelation for
you. His choicest work is all in the "Émaux et
Camées,"—a little book you can read in one morning, but having read, will re-read a thousand times.
The "Symphonie" is in it, — and perhaps fifty other
brief pieces, nearly all in quatrains. I think it the
most perfect verse that was ever made in this world;
it is just what its title implies, — jewelry of words,
the art of a mighty lapidary. There you will see the
syllables "that shine like phosphorus when rubbed."
There are many beautiful things in Gautier's other
volumes of poetry, but scarcely anything to compare

with the "Émaux et Camées." Certainly Victor Hugo never even approached Gautier in this special kind of verse. And if you have not read Gautier's "Contes et Nouvelles" (two vols.) you will have another surprise. I translated and published some; Andrew Lang did the same thing after me, but infinitely better (I believe he abused my translation in his preface). My favourites are "Arria Marcella;" "La Morte Amoureuse;" "Le Pied de Momie;" "Une Nuit de Cléopatre." But you will find wonderful things besides. Of course you have read "Mademoiselle de Maupin," — that miracle of sensuous art. I was very fond of all the Romantic School; next to Gautier as a prose-writer, I was bewitched most, I think, by De Nerval's "Voyage en Orient," with its tremendous legend of Solomon and the Queen of Sheba; and, though shocked, I felt a surprise of pleasure in the wonderful insanities of Baudelaire. Of Flaubert I only liked what most people dislike, — "La Tentation de Saint Antoine," — besides the wonderful "Trois Contes." "Madame Bovary" is pure realism; and I hate pure realism. I still believe in the Romantic School. Loti partly belongs to it. The realistic school seems to me played out, since Maupassant went mad; and the abominations (how clever they are, nevertheless!) of Richepin ("Les Blasphèmes," "La Mer") will not kill that quality of romantic verse of which they were an unintentional caricature. Among the severer writers of the romantic school (Gautier called them presbyopes) I love Mérimée in all his work, — historical, etc., as well as romantic. He alone has something of an English quality, beautifully shown, I think, in his studies of Russian history; "Les Faux Démétrius," and "Les Cosaques d'Autrefois." Somehow or other, Daudet and Zola and Bourget do not seem to me to have the enduring qualities of those older writers. They seem rather varieties of the Goncourt breed; therefore all visibly artificial. They cannot write from an overflowing imagination and a big heart, — like Hugo, Gautier, Mérimée, De Nerval; they write from notebooks, and dabble in philosophy and medicine. If I can find at Nagasaki anything good that I think you would like, I will get it.

For I'm off, in a day or two. My next letter will be from Nagasaki. I don't think you could bear the heat in Kumamoto now; I like it, except at night, when there are no windows to open, and the mosquitoes are very atrocious.

Mason has written me a delightful letter, but says I must n't write to him again for a time, as he is going away to Yezo.

By the way, he never sent me the Oliver Cromwell, — or at least, I never got it. It makes no difference, as I shall be away; but I mention the fact merely for fear the book might have been sent and not delivered, — like Lowell's letter.

Ever most truly,   LAFCADIO HEARN.

July 16, 1893.

DEAR CHAMBERLAIN, — . . . Oh! I love Heine. Yes, I saw the marvellous translations in *Blackwood*, — among others "The Pilgrimage to Keo-

laar" which will haunt me as long as I live. I have
read Bowring's translations of course; they are
rough. I read the translations by Emma Lazarus
(a pretty little Jewess who died in 1885, I think);
some were delicious, — especially the ghostly pieces
"Don Ramiro," etc., and that awful satire in which
the young lady who had been abusing the Jews in a
frantic way, allows herself to be seduced by a noble
knight, who thereupon informs her that he is the
son of the most famous and most learned Israel of
Saragossa. I also read the French prose-versions of
Heine, — superintended by himself. Indeed I liked
the prose-versions better than anything except the
translations in *Blackwood*. I never understood the
beauty of "Faust" till I had read Hayward's prose-
translation. The verse of Taylor and others seemed
to mask the meaning for me.

I am trying again to work at my theory of the
Eternal Feminine in its influence on Western æsthetic thought, but I have no heart in the work for
the present. I shall wait for a happy reaction to
develop the ideas more. What can one do in a city,
without temples, art, or courtesy? Still Kumamoto
is better for me than Tokyo could be, or Kanazawa;
the people know me, and I have much leisure and
rest, and the climate is warm. Perhaps I can find
a student sometime who has studied Buddhism, and
employ him for a year or two. But nothing is so difficult as for a foreigner to find an honest Japanese
helper. Even my little boy turned out badly, and
I had to send him away, after he had given us all
a world of trouble.

What a moral disintegration seems to have come upon the country. Here are fishermen at war, farmers at war, politicians killing each other, students fighting, a general increase of crime, etc. Japan won't be the best place in the world after another generation.

Ever most truly,

LAFCADIO HEARN.

July 16, 1893.

DEAR CHAMBERLAIN, — I have to write a line more to ask you — at your own convenience — to tell me whether the Japanese word *mayoi*, in the sense of the fascination of woman, can have any Buddhist affinity with the Sanscrit *maya* "illusion." I hope it has; but nothing is so insane in these days as to hazard an etymology without being "everlastingly sure."

I send a photo of Pierre Loti,—taken, I think, about eight or nine years ago. It is not the sort of face to encourage affection; but it is very, very Latin, — keen, fine, and hard. I don't see much heart there, but there is intense life, and great sureness of self.

The well has been cleaned. And there have been rites paid to the God of Wells. Do you know that in all the wells little fishes are kept, — to purify the water? — funa? Those in my well are rather large. I suppose the custom is founded upon centuries of experience. In learning about the fish,—regarded as the servants of the Well God, — I also learned the meaning of the old phrase *funazamurai*, — so often repeated in the Chinshingura.

Ever with best regards,

LAFCADIO HEARN.

July 22, 1893.

DEAR CHAMBERLAIN, — I predicted a letter from Nagasaki; but the prediction I found too difficult to fulfil. In fact I fled away from Nagasaki, — and propose to relate to you the history of my adventures, or some of them.

I left Kumamoto on the morning of the 20th, alone, en route for Nagasaki via Hyakkwan. From Kumamoto to Hyakkwan is about one and one-half hours by jinrickisha. A dirty little country village in a sea of rice fields, is Hyakkwan. The people are simple and good. I found one of my students there studying Chinese. Then I took a boat for the steamer. The boat was a broken-nosed boat.

The boat left the creek and wriggled over a sea, still as the silent sea of Coleridge's poem, unto the distance of four ri. It was tiresome. Then it stopped and waited; and for more than an hour, I watched the water surface sinuously moving with a queer motion as of reticulated stuffs being pulled in opposite directions, network of ripples above network of ripples. There was nothing else to watch. At last I saw an inverted comma on the edge of the sky. It came nearer. Finally I heard a scream of steam that filled my soul with joy. But it turned out to be the wrong steamer. I waited one more hour in that boat, and the right steamer appeared.

Except the Oki steamer I never became familiar with such an instrument of torture. Her name was the *Taiko Maru*. She was built only for kimono or yukata, and for the squatting position. The heat was that of the drying room of a steam-laundry.

There was nothing to drink but tea. I slept on the tatami, comfortably, with my head on a pillow of leather paper stamped with the curious figure of an elephant-headed Karashishi. Had I donned Japanese clothes instead of a duck suit, I would have been comfortable. But as I was going to a European hotel, I dressed according to the code, — for which I was very sorry later on.

We reached Nagasaki at 3 A. M., the blackest hour. A coolie promised to take me to the hotel, but took me a mile away from it and then said he did not know where it was. I took my baggage from him, and found a belated kurumaya to take me to the hotel. It was locked up. I put my shoulder against the gate, and it opened and I went up steps between heights of clipped shrubbery and ranks of flower pots filled with ornamental plants into a piazza, full of rocking-chairs and lamps and silence. There I waited for sunrise. Sunrise over the bay was really lovely; — I saw strips of gold, like those of the old ballads. And at last the house woke up and I got a room.

But it was too hot to stay in the hotel. A dead heat, worse than any tropical heat I ever felt, and getting worse as the sun rose. I hired a kuruma and rushed about. I saw the beautiful city in the most beautiful light possible; I climbed the hills; I visited the new metal torii. Let me assure you that it is very ugly, — that torii; it is the ugliest I ever saw in Japan. It is monstrously shaped, — looks top-heavy, — has no grace, and is of a sooty stove-colour. Whoever made the design ought to be killed with the edge of the sword.

Then I got breakfast and went out again. The sum of my impressions was that Nagasaki is the prettiest seaport I ever saw, — full of picturesqueness and quaintness, — made for artists to etch and for photographers to photograph. But I could not buy anything I wanted, or find anything I wished to find in a Western line. Very few foreigners, — and no books, — nothing to pick up, — no supplies to be had except in large quantities.

As the day grew hotter, I began to grieve exceedingly that I had put on a duck suit, and had gone to the Bellevue Hotel. Comfort inside of Western clothes and Western architecture in such heat was out of the question. Not even in Venezuela, in the hottest hours of the afternoon, did I ever feel such heat. In the hotel I heard the guests say they could not sleep for the heat. There was nothing for it except iced drinks at twenty-five cents. I drank about four yen worth, and was angry with all the world, because I could not strip or be comfortable. By six o'clock I determined to flee away. The heat was hell, — and though I like heat, the combination of heat and stupid convention is something beyond my power of endurance. If I had to wear European clothes and live in a European house in such heat for one week, I should go crazy or die. I resolved to flee away from Nagasaki at once.

In a Japanese hotel one can always be comfortable and naked. In a Japanese hotel everything you want to buy is found for you. In a Japanese hotel arrangements are made to take you anywhere you want to go. In a Japanese hotel they buy your

tickets for you, and accompany you to the steamer
or railroad. But in the beastly Western hotels, nobody will even answer a question. There is nobody
to ask, except depraved Japanese servants who
understand no language when asked to take any
trouble. I got a kuruma and went to a Japanese
steamship company, and begged them, in my bad
Japanese, to get me outside of Nagasaki as quick as
possible. To my surprise they understood and sympathized with me, and promised to send for me at
3 A. M. I waited in the hotel till the heat became so
atrocious that even the mosquitoes had not strength
to bite, — then I tried to go out. But men wearing shirt-tails asked me if I "wanna nice gil," — so
I went back again, and sat in the stifling veranda
until 3 A. M. Then the Japanese Company sent a
man and a sampan for me, and took me away. And
I blessed them therefor.

Got out of the harbor by half-past three, on the
Kinrin Maru (an old acquaintance), with a ticket
for Misumi. From Misumi I was told a small
steamer would take me to Hyakkwan. Got to Misumi at 9 A. M. But there was no small steamer that
day.

At Misumi there is a hotel, the Urashimaya, built
and furnished in Western style, — as much superior
to the Nagasaki hotel as the sun is superior to a
farthing candle. Also a very beautiful woman, —
graceful as a dragon-fly, — with a voice like the
tinkling of a crystal wind-bell, took care of me, hired
kurumaya, gave me a splendid breakfast, and
charged me for all the entertainment only forty sen.

She understood my Japanese, and talked to me, and I felt like a soul suddenly reborn in the heart of a luminous lotos-flower in the garden of Paradise. Also all the maidens of the hotel seemed to me *tennin*, — since I had just escaped from the most frightful place of sojourn that exists in this world. And summer mists bathed sea and hills and all distant things, — a world of divinely soft blue, the blue of iridescent mother-of-pearl. There were a few white clouds dreaming in the sky; and they threw long white trembling lights on the water. And I dreamed of Urashima. The small soul of me drifted out over that summer sea, — steeped all in the blue light, — and in the fairy boat there was a maiden standing, more beautiful than the blue light itself, and softer, and sweeter; and she said to me in a voice that seemed to come from a thousand summers back, — "Now we will go to my father's palace, the Dragon Palace under the waves of the South." But I said, "No; I must go home to Kumamoto; — I have telegraphed, you see." "Then you will pay the kurumaya only seventy-five sen," she made answer, — " and you can come back again when you wish, because you will not open the box." And in this day-dream there came to me the interpretation of the divine old story; and I learned the mystery of it and the meaning. I put the box into my heart of hearts, and went away.

Hours I watched the blue world, and wondered at the loveliness of it, and thought of the old Gods and their ways, — though along the road ran a line of telegraph poles. And upon all the telegraph top

wires sat rows of little white-breasted birds. I saw
they always sat with their heads toward the road.
They watched us passing without fear. I counted
hundreds. Not one sat with its tail to the road, —
not even one. All seemed waiting for something. I
kept on counting them till I fell asleep in the kuruma, — and floated away somewhere in a phantom-
boat; and the daughter of the Dragon-King stood
over me and smiled and said, — "You will pay the
kurumaya only seventy-five sen." . . .

Drums awoke me, — peasants in all the villages
invoking the rain. No rain; only white clouds, —
ghosts of clouds that died a thousand summers ago,
— or perhaps that summer mist that escaped from
Urashima's box. (Really he was foolish to open the
box. I remember opening such a box long, long ago.
Therefore my soul became old.) Always the birds in
rows on the telegraph wires, and not even one with
its tail turned to the road. There were picturesque
scenes. Nagahama village was pretty. It possesses
a great spring at the foot of a hill. There boys and
girls were bathing together. I stopped to look at
them. A young girl lifted a bucket of cold water to
give the runner to drink, and her light dress opening
with the effort showed the ripeness of a youth sweet
as fruit before it has become too soft. Always beating of drums at every village for rain.

The kurumaya deserts me. Is succeeded by a
fraud. I discharge the fraud in the middle of rice
fields and tramp on alone, carrying my own baggage.
Kumamoto is still three and one half ri distant. The
little birds watch me from the telegraph wires. Ex-

traordinary semi — quite different from those of Izumo — cry piteously and utter plaintive squeals when seized by little boys. Of course it is like squealing with one's feet instead of with one's mouth. But being directed by will, and for the purpose of exciting compassion, the squeal is equally pathetic.

Then I find a good kurumaya and proceed. I get home as the shadows lengthen. The sun has flayed my hands, and I have eaten nothing since nine o'clock, and I have not been in bed for three days, and I have not a dry thread on me. But I am home again, and therefore supremely happy. Nagasaki exists for me only as an evil dream of a hotel in hell, — with the seven deadly Sins for waiters. Certainly I shall never see it again. It is the hardest place to go to, or to escape from, in the whole world. When I was in it Kumamoto seemed to me displaced by magic to the distance of 100,000 miles, beyond long successions of typhoons and mountain ranges. I am again in a yukata, — upon tatami, — in real Japan. Of my trip I have nevertheless some pleasant recollections,— and a pretty fan, representing mountains and summer-sea, and bearing the name "Urashi-maya." At sight of it the vision and the dream return. I will often see them again; for the box will never be opened. But I was obliged to disobey the daughter of the Dragon-God in one thing; I paid the kurumaya,— three kurumaya,— one yen and twenty-five sen. Had they only known they could have made me pay one hundred and twenty-five yen.

"How much," my wife asks me, "would you

accept on condition of spending a week more in the Bellevue Hotel, Nagasaki?"

"Surely," I answer, "no sum earthly. Only the promise of perpetual youth in the palace of the Dragon-God for a thousand years, or a transportation to the Paradise of Amida Buddha."

Ever with best regards,

LAFCADIO HEARN.

August 16, 1893.

DEAR CHAMBERLAIN, — I have been a little neglectful, because of my reverie about Urashima, called "The Dream of a Summer Day," which I am now sending to Boston. Many, many thanks for your kindness in having the text looked up for me. And do you know, the beauty of that word Elysium greatly grew as I contemplated Horai, and felt that it could never be made to convey any idea to an English reader, and that only the Greek word could render the idea of ghostly happiness properly? . . .

The great plague of summer nights here is insects. So came the goblins about Saint Anthony. Two curious beetles, one of which is shaped hexagonally, are especially tormenting, — as they produce when alarmed the most atrocious conceivable smell. On the other hand, the singing insects are wonderful. A cricket called "junta" is very musical here, more than in Izumo, — and really seems to talk. Other creatures at night sing like birds. One of these is cooked and eaten by geisha to make their voices sweet.   Ever most sincerely,

LAFCADIO HEARN.

DEAR CHAMBERLAIN, — I have just got your letter, and a copy of the *Advertiser* which makes me glad that I changed the sentence about the sailors in proofs. I have a great mind to subscribe for the *Advertiser*, and stop reading the *Mail;* — I am so sick of all the stuff about missionaries and Christianity. Why can't a newspaper have mercy on people who don't care to have religious stuff forever thrust under their noses? I see the missionaries are still telling the people they are savages, and idolaters, etc., and have been making a row at Bakkan, among other places. There's no truth ever told about these matters; what the missionaries really do is never published.

I wonder if the Archduke's Indian servant is a Sikh. Travellers write that the Sikh policemen and troopers look like demigods or kings; and some illustrations in the London *News* gave me the same notion.

It rejoiced me to hear of your living in the Japanese wing, and in yukata. I am sure it is the very best thing you could do for health in this hot season. Foreign dress soaks through almost immediately, and then becomes a wet wrap which, breathed on by a cold wind, chills the lungs at once. I have been wearing considerably less than a yukata lately during the hottest part of the day; but when I go out in a white suit I wonder how any Japanese can don yofuku in July and August. No matter how thin, a tight-fitting dress is a torture in this heat to anybody accustomed to the kimono.

I had a long letter from the editor of the *Atlantic*.

He wants sketches of real Japanese life (sketches showing emotional character): doesn't care for religious or philosophical sketches. He wants, in short, exactly what I want, but what is very difficult to find. The fixed policy in Kumamoto has been to conceal everything from me, and although there is an approach to kindness in other directions, this policy is not likely to change much. I must devise some means of defeating it.

Reading over some part of "Things Japanese" the other day, it occurred to me that I might be able to speak of something not known to you about the household bath. Of course it is only a suggestion. It is true, as you say, that all the members of a household, in hierarchical order, use the same water. But the simple statement of this fact might create a wrong idea in European minds. The rule in such cases is worth recording. It is that each person washes outside the bath, and thoroughly rinses the whole body outside the bath, with hot water from a kanadari or other vessel, before entering into the tub proper. Consequently, in a household where this rule is observed, the servant girl who bathes last, will find the water nearly as clear as the Inkyo who bathes first. All the real washing is not done in the bath at all. And in some bathing-places, I have seen this rule strictly observed by hundreds of people, — as at Kitzuki. Of course among the poorer classes there is less nicety.

I have been studying De Quincey, Whittier, and the old ballads to pass the time (all sent me from Boston). How our tastes change with years. Half of De Quincey's charm has forever vanished for me; and I perceive qualities which repel as much as qualities which attract. Whittier charms me much more now, — though, of course, he was no scholar, nor even a really great poet. And what most puzzles me is the intense sympathy he forces me to feel for religious emotions I do not share, and for a simple faith which I know to be a delusion, to be philosophically all wrong. It is like hearing a great congregation singing "Nearer, my God, to thee." No one can hear it without feeling his heart swell, — whether he believes in a soul or not. Such is Whittier's simple music, — and yet still sweeter, because for the dear old man, no sect ever really existed, and his Christ was no Jew, but only a phantom Christ (representing the wish of the world to believe that goodness is divine, and that everything wrong in this life will be righted). Without some such beliefs life would be very hard, surely, for those incapable of evil.

Ever faithfully,
LAFCADIO HEARN.

P. S. Edith Thomas is a poet I want to introduce to you some day, if you do not know her well. She will be a surprise and a pleasure.

P. S. 2. I agree with you about the power of that sketch you like in Kipling's last. Kipling only has seized that astonishing fact, and pulled it into the light, about the doing of the world's work by boys, — "Kingly boys" he rightly called them in his verse. I doubt if any other country but England produces them; and in any event no other country could find employment for them. They are the results of the same school system that made a Clive. Much as may be said against the English educational system, — its brutality, its hardness, — the product furnishes an iron fact in reply, not to be removed. Race, of course, is a consideration; but no other race could have such a system. It is a training from childhood in self-mastery as a means to the mastery of men; — so that a boy of nineteen can, in a serious emergency, run the great Indian empire. While the prime necessity of life is intelligent fighting capacity, such training is as valuable as it is wonderful. It does not, however, produce the great minds as a rule, — does it? They require a gentler medium. I am not altogether in sympathy with the worship of Force in our century, — are you? But though surely not the highest subject of contemplation, it offers spectacles of splendour worthy of all art.

Ever,

LAFCADIO HEARN.

August 23, 1893.

DEAR CHAMBERLAIN, — We've been having typhoon weather down here too, — with sudden changes of atmospheric pressure which stupefy one in the middle of the day. This morning, for instance, I was full of poetry, — trying to write a tropical story. I was getting along gloriously, when the barometer suddenly descended and crushed all my fancies as a butterfly is crushed by laying a ten-pound weight on it. I suppose all writers who ever

lived must have had severe struggles with the
atmosphere. In the tropics, you know, only certain
hours in the morning allow of work.

That reminds me of Bates. You will find him a
little less delightful than Wallace, but still delightful.
And pray notice especially the beautiful emotional
passage at the close, — and his meditations about
returning to civilization from Para. What disap-
points me a little both in Wallace and Bates is their
indifference to those large and awful aspects of
Nature which Humboldt could feel. They are not
poets; they are not sensitive to what would be for
you or me perpetual exaltation; their science keeps
them wholly on the watch for the microscopically
wonderful.

I ordered about five months ago Symonds's
"Renascence," but never got it, — and never will
from the same house, as I have made up my mind to
buy nothing more from K. & W. You will find the
work somewhat prolix, but of rare interest nevertheless. The man who has best succeeded, however, in
putting some phases of mediæval Italy before us
in artistic guise is, I think, Yriarte. You have seen
his wonderful works on Florence, Rimini, Venice,
and the touching monograph on Francesca. The
trouble is, of course, that these books represent only
chapters, and that they are as expensive as they are
beautiful. Oh! to live in Paris, just for the sake of
books!

His Austrian Highness made the Nagasaki folk
very angry. He went incog to the shops, while the
big residents were waiting for him at the landing. So

they thought he was only a naval officer, and let him
make very cheap bargains. Great was the wrath on
finding out who the customer was. . . .

Ever most truly,

LAFCADIO HEARN.

August 28, 1893.

DEAR CHAMBERLAIN, — I don't wish to perse-
cute you with letters; but this is the close of the
leisure season, and I want to make the most of it,
— and I forgot some things.

Here is one: — At the Nagasaki Hotel I saw two
large bookcases. I looked into them through the
locked glass, and saw a glorious half-Republican,
half-poetical, choice of books. All Voltaire, I think,
— and Diderot, — and Taine, — and Renan, —
and Michelet, — and Baudelaire, — and Flaubert,
— and Maxime du Camp, — and a splendid Balzac,
— and almost everything I could wish for. A mind
kindred to my own had formed that library. Two
large bookcases; — all the books in clumsy colonial
bindings. A Japanese boy, to whom I had been
a little kind, and who appeared to be terrified
when he spoke to me (he always looked about to
see if the other Japanese were watching him, — for
they used to abuse him whenever he spoke to me),
asked me if I would not like him to get the key, —
so I could read. As I had little time before me, I said
no. At 2.30 A. M. — the landlady first spoke to me.
She had been called out of bed by anger, — because
a Russian lodger had not only gone away without
telling her, but had sent three young tittering girls

to occupy his room during his absence. In her desire for sympathy she told me that although the *Russes sont les amis de la France,* — *ils ne sont pas les amis de la France jusqu'à ce point là!* I sympathized, and she told me she had lost her husband only four days before. I spoke of the books. She said: "Oh, yes, my husband was very instructed! — he collected all those books. We were long in the silk business; then we had a French newspaper, *L'Echo du Japan.* My husband's sickness forced us to come here. I am now alone and must be très sévère." She spoke charmingly, with grace and intelligence, — a fine keen woman of the world, — probably over forty, but looking younger. Then, with a charming bow, she bade me good-night. The desolation of the house and of her own brave worldly little soul still haunts me; and I wonder often, situated as she is, surrounded by Japanese whom I can plainly see to be rascals, what she is going to do. May the Gods protect her, and forgive me for having abused her beautiful but most d—bly managed hotel.

Oh! you must be happy to-day! It is Aki. The sunshine is whiter. Emerald and ruby lightnings, — the flash of dragon-flies, are playing everywhere. All the shadows are sharp as the edge of a knife. The Season of Great Light.

Ever most truly,

LAFCADIO HEARN.

August 30, 1893.

DEAR CHAMBERLAIN, — Edith Thomas is perhaps the best of American poets, after Aldrich and

Holmes; — she has written only short pieces, but all
are exquisite in thought and finish. She is a new
growth, — not yet very famous. I can recommend
her without fear to the severest critic on earth. I
met her in New York, — to thank her for the pleasure her work had given me in the tropics. A thin,
sepulchral, black-robed, goblin-like creature, — and
yet radiating goodness through her mourning, — a
light oozing through a pitcher of obsidian. She seems
to know life only as concrete pain. And still her
work has a lightness, a spring-glow, a beauty that
would seem inspired by the possession of all earthly
happiness.

   . . . I am not insensible to the charm of popular
faith in Catholic countries. You know I have
always written tenderly of it. But I can't dissociate
the thing called Christianity from all my life's experiences of hypocrisy, and cruelty, and villainy.
—from conventional wickedness and conventional
dreariness and ugliness and dirty austerities and
long faces and Jesuitry and infamous distortion of
children's brains. My experiences have been too
heavily weighted with all this to allow me to be
just. I can't. I never, never found religious beauty
in a church, — never out of the heart of a man or
a woman of the poorer classes, — no! the poorest
classes. I know I am rabid. I can't help it, but I try
to control it in my writings. By the way, I have
heard that I can get a permit to go to Manila for
several months if I make application next year.
I wonder whether they would wall me up alive
if I went into one of their fortress-like convents.

I am writing a sketch to be entitled "The Stone Buddha," a revery on eternal mysteries at the foot of an old Shaka in a cemetery behind our college. The thing has been growing slowly in my mind during more than a year. Therefore it ought to be something good, perhaps you think. But I fear not. It will be very short indeed.

The other day I got lost in the mountains. What a fearful thing to lose one's way in a confusion of valleys, — each exactly like another, and all the paths, between rice fields and barley fields twisting into infinite mysteries. A kind peasant guided me home, after I had lost myself out of sight in a wood, trying to escape from the maze.

I have promised to ask if you collect Japanese almanacs, for 200 or 400 years back. Having done so, my conscience is relieved.

Ever most truly, LAFCADIO HEARN.

September 1, 1893.

DEAR CHAMBERLAIN, — Many thanks for the *Advertiser*, and the kind loan of Zola's last, — which I wanted to read. . . .

Tell me, do you think a mathematician can be a poet? — that is, do you know any mathematician who is? I do not mean that the mathematical faculty *per se* is antagonistic to the feeling that creates poetry. But the mental cost of the faculty (physiologically, the nerve cost) is so great that it seems to me to leave simpler faculties undeveloped, or atrophied. You know that a want of sympathy is said to be characteristic of mathematicians.

I must write you my sensations about Zola so soon as I have devoured him. Jules Lemaître, I think, first did real justice to Zola. Zola has always believed and proclaimed himself a realist. If there is anything which Zola is not, — it is a realist. His mind conceives the horrible as Doré's mind conceived the ghastly and the nightmarish. He is the idealist of the Horrible, the Foul, the Brutal, the Abominable. In this, he is greater than any man who has followed the same impulses. As you say, I cannot find that anything but evil can be the general outcome of such studies of human nature. Swift had the same spirit. It is a morbid one, of course. But Zola represents the extreme swing of the pendulum between severe reserve and frantic license. His school must die with him. He himself has done so much that no one will ever again in this century try to follow him. I am sorry you read "La Terre" last. The best of the series, I think, is "Germinal," and after it, "La Débâcle." You must have read "La Débâcle." The chapter containing that description of the rushing by of the Prussian artillery shows Zola at his best, — a tremendous nightmare. There is nothing obscene in "La Débâcle," scarcely.

(I see even Anderson makes serious mistakes. He confounds Kotoshiro-nushi-no-kami with a totally different deity, — representing him as a child of Izanami and Izanaji.) After all I can't make much worse errors in my book than much better men have done, eh? But for this, I have to thank Kojiki, above all else.   Ever faithfully,

LAFCADIO HEARN.

September 3, 1893.

DEAR CHAMBERLAIN, — Well, I've read " Le Doc-
teur Pascal;" and after reading it, I read the *Times's*
criticism. It was a good criticism from the analyt-
ical side, but struck me as wrong in two points. I
confess I have not read all the " Comédie Humaine"
(I never had a chance to borrow it, and did not care
to buy it, because there was higher literature to buy).
But Balzac was a great artist in ideal lines quite foreign to Zola's genius. Take for example " La Peau de
Chagrin;" — the terrible human symbolism of that
story will keep it forever among the great Parables
of World Literature. Take the wondrous " Contes
Drôlatiques" (with the equally wondrous engravings by Doré); — take, in spite of Froude's fierce
denunciations, "Le Père Goriot." There is a great
deep marvellous art there, — a spontaneous giant
utterance of art, coupled with strangest delicacy.
There is vice and horror; but how beautifully balanced with virtue and heroism! Balzac has tenderness; Balzac has vast sympathies; Balzac has the
charm of highest imagination. Where is Zola's tenderness? where are Zola's sympathies? and how
enormously morbid is Zola's imagination. Nothing
will ever, I think, persuade me to place Zola above
Balzac, — though I confess Zola's greatness. The
Times's critic seems to treat Zola's scientific theories
seriously. I don't know that they would bear real
scientific analysis at all. Doubtless his details are
carefully studied; — I speak only of his plan, his
whole plan. Starting out with the undeniable fact
that Zola's studies are essentially morbid in spirit,

his theory, however seemingly scientific in the small
limits of a single story, must prove itself vicious on
the larger scale of twenty volumes. The Jukes' episode of heredity would not be a justification. However, I am not competent to deal with the facts
here, — only with the general value of a result obtained upon an unreal, because a morbid, basis.

The other statement of the *Times's* critic I could
not agree with, would be his suggestion that this is
perhaps the best of Zola's series. To me it is one of
the weakest of all. It has a few nude pictures of a
woman "divinely slender and young" who compares
the beauty of her own flesh to satin and milk and
snow. These are pretty; but they are mere sensual
genre-studies. They don't compare with that monstrous personification of machinery in " Germinal,"
or the battle pictures of "La Débâcle," or the wonderful figure of the Jew banker in " L'Argent," as
works of art. And there are no other pictures in the
story, — real pictures, — except that of the Spontaneous Combustion. (By the way, I may be mistaken, but I am under the impression that Spontaneous Combustion of this sort is a myth.) Still the
book is a great book, — well worth reading. And
the characters seem wonderfully alive. I would not
care to read it twice (the test of the highest art);
but I would not miss reading it once.

After reading Zola, the sky always seems less
blue, and the sun much further away. By the way,
did you ever see "Les Soirées de Médan"? Zola
seems to me at his very best in "L'Attaque du
Moulin." I think there are six stories in the book, —

each written by a different pupil of Zola. (Only one afterwards rose to greatness, — Guy de Maupassant.) And indeed Maupassant never excelled the story he contributed to "Les Soirées," — "Boule-de-Suif." All the stories except Zola's (!) are diabolically immoral; but it is the immorality of artists, — not feeble, but vigorously cynical, like the art of Diderot's or Voltaire's "Contes." "Le No. 7" is a very fine piece of brutal realism. How curious that the man who did it could never do anything else!

I have been trying to think what all this sort of work will produce in time. Its own time is already past; but all that has ever existed as a popular vogue must continue to exercise some influence in another way. Perhaps the effect of this pessimism may, after all, prove less of value in the reaction it provokes than in the new perceptions of life's problem which it forces. However morbidly exaggerated the teaching of it, there may have been need of such teaching. It is true that we advance by ideals; and yet we must not allow the Ideal, as a mere abstract, to veil from us the real horror and misery and pity of struggling life. Perhaps the fault of the old idealism was its artistic exclusiveness; and Zola was right in calling it a "drawing-room Idealism." Such art could appeal to a very small section of the human mind. The future needs a fiction to appeal to the hearts of all who can read and feel. The cunning of it is given to but few; — yet I think Rudyard Kipling is of those thus favoured by the Gods.

Ever most truly,

LAFCADIO HEARN.

September 7, 1893.

DEAR CHAMBERLAIN, — I suspect you are more than right about a want of something in Symonds. The *Atlantic* critic said it was the lack of the story-teller's power, essential to the really great historian. I think, too, that Symonds must have felt the hand of Death upon him, and have handled his material hurriedly, — without that thorough digestion of it necessary for dramatic effect.

I have never been in Italy since a child, and know it only from books. When six years old I spoke two languages, — Romaic and Italian, both now utterly forgotten. But what a delight I should have to visit Italy now. From my reading, and from pictures, I suppose what you say about the inferiority of the Italian Cathedrals must be true. Indeed the climate could scarcely be suited to Gothic architecture, eh? But I would like to know whether Milan is an exception in your judgment. Taine says it is not. But Tennyson cries, —

> O Milan! O the chanting choirs, —
> The giant windows' blazoned fires, —
> The height, the depth, the gloom, the glory! —
> A mount of marble, — a hundred spires!

Now this does give an idea of imperial Gothic magnificence. But is it true?

On the subject of Japanese smells. No one who has lived much in the tropics is likely to be bothered by smells in Japan, — except when feeling unwell. I was only badly bothered in Oki. I fear you could not bear Saigo; for even the Japanese, in all their houses there, keep incense burning. Though very fond of daikon, I don't like to smell it while being cooked; and the smells made by the scavengers are, of course, severe temporary trials. In Tokyo I never noticed any smells, nor in Kyoto. The sense of smell varies much in different persons. A friend in the Southern States had such a faculty that he could track a deer by scent, as well as one of his own hounds. He was a polished gentleman of the old school, and appreciated delicate odours; but he told me that his faculty was a great suffering to him. There is certainly no doubt of one fact, — that by living constantly in the midst of any particular odour, one finally ceases to detect its existence.

What you say about the great poets is most true. Still, I think we lose a great deal of pleasure by confining ourselves to the Masters. I read every poet I can get hold of. I read therefore a vast heap of rubbish. But I am rewarded by the discovery of rubies, and diamonds, and emeralds. Take Joaquin Miller. No man has written at times more absurdly. But what divine surprises and jets of light he has at times, — as in that magnificent outcry to the Plains, beginning with the words "Room!—room — " or as in that verse, —

> I saw the lightning's gleaming rod
> Reach forth, and write upon the sky
> The awful autograph of God, —

or in those lines from the "Ship in the Desert":—

> A land of Silences, — a land
> Of shoreless deserts strewn with sand
> Where Desolation's dwelling is; —
> Where, wandering from day to day,
> You say, "To-morrow sure we come

> To rest in some cool resting place," —
> And yet you journey on through space
> While seasons pass, and are struck dumb
> With Marvel at the distances. . . .

I quote from memory; so may do injustice to my favourites. But I must venture to close by trying to quote from James Maurice Thomson. Who cares for James Maurice Thomson? Yet he wrote "Atalanta's Race": —

> When Spring is old, and dewy winds
>   Blow from the south, with odours sweet,
> I see my love, in shadowy groves,
>   Speed down dark aisles on shining feet.
>
> She throws a kiss, and bids me run
>   In whispers sweet as roses' breath;
> I know I cannot win the race,
>   And, at the end, I know is death.
>
> Yet joyfully I bare my limbs,
>   Anoint me with the tropic breeze,
> And feel through every sinew run
>   The vigour of Hippomenes.
>
> Oh! race of Love, we all have run
>   Thy happy course through groves of spring,
> And cared not while we lost or won
>   For life or death, or anything!

Imagine how utterly foreign to Japanese feeling all this! Could not even be explained.

Faithfully ever,

LAFCADIO HEARN.

September 9, 1893.

DEAR CHAMBERLAIN, — Conder's book on Gardens rather knocks my attempt to write about the philosophy of the Eternal Feminine, —West and

East. I had imagined no sex-idea connected with Japanese love of nature. But it seems there is a sex-idea, and a pairing idea even, in the arrangement of stones. Of course it is different from our idea. But it is there. All my Japanese experience convinces me of this fact: "*There is nothing absent from Japanese life which we imagine to be absent; all we have is there, — only the colour is different!*" My first ideas were like Lowell's, about the absence of individuality. There are millions of individualities, but one has to live close to them to discover them. They are strong, but their tints are not the same.

I believe I may have been vaguely half right. Our sexual idea is probably nude and Greek, and that of the Japanese robed and Oriental. Perhaps Japanese art might say to the Western idealist something like what a Minister of Spain said to the fellow who wanted to present the Queen with a pair of silk stockings, "Know, sirrah! that the Queen of Spain *has no legs!*" Might not Japanese art, as I suggest, observe to us, "Know, sirrah! that Nature has sex, but not any geometrical lines of thigh, breast, or of those parts which inspired your Venus Kallipyge, and which you are always thinking about!" Yet I don't see how to say this in an English essay with proper convincing force.

The other day I was astonished to hear the bamboo curtain suspended in front of doorways called a kirishitan. Asking for explanation, I was told this: The peculiarity of the bamboo curtain is that it prevents any one outside from seeing into the house, while those inside the house can see through it very

plainly everything which happens outside. And this
is like magic. Now a Christian is a sort of wicked
magician: therefore the curtain is called a Christian. I suppose this must be from the days of the
padres. What do you think of it for an etymology?

If you ever do get to work on that much-to-be-
hoped-for illustrated edition of "Things Japanese,"
don't fail to call on me for anything you think I can
offer in the line of contributions.

Ever most truly,
LAFCADIO HEARN.

September 14, 1893.

DEAR CHAMBERLAIN, — The first of your two unanswered letters brought me woeful ideas; — I tried
to answer it, but failed to do so to my own satisfaction. I found fault with your doctor, and with Miyanoshita, and with all sorts of things, — without
being able to suggest any more satisfactory means
of improvement. But your next letter brought me
joy; and I am full of hope again that you will pass
a good winter.

I am ashamed to say I know little of Pascal except
the "Pensées;" but I am going to send for him and
read him through, — together with Rousseau and Boileau, whom I have known hitherto only by detached
works. What you tell me about Symonds is simply
awful. It was especially the Italian literature of the
"Renascence" I hoped to be made acquainted with.
Yriarte, in his "Un Condottiere au XVI siècle,"
made me hungry for more knowledge on the subject.
Rossetti gave us delicious specimens of the pre-

Raphaelite poets, from 1200 to 1300; but how fill up
the awful lacuna that Symonds has left. By the
way, I suppose you know the French have reprinted
Burchard, — in Latin, of course, — the terrified
secretary of Alexander Borgia. I think the publisher is Ernest Leroux. What a reading that would
be!

You are right about Holmes being very light as a
poet. I think you would like Aldrich more on closer
acquaintance. His "Judith" is worthy almost of
Tennyson. Bret Harte, I think, is great in his pathos
and his weirdness, — especially in such pieces as
"Concepcion de Argillas," "Por el Rey," — "Miss
Blanche's Rose," etc. . . .

My grind has begun again. This term twenty-one
hours a week. Every year, I remark, they try to
make my work more practical, and less theoretical.
I have no books, and now three fresh conversation-
classes. Japanese students *do* seem to lack one
thing, — spontaneity. Conversation must be always painfully forced by questions. Original questions, original suggestions, original ideas are seldom uttered. They are written sometimes; but out
of four hundred — no, out of fully one thousand
— that I have taught, I do not remember ten accustomed to ask or to say original things. Perhaps there were eight. Out of that eight, two are
dead.

I have no belief in the worth of a literary course
for Japanese students. The standard is too low. No
class has sufficient mastery of English to feel an
author, nor even to understand the difference be-

tween poetry and prose. "Teacher! it is no use to put that into rhyme for us — we see no difference between prose and verse." I fancy the literary course in the University itself must be of little value to those who follow it. The great rush is to the Law! The reason seems to be that this branch of study requires especially the strong faculty of Japanese students, — Memory; while the Scientific and Technological branches require a faculty seldom developed among them to any high degree, — Mathematics. At least I imagine this to be the case. One disheartening fact the teacher has to face is that he need never expect to be able to influence his classes much through imagination — so powerful an auxiliary elsewhere, — not because his students have no imagination, but because he can offer them nothing capable of stimulating such imagination as they have. Now what the devil is the use of trying to teach English literature to a class totally insensible to European imagination? It is pure waste of time and money.

. . . The weather has become diabolically changeable — approaching winter. Heavy shock of earthquake the other night.

Ever faithfully,
Lafcadio Hearn.

September 16, 1893.

Dear Chamberlain, — Many thanks for the *Eclectic* which I read with much pleasure, and return to-day by this mail. I see that Pearson's book is making a great sensation. As I wrote to you long ago, I have been inclined to the same conclusions as Pearson reaches, for some years; but I arrived at them by different methods. My life in the tropics taught me what tropical life means for white races, — after the trial of three hundred years; — America taught me something about the formidable character of the Chinese, and taught me also the enormous cost of existing civilization to the Western individual. I think it highly probable that the white races, after having bequeathed all their knowledge to the Orient, will ultimately disappear, just as the ichthyosaurus and other marvellous creatures have disappeared, — simply because of the cost of their structure. There is something very sinister in the fact that the cost of life to an Englishman is just about twenty times the cost of life to an Oriental, nor does the difference of the two in mental capacity and energy by any means correspond to the difference in ability to live. I have sent for Pearson. His critics are very amusing so far. The Reverend one finds fault with him because he does n't consider "Gawd" as a factor in the case; — Harrison, because he does n't count upon Idealism, whatever that may be, as a factor. Idealism, in one sense, certainly leads to moral and æsthetic development; but neither moral nor æsthetic development can be counted on as factors in the mere struggle to live; — while we are bound to recognize the terrible truth that "the law of Murder is the law of growth."

Please just glance at the English words at the top of this "ad." from the *Asahi Shimbun.* You will not venture to include this display of Westernization in

"English as She is Japped;" but it will serve to lighten the humours of a gloomy day.

Ever most faithfully,

LAFCADIO HEARN.

September 20, 1893.

DEAR CHAMBERLAIN, — No, you never told me about that delightful old man before: it was one of the subjects, however, which I wanted to talk with you about if we ever got time, — because I knew from the preface of "Things Japanese" there was a romance there. What a charming sketch you could make, or give to me to make. Perhaps you are the only one in all Japan who could make it; — for the old men are all dead or hidden away in that obscurity which precedes death. Besides, even if one could now find such an old man, he would not now be so charming: he would have seen too much of the new, he would be changed in soul and in costume; he would have laid aside much of the beautiful naïveté which you saw, together with his queue and his swords.

Each new generation of students seems to me a little harder-featured, more unsmiling, more sullen, more lacking in spontaneity, and less courteous, than the preceding. I don't much love them. They are very, very queer in Kyūshū. While my old Izumo boys still write to me, these seldom even say good-bye to ANY of their teachers *before going to Tokyo*. This year, indeed, they sent me a deputation; but last year none; and the other teachers have told me that, on their return from Tokyo during the vacation, they don't even call on their old masters. There is something dead wrong in this brutally apathetic attitude of teachers and students; and that something wrong must have an ill-effect upon the after-life of both. I don't like it; and if all government-schools are so, I had rather teach — were it possible — in a Buddhist charity school.

. . . A curious instance of Japanese character came to my notice the other day. I was informed by letter that some Christian students, among whom was one of my old pupils, had been trying to obey the teaching of some beastly bigot by refusing to show respect to the *shades* at some Shinto temple. They were not kindly treated by the other students, as you may imagine. I sympathized much with one of them, — a very sweet-hearted boy, — and wrote him a long letter of explanation and reproach. I put the matter on the ground of common-sense politeness and common heart-religion. Then I hesitated. I felt convinced that if I sent such a letter to English students, on the same sort of an occasion, the result would be pure mischief only. Finally I sent it to a teacher, instead, requesting him first to read it, and to hold or deliver as he deemed best. He delivered. To my pleasant surprise, the result has been of the happiest. The Xn boys held council, discussed the points, and nobly confessed in a public way they had been misled. They remain Xns, but I don't think, from what has been told me, that they will make any more such mistakes. This is quite nice, — is n't it?

September 23, 1893.

DEAR CHAMBERLAIN, — My old Inkyo has amusing small misfortunes. He likes to go out for a walk, but generally loses his way, — and tries to help himself home again by looking at the tops of the mountains. Sometimes he succeeds. But when the day is foggy, and he cannot see the mountains, he has to ask. And as he speaks the old Izumo dialect, and cannot understand the Kumamoto folk at all — the questioning avails him nothing. So he sits in a store somewhere and waits till we send out to look for him. Then, when we get him home, he tells us the history of his adventures — which are always funny. To-day they picked his pocket in a crowd. It is a great crazy-festival day (Hachimau), — on which they drive horses through the streets, curiously caparisoned, with shouts of *Boshitari! Chosen Boshitari!* said to be a memorial-cry from the time of Kato-Kiyomasa, who prayed to Hachimau before going to *Chosen.* It is a rough festival! At all the larger houses the horse is halted; and the crowd is supplied with sake and salt fish. I contribute, of course. Each street has its own horse, and its own band of runners — in gay attire; and all bands have a captain, who superintends the visits, and sees that the sake is given only to his own men. So nobody is imposed on. But the old man went out to see a dance — a *No* dance; and fell among strangers. His loss was trifling; but he became impressed by the difference between Kyūshū and Izumo crowds.

The other night we had a singular festival next door. A teacher of dancing — an old woman of our neighbourhood — died last year; and on the anniversary of her death, her *ihai* were placed on a platform erected for the occasion next door, and offerings set before it. Then all the little girls she had taught — from four years up — were brought to dance before the *ihai* to please her spirit. The dainty little fairy darlings. I went behind the scenes and saw all the dressing. The children were all faultless till the dance was over — but then being tired they would cry a little; and their mothers would carry them home, — looking like wonderful dolls in their tiny gorgeous Kagura-dresses. Surely a Japanese baby-girl is the sweetest thing in all this world.

Beyond the other side of the garden I hear and see something much less pleasing — the training of a little geisha. The child is very young; but she is obliged to sing nearly seven hours every day. I can tell what time it is by the tone of weariness in her voice. Sometimes she breaks down and cries to be let alone in vain. They do not beat her — but she must sing. Some day she will revenge herself on the world for this — and "sarve it right!"

The tsuku-tsuku-boshi is not yet dead; but it sings only at long intervals. There is great heat still — alternating with spells of sudden cold — each a little bit sharper than the last. Here winter and summer come and go by sudden jerks. What a funny country it is. There is nothing steady or permanent in Nature. There is nothing steady or permanent in the race-character. And for fear that anything should be allowed to evolve and crystallize into anything resembling order, everything is being constantly remodelled and removed and reformed! What, *what* can come out of all this artificial fluidity!

      Ever most truly,

        LAFCADIO HEARN.

            September 24, 1893.

DEAR CHAMBERLAIN, — The pendulum has swung to the right again; and the blue devils have vanished; and Kumamoto seems a good place to stay in for another two years. What do you think of that! — I wonder whether Watson's poems had anything to do with it. I have by no means read them all yet. This poetry is like wedding-cake: one must eat only a little at a time. "The Dream of Man" is high sublimity; and urged me to fresh work at once on my "Stone Buddha." I was considering exactly the same puzzle; but my theory, luckily, is quite the reverse. It is that the motive and creative power of the universe are burnt-out passions and fears and sorrows, which only transformed as forces by death must continue to make birth and rebirth till such time as they reach a second and supreme form of transformation by the triumph in all worlds of Buddha's own theory. Alas! I can't write poetry.

Reading the introduction, or dedication, to "London," there flashed to me memory of a mightier poem of the same kind by a smaller poet: — do you remember the colossal power of Alexander Smith's "Edinburgh"? Smith could not have written "The Dream of Man," but he felt the grim heart of a city as I think no one else — certainly no Latin — ever felt it. Indeed Latin lands have not yet developed that awful thing, an industrial centre, as the English and the Americans have, — the industrial centre, whose blood is steam, whose nerves are steel, — devouring the weak, consuming the strong, — the machine in whose cogwork each man knows himself caught and doomed to whirl forever.

There are bits here and there that make me think of Villon. (Of course you know Payne's wonderful translations.) I was a little startled by the verses on Oscar Wilde. Why do we feel that a poet like Watson has no right to be a mocker, to say cruel things to his fellow man? We feel the same in reading Tennyson's terrible satire on Bulwer Lytton, and Browning's brutal anger at Edward FitzGerald. I think we regard it as we regard an obscene poem by a priest, or in other words a sort of sacrilege to self. We have not yet learned (as I think we shall some day) to confess aloud that the highest poetry is a religion, and its world-priests the true prophets and teachers. But we feel it. Therefore we are shocked and pained when these betray any sign of those paltry or mean passions above which their art at other times lifts us.

To-day I must tell you the Legend of my house. There are, you know, two kinds of Haunters in Japan, — the Living and the Dead. He who built this house to spend his age in was happy in all things, except a child. So he and his wife made agreement with a girl to bear a child for them, under certain conditions: Rachel and her handmaid. She gave him a boy; and he sent her away, — hiring a nurse for the boy. But he did not keep his promise in all things, — and even his wife blamed him. Whereat he said nothing. Presently, for the first time in his life, he fell ill. The physician (a garrison doctor), after trying what could be done, declared he must die. The Kannushi told him why — "there was an *iki-ryo* in his home." So others said. Then remorse seized him. They tried to find the girl. She was gone — lost in the forty millions, God knows where. And the days dragged in uttermost pain. Then came a *hyakusho*, saying he had heard where the woman was; he might be able to bring her back within a week. But the sick man said, — "No, she would not forgive *in her heart*, it is too late." And he re-turned his face to the wall and died. Then the widow, and the little boy, and the pet cat went away; and I took up my dwelling in the house. The *iki-ryo* has passed.

Ever faithfully,

LAFCADIO HEARN.

September 27, 1893.

DEAR CHAMBERLAIN, — To-day there came to the school the whole Normal School of Kiu-Kiu, — the Shihan-Gakko of Horai. They were received in the Gymnastic Hall, where all our boys were drawn up in hollow square. Then the first student of our highest class made a speech of welcome; and the first of the Loochoran students responded briefly. The director was a Japanese.

Except that the islanders had darker skins, they looked just like Japanese. They wore white cotton

trousers, and short close blue jackets. They go
hence to Dazaifu, to visit the Temple of Tenjin, and
to Hakata, etc. What impressed me was the curious
formalism of the whole reception. It ought to have
been (by European code) highly enthusiastic. It was
all silent and expressionless as a phantom meeting,
— though the classes were broken for it. What curious souls! — How much would I not give to be able
to see into them!

I have conquered the first vexation of licking my
cubs into shape. They are good boys, — as a whole;
but each new class comes in absolutely savage.
Only the Gods know how they have been trained. It
takes real trouble for a while to get them into the
regular drill. And you know how a foreign teacher
is placed — he has no moral support whatever, and
must smooth everything himself. I have never been
obliged to complain — but I feel, if I did, that the
blame of the result would be rather for me than for
the offenders. The whole idea is that a good teacher
should be able to keep his crew in hand; if he complains, it is a sign that HE is wrong! There *is* some
sense in the policy, but it is too d—bly *general.*

Speaking of the oddity of the reception of our
guests from Horai, reminds me of another queer fact
I want to chat with you about. It affords a striking proof of the fact that any foreigner who, without
very considerable experiences, ventures to draw in-
ferences about Japanese conduct is sure to be dead
wrong.

You remember my story about the *iki-ryo.* It is
true, of course. Now listen to the odd sequel. The

people blamed the girl very much. They attributed to her the death of the man who had been unkind to her. They sympathized with her, but they blamed her.

Here comes the puzzle. Why did they blame her? Perhaps you don't perceive the whole face of the puzzle yet. She was not blamed as a witch. She was not blamed for sorcery. But she was blamed for the death — caused by the haunting of the *iki-ryo*.

Now the sending of an *iki-ryo* is not *voluntary* at all. Other Things (with a capital "T") may be sent. But an *iki-ryo* goes forth quite independently of the will of the person from whom it emanates, and even without the knowledge of that person.

How then could the people blame the woman for the coming of the *iki-ryo* and the death of the man?

Well, they blamed her for being TOO angry, — because anger secretly nursed *may* cause an *iki-ryo* to form, and therefore she ought to have known better than to allow herself to be so angry!

Who could divine such an explanation of the facts in the case? Eh?

Faithfully ever,

LAFCADIO HEARN.

October 2, 1893.

DEAR CHAMBERLAIN, — I think you are right about Etagima, — especially as my little woman would be very lonesome in such a place. What attracted me especially was the idea of the divine Sea, — the smell of it, — the swirl and the sound of it and the soul of it, — a chance to swim every day, and to watch the changing face of the water. That would be heaven, — in days to come.

I don't know how to praise Watson. He is fine, fine! — delicate, deep, penetrant. I am going to return him, together with the Pascal. What a genius was P.; yet one cannot help regretting that so much genius and wit and charm of style had to be used up simply in attacking error. What would not Milton too have given us had he not wasted his eyes and his years in polemics?

Would you not like to read Froude's "Spanish Story of the Armada"? And I will soon have Pearson for you. He is a little ponderous; but a thinker worth feeling. He is not, however, a man of magical style, like Harrison, who grips your hand, and makes you feel the warmth of the pulse in it. Pearson has no pulse. He is just as cold and keen as Herbert Spencer, to whom, curious! — he makes but a single reference, though I can see that Spencer was his intellectual milk. How selfish authors sometimes are to their teachers! . . .

I have been studying Japanese babies. I have none of my own yet. But there is a pretty custom. When a woman is about to become a mother, she borrows a baby; and it is thought an honour to lend it. Of course it is petted extraordinarily; but no amount of petting could spoil the child now in the house. It is only six months old, but expresses in a supreme degree all Japanese virtues. For example, it never cries or shows vexation. It invariably smiles when smiled at. It is docile to the degree of going to sleep whenever bidden, and of laughing immediately as soon as it is awakened. Sometimes I feel downright afraid of it; it knows infinitely too much; and I strongly suspect that it still remembers all its former births. My own child certainly will never be such an angel. This is the Buddha himself. I wonder that lotos flowers as large as chariot wheels do not rise up through the floor, and that all the dead trees in the neighbourhood have not begun to blossom.

Another visitor comes of its own accord. It is a girl; and its name is Bamboo. It is fourteen months old. It walks into the house, and gravely salutes each inhabitant. Then it points to each tree in the garden, and says "Ki!" Then it points to the stones and says "IS' I!"; always putting its finger to its mouth afterwards. Each day it has a new word. It loved me till it saw me one day in *yofuku*. I fear its ancestral recollections are not good; for it cried loudly and fled, — mistaking me for a policeman (all in white). Now Missy Bamboo is the child of poor but honest parents. But, O Missy Bamboo, what were you in the previous birth? that you should fear a nice, good policeman?

Ever most truly,

LAFCADIO HEARN.

October 11, 1893.

DEAR CHAMBERLAIN, — I am thinking it is time to write you — though there is no news. Suppose I write you of one day of my life as a sample. I don't see why I should n't — though I would not write it to anybody else on either side the world.

Morning, 6 A. M. — The little alarm clock rings. Wife rises and wakes me, — with the salutation *de rigeur* of old Samurai days. I get myself into a squatting posture, draw the never-extinguished *hibachi* to the side of the *futons*, and begin to smoke. The servants enter, prostrate themselves, and say good morning to the danna-sama, and proceed to open the tō. Meanwhile in the other chambers the little oil lamps have been lighted before the tablets of the ancestors, and the Buddhist (not the Shinto deities) — and prayers are being said, and offerings to the ancestors made. (Spirits are not supposed to eat *the food* offered them, — only to absorb some of its living essence. Therefore the offerings are very small.) Already the old men are in the garden, saluting the rising sun, and clapping their hands, and murmuring the Izumo prayers. I stop smoking, and make my toilet on the *Engawa*.

7 A. M. — Breakfast. Very light — eggs and toast. Lemonade with a spoonful of whiskey in it; and black coffee. Wife serves; and I always make her eat a little with me. But she eats sparingly, — as she must afterward put in an appearance at the regular family breakfast. Then kurumaya comes. I begin to put on my *yofuku*. I did not at first like the Japanese custom, — that the wife should give each piece of clothing in regular order, see to the pockets, etc.; — I thought it encouraged laziness in a man. But when I tried to oppose it, I found I was giving offence and spoiling pleasure. So I submit to the ancient rule.

7.30 A. M. — All gather at the door to say *Sayo-*

nara; but the servants stand outside, — according
to the new custom requiring the servants to stand
when the master is in *yofuku.* I light a cigar, — kiss
a hand extended to me (this is the only imported
custom), and pass to the school.

(*Blank of 4 to 5 hours.*)

Returning, at the call of the kurumaya, — all
come to the door again as before, to greet me with
the O-Kaeri; and I have to submit to aid in undressing, and in putting on the kimono, obi, etc. The
kneeling-cushion and *hibachi* are ready. There is a
letter from Chamberlain San, or Mason San. Dinner.

The rest eat only when I am finished: because
there are two ukyo, but I am the worker. The principle is that the family supporter's wants are first
to be considered, — though in other matters he does
not rank first. For instance, the place of honour
when sitting together is always by age and parentage.
I then take the fourth place, and wife the fifth. And
the old man is always then served the first.

During the repast there is a sort of understanding
that the rest of the family and the servants are not
to be disturbed without necessity. There is no rule;
but the custom I respect. So I never go into that
part of the house unnecessarily till they are finished.
There is also some etiquette about favourite places,
— which is strictly observed.

3 P. M. 4. — If very hot, everybody sleeps, — the
servants sleeping by turns. If cool and pleasant,
all work. The women make clothes. The men do all
kinds of little things in the garden and elsewhere.
Children come to play. The *Asahi Shimbun* arrives.

6 P. M. — Bath hour.

6.30–7.30. — Supper.

8 P. M. — Everybody squats round the *hako-hibachi* to hear the *Asahi Shimbun* read, or to tell stories. Sometimes the paper does not come, — then curious games are played, in which the girls join. The mother sews at intervals. One game is very original. A piece of string is tied in a large loop, and a number of little loops and ends are made with short pieces of string. Then the large loop is spread on a velvet zabaton, so as to form the outline of the face of Otafuku. Blindfolded, then, the players must put the other loose ends and bits of string inside the circle, so as to make the rest of the face. But this is hard to do, and every mistake produces extraordinary comicalities. But if the night is very fine, we sometimes go out — always taking turns so that the girls get their share of the outing. Sometimes the theatre is the attraction. Sometimes there are guests. I think the greatest joy, though, is the discovery and purchase of odd or pretty things in some lamp-lit shop at night. It is brought home in great triumph, and all sit round it in a circle to admire. My own evening, however, is generally passed in writing. If guests come for me, the rest of the family remains invisible till they go away, — except wife, — that is, if the guests are important. Then she sees to their comfort. Ordinary guests are served only by the girls.

As evening wanes, the turn of the *Kami-sama* comes. During the day, they received their usual offerings; but it is at night the special prayers are made. The little lamps are lighted; and each of the family in turn, except myself, say the prayers and pay reverence. These prayers are always said standing, but those to the *hotoke* are said kneeling. Some of the prayers are said for me. I was never asked to pray but once — when there was grief in the house; and then I prayed to the Gods, repeating the Japanese words one by one as they were told to me. The little lamps of the *Kami* are left to burn themselves out.

All wait for me to give the signal of bed-time, — unless I should become so absorbed in writing as to forget the hour. Then I am asked if I am not working too hard. The girls spread the futons in the various rooms; and the *hibachi* are replenished, so that we — i. e., I and the men only — may smoke during the night if we wish. Then the girls prostrate themselves with an *o-yasumi!* and all becomes quiet.

Sometimes I read till I fall asleep. Sometimes I keep on writing—with a pencil in bed—but always, according to ancient custom, the little wife asks *pardon for being the first to go to sleep.* I once tried to stop the habit — thinking it too humble. But after all it is pretty, — and is so set into the soul that it could not be stopped. And this is an ordinary day in outline. Then we sleep.

Faithfully ever,
LAFCADIO HEARN.

Saturday, October 13.

P. S. There is a frightful storm — so that I would not ask anybody to go to the mail; and I have pulled open the envelope of last night's letter to add a line or two.

I am working out an essay — a philosophical essay on " Jiujutsu," promised to the Boston folks by December. Could you give me any of your own thoughts about the reaction against foreign influence, and its future possibilities. Of course I want the pessimistic view (from the Western side), — viz., that the reaction belongs to the deepest instincts of the race, and *will never pass*. I am taking this side. I don't mean to say I am sure of my position. Who but the Gods can be sure of anything. But I am taking what I believe the most probable view. What I would especially like are sample-facts of a startling kind — something that will whiz through the imagination like a splendid mad wasp. All reactions ought to be summed up if I can do it — moral, educational, religious, commercial. I don't mean to ask you to sit down when you don't feel like it to write me, but to dash off a few ideas on paper for me when you *do* have time and inclination. Even a word may stir up a universe of fancies: I want hints at least. You are in the nerve-centre, and I am only at a very small remote ganglion — so to speak.

Earthquakes increase in frequency. The boy Tortorie being carried across the street the other day might have caused the last one. I am more and more inclined to think him a Bosatsu. He has been taught to hand me letters and papers, — and though only six months old he does it always with a smile, (not taught at all, the smile, — *must* be ancestral habit). Then he watches me open them. I am quite afraid of him, and sure that he knows more than I. To cause him fear is utterly impossible; nor have any experiments sufficed to make him exhibit grief or wrath. It is all very well to say this means only perfect health; it means the influence of faith or character for one thousand years, at least.

October 11, 1893.

DEAR CHAMBERLAIN, — Won't you think me dull? Well, I have malaria, — it is nearly over, but it always stupefies me, — so that I can't write well. I trust the autumn weather is dealing gently with you.

We had great games here yesterday in commemoration of our foundation. I liked the games in Izumo better, because of the beautiful old loyal spirit they showed, love of the Emperor, love of country. But these were interesting, too. What especially impressed me was the military song chanted by two hundred young men, all keeping time with their feet and bringing out the last syllable of each line with a report of emphasis like a crash of musketry. I thought I saw for an instant a flash of Japanese soul, — the old military spirit. Oh! what pains should be taken to preserve it! — and yet those in power do so little to cultivate it. I could really cry with vexation when I think of the indifference, — the ignorant, blind indifference of the Educational Powers to nourish the old love of country and love of the Emperor. The fencing was rather savage, but quite skilful. I am convinced, however, that the French school founded by the terrible mulatto, Jean Louis, is the only one that will survive. Point will always win against edge. I believe our soldiers are drilled in the French style.

There was an idiot of a missionary — a simpering gawk — who wanted to show his Western superiority; and I knew by one look at the man that he was going to make an ass of himself. He did. He tried to throw the hammer and was beaten most absurdly by a boy of sixteen, and he tried to run a race, and was beaten badly by a man with much shorter legs. A foreigner is a fool to contend when not invited. If he is a good man, and wins, — it is no credit to him, as he is usually a giant compared with the contestants; and if he is beaten, the exultation shown at his defeat seems to say, "You have disgraced your nationality." I fancy the sly mockery of yesterday, however, was especially due to the man's being a missionary. Sneers of "senkyoshi!" were pretty audible in all directions.

I finished my "Stone Buddha" and sent it away. Whether it is good or bad, I can't even surmise. I am working now on a philosophical study of "Jiujutsu."

Every day has its revelations. What seem to be mountains turn out to be only clouds; the horizon forever recedes. Of Japan, I would say with Kipling's pilot: "And if any man comes to you, and says 'I know the Javva currents, don't you listen to him; for those currents is never yet known to mortal man!'"

Ever faithfully,
LAFCADIO HEARN.

October 31, 1893.

DEAR CHAMBERLAIN, — It was very pleasant to hear you smacking æsthetic lips over the splendid savour of Gautier; — you can feel now how apt Baudelaire's epithet applied to him, — "Le parfait magicien des lettres françaises." Then you expressed him exactly by saying "the thought is the word." As a mere pure artist I suppose, in spite of all the carping there has been about his work, he has not any equal in all European verse. We exact thinking now, as well as art, — and perhaps it is well, since the mere mechanical mastery of verse is common to a whole world of poetasters. But there is really an art in Gautier that lifts every word into the world of thinking, and that makes one almost ready to believe in a new Gnosticism, — that words are Beings which reveal their souls only to the elect.

You ask if I have any more "delightful surprises." Really I don't know. I studied the Romantic School pretty well; and perhaps if you have not paid much attention to it, I might be able to make suggestions you would like. But, of course, there is only one Gautier. I should like to know how you will feel about his prose, — "Arria Marcella," "Une Nuit de Cléopâtre," "Le Roi Candaule," the delicious "Morte Amoureuse," "Avatar," etc. If you like him, perhaps you would like De Nerval. Gérard de Nerval's "Voyage en Orient" (two volumes, Lévy, f.3.50) seems to me the most wonderful thing of the kind ever done. You know he went to Africa, married a Mussulman wife, who naturally hated him (because he was mad) and ran away from him.

He wrote the marvellous "Legend of Solomon" and "Queen Balkis" for that history, — the work which inspired Meyerbeer. It would have been put upon the operatic stage, but the conception proved like one of John Martin's pictures, — too supernatural in depth and breadth for any stage. He translated "Faust" very beautifully. Besides the voyage you might like his "Filles de Feu," beautiful, sober, sad, ghostly sketches, betraying the incipient madness that was at last to drive him to suicide. Doré, I think, made a picture of that suicide; but the police broke up the lithograph stone and suppressed the work. Anything of De Nerval's would please you. There is a marvellous mediæval story by him, — "La Main de Gloire," — worth anything in the narrative part of Hugo's "Notre Dame." But I cannot now remember what book it was in.

Should you be able to bear the fiendish and monstrous mixed with rare queer art, you would be greatly impressed by two volumes of Baudelaire, — "Les Fleurs du Mal," and "Petits Poëmes en Prose." The former work placed Baudelaire third among the Romantic poets, — first, Hugo; second, Gautier. I can't say I was much impressed by Leconte de Lisle; — nor by any others of the swarm of Romantic poets.

Of course you have read "Madame Bovary." But perhaps you have not read Flaubert's "Tentation de Saint Antoine," "Les Trois Contes," "Bouvard et Pécuchet," "Salammbô," — four books each of which would seem to have been written by a totally different person. Flaubert represents the extravagance of the Romantic laboriousness of art, — the exaggerations that preceded the Realistic reaction. But he is very great; and not *tourmenté* to the extent of the brothers Goncourt. Since Swift, I think no such satire ever was written on human nature as "Bouvard et Pécuchet." But don't try to read "L'éducation sentimentale" if you have not already done so; in spite of its title it was a shocking failure in all respects. Flaubert was a victim of epilepsy; his affliction ruined some of his best efforts.

The perfection of vital Romantic prose, however, seems to me to have been first reached by Loti. Here we may disagree. But let me remind you that you had the misfortune to read the worst works of Loti first, which is a misfortune in the case of any author. Perhaps if you would read his "Roman d'un Spahi," "Mariage de Loti," and "Fleurs D'Ennui," you would feel as I do. Loti's work is represented by a curve —

"Roman d'un Spahi"

"Mariage de Loti"   "Fleurs d'Ennui"
"Aziyade"   Five works, each
                                          weaker than
                                          the last.

I really think the prose of those three exotic books ought to charm you even more than the poetry of Gautier, and in an equally subtle way.

It is no harm to ask you if you have read the "Contes Drôlatiques" of Balzac, either in the quaint but easy French or in the excellent English "Droll Stories" (by Chatto & Windus) with Doré's four hundred and twenty-five marvellous illustrations. The book is cheap; but it ought not to be read without the illustrations. Comparing the French with the English version, I found that, although the translation is wonderful, many Rabelaisian expressions have been toned down. But I notice that the book is having a great influence even upon the higher criticism. I see references to it constantly. Of course it is more daring than Gautier's "Mademoiselle de Maupin." But "de Maupin" is only an artist's dream; the personages of the "Contes Drôlatiques" are all alive. And the stories are not all droll; there are some which are in the highest degree pathetic. Even the drollness is terrible: it was the humour lighted by the fires of the stake, or shadowed by the gibbet of Montfaucon. Of all the wonderful things in that book, perhaps the most wonderful is the story of "Le Succube." The Parisian publisher is Garnier Frères.

Well, I won't tire you with any more literary chit-chat to-day. Let me say your letter about the Reactionary Movement completely revolutionized my work, — caused me to remodel it completely. As I told you, even a suggestion may work wonders for me. What I wanted was your point of view, and having got it, I reasoned "why"? The answer to the "why" settled the dilemma I was in.

Two points in the letter occur to me to speak of. It may be true as you say that this tone of the nation is Jingo; but you did not quite understand the feeling of your humble servant. It was the contrast between the artificial character of loyal expression as I see it here, and the sincere heart-rooted character of loyalty in Izumo that impressed me. Now I think this is partly due to the insincere and artificial character of the teaching of the national feeling. In Izumo it was the real old-fashioned soul-thing; here it is done, with a cynical smile in the sleeve.

The other point was about the missionary property. Really I can't see that the Japanese are wrong at all. First, the property, being acquired in contravention of law, and by fraudulent evasion of that law, might quite justly be confiscated. Secondly, as the money was given professedly for the Japanese Church, and not for the support or convenience of foreign missionaries, the native Christians have a moral right to demand its cession as a test of the sincerity of foreign religion. Personally, of course, I think the missionaries ought to be put on a small ship, and the ship scuttled at a reasonable distance of one thousand miles from shore.

You said a very nice thing about Mason in one of your letters, that he was "always sane." I can't pretend to be always sane. Indeed I may confess I have been practically insane for a great part of my existence. You will therefore not be surprised to hear me say that I wonder how you can read the Yokohama papers without going mad. The *Herald* you sent me spoiled two meals for me. The extracts were all right, but the comments. I never open the *Mail* any more; I am afraid to. It only spoils my temper and my work. So I envy you. You can look down upon all this, as you say, "with amusement." I cannot even think of it without feeling just as you would feel to see some cowardly or base action very close to you. You see the race struggle much more philosophically. Doubtless it is the best way. I feel, too, the absurdity of any struggle against eternal laws. But, nevertheless, those few insane ones who believe themselves able to fight the Infinite, do accomplish something; they effect some delays in disintegration, and preserve in their protests the memory of something beautiful that might otherwise be lost.

Which reminds me of the absurd episode at the close of your last letter, the episode of the drunken sailors. It set me to thinking what is the value of obscene vulgarity in evolutional processes. And I came to the conclusion that the coarseness and roughness and brutality which most shock us abroad, have their indirect value as social checks, — brakes. They are a perpetual mock and menace to sentimentality, and prevent certain exaggerations.

Ever faithfully,

LAFCADIO HEARN.

Oh! I must add the following from a recent composition. "Autumn has becomed. It is the season when the sound of the rivers sink us into deep association. And the mountains are lonely, having lost their ADDRESSES." (He meant their beauty.)

DEAR CHAMBERLAIN, — The more I read Kipling's "Rhyme of the Three Sealers," the more I am astonished at the immense power of the thing.

It gains with every reading. And how little of the world's modern fiction and poetry does this! It is the sign of *true* genius, — the perfect imagination that reaches its goal by unknown methods. There is, indeed, the trouble you spoke of long ago, — that it is written in a dialect, so to speak, which may change rapidly. Still, I doubt if our rough speech changes much more rapidly than does our refined tongue. The English of the eighteenth century is not the English of to-day, though we understand and admire it. Kipling must last, anyhow, a hundred years, — that will make his best work classic.

But what are "sheer strakes," "chocks," "bends and butts," "cleats," and "topping-lifts"? You will confess that, though mysterious to the landlubber, there is a blocky, bumping, raking force, even in the sound of them that tells. Yet again, *what* — oh what is a *holluschickie?* Is it a kite? — a pi-yoro-yoro? Weird and funny at once — is n't it?

And we'll go up to the wrath of God as the *holluschickie* goes.

But he'll lie down on the killing-grounds where the *holluschickie* go.

But it seems to me that, leaving the descriptive art of the thing out of the question as above all praise, Kipling reaches his supreme art in the two simple lines, —

And west you'll turn and south again, beyond the sea-fog's rim,
And tell the Yoshiwara girls to burn a stick for him. . . .

It is, of course, the very first time that any Western writer ever succeeded in making infinite poetry with that much befouled word; — there is more art in

that one line than in all "Madame Chrysanthème."
But that is n't the wonder alone: the wonder is, that
with that simplest touch, a whole world of pathos,
— the whole romance and better nature of the rough
sailor appears, — his rude tenderness, — his superstition, — his isolation, — his vague empiric education by travel, teaching him that one faith may be
good as another, — his consciousness of no hope from
his own by the breaking of every law, human and divine, — and fifty other things! That is sheer magic.
One word more would have spoiled the effect. One
word less would have rendered it impossible. And
no genius — not Victor Hugo — could even have
changed a word without ruining the perfect balance
of the whole infinitely pathetic utterance, — the
moral of it, — the poetry of it, — "the pity of it."

I won't try to praise the rest of the astonishing
study, — the sudden change of feeling from anger to
kindness, — the change of the *modern* man, wicked
only for a reason, for a profit, — good underneath
all. But one could write a book on the thing.

Ever faithfully,

LAFCADIO HEARN.

DEAR CHAMBERLAIN, — I think your version of
the origin and necessity of the rhyme alternation—
as expressed in the treat just received from you
— must be correct. What I ventured on was only
a theory as to the period of the adoption of certain
rules to govern the use thereof,— and as to a possibly romantic origin. We may both be right: certainly you must be. As for me, I find this in Saints-

bury, — regarding the Provençal *causo:* "Here the
rhymes were interlaced, and the alternation of masculine and feminine by *degrees observed.*" (End of
11th and beginning of 12th — lasting to 13th century (1st Period.) Best work (2nd Period) of the
thirteenth century, — referred to in the above
lines.) Saintsbury thinks that of Provençal poetry
only the lyrical form affected Northern French as a
literary influence. But he also thinks the Northern
lyrical work published in Bartsch's "Romanzen und
Pastourellen" (Leipsic, 1870) was indigenous. The
question you bring up is not touched by him —
probably never occurred to him. By the way,
since you tell me you have not paid much attention
to Provençal, I am *sure* the early work would delight
you; and I am almost sure the *felibres* would charm
you. I have not studied the tongue itself, — only
made out beauties cited in works on the troubadours, etc. But I would like to coax you to experiment with the modern Provençal, in the shape of
Mistral's "Mireille." Leroux (?) has published a delicious edition of it at four or five francs, I think,
with the Provençal text on the left page, and a parallel prose modern French translation on the other.
It is beautiful, I think: I loved it. Wish I had a copy
to send you. But I was beaten out of my library —
nine hundred and fifty volumes about — by a smart
Yankee doctor in Philadelphia. Vanity and vexation of spirit! I believe the modern Provençal is a
splendid introduction to the elder form — so they
say. Some of my New Orleans friends used to speak
it well. It sounded like invertebrate Spanish mixed

with Italian. I have no copy of S. Prudhomme's
poem, or I would be so glad to send it you. I never
had his complete works, — nor even the delightful
Parnasse collections: I used only to pick up bits and
scraps of the *Parnassien* school in the French
reviews and in the *Figaro*. But were I sure of things
I would spend one thousand yen to-morrow for
French books. Prospects are so uncertain, however,
that I must abandon literary luxuries. I study now
only "thinking books" — *la raison sans mélange?*
And I am almost ashamed to confess one base indulgence in luxury of recent date — a complete
set of Goethe. Of course it's solid thinking in a certain sense, — but not the kind of thing one should
buy unless able to purchase lots of pure literature.
Clifford, Stevens, Bain, Huxley, Galton, — those
are the men I *ought* to read.

I wrote an extravagant note to you yesterday
about Kipling's last. But it really expressed my
conviction and feeling. The thing is wonderful, and
haunts me asleep and awake.

What you say about the hope for a nation willing
to sacrifice life for an idea is certainly the grand
truth — that which stills the angriest hopelessness
as oil smoothes the waves. There is, indeed, that
hope, — if the detestable officialism can be choked
to death in another twenty-five years. The friend
who has been lifting corners of the veil for me,
showed me to-day the reports of the old Sapporo
college under American management.

Well, that was a school. But what is it now? And
what are the middle schools changing into? Is it

possible there may come at last a general failure
of the whole system — as in Korea. The very zeal of
the beginning gives one that fear.

Faithfully,

LAFCADIO.

P. S. I will copy that Kumamoto Rojo, and send
the copy whenever you wish — preferring with your
permission to preserve the original MS.

It has occurred to me that you might have been
thinking of the Daikokumai Ballads, when you suggested a paper for the Asiatic Society. I did not
finish working at them, — but will later on. Should
you wish them, tell me. The only trouble is, they
won't be of any value as literal translations — which
is what the Society should certainly have, —
should n't it? I will write later about other things.

My old Japanese grandfather does not hear well,
and is not often talkative. But he sometimes tells
queer tales of the past. The appearance of an English man-of-war off Osaka in his youth was the subject of his last narrative. The idea about foreigners in those days was apparently superhuman,
for the servants of the samurai nearly all ran away
from them, when ordered to the beach. If I could
write the old man's exact words, you would enjoy
his narrative. It struck me, while I was hearing the
interpretation, that if the old men still living could
be induced to write down all their reminiscences,
out of the mass extraordinary interest could be
extracted.

Ever,

L. H.

DEAR CHAMBERLAIN, — Your kind letter from Miyanoshita has just come. Indeed, I have no sensitiveness about criticism, — even upon my own work; — I had feared having offended in a purely conventional matter only. I like a very savage criticism on a book next to a very sympathetic one. And *you* — who have the most preëminent imperial right to criticize *any* critic! — never could I dream of protesting against your most perfect frankness of like or dislike to my hobbies. No: indeed! When you agree, of course I feel glad; and when you don't I sometimes feel disappointed — at not having been able to give pleasure: that is all.

What is more, I know you are right from one point of view about Gautier. The Romantic movement, which he really headed, was a protest against *all* conventions, — moral and otherwise, — in the name and for the sake of beauty alone. This pagan principle is recognized still by schools of art and literature — without extravagance, of course — and all general sweeping extremes entail terrible errors. Mallock's criticisms are often, I think, abominable; but he told the plain truth when he said that Gautier (in "Mdlle. de Maupin") had sung the praises not only of natural but of unnatural lust. Other Romantists did nearly as ill. They all sowed a crop of dragon's teeth. Preaching without qualification the gospel of beauty — that beauty is *truth* — provoked the horrible modern answer of Zolaism: "Then truth must be beauty!"

It is not the highest art, of course, this worship of beauty. We cannot to-day touch the skirts of

Greek art, — yet we feel the realized ideal that one marvellous race, and only one, had a divine glimpse of, is not the highest *possible*. The highest must be aspirational, — like music, — aspirational with all its spirings of utterance piercing into the Future. But I think that every school contributes some tone, some colour — else unobtainable — to that mighty future scale of emotional harmonies of which the depths and the heights are still invisible to us — just as the possibilities of colour are still but faintly guessed at by us. Sense alone — pure or impure love of mere beauty and light and sweetness — cannot give the highest tones, — nor the deepest; but they help to do something for the evolution of the middle lines, which the loftier and the deeper powers cannot make — yet without which they would remain but dimly visible.

For this reason I imagine we are not wrong to praise and admire even the art of Gautier and of the senses. Some sensualism is a good thing for human nature. It softens. Now I like that " Arria Marcella," — that reverie which expresses the whole regret of the nineteenth century for the dead Gods and the dead paganism, — which re-creates the past for a night, and lives forever after haunted by the unspeakable melancholy of the broken dream. Is it not truth — the longing of every lover of the antique beauty — the dreams of every passionate student in the spring of thinking life? We have all had it. Surely never to have had it would leave life more colourless and less sensitive than it ought to be.

About the impossibility of a courtesan ever being a heroine, I am not quite sure. Two great novels — one by Wilkie Collins and one by Charles Reade — seem to hint that, even in that society where the courtesan is degraded as in no other epoch or century, a courtesan may come very near to being a heroine. But the condition varies much with country and customs. However, let us only touch the higher literature. I think at once of three books I would not like to deny supreme merit to, — the "Manon Lescaut" of Prévost, still a perfect classic after one hundred and sixty years' test; — the "Rolla" of Alfred de Musset; — and the powerful "Carmen" of Prosper Mérimée, which inspired so noble an opera — an opera that still haunts me with its Havanese airs, its tantalizing of tropical passion, its merciless lesson of the fall of those who love *Ill*. Now those three are courtesans. It is true they are — in two cases — curses and terrors; but that great novels may be written about them strikes me as quite possible. But, oh! *what would* you think of Balzac's "La Belle Imperia"? Certainly you would judge it more harshly than Froude has done "Le Père Goriot." And both you and Froude are right — though I don't think *wholly* right. The spiritual sense in both — the Northern Gothic aspirational sense — is too deeply offended by the unspiritual element of such tales to acknowledge they can have any charm for a higher mind.

You ask me to recommend some books I like, and I may venture to try something in the larger and stronger way that I imagine you might like. But I am not sure. (I have been "out of the run" for five

years; — so I have missed much.) But I would like
you to *try* what I believe to be the most powerful
emotional novel of modern times (the French version)—"Crime et Châtiment" of Dostoievsky, if
you have not already read it. It is a crucifying thing
to read, but it goes down to the deepest fibres in a
man's heart. This is a greater book even than Tolstoi's "Cossacks." I like the Russian writers, very,
very, very much. I think Tourgueneff's "Virgin
Soil" greater than Victor Hugo's "Misérables." I
think Gogol cleverer than our cleverest society
novel writers. And I like the *little stories* these men
write,—the delightful little stories of Tourgueneff,
— the "Nouvelles Russes," etc. There is so much
in little stories! You might not like "A Lear of the
Steppe," etc., but you would like, I think, "Les
Reliques Vivantes," etc. (Except Dostoievsky: I
only want my worst enemy to read some of his *short*
stories.)

Only one living French writer writes tolerably
sane short stories worthy to compare with those of
the Russians, — Daudet. Daudet's short stories
of the Franco-Prussian war struck me as greater
works of art than even "Le Nabab," "Froment
Jeune et Risler Ainé," etc. They have not the
comical power of the same class of stories by De
Maupassant, but they have what De M. never
possessed — deep human sympathy.

And I might venture to ask if you have tried
Björnson? If you have not, and should attempt
"Synnöve Solbakken," I fancy you would like to
read everything else he has written. The puzzle of

these Norse writers is their enormous force combined with childish simplicity. Take up a volume, and you think you are reading a book for babies. All at once tremendous passion shows itself, masters you, and shakes you into profound respect. Andersen's charm, you know, was marked by this same power. These Northmen never condescend to look for ornamental words, — they have no devices, no tricks at all, — nothing but great huge, smooth, frank strength. They are my despair! I could *never* write a page like Björnson though I studied for a century. But I could imitate in English a Florid Romantic. Ornamental luxurious work is n't the hardest. The hardest is perfect simplicity.

And I find myself thinking of Taylor's noble poem, "Lars," and that made me think of American writers. You spoke not very admiringly of Holmes one day; — but did you ever read "Elsie Venner"? I fancy you would like it. However, I won't say anything more about American writers to-day.

Ever most sincerely,

LAFCADIO HEARN.

P. S. A Japanese Riddle.
(Do you like riddles? I do — only when I can find the answer. I don't like the others much, — because they may turn out to be Sphinx-riddles; and I am afraid of being devoured.)
This is from the local newspaper: —
Young Kyūshū farmer goes into a public bath, finds the water too hot for his taste, and cries out, "This is Jigoku." Grizzled relative in the bath ex-

claims to him, "You are an animal!—why hair upon your face have you not got? Suppose I *was* in the Penitentiary—I am your relative!" Young farmer vainly tries to apologize;—says he had no double meaning. Relative proceeds, "You are a *mushi;* you are a child new-born. Give me back your wife: she's my blood! What right has an insect like you—who knows nothing about living—to a wife?" Young farmer says, "All right!" Goes home, tells his wife all, pets her, and sends her to the relative. Two days later goes to the house of Jigoku—calls out the returned wife, and whispers her to go to another relative's house at once. Wife goes. Young farmer then enters house, and kills ex-penitentiary relative with the edge of the sword. Returns to other relative's house and embraces wife. Wife and husband bathe, dress, feast, and *compose poems!!* Then both kill themselves.

Now all this is very, very puzzling. What public opinion under the circumstances could force a man to send back his wife for the mere asking? Then why the necessity of killing? Why the perfect, joyful acquiescence of the wife, and the universal sympathy with the dead, and the general opinion of the *murdered party as guilty of murder.* What strange ethics!—what strange pride and power of purpose!

"And if any man was to come to you and say, 'I know them Javva currents,'—don't you listen to him; for those currents is never yet known to mortal man," . . . etc.

L. H.

DEAR CHAMBERLAIN, — Many sincere thanks for
kind letter and the enclosed kind notice of the Introduction. Whether you will like *all* the book
equally with what you have seen of it, I cannot say;
but as H. M. & Co. never publish anything *very* bad,
you will not, I think, find your ventured criticism
untrue. Perfect equality of tone through a book of
this kind is scarcely possible; — for one page written
for print, perhaps ten have been suppressed. . . .

I am sorry I cannot tell you anything satisfactory about good works of a special kind on modern
French prosody. Perhaps Saintsbury's history of
French literature will contain some valuable references — but I do not know to what date he brings
up his history; and the existing schools have brought
in some new ideas. It strikes me that both in prose
and poetry Gautier is essentially alliterative, as in
the line, —

> Une grace atroce, —
> La grace du gladiateur.

And the crispy crunchy sudden thawing into softness of the Symphonie, —

> De quel mica de neige vierge,
> De quelle moelle de roseau.

I am sorry to have praised to you stories you do
not like — though your beautiful criticism of the
dramatic element in "Le Roi Candaule" shows you
were not *altogether* disgusted. My excuse is that
besides the fact the "Morte Amoureuse" is regarded
as Gautier's most remarkable story by critics of the
highest class, it has been translated by Lang, under

the title of "The Dead Leman," and it was thought worthy of a sonnet by Swinburne, who is certainly a good judge. "Arria Marcella" I like even better; but I suppose you will be still more disgusted with it.

I think your idea about a possible limit to Chinese emigration and acclimation would be, if fully supported by facts, the only powerful argument possible against the predictions of Pearson. Unfortunately, perhaps, the facts *seem* to be the other way. China can send streams out from three of her own different zones of climate; and her people pour into Siberia as well as into Singapore. I have seen Chinamen everywhere in the West Indies. They are getting all the small-shop trade into their hands in some of the islands. They settle on the Pacific coast from Canada to Southern Chili. Panama alone proved a deadly climate to them; but the West Indian negroes also died there, and faster.

A suggestion apropos of prosody. Sidney Lanier met the difficulty of vexed questions about metres and their names by a curious book that *might* please you — if you do not know it "The Science of Verse" (Scribners). He gives all the measures in music, and thinks *that* is the quickest way to teach the art of poetry. It is certainly the most natural. The only trouble is that the student should know music as a preliminary to being taught by such a method.

Many thanks for kind telegram. All well.

Ever very truly yours,

LAFCADIO HEARN.

December 3, 1893.

DEAR CHAMBERLAIN, — . . . There is a whole world of evolutional suggestion in that letter of yours, — especially in the passage of it relating to the influence of musical development upon language forms. It seems to me to explain a host of riddles. The other day while labouring to do something with the terribly dull narrative of another Japanese ballad, I came to a sentence relating the return of a mother from the dead, and could not help comparing it most unfavourably with a similar episode in the "Kalevala," which always seemed to me one of the most pathetic and beautiful in human literature. The Japanese text is dead as a door-nail. But the Finnish race is truly musical. So profound the relation between music and emotional speech, that I suppose, however deeply felt, emotion can never be strongly expressed in a tongue which music has not largely aided to evolve. It is not simply that the *words* won't cry out, but that even the thought behind the words never can be fully uttered, but only *suggested*. Are not the daintiest Japanese or Chinese poems, after all, suggestive rather than expressive, — and for this very reason? — though our own common ballads are full of powerful feeling, as well as full of music.

What you call your *theory* as to the *rime riche* seems to me to rise far above theory, — to supply a very adequate explanation. Here, however, I am too much of an ignoramus to discuss the matter. I read nothing on French philology except Brachet's "Historical Grammar," and the wonderful phonetic history of the language prefixed to his Etymological French Dictionary (the Macmillan ed. U. S.), — explaining a sort of musical, or tonic "Grimm's Law" discovered by Helmholtz, — was n't it? But I could not master all that so as to utilize it seriously: indeed I never tried. I can speak of philological matters only from the general standpoint of the Synthetic Philosophy. According to *that*, in spite of the effort to preserve it, the rhyme of the final syllable would seem doomed beyond hope, — especially, according to the opinion of the German philologist you cite, that the tendency is now to withdraw the accent further back.

Shelley and Byron both use the "rich rhymes," as you call them, in some of their comic and satiric work, — but not, I think, in their finer verse; and none, perhaps, could be found in Tennyson, Rossetti, or the best singers. The word "rich" strikes me as a euphemism, — unless it had the sense of cloying, — of too many raisins in the pudding. I cannot quite understand why what is certainly bad in English, should seem not bad in French.

With the reading of your letter there has come to me the idea that some of the old French measures might have been evolved in a way that would explain the order of the alternation of the feminine and masculine rhymes. The feminine, in quatrains, belongs always to the preponderating line, — does n't it? Thinking of those queer mediæval student-songs, of which the first line was — say Latin, the second French, the third English, the fourth Spanish, etc., — it occurred to me that the fusion of a Northern with a Latin tongue would certainly result in popular efforts to shape new metres — metres which might represent a sort of compromise between the ancient and the newer forms. The predominant language would give the predominant quality, after the fusion, to any measure of this kind. Our own ballad measures appeared only after the conquest. Again there is this possibility — perhaps (?) — that in early measures of four there would have been only two rhymes — as in our own early ballads, the masculine rhymes not being at first used at all. In our old ballads the second and fourth lines only rhyme, — in ninety-nine cases, perhaps. But the mere weakening of the tonic accent you speak of would also be a reason, the creative effort following the direction of least resistance — *basing* its work on the feminine rhymes. However, this is all the guess-work of a man so ignorant about philology that it may be impertinent for him to guess at all. I have an idea that the historical prosody of French is rather fully treated, in a very pleasing way, in the great modern works on the poetry of the troubadours and trouvères, and on the literature of old Provence. I say "idea" because I read many extracts from these books, at a time when I was trying to study Mistral and the modern Provençal singers. I cannot (horrible to say!) remember a single name. But probably nothing of solid value produced in France could have escaped the omnivorous German philologues.

Wife is well, and running about as if nothing serious had happened. The boy is everything that

I could wish — except one thing. After all, he is going to be fair-haired and fair-eyed, and not much like a Japanese. Something of the Hearn family not in Lafcadio Hearn at all is developing very strongly in him. I've mapped out all his little future. Mason's advice is right — I think, confirms my own resolve. This little being needs my whole life, time, strength, care — everything I can give before going to the *hakaba;* — I shall barely be able to freight and supply the ship for its voyage. No more life-ships shall be launched! — I am rather proud, however, of this one, and not much afraid of the future therefor.

I fear it will tax patience to read such a long epistle, — but your last was so brimful of suggestions that a brief reply was out of the question.

Ever, with grateful regards,

Faithfully,

Lafcadio Hearn.

December 13, 1893.

Dear Chamberlain, — You are beautifully right about Hugo in his nobler moods. He is simple, — but carries in his simplicity what Clifford calls "cosmic emotion."

About the accents, — well, I never studied the question; but *is* it really the accent that makes the difference? I did not think it was. "Nearest" and "dearest" and "clearest" seem right to me simply because the sound suffices to fix their meaning most clearly. Not so exactly with "near" and "veneer;" — there the second part of the dissyllable is a perfect repetition in sound of the monosyllabic word.

It only struck me about this way: — When the termination of any polysyllable contains the exact sound of another word with which it is made to rhyme, the rhyme is unlawful — becomes a sort of bastard pun. (Is n't this almost right?) And no two words of different meaning but similar sound can be used as rhymes — such as "sewn" and "sown " — or "tern" and "turn"—for like reason. It seems to me the question is rather of meaning than of accent,— that the accent only is explanatory. In "nearest" and "dearest" — the suppression of the initial consonant leaves no intelligible remainder; — "*earest*" having no meaning. But in such unlawful rhymes as "polite" and "delight," the suppression of the only differently sounding parts of the word leaves remainders with not only the same sound, but the same possible meaning — to the ear.

Oh dear! I am sorry (for myself only) that you already have the book I wanted to give you. The engravings are delightful — are they not? Then you probably know whether the work contains anything that I could build upon. I have reached that stage at which the collector finds his legends grouping themselves — each new fact only reëchoing an idea already received several times. This is sterilizing to fancy. I am always in the state of hope for a new sensation, but seldom get it. The little book of Kwannon I have, — full of queer little pictures. I would like to get some good things out of the Kompira book, however; for I hope to make something of the trip in a literary way. In a financial way, I never expect to make anything. No publisher ever paid me anything except under threat of a lawsuit, and then as little as possible. The pay of the magazines is about twenty dollars a page; the *Atlantic* paying less than half that; — but other magazines than the *Atlantic* spoil a man's work, caricature it with beastly illustrations, and take only what will feed the popular man. You know the popular man wants nothing fine. On the contrary, the *Atlantic* goes in only for fine work; but they want it *too* fine. They are forcing me into philosophical writing. Perhaps it is the best thing possible for me at the present — because I can obtain no help for any lighter kind of work, and can get no material; but it condemns a man to a very restricted audience. In order to read such stuff at all, the audience must have become well-crammed with book-lore of a special character.

Perhaps you would like Sully Prudhomme He has written exquisite things — *some*. And perhaps you would like bits of Louis Bouilhet. I made a translation of S. P.'s "Les Yeux;" but I fear it is a desecration. Of Bouilhet, I venture a version, — I can't give you the original, as I found it only in Maxime du Camp's "Souvenirs," which I no longer possess. Please don't think of the faults in my verse: it is only the strangely weird *idea* of the poem that I would call your attention to: —

THE MUMMY

Startled, — as by some far faint din
  Of azure-lighted worlds, — from sleep,
The Mummy, trembling, wakes within
  The hypogeum's blackest deep, —

And murmurs low, with slow sad voice:
"Oh! to be dead and still endure! —
Well may the quivering flesh rejoice
That feels the Vulture's gripe impure!

"Seeking to enter this Night of death,
Each element knocks at my granite door: —
"'We are Air and Fire and Earth, — the breath
Of Winds, — the Spirits of Sea and Shore.

"'Into the azure — out of the gloom
Rise! — let thine atoms in light disperse!
Mix with the date-palm's emerald plume!
Scatter thyself through the universe!

"' We shall waft thee far over waste and wold; —
Thou shalt be lulled to joyous sleep
By leaves that whisper in light of gold, —
By murmur of fountains cool and deep!

"'Rise! — perchance from thy dungeon dark
Infinite Nature may wish to gain
For the God-like Sun another spark, —
Another drop for the diamond rain!'
. . . .
"Woe! Mine are death's eternal bands! . . .
I feel *Them* come, as I lie alone, —
The *Centuries*, heavy as drifted sands
Heaping above my bed of stone.

"O be accursed, ye impious race! —
Caging the creature that seeks to soar,
Preserving agony's weird grimace
In hideous mockery — evermore!"

Do you know, — whenever I get very despondent,
I feel just like Louis Bouilhet's mummy; — I think
of the far azure-lighted worlds, and I feel the years,
like sand-drifts, heaping all round the soul of me.
Ever very faithfully,
LAFCADIO HEARN.

December 14, 1893.

DEAR CHAMBERLAIN, — What you said in your last letter about the effect of darkness upon you in childhood, haunted me: I thought I would revert to it another time. And now that about one hundred compositions have been corrected, I can find a chance to chat about it.

You specified nothing: I understand the feeling itself was vague, — like many other feelings of childhood of which the indefiniteness itself is a fear, — a sort of mysterious depression of which you could not yourself have told the cause. (This I also remember, — but it became coupled with other unpleasant sensations of which I shall speak presently.) It seems to me these feelings of earliest childhood — so intense and yet so vague — are the weirdest in all human experience, and that for the best of reasons: *they are really ghostly.* Not of our own experience are these; — they of the dead — of the vanished generations behind us; — and I am not sure but that our pleasures are equally weird at that age. I remember crying loudly at an air played upon the piano, — in the midst of a fashionable gathering;—and I remember people (long buried) whose names I have quite forgotten, making their voices and faces kind, and trying to coax me to tell what was the matter. Naturally I could not tell; — I can only vaguely guess now; I know the emotions stirred within my child-heart were not of me — but of other lives. But *then* I had to give a reason: so I lied. I said I was thinking of my uncle who was dead (though I never really cared for him at all). Then

I got petting, and cake, and wondered, young as I was, how I had been able to deceive.

Have you not noticed how utterly the psychologists have failed to explain the Fear that comes in dreams? The suspension of will-power is given as an explanation; but that will not do, — because there is frequently loss of will-power in dreams unaccompanied by the *real* fear of nightmare. The real fear of nightmare is greater than any fear possible to experience in waking moments; it is the highest possible form of mental suffering; it is so powerful that were it to last more than a few instants it would cause death; and it is so intimately linked to feelings of which we know nothing in waking hours — feelings not belonging to life at all — that we cannot describe it. It is certainly well that we cannot. Now I have long fancied that this form of fear also is explainable only by the inheritance of ancestral memories, — not any one painful experience, but the multitudinous fears of a totally unknown past, which the Gods have otherwise mercifully enabled us to forget. The memories themselves are indeed gone, — only the sensations of them remain, stir into life at vague moments of sleep, and especially in the sleep of sickness, when the experiences of real life grow faintest in recollection.

Well, when I was a child, bad dreams took for me real form and visibility. In my waking hours *I saw* them. They walked about noiselessly and made hideous faces at me. Unhappily I had no mother then — only an old grandaunt who never had children of her own, and who hated superstition. If I cried for fear in the dark, I only got whipped for it; but the fear of ghosts was greater than the fear of whippings — *because I could see the ghosts.* The old lady did not believe me; but the servants did, and used to come and comfort me by stealth. As soon as I was old enough to be sent to a child-school, I was happier, — because though badly treated there, I had companions at night who were not ghosts. Gradually the phantoms passed — I think when I was about ten or eleven I had ceased to fear. It is only in dreams now that the old fear ever comes back.

Now I believe in ghosts. Because I saw them? Not at all. I believe in ghosts, though I disbelieve in souls. I believe in ghosts because there are no ghosts now in the modern world. And the difference between a world full of ghosts and another kind of world, shows us what ghosts mean — and gods.

The awful melancholy of that book of Pearson's may be summed up in this, I think, — "The Aspirational has passed forever out of life." It is horribly true. What made the aspirational in life? Ghosts. Some were called Gods, some Demons, some Angels; — they changed the world for man; they gave him courage and purpose and the awe of Nature that slowly changed into love; — they filled all things with a sense and motion of invisible life, — they made both terror and beauty.

There are no ghosts, no angels and demons and gods: all are dead. The world of electricity, steam, mathematics, is blank and cold and void. No man can even write about it. Who can find a speck of romance in it? What are our novelists doing? Craw-

ford must write of Italy or India or ancient Persia;—
Kipling of India; — Black of remote Scotch country
life; — James lives only as a marvellous psychologist, and he has to live and make his characters live
on the Continent; — Howells portrays the ugliest
and harshest commonplaces of a transient democracy. What great man is writing, or can write
of fashionable society anything worth reading, or of
modern middle life, — or of the poor of cities, —
unless after the style of "Ginx's Baby"? No! those
who write must seek their material in those parts of
the world where ghosts still linger, — in Italy, in
Spain, in Russia, in the old atmosphere of Catholicism. The Protestant world has become bald and
cold as a meeting-house. The ghosts are gone; and
the results of their departure prove how real they
were. The Cossacking of Europe might have one
good result, — that of bringing back the ghosts, —
with that Wind of the Spirit which moves the ocean
of Russian peasant life for the gathering storm.

Sometimes I think of writing a paper to be called
"The Vanishing of the Gods."

Perhaps you are tired of theories. But I want to
speak of one thing more,— a *theorizer*, a beautiful
French boy of seventeen, whose name was Henry
Charles Reade. He died at seventeen. Friends
who loved him collected his boyish poems, and
printed them in a little book, — seven or eight years
ago. One of these poems expresses a sensation only
a psychologist of power could explain. It relates to
what Spencer tells us is relative to all antecedent
experience. I offer my own "overdone" translation

of it — because I have not the original. The original
was more simple, and in all respects worthy of a better rendering; but the idea is as follows: —

> I think that God resolved to be
> Ungenerous when I came on earth,
> And that the heart *He* gave to me
> Was old already ere my birth.
>
> He placed within my childish breast
> A worn-out heart, — to save expense! —
> A heart long tortured by unrest
> And torn by passion's violence.
>
> Its thousand tender scars proclaim
> A thousand episodes of woe; —
> And yet I know not how it came
> By all those wounds which hurt it so!
>
> Within its chambers linger hosts
> Of passion-memories never mine, —
> Dead fires, — dreams faded out, — the ghosts
> Of suns that long have ceased to shine.
>
> Perfumes, deliriously sweet,
> Of loves that I have never known,
> It holds, — and burns with maddening heat
> For beauty I may never own.
>
> O weirdest fate! — O hopeless woe!
> Anguish unrivalled! — peerless pain! —
> To wildly love, — and never know
> The object wildly loved in vain!

Certainly the lad who could write such a poem at
sixteen might have been a poet if he lived, — don't
you think so?

LAFCADIO HEARN.

January 12, 1894.

DEAR CHAMBERLAIN, — Twenty thousand thanks
for your kind criticisms. As to the general verdict,

it is the very highest I could wish to obtain from you. To write about such matters at all, situated as I am, is a hazardous thing, — having *no one* whoever to exchange ideas with by word of mouth.

Of course your illustration of the Chinese love of rhyme (and indeed I ought to have remembered Legge's illustrations) knocks one of my suggestions out of existence; and I shall suppress it. Thanks also for notes on the margin, or rather queries. The ugliest one, that is, the only one I can't answer at all, is the query about quadrupeds. I never have been able to satisfactorily explain to myself the contrast offered by the drawings of cats, dogs, horses, and, above all, cows, — to the marvellous drawing of insects, flowers, landscapes, and en masse, or as figures in a landscape, even men and women. I can't think it is the mere difficulty of size. Why should a cow be drawn so much worse than a dragon? Yes, that is an ugly matter to get over. But, of course, I presumed in my article to refer only to things not suggestive of sex; — horses and cows, etc., certainly are. Why should a Japanese artist astonish the world with drawings of monkeys, and not be able to draw a cow? Here again, my theory has to face a series of exceptions I can't get over. All I can venture is this: — From the intrinsic merit of the art itself I cannot help suspecting (or, if you like, wishing to suspect) that there may have been social conditions, conventions, or disabilities of some sort which checked the development of that art in one direction, — or perhaps traditions which checked it, or perhaps other causes connected with

the religion, the agriculture, etc., of the people. All
this may seem wild. But the common explanation
that large subjects were beyond the range of Japanese art does not strike me as tenable. However, here
I must acknowledge my ignorance.

As to the two queries on Wordsworth: — I did
not mean to call Wordsworth obscure, but I think
Tennyson is more lucid, simpler, requires much less
mental effort to follow. There is great depth in
Wordsworth; — I confess I have to re-read stanzas
several times to get the meaning clear. Parts of the
"Ode to Immortality" I think you would acknowledge hard reading. That Wordsworth conceived
Nature as Intelligence is alone a good proof of his
depth. And I must confess my sympathy with
Arnold's criticism that one must wade through a vast
heap of rubbish in order to get all the beauties of
Wordsworth. On the second query, it is true that
Wordsworth is much less characterized by the anthropomorphic spirit than other poets, — as he is
also less imaginative; but when he does describe, he
can look even at houses anthropomorphically, —

> Dear God! the very houses seem asleep,
> And all that mighty heart is lying still!

However, the question is: — "How do we see the
beauties of Nature?" (By "we" understand the
artistic West.) Do we generally see them with the
coldly moral gaze of Wordsworth, or do we not
rather see them through the passional delight of
Shelley? — or the fantastic fetichism of Coleridge?
— or the spirit of the Amourists? I think artists

generally certainly do not look at Nature like
Wordsworth. That you yourself cannot, your lines
about Fuji plainly show, and your much more
beautiful lines about the colour of the scenery at
Miyanoshita. Wordsworth represents for me the
cold theological view of the world; we have to love
him, because he touches infinite truth betimes, but
surely he was immensely deficient in sense of imagination! Never in his life could he have felt
Byron's lines, —

> They looked up to the sky, whose floating glow
> Spread like a rosy ocean, vast and bright;
> They gazed upon the glittering sea below
> Whence the broad moon rose circling into sight; —
> They heard the waves plash, and the wind so low,
> And saw each other's dark eyes darting light
> Into each other; and beholding this
> Their lips grew near and clung into a kiss.

He describes sensation almost miraculously, — but
the sensations are rarely very fanciful.

Be the intellectual world as it may, however, the
vast middle class abroad certainly seem to feel that
all beauty is feminine, and the exceptions in any
class should not break the rule. But in regard to
what I said of terrible beauty, even Wordsworth's
"Yea! Carnage is thy daughter!" is an example.

Of Corot, I can't speak; I only saw engravings.
But I think the charm of colour, of sound, of perfume, are all (in spite of Grant Allen's beautiful
book) related (to-day) to our passional sense. That
German music should have crowded out Italian for
a time only proves that we are rising higher into the
ether; the passional music will come back to favour,

etherealized and infinitely more powerful as an
emotional influence. Of course, I am not supposing
that you suspect me of a tendency to hard and fast
rules. There are no general rules of a sharp sort; but
to insist upon absolute accuracy would kill speculation and paralyze fancy, — would n't it?

Mason's criticism is partly right from his point of
view as expressed in his letter, I think. But I also
think that neither in this article nor in a previous
one did he quite understand my drift, which was
psychological. I still think, as you say, the foreigner
does not see the real Japanese life, even under the
most favoured conditions. Only the other day, at a
Japanese house, my host, drawing his child to his
breast, and caressing it, said to me: — "We cannot
do that among ourselves, and the little fellow knows
he has not any right to come near me [meaning cud-
dle up to him] when there are guests. But as you
are a foreigner, you will excuse him." In Izumo, I
noticed contrary signs, proving that the conduct of
husband and wife to each other is by rigid rule
purely formal under observation; even the pretended
throwing aside of formality is formal. Of course I
have learned something of other lives, — but not
by my own observation. The emotional side, even
in the case of death, is forever hidden, not from us
alone, but from all. I heard the other day of trage-
dies that astounded me. The sufferers — fellow
teachers — never interrupted duty, nor hinted of
their loss or suffering in any possible way. They
would have thought themselves degraded to have
done so.

And now for the big? — Are you really surprised that I think evolutional philosophy has enormously spiritualized our idea of woman and made her infinitely more precious? Well, it is true I have seen no books written upon the subject; but the doctrine entails the result I specify. Here I would wish to be able to talk; to explain my thoughts on paper fully would take too long. I can only suggest. The physical or material facts of evolution are terribly beautiful and wonderful. But what is infinitely more terrible and beautiful and wonderful is the psychological story of evolution. Let us think of a sweet young pure girl, with the mother-soul (mutter seele?) in her but half-fledged. According to theology, what does she represent? A freshly created being, moulded by an imaginary God. According to materialism, what is she? A perfect female body, brought into existence by material laws, and destined to live and perish like a plant, a human polycotyledon. According to evolutional philosophy, what is she? Not ONE, — but countless myriads of millions of dead in ONE LIFE MANIFESTATION, — an incomprehensible Multiple, that has appeared but once in the order of the Cosmos, and never can appear again.

But that is only the barest definition. Why is she beautiful? Because in the struggles of unknown millions of years between the tendency to beauty and the tendency to ugliness, — the beautiful triumphed over unspeakable obstacles and won. Why is she good and sweet and lovable? Because by the sacrifices, and the love, and the sense of goodness acquired by countless millions of mothers, — in spite of all conceivable suffering and pain and terror and fear and wickedness, — the sum of all the unthinkable multitude of tendencies in the race to goodness triumphed to appear in her. A good man, a good woman, seemed a small matter a century ago, — men and women were, as for Heine, Nos. 1, 2, 3, — 11, 12. But when we learn scientifically at what awful cost of suffering and struggle and death any single moral being is evolved, surely the sense of the value of a life is increased unspeakably. And on the other hand, — how much more terrible does a crime appear. For of old a crime was a violation of the laws of a country, a particular society, a particular theology. But in the light of the new philosophy, a real crime becomes a crime against not only the totality of all human experience with right and wrong, — but a distinct injury to the universal tendency to higher things, — a crime against not humanity only, but the entire Cosmos, — against the laws that move a hundred millions of systems of worlds.

Years ago I wrote a story I am now ashamed of; but I cut out a paragraph and send it, because it embodies some of my fancies on this topic. Still, I can't write my thoughts to you; they are things to talk over only. Thousands of illustrations only could satisfy me.

Then there is this other very awful thing. Here is a woman, for example, who is good, sweet, beautiful. Since the being of the world, all life, all humanity, all progress has been working against evil and death in one line. The end of the line only is visible.

It is that girl. She represents the supreme effort. But she is a creator. Her place is to continue the infinite work of the dead. He who weds her has an awful responsibility both to the dead and to the unborn. To the dead, if he should mar their work. To the future, if he plant in that bosom a life incapable of continuing the progress of the past. But this is too long. Are you not tired?

Ever most truly,

LAFCADIO HEARN.

DEAR CHAMBERLAIN, — Looking over Saintsbury's "French Literature," which I received only to-day, I find in regard to the origin of the alternation of masculine with feminine rhymes, a remark. As I guessed, you will remember, from our own poetry, — it seems the alternate form began with Provençal, in which the earlier form was eight-syllable lines rhyming together, pair by pair, and, subsequently, the form changing, the alternation of feminine and masculine began. This would be the natural evolutional process, of course. But that the invention was Provençal, and made just perhaps about the time of the amorous feeling which created the courts of Love, would, I think (though Saintsbury says nothing about it), account for the first place being given to the feminine.

In the accompanying volume ("Specimens"), also received to-day, I find that Saintsbury, who both in the Encyclopædia Britannica and in his "History of French Literature" characterizes "La Morte Amoureuse" as the most perfect of all French short stories, actually cites three pages of it as the only prose sample of Gautier's best work. On the other hand, I certainly cannot agree with Saintsbury that Baudelaire's "Fleurs de Mal" "were never popular" or worthy to be, — nor that Zola and the Realist school are insufferably dull, have no art-sense, and owe their existence to the appetite for vice. I have not read him all, of course; but while some of his criticisms both delight and surprise me, others strike me as showing total inappreciation of the character-istics of the writer. Certainly, it would not be well for us if we had to accept the judgment of any one literary critic as final. It is only through conflicting opinions that we reach the secret both of the faults and the merits.

I noticed that the presents manufactured this year show less of innovation than last year. The figured silks, haori linings, etc., were among the most beautiful things I ever saw, — chrysanthemum blossoms, flower sprays of divine colours (including an unforgettable blaze of iris-blossoms), — dragons and clouds, — birds, etc., and landscapes. The only unpleasant break in the hundreds of designs I saw was one representing Lieutenant Gunji and Lieu-tenant Fukushima exploring ripples and deserts of damascening. These were costly; but perhaps the simplest things were even more charming. I bought piles of towels, because they were just as good as kakemono. Some were figured with Chinese poems and Japanese poems; — some had scenes from plays; — and some scenes from Oguri Hangwan (!); not to speak of views of Matsushima, Fuji, etc.

The sake cups were less vulgar than last year; but I saw one horror, the word BEEF (sic) in gold letters upon fine porcelain (made as presents from butchers!)

From Nagasaki I got a Consular letter with extraordinary spellings; — I enclose as a curiosity. I have written a long answer asking advice, but hesitate to post it. My folks won't hear of becoming English citizens, and losing power of acquiring property in the interior. If the Consul Quin is a good fellow, he might write to me; but I feel again he might snub me, etc.

It has suddenly occurred to me that my reference to masculine and feminine rhyme alternation in Provençal is childish, — as I forgot that I did not know whether in that era the rhymes were thus named at all. What might again be considered, however, is the appearance, in early French poetry, of verse *in two languages*, — one line in Latin and one in Romance, alternately. Your question is certainly most interesting, but difficult to solve. Perhaps it can't be certainly solved at all, because the early ballad-poetry of the Northern French dialect has completely disappeared, if it ever existed, which some doubt.

I fancy I may have discovered the truth about all that disgusts me in government schools. One said to me yesterday: "There is little love between students and teachers and little zeal in the teaching, — simply because the government schools are official nurseries. The teacher may be in love with his profession, but he may not. He is merely a govern-

ment official in hard fact. He regards teaching as a
step to rank, and perhaps to public life in the capacity of a foreign representative, or a Tokyo office-
holder. He is appointed not for his abilities, but for
his relationships or his utilizeability, so to speak.
The students understand the position perfectly
well, and act accordingly. There is no more respect,
much less reverence."

Let me tell you a rather pleasant story of local
life. An old shopkeeper who sells us lacquerware had
a queue, — like not a few other old shopkeepers in
Kumamoto. He professed to detest all Western
manners, dress, ideas; and praised the *tempora
antiqua* without stint. Whereby he offended young
Japan, and his business diminished. It continued
to diminish. His young wife lamented, and begged
him to cut off his queue. He replied that he would
suffer any torment rather than that. Business became slacker. Landlord came round for rent. All
three were samurai. Husband was out. Landlord
said, "If your husband would cut off his queue he
might be able to pay his rent!" "That is just what I
tell him," said she, — "but he won't listen to me."
"Let me talk to him!" said the landlord. Queue
comes in, out of breath, and salutes landlord. Landlord frowns and asks for rent. Usual apologies.
"Then you get out of my house," says the landlord,
— "get out at once." Queue cannot understand
old friend's sudden harshness, becomes humble in
vain, — makes offers of his stock in payment.
Landlord says, "Hm! what?" "Anything you like
in the shop?" "Hm, word of honour?" "Yes."

Landlord joyfully to wife, "Bring me a scissors, quick!" Scissors is brought. Dismay and protests checked by the terrible word "Yakusoku." Off goes the queue. Owner mourns. Landlord laughs, and says, "Old friend, I make you now a present of the three months' rent; you owe me nothing." Business begins to improve.

Ever most truly,
LAFCADIO HEARN.

P. S. I feel the power of the anti-foreign reaction. The sudden hiss of hatred with which I am greeted by passers-by sometimes, in unfamiliar districts, convinces me that foreigners in the interior would have an ugly time in case of political troubles of a very likely kind. The only hope for Japan is a return to autocracy.

January 22, 1894.

DEAR CHAMBERLAIN, — I have just had your letter and a new big batch of proofs at the same time, up to galley one hundred and eighty-two, — makes, I think, over seven hundred pages already, but more to come.

However, I want to chat first. Yes, after I posted my last letter, I thought to myself, "He has got me on Wordsworth; I can't make out a case there. I must give in." Indeed I think more of the Latin poets, I suppose; I think of the Latin prose-writers, like Gautier describing the hills *qui ondulaient comme les hanches d'une femme*, when I write those things. And you are right; the world is n't all paganized yet. Still, I fancy our artistic classes do at the present

time feel Nature more in the Latin way than they
did in Wordsworth's era, — feel her something like
Symonds did. Your comparison about Wordsworth
— beautiful as a swan when he glides along with the
current of a subject befitting his powers, and wad-
dling clumsily when out of it — is delicious. By the
way, Baudelaire has a touching poem about a frig-
ate-bird, or albatross, which you would like, — describing the poet's soul superb in its own free azure,
— but helpless, insulted, ugly, clumsy when striving
to walk on common earth, — or rather, on a deck,
where sailors torment it with tobacco pipes, etc.

But about Japanese art. I, too, thought of the
anatomy question. It did not solve the question for
me. Why? Because *I don't believe the Greeks knew
anything about anatomy.* I say this after a careful
study of Winkelmann and the monuments so match-
lessly engraved by the Society of Dilettanti (what
would I not give to have the edition I saw!), and the
engravings of gems, etc., etc. The astounding thing
is that the great Italians who studied osteology —
who drew the skeleton before covering it with
painted flesh — never approached the commonest
Greek outline. Did the Greeks ever dissect? It
strikes me their religion would have rendered that
impossible, and their humanity. How did they manage? What is the awful, — really *awful* secret of
their knowledge of grace? We know the geometrical
rules for the face. But those for the limbs, — those
long, lithe, light, wondrous limbs! and the torso, —
and the divine symmetry of the rest, — we cannot
find. We know they drew by rule, squaring off the

surface with cross-lines first. But what was the rule? And how did they find it? And the muscles of the Farnese, — the suppleness of the miraculous Aphrodite, — the abdominal lines of the Apollo, — nay, the mere set of the limbs of the smallest nude figure on a gem! Yet they cannot have studied anatomy at all in the modern sense. No; they loved the body, — they found the secrets of the divine geometrical idea of it through the intuition of that love, possible only in a time when there was no sense of shame or shyness or what we call conscience about sexual matters in themselves. I can't think scientific knowledge of anatomy could have helped them much in groping for the pure ideal which they found; it would rather have balked them. And I don't think ignorance of the subject would alone explain the Japanese incapacity in the anatomical direction.

Strange to say, however, yesterday I saw an artistic cow! Really! I had been invited to look at some kakemono by Ippo, and lo! — the first was a *running* cow. It was very good. But why? Curiously enough the cow had been drawn *exactly like an insect;* the figure was about as large as this sheet, and foreshortened, — the hind quarters being turned toward the gazer. What the artist had caught was the motion, — the queer crooked lumbering knock-kneed motion of the cow. I don't believe he could have done it on a bigger scale at all; he could not have then given the sense of the gawky movement.

I found this in the *Athenæum:* —

> "Give me thy dreams!" she said; and I,
> With empty hands, and very poor,

Watched my fair flowery visions die
   Upon the temple's marble floor.

"Give joy!" she cried. I let joy go; —
   I saw with cold unclouded eyes
The crimson of the sunset glow
   Across the disenchanted skies.

"Give me thy youth," she said. I gave;
   And, sudden-clouded, died the sun; —
And on the grey mound of a grave
   Fell the slow raindrops, one by one.

"Give love!" she cried. I gave that too.
   " Give beauty!" Beauty sighed and fled,
For what, on earth, should beauty do,
   When love, who was her life, was dead?

She took the balm of innocent tears
   To hiss upon her altar-coal, —
She took the hopes of all the years,
   And, at the last, she took my soul.

With heart made empty of delight
   And hands that held no more fair things,
I questioned her; — "What shall requite
   The savour of my offerings?"

"The Gods," she said, — "with generous hand
   Give guerdon for thy gifts of cost;
Wisdom is thine, to understand
   The worth of all that thou hast lost."
                   (E. NESBIT.)

It strikes me that the workmanship might be vastly improved; but the imagery, the thought, the moral of the verses are true poetry in spite of the flaws.
            Ever truly,
                LAFCADIO HEARN.

Mason likes dreams. I send a sample of a genuine one, described as exactly as I knew how, — without any additional imaginings.

P. S. I forgot another thing. You are certainly right in holding that both sexes ought to be equally exalted by the philosophical idea of character evolution. We do not disagree there at all. But of course, each sex studies the other as a something apart from itself. I, writing from the masculine point of view, think of the woman in the reverential fashion for a purpose.

There is this, however: — The perfect woman appeals to us through the evolution in her of those particular qualities which latter-day faith especially dwells on as divine, — devotion, mercy, pity, infinite love, tenderness, — all those soul-things that the world's bitterness and struggle make us wish for, — all those things which are to make and soften the peace of the future Age of Gold. But the ideal man cannot be figured in this wise; we cannot divest him of the aggressive, — we cannot admire him even without recognizing in him some latent capacity of inspiring fear and some potential hardness of soul. As a matter of stern physical fact, the man is really the superior being, — morally as well as physically; his whole nature is one of greater massiveness, his sympathies are larger and deeper, his sense of justice incomparably higher and broader, and woman *never* can be his equal for plain physiological reasons. But in the present unhappy condition of the world, *it is only the woman who really sees the man;* it is only for her that he takes off his armour and mask.

L. H.

January 27, 1894.

DEAR CHAMBERLAIN, — Your letter was a great
pleasure to me for more reasons than one, — especially, however, because giving what a man is
always most hungry for in this world (unless he is a
Diogenes) — sympathy. First, about the registration
question: — Perhaps your idea of my destiny is
prophetical, and I may again be a traveller. I think
I ought to travel *a little* for literary material. But I
cannot imagine any circumstance, except banish-
ment by the Tenshi-sama, that should prevent me
from making my home in Japan. Indeed, I never
thought about such a possibility. The only grim
outlook is death, — because I am much older than I
like to be; in that case English citizenship would be
of no use to my folk. As for my wife, she is only a
simple sweet-hearted country-girl; she would never
feel at home in the life of the open ports, or be able
to mingle at ease in the Europeanized circles of their
Japanese society. Again, none of my folks know
anything about business; — they would be easily
deprived of anything. I could leave them in any of
the settlements; but as for myself, I can't imagine
anything which could separate us indefinitely in
life. Leaving the moral question aside altogether —
though it is a stronger one than any — there comes
the consideration of the facts, thus: The Japanese
are still the best people in the world to live among;
— therefore why wish ever to live elsewhere? No
one will ever, or could ever, love me any more than
those about me now love me; — and that is the
most precious consideration in life aside from the

mere capacity to live. The ugly questions are death and lack of employment. The latter is quite possible. The former is important. In either event, it were better that mother and son were able to live in the interior, and own their own homestead, and have a little revenue, and take care of each other until better times. There's the odds. Yes, as you say, it is a hard nut to crack; but I fancy the safe side is that suggested by the family instinct — they have all decided not to risk loss of citizenship. The patriarch, of course, considers me only an adopted son; and thinks that Izumo should always be the family home.

What you say of Japanese costume as a protection by mimicry is glorious. I should like to meet the Japanese who had shrewdness enough to say so delicious a thing! The fact struck me a good while ago (and I embodied it in my article on "Jiujutsu") that the Japanese have never really adopted European costume at all. It is worn only outside the house; the *reifuku* as a *business uniform*, the *yofuku* as a military uniform. Even the officers of the garrison resume at home the kimono, obi, haori, and tabi. The Kencho officials, the judges, the Governors of provinces, the teachers, are, at home, each and all, just as much Japanese as they were a thousand years ago. The students even hate the uniforms and confess its value only as a military garb.

What you say about the French rhymes again is of extreme interest to me, — showing how enormously complicated the most apparently simple subject always proves under the examination of a thinker. I believe everything you say about the "pause" — value of the single rhyme, etc. But the question first suggested by you — the precedence given to the feminine rhyme — would not be solved by any of these discoveries, I think; — although they would explain the *raison d'être* for the retention of the rule. I don't think it was a gradual evolution, — though it may have been; because far, far back in the history of French literature it still appears, and because exceptions would only prove the rule by their comparative rarity. I still imagine (and will do so until a proof to the contrary turns up) that the solution is to be found in the old rules of Provençal lyric poetry, — which strongly affected the Northern lighter verse that it preceded, so far as we are able to learn. Of course, this idea leaves out the supposition, for which no positive proof exists, that a mass of Northern ballad literature, antedating the "Song of Roland," etc., has been lost. Saintsbury thinks this an unsubstantiated conjecture; and the extraordinary vitality of ballad literature elsewhere is in his favour.

I suppose you can scarcely have failed to observe the extraordinary benevolence exercised toward students throughout the country. Every official and every teacher — or nearly every — has a number of shosei in his house. Nominally they should support themselves, but I fancy they are in all cases largely aided, even as to food. What you may not have noticed, perhaps, is that in modern Japanese houses of a fair class — such as my own — *special architectural provision is made for shosei.*

There are two or more small walled-off rooms (solid
kabe-work) contrived about the entrance which are
called "student-rooms." The *soshi*-business in
Tokyo represents only the perversion of this bene-
volent custom to political ends. I myself intend, if
things turn out pretty well, to take an Izumo student or two later on, and help as far as can reasonably be expected. I am often asked by local students, but as often refuse; for others have prior
claims, and, besides, my present house is too small.

The native benevolence does not draw the line
at shosei. I know a *number* of cases of hard-worked
teachers contributing regularly every month to the
university expenses of boys whom they have taught.
I asked, "Are they really grateful?" of a very cynical professor. He said, "Yes, I believe they are;
— they are grateful to their Japanese teachers for
personal favours." I said, "But they are not
grateful to foreign teachers?" He answered, —
"Well, no: that is quite a different matter." Then
I wondered whether this is not just because we
foreign teachers are really so much more selfish
towards them — for reasons we cannot help, of
course.

Lastly: — The benevolence of the teachers does
not stop there. Special teachers devote their whole
spare time to unpaid, gratuitous teaching, — in
many instances. Take jiujutsu! Our present teacher,
a disciple of Kano's, builds here at his own expense,
in his own residence grounds, a jiujutsu hall, and
teaches all his spare time without a cent of remuneration. Take natural history! The least sympathetic

of all the teachers gives his whole leisure to extra labour in this direction. Perhaps it is the very excess of such kindness on the part of the native teachers which creates the feeling of "offness" between the foreign teacher and the students. His greatest kindness suffers terribly by comparison.

Again the foreign teacher is trusted only as an intellectual machine. His moral notions, his sympathies, his intuitions, his educational ideas are not trusted at all; — a Japanese teacher is always consulted by preference. There seems to be the set conviction in every official mind that a foreigner *cannot* understand Japanese students. Indeed I suspect that those among us who sympathize with them, and wish to know them, may really understand them much better than they can understand us, — which is saying a good deal, — just because of this solid conviction about our mental incapacity. . . .

Ever most truly,
LAFCADIO HEARN.

Extract from a composition now before me: —
"I think the orders of the Mombusho are very cruel to our students. According to this document, the students must be very humble to their masters. We are giving the money for thanks for our lessons. The masters, who are *only* obliged to teach us, have no affection for us, — so that we also have none for them. Whenever by chance there happens any disagreeing between teachers and students, then the students seem in the teachers' eyes to be venomous snakes, and 'the cruelty carried up to our

head,' so that anger is more encouraged than ever. (I don't quite understand this.)

"In Japan there used to be good customs, — to honour His Majesty Our Emperor, to love our parents, and to reverence the old. Now the only precepts are about carefulness. Our hearts are infected with European false-hearted customs."

Well, — but is n't it true?

L. H.

January 30, 1894.

DEAR CHAMBERLAIN, — I am really overwhelmed, and can't say much in way of thanks. The translation delights me beyond all measure; it is exactly the thing I dreamed of! — transliteration and all. As I began to read it I began to sing, — for the whole thing flashed with melody at once, — the new jerky, menacing, clarion-style, — with all the emphasis phalanxed at the line-ends, like bayonets. It lives; and I am going to try to versify it. I am very weak and inexperienced in versifying, however; and it will take time. Then I will offer you the sample, to be judged. Your MS. I will always preserve as a very dear thing. But do not ever take such trouble for me again, — because it would only make me ashamed. Of course, I shall try to use the song for the Kumamoto paper in my own way, if you wish. . . .

Is n't Lowell much like those tropical fruits that are ripened only by sun? He has had none of the frost of life to sweeten him. Tropical fruits, you know, are terribly disappointing, — though very

lovely to the eye. You must go North, and far
North, to get the fruits that have the true rich flavour and nutritive force. They have been ripened by
sharp winds and frosts. So with men, is n't it? The
man who has not suffered, has had only half of his
nervous system developed. He can touch and feel
life on one side only. It is the man who has had to
fight with the world's rough weather that can feel
life to several dimensions. Hence that Goethe-
verse you know so much better than I do, —

> Who ne'er his bread in sorrow ate, —
> Who ne'er, the lonely midnight hours,
> Weeping upon his bed hath sate,
> He knows ye not, Ye Heavenly Powers!

And so the whirligig of Time works! Would it not
be enough to make one doubt the Unutterable, were
all powers and privileges of feeling, seeing, and thinking possible to ripen only by fertilizing the life-soil
with gold-dust? The Eternities and the Immens-
ities seem to equalize things pretty well after all!
Perhaps the highest sympathies cannot be evolved
at all without subjection, for some time at least, to
the discipline of pain.

Just as you suppose, the house revolves around
the little boy now; I have greatly fallen into oblivion. How good the Japanese are to children, — even
the most extravagant things said do not tell. The
little creature's eyes, though, are bright blue; and
I wonder whether his possible foreign appearance
would cause him any trouble with future schoolmates. In Kumamoto children are not gentle. The
old grandfather is the most delighted. He used to

take care of the children of the Daimyo of Izumo
(Matsudaira Dewa-no-kami, I think) in his youth,
— and is accustomed to children; besides, he has
still the heart of a child. He sings the lullabys of
long ago, and among many others one which goes
something like this: —

> Tsuru sennen
> Kame wa mannen, —
> Urashima Taro, hassen zai,
> Tobo Saku
> Hyaku mutsu;
> Take-Uji Daijin
> Sambiaku yo:
> Inagaki Kaji-Wo
> Kono tori.

(He is *great-grandfather* by the adoption only of my
wife by his son. She was a Koizumi, daughter of a
samurai of much higher rank, — old Karo stock.)

I did not believe it was possible for one child to
give constant labour, night and day, to seven persons; yet such is the fact. If I protest, I am asked
to help — which does n't suit my occupations; besides, the child feels strangely afraid of me: I am
so clumsy!

I made a speech by request Saturday on "The
Future of the Orient," and I think the students are
going to print it. I never sent you any of my printed
speeches from Matsue, — there was nothing in them
that would not have seemed platitude to you. If
this be printed, however, I will send it, as it is a sort
of philosophical history of the invasion of the Western Barbarians, — a supplement to the views of
Pearson.

The secret of many enthusiasms evoked by national song must be, I imagine, hidden from those
of alien race and experience. I was horribly disappointed by the "Ranz des Vaches:" perhaps one
must have lived in Switzerland to understand it.
Songs there are, like the "Marseillaise," which explain their history by the melody alone: so powerfully do they reflect the emotion of an hour. But
I doubt whether even so splendid a song as the
"Death of Nelson," with its shouting lines, —

> England expects
> That every man
> This day will do his duty, —

could be fully understood by any Latin. And what
would an Irish or Scotch air mean to an Italian or
a Spaniard, in most cases? Association is the great
witchcraft. Still there are songs which combine the
triple charm of poetry, melody, and association.

"Patti is going to sing at the St. Charles," said
a friend to me years ago: — "I know you hate the
theatre, but you *must* go." (I had been surfeited
with drama by old duty as a dramatic reporter, and
had vowed not to enter a theatre again.) I went.
There was a great dim pressure, a stifling heat, a
whispering of silks, a weight of toilet-perfumes. Then
came an awful hush;—all the silks stopped whispering. And there suddenly sweetened out through
that dead hot air a clear, cool, tense thread-gush of
melody unlike any sound I had ever heard before
save — in tropical nights — from the throat of a
mockingbird. It was "Auld Lang Syne" only — but
with never a *tremolo* or artifice; — a marvellous, au-

dacious simplicity of utterance. The silver of that singing rings in my heart still.

There is no song which moves me so much, — not because of the "intolerable pathos" only — as Matthew Arnold calls it — of the words, nor only because of the souvenir of the divine voice. But there is a dream fastened to that song, — the dream of an Indian city stifling in reek of pestilence and smoke of battle, — trenches piled with sweltering corpses, — grim preparations against worse than death, — the sense of vast remoteness from all dear things, — and the sudden lighting up of all those memories which grow vivid only at the last hour. And then, like one of those memories itself, — startling beyond all startlingness, — the Highland piping beyond the walls, —

> We twa hae paidl't i' the burn,
> Frae morning sun till dine;
> But seas between us braid hae roared
> Sin' Auld Lang Syne.

I believe it was first the clan call of the MacGregors; — then "Auld Lang Syne." What was Beethoven to *that?*

Well, your mere statement of the history of the existing military songs of course kills all hope of finding in them anything corresponding to sincerity of thought and true emotional art. Such merits belong only to spontaneous work, and especially to the creations of the people. Only the melodies and the historical or local suggestions can therefore account for the excitement these new songs produce; — and the most one could attempt would be to give the lilt and an occasional suggestive fragment, — in a purely literary study of them. On the other hand, their *Zeit-geist* quality is of the most extraordinary, and worthy of a very elaborate essay. The idea of "Supensa" and "Dawin" is too enormously grotesque! — what a study you *could* make! The romance would n't be on the surface, — but deep down under the whole thing there is certainly the broad interest of a race-effort for independence. It would apologize for the atrocities of many an utterance. "Supensa"! ! — "Da-win"! ! !

I read Kipling's ballad three times last night, and every time I found new surprises in it. Queer how he hits the local colour and the exact human tone always. I used to chat while stopping at Carey's in Yokohama with just such men and the sealers. I rather like seamen, engineers, — all that hard class. They can tell you wonderful things; and their talk is never dull. But to use it like Kipling one must have worked with them, lived their life. I always fail in trying to work out one of their yarns; the stage of the action is too unfamiliar to me.

Since you are indirectly responsible for my horrid mistake about Mr. Okakura's observation, I will revenge myself by offering you a caricature in words of Sully Prudhomme's, —

> Bleus ou noirs, — tous aimés, tous beaux,
> Des yeux sans nombre ont vu l'aurore;
> Ils dorment au fond des tombeaux
> Et le soleil se lève encore!

If you are disgusted, remember it is your own kindest fault.

I must write some curious Kumamoto news to you in a few days. The contradiction of facts and feelings throughout my notes to you may amuse you; that contradiction, however, reflects the conflict of the still uninterpreted existence about me. And my letters are too prolix and gushy, I know; but if I stopped to polish them, I would never get through, nor would I feel quite honest.

With sincere thanks,

Ever faithfully,

LAFCADIO HEARN.

February 2, 1894.

Pendulum on the left.

DEAR CHAMBERLAIN, — The heading does not imply that I feel out of sorts, or dissatisfied, or lonesome.   It signifies only that in spite of the most obstinate optimism, perceptions of the pessimistic sort are forcing themselves upon me. As the last page of my optimistic volumes left for Boston, I said to my own soul, — "Oh! you foolish thing! what an illusion it all was!!" My soul made no answer. She only looked down on the ground.

Smallness, after all, is the word. You called attention to the multitude of words in Loti expressing smallness. He saw outwardly and on the surface only. Yet one who sees inwardly is forced at last to think of smallness. After all, what is there large in Japan except Fuji, and the ranges? What has man made that is large? What has he done that is large? What does he think that is large? What does he feel that is large? His gods are ghosts only, —

who eat tiny, tiny, tiny repasts. His cities are vast
collections of wooden huts. His temples are scarcely
better. His castles are mere timber barricades.

And very small his imaginations are. What is
large about them? His poems, which are only
tiny pictures? — his deepest sentiments of heroism
which he shares with the ant and the wasp! — his
romances, mediævally tiresome, yet without any
of the strength of our own mediævalism! Always
details, — details *infinite* in number and variety,
infinitesimal in character. And to-day, what is his
tendency? To make everything that he adopts small
—philosophy, sciences, material, arts, machinery; —
everything is modified in many ways, but uni-
formly diminished for Lilliput. And Lilliput is not
tall enough to see far. Cosmic emotions do not
come to Lilliputians. Did any Japanese ever feel
such an emotion? Will any ever feel one?

I watch with amusement the tendency to the
disease which the *Saturday Review*, or somebody
else, called "Specialistitis." Does not the difference
between the average Japanese mind and the average European mind seem to be something like the
following: —

Thinking in small detail	Thinking in relations
OBJECT	OBJECT
Ideas, habitually dissociated, and never synthetized, would never produce any line of thought capable of giving any result.	Ideas habitually coördinated and synthetized, would unite into a single line of thought.

And then again the comparative difference in *mass* between mere feeling in Western and in Japanese people! When I think of what is expressed by a musical emotion, — a mere memory of Verdi; — by a Greek marble; — by a religious exaltation; — by a Gothic church; — by a poem — how enormous the difference *in volume* of life. We are *Brobdignagians!* And yet, perhaps, the future is to these races! The age of giant feelings, like the age of giant mammals, may be succeeded by an era of smaller life — a life without dreams and aspirations above the material. Do you know Quinet's tremendous prose-poem about the Cathedral?

But in a purely, hopelessly industrial age, what would be the use of dreams? And that age is coming. Then the men who are giants will all starve to death; and the earth will be peopled by the extremely small, and governed by extremely small ideas.

Ever most truly,
LAFCADIO HEARN.

February 12, 1894.

DEAR CHAMBERLAIN, — I have been silent for some days, being crazy with the labour of reading, revising, and indexing 490 plate-proofs. Therewith came a letter which will not please you, — but which I enclose, as a duty.

I think your love of indexing is simply an indication of your force of purpose. The only way to face a painful thing satisfactorily is to train one's self by sheer strength of will to love it. This can be done; and you seem to have done it. But I suspect it is a comparatively recent feeling because you never indexed the "Kojiki," which greatly needs indexing. I hate — detest — abominate indexing; but I will gladly help some day to make an index for the "Kojiki," if you want. Such an index would have to be enormous.

A subject on which we are as "two souls, etc.," is chess — *perhaps*, mathematics and kindred things: all forms of calculation for the mere pleasure of the exercise. I have not even the *faculty*, which is an awful confession. What I can't understand is how so amiable a man as Mason can be a good chess-player, — or how, being a good chess-player, he should not be a first-class man of business, — a big merchant, etc. Strong chess-players, mathematicians (except the crazy sort), and all men with remarkable powers of calculation seem to me to have all the qualities for success in big things; — but they also seem to be rather *hard*. It is difficult for me to imagine Mason as a good chess-player, simply because he is so delightful a letter-writer.

"A South American Republic!" I believe it. Spencer's explanation of the Spanish-American incapacity for autonomy is the half-breed blood. The *Indian* ancestral impulse overpowers all tendency to social integration of the highest kind. The Japanese have not this trouble to contend with. But they have others, — shared perhaps with the Spanish, whom they most seem to resemble (i. e., if they can be said to resemble any Western race at , all). The Northern capacity for autonomy is immemorially old, racial, and is physiologically represented by enormous capacity of self-restraint by judgment. One should suppose, on a superficial view of things, that the highest self-restraint was exemplified in the Japanese race. But I am convinced that it is n't. Remove the necessity for religious and social submission, and they will show no self-restraint at all. Why? Because the self-restraint of the Northern sort requires *large*-mindedness. It is rendered possible only by large, straight, powerful apprehensions of general truths, and the general effects of general causes. The ability to think in relations, and in abstract relations, alone accounts for the existence of England. Will the Japanese learn to think in relations — *as a people?* Not before the sun dies, I fear. The men who now think in relations are — the old masters of the Buddhist philosophy! Not the politicians, nor the students, nor the native teachers.

I think it will be Korea over again — in regard to public education. The first enormous burst of zeal has been succeeded by a number of reactions, — all tending toward a dimly visible end, — a universal crash. The impossible was attempted at the beginning; — then preference was given to the possible. The teaching of English was restricted every year. The foreign teachers and managers are being got rid of as quickly as possible; — and the institutions founded and operated by them are falling into degradation year by year. Instead of trying to keep up the fabric, the appropriations are annually decreased. Compare the Sapporo College of 1871 with that of to-day! The incomes of the Middle

Schools are being reduced. The remuneration of all foreign teachers has been reduced. The *systems* of teaching devised for perpetuity have all been abandoned—except *perhaps* in Tokyo. There is no *system* elsewhere. To establish a system would be impossible now. To establish discipline would be impossible. To dyke back in any way the constant movement toward utter disintegration would be impossible.

Lest any efforts should be made to establish a system, to enforce discipline, to crystallize anything, — all educational officials and all other officials are being perpetually removed from place to place. Here we have Spencer's changes "from integrated to disintegrated movements." But all plans and purposes being fully understood, even by the public, the attacks made upon the educational system as a whole will continue; demands for further reductions in expenditure will be regularly made and acceded to; — the Mombusho will certainly become what Hasegawa Tai already called it, — a *bakemono-yashiki;* the students will revolt, desert, or disappear; — and the things will disappear also from want of funds to prop them up. I think it is reasonable to expect that, in spite of Japanese pride, the Higher Middle Schools will shortly (i. e., within a decade) vanish. They will probably be first changed in some way so as to cover up the shame of their abandonment, — and gradually dropped. Kencho schools will follow, — by the hundreds. Government will drop education perforce; and it will have to be all reconstructed by private effort. This seems possible to many. To me it now seems much more than possible. The military and naval schools promise to last a little longer. But how much longer? Assuredly there will be also a reaction in that direction.

One reason why I think thus *bluely* is that Japan naturally but unfortunately overestimated her physiology. Mental capacity *is* nervous capacity. . . .

I think that universal education, just like universal suffrage, etc., is a humbug in every country. It seems to me especially so in Japan. Why waste the national forces in the effort to bestow it on the millions who cannot profit by it, and to whom therefore it can only be made pernicious? In this school, certainly only a third of the scholars ought to be allowed to remain. The rest are wasting their youth. Men of marked capacity alone ought to have the highest opportunities. A reform in higher education ought to mean the remodelling of the system for the sole benefit of extraordinary capacities.

I should like to be mistaken about all this. But the pendulum won't move any more. I feel it is no use to pretend to one's self that the race is equal to its own ambitions. I feel it is no use to optimize about anything in relation to it. That is bad, — is n't it? The opening of the country was very wrong, — a crime. . . . Fairyland is already dead; — perhaps the anti-foreign feeling at present is no more than the vague national consciousness of what must come. "That which ye fear exceedingly, shall come upon you," — saith Isaiah.

Ever most faithfully,
LAFCADIO HEARN.

February 16, 1894.

DEAR CHAMBERLAIN, When you reissue "Things Japanese," perhaps an extra line or two about baths might be of interest. The custom of *singing* in public baths is worth commenting upon. In Tottori there is a famous "o-furo-uta."

I have been thinking how disappointing Japanese song-titles are. From a Western point of view the titles are most suggestive — but nothing suggested is to be found. Your criticism seems to be just; "apples of Sodom and ropes of sand."

Perhaps the condition of the Japanese dog is one thing which tells powerfully against our beliefs about the influence of Buddhism upon the treatment of animals. The Japanese dog remains very close to the primitive wolf or jackal. The "chin" makes only an exception to the rule. We must talk of the *dog* in general. What a difference between the Western and the Japanese dog! How different the gaze, the intuition, the memory! And how utterly deficient the Japanese dog in gratitude! And how indifferent to the question of who owns him. He is still pretty savage, — occasionally shows it in very ugly ways. He feeds his young exactly like a wolf, — chewing up, half-digesting, and then re-gorging for the benefit of the pup. He is curiously cunning, — but in a savage, sneaking way.

A great russet brute lies on the sunny half of the street facing the college. He lets the children play about him, but is n't demonstrative; Japanese dogs never are. He is apathetic in demeanour. I notice his sharp ears suddenly prick, and his sharp

eyes aim for a minute far down the road. That
means inward emotion; but what it is I can't imagine, because he deliberately turns his head the
other way, and stares at the smoke of the Aso-San.
Presently I discern—far, far away — the cause of
the momentary emotion, coming at a lope. It is a
dog of foreign breed, — setter build, — long, light,
with silky, drooping ears. Approaching, his very
large eyes get bigger. He sees the red bulk lying in
the middle of the road. A moment he hesitates;
but the wolfish muzzle is pointed toward Aso-San.
There is a chance. The Gwai-koku-jin "spurts" to
pass. But at exactly the right moment the red jaws
take him by the back. Oh! the agony and the howl-
ing! The foreign yowls, yelps, desperately fights.
The native does n't make a sound, — he only bites.
For half a mile he follows the fugitive, — rolls
him over, — turns him in circles, — torments him
into frenzy. At last he comes back slowly, and lies
down again, without a sign of excitement, among the
children. A peasant strides along with his horse,
and scowls at the dog. The late warrior suddenly
changes to jackal, — because the peasant happens
to have a bamboo. Such a combination of cunning,
ferocity, and cowardice is not of the civilized dog.

I have not yet been able to find a civilized cat.
There must be some, but they are very rare. Shyness and treachery characterize most of them.

The horses I don't understand at all. Never
have I seen one struck. The peasant marches along
with them, speaks gently to them, does not ask
them to labour harder than himself. I followed one

day, for fully two miles, a peasant who walked
behind his horse, holding the ends of two heavy
planks fastened to the animal's back. The motion
of the horse caused them to oscillate; — so the
peasant held the ends and handled them in such a
manner as to prevent the horse's back from being rubbed. I see lots of such actions. But why
are these horses so horribly afraid? They actually
whinny with fear when they hear a kuruma coming. It gives one an awful suspicion that they must
have been started out in life with a sufficient experience of pain to render all further correction unnecessary. They give one the same unpleasant impression
as performing dogs do — which is unspeakable.

This brings me to Buddhism. Surely, as you say,
it were better for Japan to have any civilized religion than none, — and the danger is that of having
none. You can't imagine how many compositions
I get containing such words as — "Is there a God?
— I don't know" — which, strange as it may seem
to you, does n't rejoice me at all. I am agnostic,
atheist, anything theologians like to call me; but
what a loss to the young mind of eighteen or
twenty years must be the absence of all that sense
of reverence and tenderness which the mystery of
the infinite gives. Religion has been very much to
me, and I am still profoundly religious in a vague
way. It will be a very ugly world when the religious
sense is dead in all children. For it is the poetry of
the young, that should colour all after-thought, —
or at least render cosmic emotions possible later on.

The Shinshu does seem to hold its own, or to

gain(?). But there are curious obstacles. The students of its schools are obliged to reverence the Head of the sect as a living Buddha, — wherefore modern ideas must be tabooed, or modified and distorted. (The same thing, I believe, in the University; for at one time it was seriously proposed to secure John Fiske for the chair of Philosophy, but the discovery that the evolution theory assailed the Imperial prerogatives ended *that* project. I am also told there is no chance of having the Spencerian or any other form of Western philosophy ably taught in Japan for similar reasons — much as they pretend to follow Spencer.) But, as I was saying, what of the other sects of Buddhism? — the enormous ignorance, the hideous poverty, the corruption? . . .

Shinto, on the other hand, has native nobility. It seems to me in many ways a noble creed; and the absurdities of its records of the Gods are not, after all, greater than those of other faiths, — either Indian or Hebrew or Moslem. But the fox-temples and fox-rites and divinations and exorcism mixed up with it, seem to have much more influence than the real thing.

Finally Christianity offers the small choice of thirty-two different creeds. And the young man of the twenty-seventh year of Meiji is disgusted. He thinks of all these beliefs as various forms of mental disease, and cannot naturally be expected to believe, without a study in advance of his years, that all — even the most corrupt — are growths rooted in universal truth.

For the educated classes no religion seems to be

the certain goal. This means, not only that the whole moral experience of the past is being thrown overboard by that class, with nothing to replace it; but it means the rapid widening of an impassable gulf between the educated and the common people — the total separation of the head from the body, — or at best a sort of *nuke-kubi* future. A ghastly business!

What is there, after all, to love in Japan except what is passing away? There are fairer lands and skies; — there is a larger — a vastly larger life — as much larger as Sirius is larger than the moon. The charm was the charm of Nature in human nature and in human art, — simplicity, — mutual kindness, — child-faith, — gentleness, — politeness. These are evaporating more rapidly than ether from an uncorked bottle. And then what will there be but memories? The one tolerably good thing yet is the cottony softness of all this life; — the let-alone spirit of it, — for it even hates work with smiles and pretty words. This *is* good, — although it means the absence of large feelings, sympathies, comprehensions. As the stronger the light, the blacker the shadow it casts, so are our highest feelings offset by evil ones of startling power. One does not meet these in Japan. But how long will this condition last? The bonds are only now being cast off; — the cage doors opened. By and by the games will begin — *circenses*.

I am through most of the indexing. Really it was more pleasant than I had anticipated — gives one such an exaggerated idea of the extent of one's work.

The book seemed to be enormous by the time I got to "Zuijin." An enormous illusion — or, rather, evocation of the ghost of old Japan.

Ever most truly,

LAFCADIO HEARN.

February 18, 1894.

DEAR CHAMBERLAIN, — Just received your delightful translations, and letter.

In these short poems, of which I think the two specimens forwarded among the most charming possible, I have always thought the Japanese just as great as they are great in art, — in colour-pictures of precise times, moods, sensations. Very, very great! Each little poem gives one the same ghostly shock that the wonderful print does — only (as in these instances) it is more subtle; for it penetrates well into the heart, — thinly, perhaps, like an acupuncture, but none the less effectively. No: these brief Japanese poems are very wonderful. I felt that when I first read the versions of De Rosny in America, and afterwards when I read your "Classical Poetry," and the more I learn of the old life, the more the conviction of the value of that poetry grows upon me. Without knowing anything about the language, I feel competent to make one observation: the poems are characterized by what we know to be among the highest qualities of Western verse, — including one of the qualities most marked in Gautier, in Rossetti, in all great modern poets, — self-control. This self-control means concentration, means simplicity, means artistic reserve,

— and therefore power. The race-character at its
antique best seems to speak here, — just enough
and no more. Of course I suppose the study of colour, form, or melody in words is not at all comparable to Western art; — the self-control is in the utterance only, the thought. The measure permits only
the briefest possible utterance, and thus assists the
art by the *cothurne étroit.*

As to genius, I am a profound, earnest believer
in genius: I think any student of the new psychology
must be. The literary curse of the century is the
want of genius, coupled with extraordinary perfection in the mastery of all mechanical form. Thousands can write absolutely correct flat prose in a
century of different forms of verse, — not only *can*,
but *do*. Hence, *what* a relief to read a ballad by
Kipling!

How genius exactly works, we shall perhaps never
know. It means, though, exactly what you say —
seeing, and seeing in lightning flashes. Perhaps it
also means remembering, — *seeing retrospectively*,
through rifts in the curtain of the past. The faculty
is, of course, explainable only by the ancestral
hypothesis: by any other, we should be obliged to
go back to the old mediæval ideas for any account
of it.

Spencer makes a very beautiful illustration of
ancestral memory. Imagine a number of coloured
negatives (each photo. negative representing an experience of a different individual); and superimpose
them. The light still passes through; the images
are blurred more or less; certain details are lost;

but the general arrangement of the landscapes, their general tone and character, and colour, will still be dimly perceptible.

If this be the general symbolic result, may there not be such exceptions as might correspond to extraordinary lucidity of the photo-impressions and their colours in the possible supposition of negatives superimposed. These might account for certain perceptivities; and, again, there would necessarily ensue the phenomena of *strengthening*, — I mean decupling or centupling a transmitted power by certain fortuitous combinations in the memory — superimposition. Only vague suggestions; but I fancy they must roughly symbolize real facts.

Ever most faithfully,
LAFCADIO HEARN.

February 25, 1894.

DEAR CHAMBERLAIN, — . . . Indeed I should like very much to read that book by Loti, and shall take good care of it. I have Pater's "Appreciations" — would you like them to read? They have fine and subtle quality, and penetrating needle-points of truth; but I fear the general effect would disappoint you. Still the book has become so famous, that I think you might like to look at it. Anything I have you would like to read is always ready for shipment to you at the drop of a postal.

Two gleams of sunshine: —

You know there are men in this world that we love the first time we look at their faces, and never cease to love. I have met two such Japanese, —

needless to say never of *this* generation. The first
was Koteda Yasusada, now Governor of Niigata.
The second was Akizuki of Aidzu, an old man of
seventy-three, Professor of Chinese in the college.
I have often spoken of him.

He came to-day to see my boy (for he had been
away in Tokyo for some months). He brought gifts,
— a beautiful plum-tree in blossom, a most quaint
vase full of sake, and (most precious of all) two kakemono written by himself, inscribed with poems in
honour or in congratulation — what should I say
— of *Herun-San-no-o-ko-san.* He is a great Chinese
scholar, and famous for calligraphy too. So I had
this Soul of old Japan in my house for an hour; —
and the Presence, like the perfume of the plum-
blossoms, filled all the place and made it somewhat divine. Were there real Kami, I know they
would come and smile and look just like that divine
old man with his long grey beard.

The other gleam of sun was less bright, but it
was cheerful, — a visit to the jiujutsu private
school. Its teacher, Arima Sumihito, long of the
Nobles' School, is at all events a man. He is a pupil
of Kano, speaks English perfectly, — the handsomest Japanese I know, — cynically polite, — a fine
aristocrat: in short, one of those types so different
from the rest that I never thought before of writing about him. The type is impossibly reserved, —
not attractive, — but decidedly interesting. Well,
I studied some marvellous things during the exhibition there; and as I watched the jiujutsu, and
studied the surroundings, the idea came to me of

a possible normal change, or reform, in the whole existing educational system. "Here," I said, "is the old samurai school, — severely simple, healthy, lovable, romantic. The students delight in this return to the old ways, — the squatting on the floor, — the perfect natural freedom, — the faultless discipline of self-control, — the irreproachable politeness, — the brotherhood between teacher and pupil —" Now could not schools be established for *all* teaching in this very way? I think they could. It seems to me now an enormous mistake for the Japanese to have tried to adopt the Western school-system, to have built monstrosities of brick, and destroyed the Oriental relation of pupil to teacher.

DEAR CHAMBERLAIN, — I'm wondering whether you sent me the *Herald* article about Leland's book with a single or double purpose — I mean with a possibly suggestive literary purpose. I thought of talking to you a long time ago about a book, — not of the Leland sort at all, but a book of extraordinary or curious personal impressions, touching only certain tones and colours of life. However, I don't feel ripe enough yet.

Leland is quite a wonderful person; but I confess to a slight ill-will towards him. The reason has been his belittling of Borrow. Now Borrow was as much greater in Gypsy matters than Leland, as Leland is greater than a police-reporter. Borrow's life was a romance; his book "The Bible in Spain," despite its forbidding title, is a delight; and his stories are

wonderful. Leland tries to belittle him. Leland's
book on the Gypsy is the dullest ever written, —
worse incomparably than even Simpson's, and Borrow prepared everything for him.

By the way, you have read Mérimée's " Carmen,"
of course, — matchless story! — but would you not
like to read the sweetest and tenderest gypsy-story
ever written? If you have not read it, let me most
humbly pray and beseech you to read J. Sheridan
Le Fanu's "Bird of Passage: A Love-Story." You
will thank me, if you read it. It is very short.
Sheridan Le Fanu is a very great artist at his best.
His "My Uncle Silas" is a terrible, but tremendously powerful novel.

DEAR CHAMBERLAIN, — I am absolutely unpro-
ductive now, hovering between one thing and another, — sometimes angry with men, — sometimes
with the Gods. But I think of many things. I have
been long writing down extraordinary passages from
the compositions of students. Some are simply
queer, — some interest because showing a thought
that is not as our thought, — some are beautiful,
as in the old Chinese utterance about the firma-
ment: —

"What thought is so high as it is, — what mind
is so wide?"

What most pleases me are subjects taken from
the memories and thoughts of the boys themselves.
I have some beauties I know to be original; and I
have often thought of an essay about them.

But of a few I am in doubt. Can this be original?

— (*Subject: "What men remember longest."*)

"When I was only four years old, my dear, dear mother died. It was a winter's day. The wind was blowing through the bushes and trees round our house. There were no leaves on the trees. Quails in the distance whistled with a melancholy sound. I remember that as my mother was lying in bed, a little before she died, I gave her a sweet orange. She smiled and took it and ate it. It was the last time she smiled. From that moment when she ceased to breathe until to-day, sixteen years have elapsed. But to me the time is as a moment. The winds that blew when my mother died, blow still; — the quails utter the same cries; — all things are as then. But my mother never will come back again."   L. H.

March 4, 1894.

Pendulum to the right.

DEAR CHAMBERLAIN, — After all, the contract did *not* go back to H. M. & Co. My little wife was too shrewd. She knew nothing about what the letter contained, but she saw by my face that I was in a bad humour. So, after duly addressing the big envelope, she posted it — in a drawer — and asked me to-day whether I should not like to have withheld some of that correspondence. You see she understands me very well. I concluded not to send it on finding it had not been sent, but to await the results of the letters. Besides, after all, I am not sure that the return of the contract would have much affected H. M. & Co.

I have given up all idea, for the time being, of ever living in Tokyo. Really, as you have more than once suggested, I think I should find it out of the frying-pan into the fire. Besides, I wonder whether Japanese life has not spoiled me for any other — at least in the temperate zone. The freedom of it, the *laissez-faire*, the softness of things, the indifference, the lonesomeness, really constitute a sort of psychological tropics. Tropical life in lat. 15°–14° destroyed permanently my capacity for physical effort; — this psychological tropic of Japanese life may have already unfitted me to endure anything resembling conventions and unpleasant contacts.

I suppose, after all, that the populations of the Open Ports of the Far East must be much more afflicted with *bourgeoisme* (if I can coin such a word) than any others, — partly because composed almost exclusively of the mercantile middle-classes, who are made by conventions, and partly because the conventions themselves, transplanted to exotic soil, must there obtain a savage vigour unknown in the mother country. Ideas and opinions must be petrified; "it has been suggested;" "it is hoped;" "it is the opinion of the community;" — must be phrases of enormous weight there, — primitive war-clubs, — stone celts! Oh, dear, I am blessed after all in not having to live where people think they *must*, only because "it has been suggested," — while within themselves thinking also, "What an infernal humbug!" There is something much worse than dwelling in a community governed by the revolver, or by Judge Lynch. And that, for me, would be to hold a situation of absolute dependence in a community regulated by lawyers, codes, contracts, and opinions dry and tough as Mexican jerked beef. Besides this conception of an open port, how innocently comfortable Japanese life is!

But why is it that these horrors do not exist in Roman Catholic countries? Do you find them in Italy, or in Spain, or in France? Zola wrote some articles once, "Mes Haines," well worth reading. He had one on religious influences in literature, — holding that Protestant influences cut-and-dried and mummified and devitalized everything, — that emotional power and high imagination must be sought for elsewhere than in Protestant countries. Here, of course, Zola fell into the inevitable fallacy of a sweeping statement. It is n't all true. But there is much truth in it. Protestantism-Puritanism — substituting conventions for spiritual beliefs — has had the most repressive effect upon social freedom and upon imaginative art. Milton towers up, as one talks, and Goethe, and a host. But Italy made Milton, and Faust is profoundly mediæval; and I think we would find that the modern English writers we love most are all men who have felt the older influences, or who have emancipated themselves from all conventions. Ruskin, Rossetti, Symonds, — how pagan or Catholic! — Browning, how bathed and interpenetrated with the soul of Italy and of the Middle Ages! — or go back further, and compare the feeling of Coleridge, Keats, Byron, Shelley, with the greys of Cowper and Wordsworth.

Is not the truth also that we English or Americans hate our "awful orderliness" (to use Kipling's word) — and all the shams and conventions that we perforce obey, and rush to Italy or to France as soon as we can get free? — (Do you know Curtis's "Howadji in Syria"? — there is such a beautiful comparison of the human soul to a camel, — the camel that weeps when approaching a city.) But what cities do city-haters hate? Venice, Florence, Milan, Rome, Genoa? — Seville, Granada, Cadiz, Alcantara? — Marseilles, Paris, Rouen? — No, — but Liverpool, Manchester, London; New York, Chicago, Boston. I believe Wordsworth alone ever found London beautiful. What London really is seems to me to have been exactly felt only by Doré. (You know his "London" which the English did not like at all.) And I say this even while wishing to be in London again, like Private Ortheris, — "for the sights of 'er and the smells of 'er," — "orange-peel and hasphalte and gas coming in over Vauxhall bridge."

But I suppose the ultimate value of conventions is this: — that they shrivel up all souls except the strongest, and that any one able to dwell among them and abide by them, and yet remain purely himself, becomes a wonder that no Latin country can produce.

I found in " Wilhelm Meister's Travels," one of these marvellous little stories by Goethe which have a hundred different meanings. Perhaps you know "The New Melusine." . . . I repeat some of the facts only to suggest one application. There was a man a fairy loved; — and she told him she must either say good-bye, or that he must become little like herself, and go to dwell with her in her father's kingdom. She made him very, very, very small, by putting a gold ring upon his finger. Then they entered into their tiny world. Everything in the palace of the fairy king was unimaginably pretty, and the man was petted greatly by the fairy-people, and had everything given to him which he could desire. He had a pretty child, too; and the old king was good to him. After a time, however, being ungrateful and selfish, he got tired of all this; he dreamed of having been a giant. He supplied himself with gold for a journey, and then managed to file the ring off his finger, — which made him big again, — and he ran away to spend the gold in riotous living. He did other horrible things, which you may remember. The character of the fairy was altogether Japanese — don't you think so? And the man was certainly a detestable fellow.

I have become much more interested in the jiu-jutsu teacher I spoke of the other day, and I want to try to cultivate him. His slightly frigid politeness tells me that I shall never get very close to him; but he is certainly a remarkably "fine gentleman" as well as an amiable man in a general sense, and perhaps I shall have some experiences worth writing about to you.

Of Seki-Baba, whose images used to be placed under bridges, and of the bridge-superstitions about coughs and colds, you may some day like to know. They are naïve and interesting.

While the winter lasted the weather was heavenly. Now is the season of close warm air, mould, rain, and (what you don't especially like) atrocious smells. I wonder what Lowell thought of that awful cynicism of yours in "Things Japanese" about that in Tokyo which "appeals to the nose."

Faithfully,   LAFCADIO HEARN.

March 5, 1894.

DEAR CHAMBERLAIN,— ... Oh! what a pleasure to get the Loti. I have only read the Japanese sketches; and they are really very fine. Of course Loti is very unjust to the Japanese woman, and has not yet even learned that to understand the beauty of another race so remote as the Japanese, requires both time and study. It does not strike a European at the first glance. He knows also nothing about their morals or manners, and his divinations are all wrong on these subjects. But aside from all his errors, is not the *general impression given* by "Femmes Japonaises," dainty, tender, graceful, mysterious and queer. His judgment of the peasant woman, of the Japanese interiors, of the love of children, are all very pleasing, however we may find fault with the details. The trip through the Kyushu country is perfection itself: I could smell the rice-fields, and cedar groves. *That* is genius! He says strange things betimes, however: —

"Il se forme à la longue dans l'air, un ensemble impersonnel d'âmes antérieures; — quelque chose comme *un fluide ancestral*, qui *plane* et qui veille sur les vivants."

(I might stagger here; I am not sure. These are *our* thoughts of the thing. But are they Japanese? I am not sure; but I *think not*. I think the ideas of the ancestral ghosts remain distinctly separated in the Japanese mind. I mean the mind of the common people. The synthetizing mind of the higher intellect might have such an ethereal notion — not that of the peasant.)

"Ces dames marchent les talons en dehors, ce qui est une chose de mode, et les reins légèrement courbes *en avant*(?). *Ce qui leur vient sans doute d'un abus héréditaire de révérences.*"

Not hereditary at all; but the impulse to make a joke was irresistible, and also artistic.

There is a delicious humour also in Loti betimes, — whether conscious or unconscious, I cannot say; but I am perfectly certain that you will not be able to help laughing after you have read the following lines: —

"Leur musique, qui les passionne, est pour nous étrange et lointaine comme leur âme. Quand des jeunes filles se réunissent le soir, pour chanter et jouer . . . nous ressentons, après le premier sourire étonné, l'impression de quelque chose de très inconnu et de très mystérieux *que des années d'acclimatement intellectuel n'arriveraient pas à nous faire complétement saisir.*"

If you don't laugh at *that*, please tell me; the *n'arriveraient pas* to me is delicious.

I may attempt a little criticism, *entre nous*.

"Surtout elles essayent de se dérober par le rire à *l'effroi du surnaturel.*"

(A Western thought, — Breton perhaps, Celtic, — not of the Orient.)

"Des superstitions vielles comme le monde, les plus étranges et les plus sombres, effroyables à entendre conter les soirs."

(A Celtic or Norse feeling applied to vague ideas of what Japanese might *seem* to believe, but do not believe at all. The deep fear, the nightmare fear of the supernatural, *has never been known in Japan.* It is not in the race.)

I will write again as soon as I have read the rest of the book. . . .   LAFCADIO HEARN.

March 6, 1894.

DEAR CHAMBERLAIN, — Well, I read Loti all through in bed last night — and dropped asleep at last to dream of the *Venise fantasque et tremblotante.*

Before talking of the book especially I want to utter my heterodoxies and monstrosities in your ear. You will not be pleased, I fear; but truth is truth, however far it be from accepted standards.

To me the Japanese eye has a beauty which I think Western eyes have not. I have read nasty things written about Japanese eyes until I am tired of reading them. Now let me defend my seemingly monstrous proposition.

Miss Bird has well said that when one remains long in Japan, one finds one's standard of beauty changing; and the fact is true of other countries than Japan. Any *real* traveller can give similar experiences. When I show beautiful European engravings of young girls or children to Japanese, what do they say? I have done it fifty times, and whenever I was able to get a criticism, it was always the same: — "The faces are nice, — all but the eyes: the eyes are too big, — the eyes are monstrous." We judge by our conventions. The Orient judges by its own. Who is right?

There are eyes and eyes, in all countries — ugly and beautiful. To make comparisons of beauty we must take the most beautiful types of the West and East. If we do this, I think we find the Orient is right. The most beautiful pair of eyes I ever saw — a pair that fascinated me a great deal too much, and caused me to do some foolish things in old bachelor days — were Japanese. They were not small, but very characteristically racial; the lashes were very long, and the opening also of the lids; — and the feeling they gave one was that of the eyes of a great wonderful bird of prey. — There are wonderful eyes in Japan for those who can see.

The eyelid is so very peculiar that I think its form decides — more than any other characteristic of the Far Eastern races — the existence of two entirely distinct original varieties of mankind. The muscular attachments are quite different, and the lines of the lashes, — indeed the whole outer anatomy.

One might ask mockingly whether to Japanese eyelids could be applied the Greek term *charitoblepharos*. I think it could. There is a beauty of the Japanese eyelid, quite rare, but very singular, — in which the lid-edge seems double, or at least marvellously grooved, — and the effect is a softness and shadowiness difficult to describe.

However, it seems to me that the chief beauty of a beautiful Japanese eye is in the peculiar anatomical arrangement which characterizes it. The ball of the eye is *not* shown, — the setting is totally hidden. The brown smooth skin opens quite suddenly and strangely over a moving jewel. Now in the most beautiful Western eyes the set of the ball into the skull is visible, — the whole orbed form, and the whole line of the bone-socket, — except in special cases. The mechanism is visible. I think that from a perfectly artistic point of view, the veiling of the mechanism is a greater feat on Nature's part. (I have seen a most beautiful pair of Chinese eyes, — that I will *never* forget.)

I don't mean to make any sweeping general rule. I only mean this: "Compare the most beautiful Japanese, or Chinese eye with the most beautiful European eye, and see which suffers by comparison." I believe the true artist would say "neither." But that which least shows the *machinery behind it* — the osteological and nervous machinery — now appears to me to have the greater charm. I dare say such eyes as I speak of are not common; but beautiful eyes are common in no country that I have ever visited.

And now I will presume to express my opinion about another heresy, — that a white skin is the most beautiful. I think it is the *least* beautiful. The Greeks never made a *white* statue, — they were always painted.

Naturally each race thinks itself the most beauti- ful. But we must not think about race in such matters at all, — only about colour *per se*, and its effect upon the æsthetic *colour-sense* in us, derived — as we all know through Mr. Grant Allen's popularization of a most complex subject — from ancestral experience in food choice. The sensation of a beautiful sunset and that of a ripe apple is not so different in origin as might be supposed.

But to appreciate the beauty of coloured skins, it is not simply enough to travel, — one must become familiar with the sight of them through months and years. (So strong our prejudices are!) And at last when you perceive there are human skins of real gold (living statues of gold, with *blue hair*, like the Carib half-breeds!) — and all fruit tints of skins, — orange, and yellow, and peach-red, and lustrous browns of countless shades; — and all colours of metal, too, — bronzes of every tone, — one begins to doubt whether a white skin is so fine! (If you don't believe these colours, just refer to Broca's pattern-books, where you will find that all jewel-colours exist in eyes, and all fruit-colours and metal colours in skins. I could not believe my own eyes, till I saw Broca.) I have seen people who had grass-green emeralds instead of eyes, and topazes and rubies for eyes. And I have seen races with blue hair.

I do *not* think the Japanese skin remarkably beautiful: the "amber" of Arnold's imagination does not exist in this archipelago, — one must go to the tropics for that. The Italian or Spanish brown seems to me much richer and finer. But I am only talking in general. It seems to me a sort of egg-

colour. Well Mahomet says that is the colour of the
houris, — but it is nothing to other colours that
exist.

Now for jet-black,—the smooth velvety black skin
that remains cold as a lizard under the tropical sun.

It seems to me extremely beautiful. If it is beautiful in Art, why should it not be beautiful in Nature?
As a matter of fact, it *is*, and has been so acknow-
ledged even by the most prejudiced slave-owning
races.

Either Stanley—or Livingstone, perhaps — told
the world that after long living in Africa the sight
of white faces produced something like fear. (And
the Evil Spirits of Africa are white.) — Well, even
after a few months alone with black faces, I have
felt that feeling of uncomfortableness at the sight
of white faces. Something ghostly, terrible seemed
to have come into those faces that I had never even
imagined possible before. I felt for a moment the
black man's terror of the white. At least I think I
partly realized what it was.

You remember the Romans lost their first battles
with the North through sheer fear. *Oculi caerulii et
truces*, — *rutilae comae*, — *magna corpora!* — The
fairer, — the weirder, — the more spectral, — the
more terrible. Beauty there is in the North, of its
kind. But it is surely not comparable with the
wonderful beauty of colour in other races.

As I write two queer memories come up before me.

(1) On board a West Indian steamer. — We had
stopped at some queer island out of our route,
to the disgust of the captain, who wanted cargo so

badly that he had to take it where he could get it.
— Then it was sugar and lemons. A brown man
came on board, the owner of the cargo, and tried
to talk English. We could not understand him at
first. He made amazing efforts, and at last his talk
became clear enough to understand. Yet he had
been a graduate both of some English university
and of Heidelberg. He had begun even to lose his
native language. Only at intervals of months could
he speak with whites. He spoke only the patois of
the negroes in the valley where he lived alone. His
plantation was worth £10,000.

(2) In Martinique, — in an unvisited, unknown
forgotten corner of the island, — a sort of happy
valley between mountains of this shape, — like the
Mountains of the Moon. Two whites — brothers —
alone there for fourteen years. They almost killed
me with kindness, for the sake of the chat. *"Et vous
êtes Anglais! Mais c'est drôle!"* Then in the night,
under the palms, we sat; and one of the brothers got
a dusty fiddle out of the Lord-of-Zombis-knows-
where; and began to play and sing a song about an
Englishman, of which I can remember only one
verse (mocking the English accent as he sang): —

> "L'autre nuit j'ai fait un rêv-e,
>   Un rêve qui me plaît;
> J'avais mis dans mon oreil-le
>   Le canon d'un pistolet,
> Et comme je pressais la manivel-le
>   La balle a pris son cours [pronounce course]
> Et je sentais sauter ma cervel-le —
>   Que ne peut-on rêver toujours!
>   Que ne peut-on rêver toujours!

(Basso extra profondo)

I wish I could get the whole of that song; it was very, very funny,—but in the tropics people are so lazy you can never get them to copy anything for you.

Perhaps the French poet was thinking of the Englishman who hung himself just because of the trouble of dressing and undressing every day. I sympathize with that Englishman. I, too, would rather hang myself than be obliged to dress and undress *à la mode*.

I wanted to write about Loti, but I shall wait till next time. Sufficient for the day is, etc.

Faithfully,
LAFCADIO.

Ah! que ne peut-on rêver toujours!
Que ne peut-on rêver tou
JOURS!

March 7, 1894.

DEAR CHAMBERLAIN,— There is very, *very* great art in Loti,—*very* wonderful art: —

Je me souviens aussi de ces silences quelquefois, après qu'elle avait dit une chose profonde, *dont le sens paraissait se prolonger au milieu de ce calme* . . .

I can think of nothing so exquisite in any English writer. The nearest approach to it that I recall are the lines in Rossetti's supremely divine "Staff and Scrip," —

And when each anthem failed and ceased,
It seemed that the last chords
Still sang the words. . . .

But how much subtler still is Loti's prose!

Nevertheless, I must confess I dislike Loti very much in this book. The Carmen-Sylva papers, with

all their art, do not seem to me the work of a gentleman. I should not wish to be intimate with the man
capable of writing them, — or, at least, of printing
them. In this case, indeed, one must distinguish
between the artist and the man. The former is a
wonder and worthy of all highest praise; — the
latter seems to me a sort of traitor and coward,
ready to sell anything for the pure egotism of
announcing himself once a royal guest. Nay, I
would go further even than that. I do not think
that on the moral side here there is any difference
between Loti and that Russian *demi-monde* who
published in England the history of her amours with
the Grand Duke. One feels even that Loti would
have done as badly if he dared, but that he is re-
strained by conventions of an order which all but
those who have nothing to lose must obey. To give
the world the history of all a woman's little weaknesses — her weaknesses in literature or in speech
or in health — would surely be thought nasty even
if the woman were only an ordinary person of the
middle class; — I cannot think but that it is even
worse when the woman happens to be a queen.
That "Carmen Sylva" made herself a topic of
public converse, by even writing for American
magazines, is true. But is it not just for that reason
that a professional man of letters should have been
silent about all that he could not praise? No: I fear
the dulness of Loti's moral sense is in inverse ratio
to the extraordinary sensibility of his perceptivities.
Take, for example, page 96; and remember that the
queen and the woman was then very, very sick, —

on the verge of insanity or death, — and how is it possible to judge of Loti's printed lines about "*puerilité,* — *blasphème d'enfant,* — *déception inattendue,*" without extreme disgust! The after-revelation does not mend matters.

But, leaving the man and his contemptible conceit out of the question, the book is a treat. The coloured pictures of Venice are certainly miracles, and one can never forget them. And there are beauties at every few pages of extreme rarity.

By the way, I am so sorry you have not read Loti's "Roman d'un Spahi" that I will venture to suggest that you ask Hanawa whether he cannot lend you a copy. He used to have one, which I gave him. — I would like you to read those earlier works of Loti, without thinking of the man except as a wonderful nervous machinery. — (As I write these lines, there comes upon me the vague unutterably displeasing after-taste of those Sylva sketches, — the sense of sickness and sorrow and all that refinement and tenderness should guard from view, — caged in long primer for public show!)

By the way, *why* can we never get out a novel so tastily as the French do? See how everything takes colour and power and beauty from the clear, large type, and grand spacing, and broad margin! But we are not enough artists in style yet. When we are, perhaps we shall set our jewels better.

Shall I not, in returning Loti, also send Pater? Many thanks for the loan of Loti.

Ever faithfully,

Lafcadio.

March 9, 1894.

DEAR CHAMBERLAIN, — I'm trying to write an essay — no, a fantastico-philosophical sketch — about Mirrors and Souls. Especially Souls. Which causes me to think about Mrs. James's version of the "Matsuyama Kagami."

Who is Mrs. James? I have read her version about fifteen times, and every time I read it, it affects me more. And I can't help thinking that the woman who could thus make the vague Japanese incident so beautiful must have a tender and beautiful soul, — whoever she is, — whether missionary or not. Of course a great deal of the charm is helped by the work of the Japanese artist, — I suppose the same supernatural being who drew the pictures for Urashima. I think more of those pictures, love them more, than any engraving ever printed in *L'Art* or *L'Illustration*. But of course to know how magical they really are, — how very extraordinary they are, — one must have lived in Japan a good while.

"Dai-Kon" for *Dai Konrei*, I suppose, — the Great Wedding. Their Imperial Majesties have given us all — teachers and functionaries — the sum of *fifty yen*, wherewith to make ourselves jocund. At the school a new Japanese song was sung; and we all bowed to the pictures of their Augustnesses, and then there were military salutes, and then, in the refectory, we drank the Imperial healths. (The ceremony of bowing is much less elaborate and graceful than in the ordinary middle schools. Only two bows are given, instead of six.)

Then "Ten-no-Heika-Banzai!" — and such a yell!
— like a real college-yell in the West. "Ten-no-
Heika-Banzai!" — not a yell, the second time, —
but a clear roar, that did my heart good to hear. I
wondered what the *third* cheer would be like. "Ten-
no-Heika-Banzai!" A tremendous roar followed and
suddenly broke into a furious song, — the song of
the overthrow of the Tokugawa dynasty. "They are
very, very much excited," said one of the teachers,
— "and that song is not a good song; it is vulgar!"
I tried to get the song; but every one to whom I
applied made unfavourable criticisms about it.
What the fault was, I can't imagine; but the song
went on till I thought the roof surged up and down
at every lilt in it. It was a very quick, swinging,
devil-may-care sort of a song, — not at all like the
solemn military measures of to-day. — Then the
pendulum moved a little more to the right. It
always does when I hear such singing. I think then,
the Soul lives; — while *that* remains there is always
hope.

To-night a procession of students with E-NOR-
MOUS lanterns, — and then an entertainment at
the school. What it will be like, I don't know. I am
going to see, — and will tell you all about it to-
morrow.

Do you think I am right or wrong about the following matter? I am asked advice sometimes, and
I urge those who ask it to follow a course of practical science or of medicine, and to leave law, literature, and philology alone (unless, in the case that
they seem to have extraordinary natural talent

for languages). The other day I got a letter from Kyoto, full of English mistakes, from a student who wanted to know about taking a philological course; — and I wrote him, very strongly advising him to study anything else by preference. The utter incapacity of most of the students to turn literary and language studies to any high account seems to me proof that only rare talents should be even allowed the chance to follow such studies.

Saturday, 10th March: — This morning I returned home from the college at 2.30, — after a night of curious festivities. About 6.00 on Friday afternoon the lantern procession left the college. There were about 400 students, — each carrying a small red lantern, — and to every hundred there was a monstrous egg-shaped red lantern, borne at the head of the column. The teachers and students sang their new song, and other songs through the city, and shouted "Banzai." At nine they returned to the college, and the festivities began.

These were chiefly theatrical, with some recitation thrown in. Unfortunately the college has no real hall, — only an enormous shed used for drilling-purposes in wet weather, and the shed is not enclosed at the sides. Kneeling on the floor, with the north wind on one's back, from 9.00 P. M. till 2.00 A.M. was trying. Still I find I *can outkneel* the Japanese *in yofuku.*

A word about the performances.

The students had arranged a nice little stage, and some scenery. The performance opened with *sam-urai* sword-songs, — each young man having the appropriate costume, with a white band about his hair, sleeves strung back, etc. This was greatly and deservedly applauded.

Then came a comedy. Some peasants appeared from different sides, singing real peasant songs, met, greeted each other, and squatted down in the middle of an imaginary field. Surveyors come to survey. Peasants protest, interfere, attack, — the instruments are slung about, — a great fight occurs; — policemen run in, and arrest all parties concerned. Next scene shows the police court. The trial is, of course, made very funny by the answers and protests of the peasants. Just after the judge has pronounced sentence of two months' imprisonment and costs comes a telegram announcing the Imperial Wedding-anniversary. Prisoners are discharged; and judge, attorneys, police, peasants, and surveyors dance a dance of exultation. The acting in this piece seemed to me very fine: I was able to appreciate the excellence of the peasants' parts.

To not bore you with too many details, I will only mention one remarkable series of subjects — what subjects? *Je vous le donne en mille.* — Why Commodore Perry and the Shogunate. The Commodore speaks English, and is surrounded by armed marines. Shogun's interpreter asks him, "Why have you come to this country?" Perry makes appropriate answer, explains, — says he has a letter from the Great American People. Interpreter reads letter. Replies that the letter is too difficult to answer at once, — so much time will be required. . . . "Sir,

next year come to Nagasaki, and wait there for the
Shogun's order. Do you know Nagasaki?" Perry
answers that he knows Nagasaki, but does not
propose to know the Shogun. He will return to
await the *Emperor's* orders.

Next scene, Ronins, Samurai, aged teacher.
Aged teacher advises his young men what to do.
Times are about to change. The duty will be to
work, — to work earnestly to make Japan great.

Last scene. Banquet of Ministers in Tokyo.
One student very cleverly represented Count Ito.
The Minister of England arises and makes a speech
about — the Imperial Wedding-festival. The French
Minister speaks on the same subject in French.
The German in German. The Chinese in Chinese.
The Russian Minister, the Spanish, and the Italian,
do not, however, speak in their own tongues. The
speeches are humorous; but more humorous still the
interpreter's part, by a young man with a magnificent voice, ringing like a gong, — who imitates,
with very artistic exaggeration, the solemn musical
antique method of reading official texts.

I may also mention a really magnificent Daikokumai — Kyūshū style, quite different from anything in Izumo, and extremely picturesque in costume and movement. Also samurai in raincoats,
disguised as peasants, singing a very small weird
humble song in a field, with their swords hidden, —
waiting for Demons, who are duly slaughtered.

Well, you would be bored if I told you any more
on paper in this mere hasty fashion. Suffice to say
the evening was a very pleasant one for me. I could

not understand the dialogue, but I could understand the acting. It seemed to me very good indeed, — like the acting of Latin students. I do not think English students are naturally good actors at all. The enormous difference in the acting of French and of English boys was strongly impressed on me in early days.

Then I could but remark the extremely strong national feeling that characterized the greater part of the performance, — the real enthusiasm of the young men, — but always with the fond regret for old samurai days, — sword-days. Whatever the officials be, the students certainly have the feeling that should be the strength of Japan.

At a little after 2.00 I fled, — too many students urging me to drink sake. I had to drink about fifteen cups, and have a headache as I write.

Faithfully,
LAFCADIO HEARN.

"The Pipes of Hamelin"

Notes — Extracts — (This is *not* a *composite.*)

"There were lived so large rats that cats could not treat them as an enemy. They increased in great many number, and all cats of town ran away to far-distance. Then the rats were free to steal all foods which put on a table for gentleman. Town-folk appealed to Town-hall, but Hall-men could not conquer.

"Therefore they advertised *that if a man would have been subdued the adversity of rats*, they shall pay him ten thousand pieces of gold. There come encient man.

" . . . Town'smen sorrowed and celebrated religiously that mount to *protect* their town." (I can't quite get the idea here, can you?)

The *following* extracts are taken from a composition to which I gave 100 marks. There were scarcely any errors, but the *variations* are amusing: —

"He took a small pipe from his pocket, and put it to his mouth. When he piped, all the rats came out of their nests and ran through the street. *He ran after them.* The faster they ran, the faster he pursued, etc., etc.

"They said they should give him only fifty pieces of gold. He became very angry, because they had broken their promise. *But he pretended as if he were not angry*, and said, 'I will show you some magic,' and he began to pipe again. Then the Mayor and all the people could neither move nor speak. All the children came from their schools, etc.

"The children were never seen again. *It became a custom in that city to celebrate a festival* [*Matsuri?*] *once a year for them.*"

(How Japanesy!)

March 13, 1894.

DEAR CHAMBERLAIN, — Can't wait for your answer any longer, — wherefore here goes Pater with Loti, for which renewed thanks. The essay of Pater on Wordsworth seems to me very beautiful — the most beautiful thing ever written on Wordsworth; — that on Feuillet's "La Morte," and that on

Coleridge are also fine. That on Rossetti is very disappointing, indeed, — infinitely inferior to the fine paper in the "Encyclopædia Britannica," — a case, in short, of IN-appreciation. But you will be charmed with the Wordsworth paper.

I forgot to tell you a funny episode of the students' theatricals. The Minister of France forgot his *rôle;* but with admirable presence of mind instantly supplied the gap in memory by reciting very rapidly, with appropriate gesture, —

> *Maître Corbeau, sur un arbre perché*
> *Tenait dans son bec un fromage, etc.*

When I, early in the dawn, do open my door and do feel the whiff of the cold, I think of Death. For Death is cold. Warmth is a great vibration; the less the vibration, the less warmth, the less life, the less thinking. In the Sun one would "think like h—," to use a picturesque Americanism, whereas in outer space, there would be absolute death. I have been told that all vibration ceases at 200 degrees below Zero? Then 200 degrees below Zero would be Nirvana. Now I love Buddhism; but the idea of perfect bliss being only possible at 200 degrees below Zero is too much for my nerves at present. Mild as the winter has been it is too long for me. — I have only two metaphysical consolations:

(1) That thought, as motion, has been proven incomparably lower than other modes of apparently non-sentient force.

(2) That perfectly extinct Buddhas, like Pragnakuta, return at will and become visible to hear the preaching of the Law, — *ergo*, they have power

of motion to escape from 200 degrees below Zero, and are under no necessity — to seek existence at 1,000,000 degrees Fahrenheit.

There is some possibility of a golden mean, apparently.

Speaking of motion, another idea has come to me. We were talking some time ago about smallness as an inherent Japanese quality. What of slowness?

The complexity of life means much more than complexity of structure; it means quantity of movement. The greater the motion, the higher the life. This is the outset of physiological psychology.

The motion may be locomotion; but the highest motion of life is not, according to present knowledge, in locomotion. There is more force in a mathematical thought than in the flight of an eagle for a mile. The highest and swiftest forms of ascertained living motion are *thoughts*.

Well, it strikes me that something very extraordinary could be written by a competent philosopher on the comparative manifestations of Oriental and Occidental movement. I can only think now of a few points of comparison, — music (popular), dancing, — writing, — daily motions of workers. The result, however, is quite startling. Think of a Scotch reel, an Irish "wind that shakes the barley," our dance-tunes, especially the Celtic, and all the expressions of our physical life under excitement. Then think of the East!

A letter has just come from you which might have been written by Herbert Spencer. You have everlastingly and instantly revolutionized my view of the case. — Every point you make is irresistible, and very large. I am sorry I cannot disagree with you enough to try to say something new; but I can't. My view was very narrow, because made by the idea of a special class. Yes, — in England there is the highest freedom between certain lines. And I suppose the bourgeois class in all countries is dreadful enough. In French country towns it is Monsieur le Cure, Monsieur le Vicaire, Monsieur le Maire, Monsieur l'Intendant, and a few military and civil functionaries who are the Law and the State. The point about savages is especially fine; for even the remotest possible conception of perfect personal freedom can never have entered into a savage mind.

The great beauty of De Coulanges's work, "La Cité Antique," is perhaps in illustrating the tyranny of antique life. No Greek of the golden Greek prime ever enjoyed so much as the faintest sense of modern civic freedom. Even the Gods were not free.

Still, you will feel inclined to grant that where the English bourgeois do insist upon "awful orderliness" — the orderliness is at least something unparalleled for line and weight and gloom, — like unto the architecture of Egypt, — something in the style of Luxor and Hecatompylis!

Ever with best wishes and thanks,

LAFCADIO HEARN.

P. S. If you have any old Korean or Chinese stamps you don't want betimes, please send two or three for a little boy in Martinique, who writes wonderful letters to me.

March 14, 1894.

DEAR CHAMBERLAIN, — . . . What you said about English freedom ran back like a powder-trail, and ignited a host of evolutional ideas that are still glowing. Of course there ought to be in England not only as much but more freedom than in Latin countries, since the race is the Mother not only of freedom but of its modern ideals, and of all the philosophy of liberty of thought. — Perhaps the strong conventions which rule certain of its social territories act only as necessary curbs to check *extreme* tendencies to freedom of action.

Do not Bacon and Hobbes give one a very unpleasant sense of being scrutinized, or rather analyzed, without sympathy? Especially Bacon. I have read little of him, and I can admire him only as one admires superior cunning. Indeed Hobbes is much the more *humane* of the two, it seems to me. — I know Plato only through extracts, — the delightful dialogues, the criticism of Lewes, and the translation of the "Republic." But all the atmosphere about him seems to be delightful as the mysterious tenderness of a great mild summer's day.

Of a summer's day I happen to be thinking, because in re-reading your paper on pilgrimages, there came to me with a vividness, sharpened by the peculiar regret which pleasant things always leave after them, memories of a day of travel three summers ago. We had reached a broad river somewhere in Hiroshima Ken, and were waiting for a ferry-boat. As the boat came, a young pilgrim, all in white, joined us and went on board. The women, of whom there were a number, began to say to each other, "How pretty he is!" and I looked. Whether it was the costume or not, I cannot tell; but it seemed to me that I was looking at one of the handsomest boys I had ever seen. He was perhaps thirteen years old. Everybody began to question him, — was he alone? — any parents? — where from, etc. He answered laughing; but what the answers were I have forgotten: they left me, however, with the impression he had no kindred and was quite alone. Then those poor women and men, — very poor, I think, nearly all peasants, — all made up a little subscription for him. I gave him ten cents. He took it with a soft laugh; and looked straight at me from under the edge of his immense white hat; and the long black laughing eyes went right into my heart and stayed there till now. Then we left him behind. As I looked again at the picture in your book, this grey dead day, the dark rosy young face reappeared suddenly with its laughing eyes, — and the gold sheet of sun on the river's breadth, — and the sense of summer wind, — and the weird blue ghosts of the hills peaking into the empty sky.

Ever faithfully,
LAFCADIO HEARN.

March 19, 1894.

DEAR CHAMBERLAIN, — . . . There is a good deal of thinking — curious thinking — among these men-students. I find the fact of existence is a trouble to not a few. "Why am I in the world — Please tell me your views?"—these are the awful questions I am sometimes asked. I cannot forbear to cite a specimen-composition. It is queer,—is n't it? —

"For what purpose do men live in this world? From the time a man is born he drinks, eats, speaks, sees, hears, feels happy or sad, sleeps at night, rises in the morning. He is educated, he grows up, he marries, he has sons, he becomes old, his hair turns white, and he dies.

"What does he do all his life? His whole occupation in this world is only to eat and to drink, to sleep and to rise up. Why came he into this world? Was it to eat and drink? Was it to sleep? Every day he does the same thing;—yet he is not tired!

"When rewarded, he is glad. When pained, he is sad. When he gets rich, he is happy; when he becomes poor, he is very unhappy. Why is he sad or glad about his condition? Happiness and sadness are only temporary. Why does he study hard? No matter how great a scholar he may become, when he is dead, there remains nothing of him — only bones!" —

And observe that the author of the above is full of humour, life, and noisy fun. He it was who personated the Minister of France at the late banquet-act.

The composition brought a memory to me. A great crime which terrifies us by the revelation of the beast that hides far down, Minotaur-wise, in the unknown deeps of the human heart, sometimes makes one think like the above composition. All mysteries of pain and sorrow stir up afresh the awful three — Why? Whence? Whither?

Well, there had been a frightful crime committed. I slept and forgot the world and all things in the dead heavy sleep which men sleep in the tropics.

Midnight within forty hours of the Equator; and there was music that made people get out of their beds and cry.

The music was a serenade; — there were flutes and mandolins.

The flutes had dove-tones; and they purled and cooed and sobbed, — and cooed and sobbed and purled again; — and the mandolins, through the sweetness of the plaint, throbbed, like a beating of hearts.

The palms held their leaves still to listen. The warm wind, the warm sea, slept. Nothing moved but the stars and the fireflies.

And the melody said, more plainly than any speech articulate could ever say, —

"Do you not feel the Night in your heart, — the great sob of the joy of it? —

"And this strange fragrance that recalls the past, — the love of all the dead who will never love again, — being only dust, — feeding the roots of the palms?"

And I asked, "Why that wonderful, inexpressible, torturing sweetness of music?"

And they said, — "*The murderer of the girl has been acquitted. They are consoling his family!*"

Faithfully,

LAFCADIO HEARN.

March 24, 1894.

DEAR CHAMBERLAIN, — I kept another letter back for a few days, because it struck me that the musical experience therein recorded — which I tried to polish up a little — might' displease you. Reading it over again, however, it seems all right enough, — and excusable at least as an illustration of how extreme artistic sensitiveness, or, if you like better, sensuousness, may be conjoined with extraordinary and savage ferocity. Some recognition of this fact alone would help us to comprehend certain phenomena of the antique society, which yet faintly survive in Latin countries. — And surely there is a very great problem behind all such facts; which proves that the instinctive religious enmity to art was not altogether wrong.

Here comes the kindest letter from you, with some bad news (for I am always very sorry to hear you have a cold), — and a delicious little envelope full of exotic stamps, — and three numbers of the *Eclectic* which I am not to return but sure to enjoy very much. Please don't give yourself more trouble about stamps; I have quite enough — more than enough — to delight the little boy in Martinique. In New York I got him quite a nice collection of African, European, and Turkish stamps, — together with some Oriental. But you have sent a number that will fill gaps in his collection. Should you *like* Pater, it would please me to have you keep him; I have digested him, and will not really have any more need of him.

As yet I can't chat much about the *reviews*, not

having read anything except the paper on the Entrance of the Prussians into Paris. One thing in that essay sums up the whole French soul,—one phrase. I mean the exclamation of the woman who, after inspecting the new arrivals, exclaimed, "*C'est dégoûtant comme ils sont distingués!*" How Greek, how pagan that terrible intelligence is! I cannot help saying *terrible:* all perceptions which show powers superior to human passion are somewhat terrible. Then the question comes whether this inherent, innate power of sharply defining things as they are in themselves — this antique art faculty (for it is nothing else) — can have the same value for a race as the enthusiasms or beliefs or senses of duty which blind men to things as they are, and show them only things as they should be. — I don't think it would be safe to try to decide so complex a question now. It involves the relation of the faculties in question to the development of the applied sciences. But I can't help venturing this,—that I fancy the belief of the Russian peasant in the destiny of his race and the power of the Holy Ghost is at least as strengthening as any possible development of pure intelligence could be, in a time of national peril.

It has occurred to me that as the blue stamps are rare, you might like especially to send a couple of new ones to English friends. As I did not buy them, but had them given to me, you will not refuse them, I hope. I enclose also an uncancelled American stamp: as for cancelled Exposition-stamps, I can send you all you wish,—should you need them.

In the *Atlantic* you will find a paper entitled "Is the Musical Faculty Masculine?" — which should interest you. I do not know the writer; but she seems to know her Spencer as well as her Schopenhauer, — though quoting only the latter. And pray be patient with "Philip and his Wife." The interest may diminish in the mere story, but the study of the woman (Cecilia's) character is really like witchcraft — so perfect it seems to me. I thought there was only exactly one woman of that particular type in the world, and that I knew her; but Mrs. Deland must have seen *numbers* to write the sketch. For one character cannot give us a type in fiction: every "fictitious" creation of genius is a composite of interrelated impressions and experiences. — Well, every day I find my extraordinary people are, after all, only common types; and it makes me feel just as I used to feel when obliged to recognize that I knew nothing about some subject on which I had imagined myself pretty well informed. — Of reading: I wish I were able to take a year's rest from all anxieties, and spend a part of each leisure day in reading to you something you would like. But that can't be — so I can only offer one suggestion — the result of experience.

I have found that by reading in the common way — looking *down* on the book — I can only read for a comparatively brief time without feeling my eyes tired.

But by *looking up at* a book I can read all day without fatigue.

I just put a high, hard pillow on the floor, lie

down on my back or side, and hold the book above me. Then my eyes don't get tired at all. The physiologist knows that the act of reading of itself increases the supply of blood to the eye,— but when one bends the head also over a book, the flow increases. This, I believe, is the explanation.

The examinations are on me. I hope to go to Kompira on the first.

Faithfully, with best thanks,
LAFCADIO HEARN.

DEAR CHAMBERLAIN, — It is not yet really settled weather, but there is the same warm lush atmosphere almost as at the time of your visit last year; and the trees are bursting into clouds of pink-and-white blossoms. The examinations are over; and I have a passport for Kompira which I may or may not use.

There is nothing very new or delightful to tell you. Only a fox-story.

Anciently where the college now stands there was a temple; and a fox used to torment the priest of that temple by assuming the shape of the acolyte, and announcing that the bath was ready, whereupon the priest would enter not a bath, as he imagined, but a cesspool — to the great diversion of the fox. After the temple had disappeared and the college was built, the memory of the priest's fox remained. Recently the postman who used to deliver letters in the neighbourhood of the school complained of being deceived by foxes; and kurumaya protested they had been hired late at night to take army-officers to phantom-villages which disappeared about them while they were waiting for the return of their fares.

Be that as it may, the students of the Daizo Koto Chugakko three days ago killed a female fox in the parade-ground. She had made her den in one of the drain-pipes. Five little blind cubs were found in it. The boys carried these to their dormitory buildings, and subscribed each a few rin to buy milk for them. So we are now cultivating foxes.

I suppose *you* must be exceedingly tormented by autograph-hunters. I receive a small number of letters from them every year, to none of which I ever reply,— always stealing the enclosed stamp, on the authority of Oliver Wendell Holmes, who told us all some years ago that such stamps should be confiscated. But yesterday the most accomplished autograph-hunter I ever came across wrote me — that is, I got his letter. It was wonderfully elegant, and stamped with a crest of blue-and-gold. Enclosed was a most exquisite sheet of paper, in another envelope,— and on that sheet of paper I was to write "a sentiment" and my auto. This sheet of paper was placed inside of a carefully addressed envelope,— stamped with *a 5-cent Japanese stamp ! !* There was cunning for you! The letter contained only the exact number of necessary words. But there was also a *printed statement* of the history of the author's collection of autographs, and a list of the names of those who had fallen victims to his wiles. And at the head of the list was printed the name of — Oliver Wendell Holmes, the champion enemy of all autograph-hunters! The assault was masterly! But I am not going to do what Oliver Wendell Holmes *does*, but only what he *tells me* to do. So I confiscated the whole. On trying to explain at home the reasons for my conduct, I found that my action was judged to be highly immoral. In vain I tried to explain. The moral evidence was against me. Nevertheless, I know one autograph-hunter who "shall be disappointed."

Ever,

LAFCADIO HEARN.

April 7, 1894.

DEAR CHAMBERLAIN, — Just back from Shikoku to find your kind letter. I thought of writing you on my journey, but as we rushed from Kumamoto to Kompira-uchi-machi and back in four days, I really could not get a chance to write a decent letter. This is partly about the Adventures of Kaji.

Before he was born, I remember expressing the fear in a letter to you that no child of mine could ever have the wonderful placidity of the little Japanese boy, Kame, whom I compared to a small Buddha. But, although in quite a different way, my boy turns out to be altogether Japanese in this excellent point. He never cries, which you will grant is quite extraordinary, — and is never sick, and likes travel. His adventures gave me proof (such as I could never otherwise have obtained) how much the Japanese love children, and how much deeper and more natural is the common interest of the people in children. Perhaps this may be partly though not altogether explained by the custom of early marriages, and the Oriental family structure. With us the long delay of marriage, and the disintegration of the family, and the difficulty of life have all combined, doubtless, to create that absence of sentiment which renders it difficult for us to be interested at sight in children not our own; and which, by reaction perhaps, helps to make Western children so much naughtier and more troublesome than Oriental children.

On the train from Kumamoto to Moji we travelled with a crowd of furious politicians, — some of whom had evidently been banqueting. They shouted as they talked, and laughed enormously, and made a great ado. This interested Kaji. He looked at them very curiously, and laughed at them; and they stopped talking politics awhile to amuse themselves by watching him. So far as I could judge, Kaji began his travels by introducing peace into the world of politics.

At Moji he was carried all over the hotel, and made much of. We took a steamer the same night, — an abominable steamer (don't forget the name!), the *Yodogawa Maru*. No first-class cabin, — but a large *chu-to:* all together on the floor. There were perhaps twenty others with us, — including a number of very sweet women. At least I thought them very sweet, — partly because they were young, pretty, and gentle, but much more because they begged for a loan of Kaji. He played with them all, and was petted very much. But he showed much more partiality for the men (I pray the Gods he

may always have this disposition: it would save him
a universe of trouble); and the men carried him all
over the ship, and the Captain descended from his
bridge to play with him. Then one old man produced the portrait of his granddaughter, a little
girl whom he said looked much like Kaji; and the
resemblance was really striking. Another passenger
gave Kaji a small book, — to read as soon as he
should be able; and little baskets of oranges, boxes
of suchi and cakes were given us by various persons.
Thus, as the "grub" furnished by the steamer was
really uneatable, Kaji supplied us with provisions.

Kaji's grandmother, who carried him on her back
over most of the distance, insisted upon certain
observances. There was a wonderful display of
phosphorescence that night: the ripples were liter-
ally created with fire, — a fire quite as bright as
candlelight, — and at the bows of the steamer there
was a pyrotechnic blazing and sputtering bright
enough to read small print by. Kaji liked the sight,
but was not allowed to look long at it: there is some
ghostly idea connected with these sea-lights which
I could not fully learn. (You know the French
phrase, *la mer lampe*.) Well, the sea really did
"lamp" that night: I never saw a brighter phosphorescence in the tropics. Even to throw a cigar-
butt into the water made a flashing like a fire-
cracker. A tug (Ko-joki) passed us, surrounded by
what seemed like a vast playing of Catharine-
wheels. — And Kaji also is not yet suffered to look
much into a looking-glass; for another ghostly
reason which I shall some day tell you about.

Setsu translated for me some conversation that took place in the cabin during my wanderings on deck, over cases of oil of Batoum. If true as to fact, it would seem that I am far more popular with the Kumamoto students than I had imagined; for some very extraordinary statements were made as to their feeling towards me by a Kumamoto official on board. Recently, however, the students have been coming very much closer to me, taking walks with me, and telling me wonderful things, — so it *may* be true.

At Tadotsu, the crew and passengers all said good-bye to Kaji. The women said, "We shall be lonesome now." Kaji laughed at them till their faces passed out of sight.

The hotel at Tadotsu called the Hanabishi is very, very pretty, — and rather old. The *oshiire* were wonderful; — the *fukuro-to-dana* (?) or *jibukuro* were marvels; the whole place would have delighted Morse unspeakably. And nowhere else in all Japan did I ever eat such fried fish! — just out of the sea. — You know Tadotsu, — so I need not describe it. Except for the modern structures, the town is delightful. Setsu said, "I saw this place before in a dream;" I said, "That is because your ancestors visited it so often." — Kaji was pleased by the shops, and we bought absurd little toys for him.

But the Kompira-uchi-machi was a greater surprise than Tadotsu. What a delicious town, — what survivals! It was just the day to see such things, — a vast warm bath of blue light, — cherries and peaches in bloom, — long vistas through hazy bursts of pink-and-white blossom, — all divinely clear. And oh, oh, oh! the queer dear mountain-climbing city, — itself a pilgrim, all robed in blue-and-white, and shadowed and hatted with unspeakable tiling, and supporting itself with staffs of bamboo, as it zigzags, singing, up to the clouds! Oh for a photographer that knew his business! — for an artist with a soul to image what cannot be described at all in words! Even Loti could not do it. Neither Nara nor Kitzuki nor anything in Kyoto nor anything in Kamakura can ever compare with the "*Saka*." The colours, — the shadowings, — the flutterings of drapery, the riddles of the shops, the look-down over the magical village to the grand blue silhouette of Sannki-Fuji! I saw on the tablets the name of "B. H. Chamberlain, English," — and I wished so much he were beside me, that I might say those things which moments inspire but which cannot be written or remembered.

Kaji's grandmother, at the bottom of the steps, took off her zori, and began the ascent very lightly, with the child on her back. I protested; but Setsu said, "No, that is mother's way: she thinks it wrong to approach a holy place with footgear." People stopped her to look at Kaji and ask questions. *I* was taken for an Ainoko by some, — Kaji seems to pass for a Japanese very well. In parts of Oki also I was said to be an Ainoko.

We made a present to the temple, following the example of "B. H. Chamberlain, English;" and the miko danced for us. They were two very pretty girls,—not painted up and powdered like the Nara virgins, but looking like the sisters of the daughter of the Dragon-King in the Urashima pictures. Kaji opened his eyes more widely, and laughed, and made one of the miko smile, even during her solemn dance. After the dance he became an object of attention. Kaji seemed to like the miko better than any other strangers of the fair sex; — for with this exception his friendships are especially masculine. I admired his taste in the case of the miko. Besides they were just at the lovable period between girlhood and womanhood, when children are very strongly sympathized with.

Our hotel was the Toraya. You know there are two figures of tigers there, said to have been made by Hidari Jiugoro, and caged in wire nets. (I suspect they are relics of the Buddhist days of Kompira.) And upstairs I found myself looking out upon the street through the legs of another tiger.. There are more than one hundred rooms, and a very beautiful garden. What most impressed me was the use of a most beautiful sky-blue plaster for the walls of the back part of the buildings and corridors leading to the *chozuba*. — A lot of geisha came and sat down on the gallery to play with Kaji. I hope that will be Kaji's last acquaintance with geisha,—although they behaved very prettily with him.

I passed over the wonderful bridge, of course; and down the avenue of stone lanterns; and we ascended the colossal toro, and saw the black skillets in which two *go* of tomoshi-abura are burned every night. But we did not take Kaji upstairs. It would have been dangerous. — I observed the curious wind-bells of bronze, hung at the corners of the eaves; the very broad tongue has almost the figure of an inverted fleur-de-lys.

I returned by a much finer boat, — the *Odagawa Maru*, very comfortable, with a good table. There were many children; and Kaji won many successes. Meanwhile I met one of your old pupils, — a young naval surgeon named Oki, now stationed at Kure, with a prospect of three years' study in Germany. A fine, long-limbed young fellow, with heavy eye-brows, and a love of innocent mischief. We talked a good deal together. I also met the new director of the Yamaguchi Higher Middle School — pleas-ant, cautious, and inquisitively official: there I saw only the surface. Oki seems to me a fine boy. He has just the necessary amount of conceit to help him through the surf of life; and exactly the dis-position that will make friends for him among the students of Munich, where he hopes to go.

We were delayed about six hours by a perfectly black night — the hand could not be seen before the face. Kaji gave no trouble at all.

But there are so many risks for a child in travel that I did not feel quite easy till we got home last night. I send a picture of Kaji. His last friendship on the railroad was with a grim-looking government surveyor, whose hand he seized from behind, while the man was looking out of the window.

(*Finis first chapter of the Adventures of Kaji.*)

What, after all, is the charm of Kompira's city?

Not certainly in any one particular thing. It is the result of a great combination of very simple things under a divine sky. This grey day it would look common enough. Another day it would look like the ascent, through blue light and sungold, into the phantom city of the Gokuraku, and the gardens where souls like Kaji's are born out of the lotus-flowers, and fed with ambrosia by miko having wings. Truly the whole place is a work of Art, — with well-chosen Nature for its living pedestal, or canvas.

And that's all about my travels. . . .

Faithfully,

LAFCADIO HEARN.

DEAR CHAMBERLAIN, — Since last writing you I have copied and mailed the index, corrected the remaining few hundred plate-proofs, worked over the preface (of which I sent you a raw duplicate), and written a metaphysical article on Japanese mirrors. So that I have been working pretty hard. Many thanks for the *Eclectics*. The second paper by the recorder of that wonderful phrase *C'est dégoûtant comme ils sont distingués* — the paper on the Commune in 1871 — strikes me as the most remarkable contribution in the three. That man, whoever he be, is a very great, large, vivid, comprehensive, sympathetic man. *What* a book he could make! The terrible realism of that story about the girl is something one will never forget. That is a master-artist. He has a gift like Froude.

Indeed I am delighted to sympathize with you

about Froude's "Short Essays on Great Subjects." They seem to me the most perfect work of the kind ever done in the English language; the "Spanish Story of the Armada" is in the same vein and of the same fibre; and I am looking forward with eagerness to his coming volume of sketches relating to the great seamen of the seventeenth century, — the Drakes, Hawkinses, etc. It is many years since I read those essays. I have most vivid recollection of the papers relating to Roman society in the period of the Decadence (including that marvellous study of the impostor Alexander); — then I can always see the figure of that terrible fighting English bishop, — Le Despenser, was n't it? — who settled the peasant revolt by attacking the whole host all by himself (*Sicut aper frendens dentibus*); — and last, but not least, the weird humour haunts me of that dream about the Railway Station and Judgment of Souls. Perhaps the fate of Western races is indeed to be decided at last by their treatment of the animal world—though this is by no means easy to show.   Faithfully,

LAFCADIO HEARN.

P. S. I have been trying to shoot with a bow. You know the shape of the Japanese bow is peculiar, and it is not held as our bows are. It is held near the bottom, and is hard to use. The bottom part is wider than the top, and the thing is tremendously long. I think mine is fully nine feet. My father-in-law, trained to arms in his youth, is expert with it. I can scarcely do anything with it; but he is teaching me. The target the first day was a metal wash-basin, covered with painted paper. His first arrow, though blunt, whistled through the basin and struck halfway through the fence. I am rather afraid of the thing,—for it would kill a man at once. I would feel safer shooting with a revolver, which I know how to manage. But I shall try.

May 10, 1894.

DEAR CHAMBERLAIN, — I think you are quite right not to care about work in MS., — indeed, I made the proposal rather through a sense of friendly duty than with any idea that it could be hailed "with joy and gladness." There is no colour in MS., and symmetry is concealed. It is like trying to read through loose tissue paper, which lumps over the page and has to be held down with the fingers. . . .

That is delightful news about your new librarian. You are really very pleasantly fixed. I am only legitimately jealous — rejoicing in all your comforts; but if you only knew what four years mean (or at least three), separated from every intelligent being in the Western sense, you would experience the grim joy of Jeremy Taylor, who held that one of the greatest delights of heaven consisted in the inspection of the torments of the damned. (By the way, I think I am wrong — that it was Jonathan Edwards.) Well, whoever it was, I don't think he meant that the S. S. are to take any *malicious* joy in the spectacle, but only that their heaven would become quite unbearably monotonous if they did n't have an occasional chance to compare STATUSES

(there's an English plural for you!) — My whole
trouble here has been the work of one man. He represents (I *think*) what is called the missionary influence in the school. Somehow or other, he has the
ear of K——. K—— is now trying to get him into
the University as assistant teacher or something —
preparatory department. But whether this is only
a plan for getting rid of him or not, I cannot be sure.
My admirer's specialty is English literature — so I
suppose I must be in his way. He has a very good
— even *wonderful* collection of books on the subject
(I don't know how he could afford them), and a
book-clerk's knowledge of titles and prices. When
I have said that, I have said all. He cannot write
ten lines of a letter without a mistake, and he cannot understand the "Lady of the Lake." But he
teaches Bacon's Essays, Burke's Speeches, Carlyle, and the Devil knows what. He also publishes
texts. A foreign teacher can only be asked about
ten questions a day — there is so little time. But
at the end of a year it figures up. Then comes out
the original editing. The youngest class but one —
a preparatory class in which no boy can write a
decent composition — was the other day being
taught by this wonderful genius — *Je vous le donne
en mille !* — the structure and history of the English
sonnet (!) out of "Barnes's philological grammar."
It is rather funny that my friend imagines himself
such a philologist that he represented to K—— the
very inefficient philological methods of the University. K—— told him to write a letter to the Minister of Education on the subject — which I have

no doubt he did. I am very kind to the horrid little beast. But my nerves are strained, — as I can't pretend to understand what I know he is doing. I pray the Gods, K—— will get him into the University, or anywhere out of this. In the University I think he would hang himself quick enough. He has been in the Doshisha, — but they don't seem to have appreciated him there. — And yet, there might be worse than he in our school. He is not of the rude rough sort — but of the small, shabby-genteel, spiteful kind; one of the kind that hates everything Japanese, and everything foreign except missionaries, who seem to be of use to him. My greatest suffering are the lectures on Milton, Nicholas Breton (!), Donne, Painter's " Palace of Pleasure," and various other known and unknown authors which he inflicts upon me. He is scandalized at my ignorance "of those Elizabethan lyrists, edited by Bullen." Can you imagine!

How many pages of scandal! Still I must howl to somebody who can appreciate the anguish! No Japanese could understand it. — Now about that poetry.

No, I never spoke much about the *décadents*. I don't understand their work — only their principles. It is Manet in words, they say. It is impressionism. Some people see much in it. I can't. The principle *must* be wrong. Psychology ought to prove it. The values and colours of words differ in all minds — as tabulated statements of word-sensations collected in the universities and schools have shown. The effect of a poem like that you sent me can only be anything to the writer's psychological cousin, — provided the cousin has had precisely the same experiences in mental preparation. I can imagine a tolerably successful application of the principle, — but the medium would have to be the language of the *greatest* (not the *great*) majority. Could a writer apply the thing to the vulgar idiom of the people — to what everybody understands (except the highly refined), I think astonishments of beauty and power might result. There are obvious obstacles, however. As the *décadents* now are, their "art" seems to me a sort of alchemy in verse, — totally false, with just enough glints of reality — micaceous shimmerings — to suggest imaginations of ghostly gold. I can't understand that thing at all. It pains my head, and hurts my soul. The only really fine line in it, —

— meurtries
De la langueur goutée à ce mal d'être deux —

(you will acknowledge a sensual but weird beauty in that!) is not original. I have read it before, though I can't tell where. I think it was better in the other form — to my taste the word *goutée* spoils the charm. The beauty is really in that psychic truth of the desire to melt into another being — the fable of Salmacis and Hermaphroditus.

Huxley says, "No man can understand Shakespeare till he becomes old." I think he might have said the same about the old Greek fables. I *now* only, turning grey, seem to understand them. I know Medusa, the beautiful woman who freezes the hearts and souls of rich men into eternal stone.

THE MOUNTAIN OF SKULLS

From a sketch by Hearn

And I have seen the Sphinx. Alkestis I have also seen, and Admetus, and glorious Herakles, and the Witch whose wine makes beasts of men,—and the Sirens singing, with white bones bleaching under their woman's breasts,—and Orpheus to whom the trees bowed down, who sought hell for a shadow and lost it: all these have been with me. But how new they now are! — how real — how deep — how eternal!

I can't let you get out of *hototogisu* and *uguisu* in that most unfair way,—because I insist that the *hototogisu* is *not* a cuckoo, and that the *uguisu* is *not* a nightingale. And I have become so accustomed to say two kuru*ma*, four kuruma*ya*, that it seems monstrous to me anybody should put an "s" to them. If you imagine that I have been writing Japanese words for four years without ever using a plural, you will believe me. It is a thing one gets used to, and fond of,—like squatting.

But it is late, and I am tired *awfully*. With best wishes and thanks for the *decadantissimum poema*, which I shall try to read once more before returning.

Faithfully,

LAFCADIO HEARN.

May 16, 1894.

DEAR CHAMBERLAIN, — Your letter went right into that much bescratched thing called my soul. I am getting rather hungry myself for the open ports. To live in a Japanese fishing-village in Oki, or Yu-Notsu, or a certain little islet I know where all the people still wear queues and the terakoya still exist might be preferable. But that would entail certain severe discomforts, — especially as my folks do not share my liking for out-of-the-way nooks and corners. Yes, I imagine one *could* be happy in the open ports. As you say, there are genuine men and women there. And they are the most beautiful cities in Japan. Kobe! — what a flood of light, with the amethyst hills massing into it; — what dreamy luminosity over Yokohama bay, with the ghost of Fuji floating over all! — what delicious quaintness and queerness and windy glory over Nagasaki! But how live there! One must be right rich, or a business man, or — a journalist? ? I have dreams. Beale has been suggesting future possibilities. I should be better off, "driving a quill," than teaching under these officials.

Some splendid boys will go to Tokyo this summer, but I suppose as you no longer teach you are not likely to see them. Still, I would like to mention one name. Yasukochi Asakichi, whom I have taught for three years, is the finest Japanese student I ever met. Though a heimin, he is patronized by the lord of Fukuoka, and will probably be sent abroad. He studies law, I am sorry to say, but he is right, — having a special high talent for it. He is extraordinarily solid in character, — massively, not minutely practical, — straight, large, thorough, and I think will become a great man. He is not only first in English, but easily first also in everything he studies, — and, quite unlike the average student, regards his teachers only as helps to his own unaided study — instead of as bottles of knowledge to be emptied slowly upon lazy sponges. — A comrade, Kawafuchi, is nearly as clever, though less solid. What a pity, however, that the really fine heads take always to law. The science-classes show no such young men: they are mediocre in the extreme.

I feel a great temptation this summer to take a run by myself to Hakodate, and plunge into the little hotel kept by Carey the mulatto there. (You may remember I lived at his house in Yokohama: he was kind, and a good man to the bones of him.) Then I could bathe once more in an atmosphere of sailors and sealers and mates and masters of small craft — in a salty medium full of water-dogs. It would be healthy for me, refreshing: I like rough men who don't get too drunk, and I get along with them first-rate. . . .

DEAR CHAMBERLAIN, — What do you think about the idea of getting up a new "Japanese Fairy Tale Series"? I have quite a number of tales splendidly adapted to weird illustrations. Is there money in such a thing?

Do you know this poem?

BRAHMA

I am the mote in the sunbeam; and I am
    the burning sun:
"Rest here," I whisper the atom; — I say
    to the orb, "Roll on!"

I am the blush of the morning, and I am
    the evening breeze:
I am the leaf's low murmur, — the swell
    of the terrible seas.

I am the vine and the vineyard,—grapes,
    winepress, and must, and wine,—
The guest, the host, the traveller,—the goblet
    of crystal fine; —

I am the net, the fowler, the bird and its
    frightened cry; —
The mirror, the form reflected,—the sound
    and its echo, I; —

I am the breath of the flute; — I am
    the mind of man,—
Gold's glitter, the light of sunrise,— and the
    sea-pearl's lustre wan,—

The Rose, her poet-nightingale,—the songs
    from his throat that rise,
The flint, the spark, the taper,— the moth
    that about it flies; —

The lover's passionate pleading,—the maiden's
    whispered fear,—
The warrior, the blade that smites him,—his
    mother's heart-wrung tear;

I am both Good and Evil,— the deed, and
    the deed's intent,—
Temptation, victim, sinner, crime, pardon
    and punishment; —

I am what was, is, will be,— creation's
    ascent and fall,—
The link, the chain of existence,— beginning
    and end of all!
                (RITTER, from *Djellalleddin Rumi*.)

I have studied this poem for years, and every time
I read it,—the grander it seems. To-day I found
the old copy I made of it in 1879 among some loose
papers.

There is n't anything new to tell you that you
could care about.   Faithfully,

25th May, 1894.   LAFCADIO HEARN.

I wish it were 1994,—don't you?   (OVER)

I forgot to tell you: —

To-day I spent an hour in reading over part of the notes taken on my first arrival, and during the first six months of 1890. Result, I asked myself: "How came you to go mad? — absolutely mad?" It was the same kind of madness as the first love of a boy.

I find I described horrible places as gardens of paradise, and horrid people as angels and divinities. How happy I must have been without knowing it! There are all my illusions facing me, — on faded yellow paper. I feel my face tingle as I study some of them. Happily I had the judgment not to print many lines from them.

But — I ask myself — am I the only fool in the world? Or was I a fool at all? Or is everybody, however wise, at first deluded more or less by unfamiliar conditions when these are agreeable, the idea always being the son of the wish?

Perhaps I was right in one way. For that moment Japan was really for *me* what I thought it. To the child the world is blue and green; to the old man grey — both are right.

So with all things. Relations alone exist. The writer's danger is that of describing his own, as if they were common or permanent. Perhaps the man who comes to Japan full of hate for all things Oriental may get nearer to truth at once — though, of course, he will also make a kindred mistake.

Ever,

LAFCADIO HEARN.

June 4, 1894.

DEAR CHAMBERLAIN, — . . . The poem of
Brahma (much finer than Emerson's) I first saw
in Longfellow's "Poems of Places," credited, as a
translation from Rumi to Ritter. Ritter, I believe,
is a German; for I could not get anything Oriental
by Ritter in English—they were all German books.
Perhaps Longfellow himself tried his hand at the
versification. I think the contradiction in the first
stanza — which might be improved, perhaps — is on
the whole pardonable considering the tremendous
antitheses and contradictions of the whole thing.
It is the Bhagavad-Gita condensed; and I suppose
the magnificence of the Saddharuma-Pundarika is
due to the same mighty source. Of translations,
I liked Burnouf's much the best. When I read such
things I am angry with my own soul that I cannot
believe,—so cyclonic is the sublimity of the verses.
They create, as I think no other verses do, what
Clifford calls "cosmic emotion." So some verses of
the Bible do, — but only because of the changes
of meaning caused in them by the expansion of
knowledge to-day: —

"They shall perish, but thou shalt remain: yea,
all of them shall wax old as a garment. And as a
vesture thou shalt change them and they shall be
changed."

The Hebrew poet's world was small. But *to-day*
— to-day when the application of evolution to
astronomy confirms the Orient faith that the cosmos
itself appears and vanishes with the night and day
of Brahma, — all being but the shadows of the

dream of a God, — how tremendous the old psalm becomes! . . .

Every once in a while, some delightful, earnest, sweet-souled man — a Tempo — comes down here and lectures. He tells the boys of their relation to the country's future. He reminds them of their ancestors. He speaks to them of loyalty and honour. He laments the decay of the ancient spirit, and the demoralizing influence of Western manners and Western religion and Western business methods. And as the boys are good, their hearts get full, and something brightens their eyes in spite of the fashion of impassiveness. — But what are their thoughts after?

A striking example was afforded me the other day, by a conversation with the remarkable student I told you of before, — Yasukochi Asakichi. I will try to reproduce it thus: —

"Sir! What was your opinion of the old-fashioned Japanese when you came first to Japan? Please to be quite frank with me."

"You mean old men like Akizuki-San?"

"Yes."

"Why, I thought them divine, — Kami-Sama; and I think them more divine now that I have seen the new generation."

"Akizuki is a type of the ideal old samurai. But as a foreigner you must have perceived faults."

"How, faults?"

"From your Western standpoint."

"My Western standpoint is philosophical and ethical. A people's perfection means their perfect

fitness for the particular form of society to which
they belong. Judging from such a standpoint the
man of the Akizuki type was more perfect than any
Western type I have ever met. Ethically, I could
say the same."

"But in a Society of the Western type, could such
men play a great part?"

"By their unaided exertions?"

"Yes."

"No: they have no business capacity, and no
faculty for certain combinations."

"That is true. And in what did their goodness
seem to consist to you?"

"In honour, loyalty, courtesy, — in supreme self-
control, — in unselfishness, — in consideration of the
rights of others, — in readiness to sacrifice self."

"That also is true. But in Western life are these
qualities sufficient to command success?"

"No."

"And the Oriental system of morals cultivated
these; and the result of that cultivation was to suppress the individual for the sake of the whole?"

"Yes."

"On the other hand, the Western form of society
develops the individual by encouraging selfishness
— competition, struggle for gain — and all that?"

"Yes."

"And Japan, in order to keep her place among
nations, must do business and carry on industry
and commerce in the Western manner?"

"Perhaps."

"I do not think there is a perhaps. There is only

a must. We must have manufactures, commerce,
banks, stock-companies — we must do things in the
Western way, since our future must be industrial
and commercial. If we should try to do things in
the old way, we should always remain poor and
feeble. We should also get the worst in every commercial transaction."

"Yes."

"Well, how can we do any business, — or attempt
any enterprise, — or establish any large system, —
or carry on any competition, — or do anything on
a large scale, — if we live by the old morality?"

"Why?"

"Because if we can do something advantageous
to ourselves or our interests only by hurting some
one else, we cannot do that according to the old
morality."

"Yes."

"But to do business in a Western way we must
not be checked by any such scruples; the man who
hesitates to obtain an advantage simply because he
knows some one else will be injured by it, will fail."

"Not always."

"It must be the general rule when there are no
checks upon competition. The cleverest and strongest succeed; the weak and foolish fail: it is the
natural law — the struggle for life. Is Western
competition based upon love of one's fellow man?"

"No."

"Sir, the truth is that no matter how good the
old morality was, we cannot follow any such moral
law and preserve our national independence and

achieve any progress. We must try to substitute
law for morality."

"It is a bad substitute."

"It is not a bad substitute in England. Besides,
at last, men through the influence of law will learn
to be moral by reason, not by emotion. We must
forsake our Past (?)"

And I could say nothing. . . .

And now I have said so many horrid things about
officials that it is high time to say something nice
about men who are not officials. Some years ago
I met in Tokyo a gentleman named Takagi, then
suffering from brain-trouble of some sort,—very
charming and gentle. I forgot all about him until
the other week when he came to Kumamoto. He
had been in the Educational Department, but was
not happy there, and being a good chemist got
employed as head man in the Sumitomo Camphor
Refinery of Kobe. The merchants liked him, took
him all round the world, and made him quite happy.
His visit did me good in an unsuspected way; for
he had been the schoolmate of some not inclined
to view me favourably, and his opinion changed the
course of events. I passed some pleasant days with
him. He possesses, what is rare in Japan, a keen
sense of humour, sharpened by foreign experience.
I was much amused by his observations about foreign countries. Of the French manner of life he
said, "They are the most economical of people:
they are careful not to spend their own money; but
they possess an infinite art in making other people
spend money." I asked him about the Chinese in

Kobe, as merchants. "There are too many Chinese, but few merchants in Kobe. The remainder are chiefly receivers of stolen goods, and dangerous characters." Takagi has the most remarkable boy I have seen; and I think of using the head (photograph) in a future book. I want to send you a copy to look at: you will agree it is fine. I am to spend some days in Kobe with him. He is a good amateur photographer, and is taking photographs of queer things for me. I think a more charming man it would be hard to find. He could never have succeeded in official life, as he has the awful habits of saying what he thinks, and being in earnest — two vices intolerable to the existing bureaucracy. As a letter-writer he is far superior to any Japanese I know — not simply because he makes no mistakes, but because he writes as honestly as an Englishman, with a very delicate, humorous way of expression peculiar to himself — always original. Should you ever have occasion to meet him, you would find him interesting in no small degree. Hinton used to be a great admirer of his — and I believe tried hard to get his services once, but without success.

The other day some Japanese books were brought me to look at. On them was the name of the father of a student now at the University. The poor old man could only pay his son's expenses by selling his library,—a wonderful library. It is all scattered now. Nothing could be more touching than the history of the sacrifices being made every day in every part of Japan for the education of sons and daughters: — the unwritten goodness is the most wonderful.

I am disappointed to hear you made nothing by
those delicious Fairy-Tales. I thought there was
a fortune in them. Sets must have been sold by
thousands. A small set I could certainly make;
but I want you to read my book first. And my
head is full of dreams. I dream of —

(1) "The Story of a Soul," — to be illustrated
with weird, but not ugly, pictures of the Meido, —
River of the Three Roads, River of Tears, Sami
Kawara, etc.

(2) "(New) Japanese Fairy-Tales" — The Foun-
tain of Youth — The Haunted Temple — The
Artist of Cats — The Waiting Stone — The Test of
Courage — The Story of an Ihai — The Ise o-fuda
— The Old Woman and the Oni — Jizo and the
wicked Hotel-keeper, etc., etc., etc.

(3) "Western Science and Eastern Faith." A
comparison of results in the form of an address.
Shall I, or shall I not try?

And again I sometimes feel like despairing of
writing to any purpose — feel like quitting everything I like, and leaving the ground fallow for some
years.

I thank you in advance for the works you are so
kindly lending. Anything genuine from the old
Jesuits I should like to see — except, of course, such
hideous trash as "Paul Anjiro." Perhaps I can make
a fine Kumamoto chapter. If I can't, I shall accu-
mulate notes, and go to Manila for a season later
on — where I can get the emotions I want.

My boy has lost almost every possible trace of
Japanese origin. Even the eyelids have much

changed. His hair has become a *bright* curly brown-chestnut: his features are all different: he is getting to be a naughty naughty English child — extravagantly English. Oh! what a devil of a time I shall have with him! I'm sure he won't be very submissive, after all. I'll have to send him to a land of sterner discipline, later on. For the moment only, good-bye, — I'll finish another letter to you soon.

Most gratefully,

LAFCADIO HEARN.

June 10, 1894.

Further Adventures and States of Mind

DEAR CHAMBERLAIN, — To-day I could not stand it any longer. I dismissed my class abruptly for the first time, and went home to write a letter of resignation. After having written it, I tore it up, and went, for the first time in my life, to the house of Sakurai (he has a brother professor in the University), — the head-master. He is civilized, having been educated in France; and I felt some confidence in him, because he allows no one to be familiar with him. I could not find him in his house: he was at an archery club. I sat down, or knelt down, in the archery shed, and looked at all those Oriental impassive faces, and my courage began to ooze away. Perhaps you don't know what it is to want to say something very private, and find your man for the time being part of a public in nowise interested in you — rather the reverse. But I stuck it out, saying now or never; and after the archery asked to see the gentleman privately. Happily no one else understands French. I went to his house, and conversed with him very guardedly, — mentioning no names, but simply giving my three years' experience of discomfort. He smiled and seemed to understand, thought a little, became suddenly impassive, and said: — "You are generally liked, —they are not polite and courteous; and besides Japanese are cold. You have no friend, I know; but I am your well-wisher, and I keep your confidence. If there be anything very disagreeable, come to me and tell me frankly, and I'll settle it as well as I can. As for your contract, that oversight was only due to your being so long here, that we forgot to ask you. When the director comes back, we settle that." I said: "I am no longer interested in staying; I am only interested in being able to go away on good terms." — I think he understands exactly what I refer to, and I think he will hold his peace to all but the director. The director dislikes the person I am troubled by, and there may be found a way to get rid of him. But the head-master, who is a perfect gentleman, would not like me even to think he understood; and I believe we talked in riddles all the time. However, I have more courage now to finish the three weeks left.

Yet Lowell says the Japanese have no individuality! I wish he had to teach here for a year, and he would discover some of the most extraordinary individuality he ever saw. There are eccentrics and personalities among the Japanese as with us: only, they show less quickly on the surface. No man can make a sweeping general statement about Japanese character in a negative sense, without finding out his mistake later. It is only by degrees, however, that one finds out they have just as much difference among them as any Orientals. But physiologically and conventionally these are less perceptible at first sight.

Won't you think me a crank, writing all this stuff? But it is part of the record of a disillusioned enthusiast. You remember my first letters from Izumo. *Quantum mutatus ab illo!* The iron — Japanese iron — has entered into my soul —

> And thro' the body of the Knight
> He made cauld iron gae, gae,
> He made cauld iron gae!

Ever,

LAFCADIO HEARN.

P. S. By the way, let me send you a typical composition: —

Subject: — *"Flowing Water."*

"The water of a river is not the same clear water that gushed from the source in the mountain. It becomes dark and muddy as it flows on, and never turns clear again. So with the life of a man. The sun always rises and sets the same: in the same way the year always comes and goes. But man grows older always, and never can become young again. One of us who was never sick till last winter now sleeps in a grave: one who was singing and laughing but a few days ago, has gone back to whence he came. One is not long wept or honoured, but soon forgotten quite. The same sad fate must overtake us all. Even our coffin must rot, and the very worms at last disdain our bones. Is this human life of ours all a dream?

"Certain it is that flowing water is not lost: it only vapourizes, and is returned to the rivers again. Yet I cannot believe that our Souls ascend to Heaven unchanged by death. Let us be happy in this world only. If even the shadow of our names remain for a few centuries, it is a very strange and delightful thing."

June 16, 1894.

DEAR CHAMBERLAIN, — . . . I have read the Charlevoix with strange feelings, and am returning it to-day. What another atmosphere was that. You can understand that I feel it, — having been so much in its modern continuation. Was it not a veritable madness? — like the Children's Crusade, — like the epidemics described by Hecker: those millions thirsting for pain and death, — those Jesuits crossing the whole world in absolute terror of arriving too late to have the chance to die. Do you know that the conviction has suddenly come to me that the great missionary successes of old Romish days can only be explained by illuminism, — not only mad faith, but contagious insanity, the capacity to communicate the cerebral disturbance to others.

Ever, in haste,

LAFCADIO HEARN.

DEAR CHAMBERLAIN, — Thanks for precious letters — even the *sharp* one, for that meant love —
and the charming discussion on the moral question.

By this time I imagine my letters have shown the
state of affairs. I made a protest which was kindly
received, with the assurance of a renewal of contract until March. Will it last? I don't know. . . .

Though I cannot but regret that I should become
useless to the Japanese Government, I must honestly confess that I approve of the abolition of
English studies. They should be permitted to those
only gifted with a natural capacity for languages;
and their indiscriminate, foolish, wholesale, topsy-
turvy teaching has been a great aid to national
demoralization. I can feel no possible sentiment
of adverse criticism on this subject. It is simply
jiujutsu. *Vae victis?* Japan experiments with
everything, and retains only what will be of use to
her — of *great* use to her. She is right. It is possible
she miscalculates her strength; but I doubt it. It is
possible she is going to play a Korean rôle, and
bankrupt. But I doubt that too. We shall be dismissed after use — just as the old Chinese teachers
must have been in former days. They cared less,
for they asked less; and they could live on rice.

Well, the Japanese Gods have treated me tolerably well: I trust in them. If I have to leave Japan
awhile, it will not be for the worst.

Now about your argument. Indeed, as you say,
there is a vast spiritual side to Western life, and
noble effort must ever rest upon a spiritual basis, —
just as in hard science the most material possible

fact rests upon a metaphysical basis. This has been
beautifully proved by Huxley. For when we even
touch the question of matter itself scientifically, the
thing vanishes further than Berkeley's examination
ever went, and leaves us in the presence of nothing
but ghostliness.

Unfortunately, however, there is what must be
termed a material side to life, — the *real* materialism. Our civilization, with all its aspirations, is
industrial and commercial — and there is no morality in that competition worth priding ourselves
upon. It is n't Yankeedom more than it is Anglo-
dom. See, for a terrible illustration of the facts in
the case, Herbert Spencer's essay "The Morals of
Trade." Business men know this. The *Eclectics*
you sent me contained several awful articles on the
same subject, written by Englishmen. The fact
seems to me that my young student is altogether
right. Without having studied philosophy, he per-
ceives that emotional morality must yield to legal
morality; and I am trying to make him consider
cosmic law *the* law to study, and he understands. I
have English business friends: men who control vast
movements of money. They do not hesitate to
speak frankly about the cruelties and the bitterness
of commercial competition. Our whole civilization
is based upon immorality — if we are to accept
either the Buddhist or the Christian system of
ethics. *There is* a *comparative* morality, of course;
but he who follows the old code must fail. What
you and I love — what we admire — what we
aspire after — does not belong to industrialism; yet

only by industrialism can any of us — even a
Spencer or Huxley or Tennyson — exist. We can
do what is beautiful or right only by the aid of
industrialism, unless, like Thoreau, we prefer to live
in the woods. A larger morality will come — but
only when competition ends. As for the condition
of woman in Western lands, I think you refer only
to the upper classes. The condition of woman in
certain classes is horrible beyond Japanese imagin-
ing.

Ever sincerely,
LAFCADIO HEARN.

This year all the people of the street have been
coming to my house on festival occasions. There is
then a great crowd always — but perfectly behaved.
In the court before the house, children, girls, and
men dance fantastically. Girls dressed as men, and
men as girls. This is to gladden the spirits of the
dead. The songs sung on the *shokonsai* were curious,
and the dances very interesting. I send a copy, —
if you think worth while, you might ask somebody
to translate them, at the usual rates. The dancers
on this occasion wore curious headdresses. One had
a wig of seaweed, — red seaweed, that made him
look either like a *Shojo* or Norse pirate (he was a
handsome fellow and danced splendidly). Another
had an *o-mikidokkuri* on his head; others *gohei;*
one an enormous *daikon*. The children danced
prettily and blessed the house with *gohei*. A string
stretched across the yard sufficed to keep back the
women and babies and street-boys. What a relief

to *feel* the atmosphere of the people, after stifling
in the atmosphere of officialism! Griffis said he had
found that to live long in Japan spoiled a man. His
meaning was wrong. But there is truth in his words.
To live among officials does poison character — fills
it with suspicions, hates, mean sensations. I can
therefore well understand certain horrors of Tokyo.

June 24, 1894.

DEAR CHAMBERLAIN, — Your telegram came
early this morning, "at the hour when the crows
first fly abroad and cry" — but three days after
the affair. It made us feel very glad; but you may
imagine that we were not easy in mind. I was
especially anxious about Mason; for I learned that
no damage to speak of had occurred in Akasaka,
but that the lower parts of the capital — those on
the flat ground — had suffered severely. Oh! dear!
what a country! No wonder the doctrine of Impermanency should have taken deep hold of the popular mind. Even the face of the land continually
changes. It is remarkable that we foreigners usually escape.

I wrote you yesterday not without qualms of conscience, — feeling as if I had no business to write
at all till I got good news.

I promised some samples of student-compositions,
which I could guarantee as *échantillons* of the standard feeling. The words of the old conservative lec-
turers may have produced the fruit, or at least
ripened it. Certainly it is ripe.

(1) "What did our ancestors contribute to the

common stock of civilization is a most disagreeable question to all of us. It is shameful for us to hear that civilization is a product of the brain of the Caucasian. Only recently the Japanese were awakened by the foreigner. *Now they have begun to sound, like a temple bell struck from the outside.* And Western institutions have been rapidly introduced.

"There was this reason for it. To a child the sun seems brighter and the moon larger than to an old man. Japan as a nation by itself is old, but as a nation of the world at large is very young. The Japanese were too easily stimulated by Western civilization, — because it seemed to them brighter and larger than it really was, as the moon seems to a child. Now the Japanese are becoming old. Experience has taught them good lessons. But even if we grant the Japanese are below the Western nations in material progress, that does not mean they are morally lower also. Christians' minds are not higher than ours. A foreigner can observe the outward conditions; but it is very hard for him to read the depths of our soul. The Japanese never struggled to get freedom or equality. They knew that men cannot find real freedom or equality either on earth or in heaven. Stars are not equal. Some are larger than others; some are brighter. None move freely; all obey laws. The Japanese are not dreamers. It is true that nearly all Japanese are cold toward religion. They cannot dream about a God. . . ."

(2) "Statistics show not only that the average weight of the students in all the Higher Middle

Schools is decreasing year by year, but also that the number of short-sighted students becomes every year greater. Is this the result of too much study, or of the want of bodily exercise? I think the former. *If the present educational regulations continue, the result will be very injurious to the next generation.*"

I reserve for a future letter some selections from *atheistic* compositions. I discourage them, but I fear I am only laughed at (good-naturedly) for my pains.

The importance of teaching scientific philosophy in the schools, instead of barren logic and dead-bones of dead ethics, seems to me more and more of paramount importance. The higher education is simply making atheists — *shallow atheists* (perhaps I am an atheist myself, but there are differences of kind) — men who disbelieve simply through ignorance and undiscerning contempt of what they see; and who think that when they have said "matter is matter," that is the end of the whole business. And this will have its effect upon national morals — not so great an effect as some suppose, because moral character is inherited. Still it will accentuate all evil inclinations in those naturally vicious or weak. One can't make this generation religious. But one might certainly devise one sensible means of inculcating the scientific fact that raw materialism is just as irrational and vulgar as any form of peasant superstition, and infinitely more injurious to the higher faculties of the mind.

There is another advance notice of my book in the *Atlantic* which I send. But read this instalment of "Philip and his Wife." I think that woman is greater than George Eliot. Perhaps she indulges sometimes in touches neither of us quite like. But for fine, terribly-perceptive analysis, — what a writer. Notice, for example, the paragraph describing her disgust with the every-day actions and ways of her husband, and the scene of the quarrel. The Gods have denied all such faculties of perception to me, — that is *creatively*. I know them only when I see them. — Then I think the practical paper on American railroads may interest you. Otherwise I see nothing to *specially* commend, — except, perhaps, the paper on Tortoni's. It seems to me to have been made up from French sources; for I read many bits of it in the *Figaro*, long ago.

I am quite sorry to hear about all the trouble you have with your Japanese assistants. I wonder if every foreigner has not had some like experience. There is a nomad restlessness in this race which really finds pain in stability, regularity, permanency of any sort. The most amiable seem to have it. Even the sweetest Japanese woman has something of this Tartar soul. Like sweet women the world over, she loves to make a nest and collect treasures; but like her possible ancestors of the steppes, her life is still the life of tents. When she rests, she strives with charming success to make everything beautiful; but she is ready to-morrow to pull up the pegs and travel a thousand ri. And what wonder — since even the ground will not stay still.

With best regards and felicitations,

LAFCADIO HEARN.

June 27, 1894.

DEAR CHAMBERLAIN, — Your letter came late
last night, and made me very glad. It is really nice
to be able to think, or at least to feel, as if one's
friends were specially cared for by the Gods. I had
no idea when I first wrote you on the subject how
much real danger there was so near you.

There is no news here to send you, even about
that tiresome subject — myself. The heat is great,
but heat makes me feel young, although I am this
blessed or accursed day exactly forty-four years old
(27th June), and if I could be where it is always hot
I think I should live to dry up and blow away. Still
I can sympathize with your discomfort, — to enjoy
great heat we should be able to dress or undress as
we please, have freedom from dust, and the luxury
of moving water — whether river, lake, or sea. I
fear Tokyo has not these.

Liquidly beautiful the sky-fire is, and everything
looks sharp as the edge of a sword, and the white
clouds seem souls of Bosatsu about to melt into
Nirvana. There is pleasure always in this Nature
— however wearisome the hard work of living (or
working) with people who have no souls. For the
Japanese officials have none. Imagine people having no sentiment of light — of blue — of infinity!
And they cannot feel possibly the beauty of their
own day as you or I do. Think of the comparison
of Fuji to a white half-open inverted fan hanging
in the sky. Of course it is pretty; it is even start-
lingly real; — but what sentiment is there in it?
What feeling do mountains give these people?

Surely nothing like the thought of Job, — "*He maketh Peace in His High Places.*" What feeling does light give them? — the light which makes us wish to pray — to thank somebody for it? Nothing like the utterance of John, — "Verily this is the message we give unto you, — *that God is Light!*" What, even, is their thought of Nature — beautifully as they mock her? Has any among them ever so much as thought the thought of the Bhagavad-Gita, — "I am the breath of winds, the light of waters — MOST ANCIENT AND MOST EXCELLENT OF POETS"? . . .

Never a one! They have lost the child-hearts that the Gods gave them, which were beautiful; and in place of them have something resembling the legendary apples of Sodom — full of bitterness and dust only.

Oh dear! oh dear! I used to think I had no soul; but since coming here I think I have, — that if I try very hard, I could discover it. Converted from various nihilisms I have become. The Western world verily seems to me now only a Titan world, but a world charged with spirit, like a dynamo with lightning. Of course there are bottled devils in multitude, as in the Arabian tales of Soliman; but what a magical world it is! — and how much does absolute exile from it mean!

I wonder how I shall feel in another few years. Would that I could go to those zones in which Nature remains primeval, — where light is divine, and where people walk forever with eyes fixed upon the ground, — looking for snakes. Then I should say to the cobra,—"Thou art my sister and my brother. Thou hast a soul. So have I. But I have been among men not having souls."

LAFCADIO HEARN.

Extracts from Compositions — showing the results of *improved* teaching by native teachers.

(1) Human life is produced by the combination of those energies which compose the soul. When a man dies, his soul may either remain un-(This is changed, or may change according to what it not bad at all.) combines with. Some philosophers say the soul is mortal; some that it is immortal. They are both right. The soul is mortal or immortal according to the change in its combinations. But those elementary energies from which the soul is made, are, of course, immortal, — etc.

(2) Why has man come into the world, and why should he struggle to succeed in life? These are questions that have remained unanswered from ancient times. Religions were introduced into the world in order to explain them. Many religions teach the existence of a God, and theorize about a paradise and a hell. *But such opinions must have come out of human wishes. . . .* etc.

(3) Some say the world and all things were made by a God, omnipotent to do as he pleases. But there is no evidence for this. If there were such a God, why did he not make only good and useful things, and exclude all badness and uselessness from the world? God is nothing but an ideal being. He has no power to influence life or death.

(4) Perhaps there is a universal energy without beginning and end which is wrongly called " God," and this energy appears as a man by its union with substance. When the union is destroyed life ceases, and the body only remains.

(5) Nothing could be more foolish than to talk about the immortality of the soul. But even were such a thing possible, the soul could not continue in the same form; — for all things in the universe are constantly changing their characters and conditions.

(6) After the death of an ice-bear (sic!), a man takes off the fur of it. So the fur is preserved for the future. But after a man dies, what remains of him but a name? . . . etc.

"The evil of the day," etc. You will see there is some excellent hard sense in some of these thoughts. The pity of it is that the half-scientific teaching hardens the mind before it half reaches the end of the matter. Then it stays petrified in materialism, or in a scepticism with no solid basis; — ergo, — the world is humbug?

July 2, 1894.

DEAR CHAMBERLAIN, — I must say that the dreariest work I ever undertook was that of putting the three Daikokumai ballads into endurable English prose. The work is nearly done, and I am very sick of it. Indeed, I could not have done it at all — except just a means of keeping my mind occupied in lieu of better work.

And now, what on earth shall I do with them?

Of course they have much interest as folk-lore, but no literary value that I can discover. There is a weird coarseness about them, too, that, in addition to their flatness, renders it impossible to use them in my new book. They would jar with everything else. Your warning to me about Japanese literature of this kind has been fully realized. There is nothing in it for me, — no poetry or thought or sentiment.

At an examination in Conversation the other day, I put the following questions to the youngest classes as exercises: "How do you ask a favour politely?" "How do you refuse a favour politely?"

I had scarcely any good answers to either, but some characteristic replies to the second one, e. g.: —

"I cannot lend you my dictionary, because I have been *stolen* my dictionary last night."

"I am sorry not to lend you my horse, for he is sick. When he had returned to his pleasure, then I will lend to you for many week."

Is n't it like your delicious rendering in "Classical Poetry," of that comedietta "*hone to kawa*"?

I can't expect an answer to this. For I hope to get away in a few days. Oh! what a long, long month — and what a dull, dead town!

Ever,

LAFCADIO HEARN.

DEAR CHAMBERLAIN, — Two most delightful letters, — one from you and one from Mason, both inviting me to pass a few days in Tokyo. I think I shall really go to 19 Akasaka Daimachi for a little while anyhow, — for I have bachelor-habits of long standing (I mean *orderly* ones, such as disturbing nothing, and giving as little trouble to others as possible), and I would feel less of an intruder than I should in going into the midst of anybody's family, for more than an afternoon at a time. But it is very, very pleasant to be so kindly thought of, and I don't know what to say to you at all. . . .

I am sorry about your spraining your hand, and have been thinking of suggesting archery as a substitute for tennis. I have now become pretty good at using the bow; but a leather glove seems to be necessary, — else the leap of the bow skins the palm. As I never practised with an English bow, I can't tell how the thing is handled; but the Japanese style is quite difficult to learn. The bow is held *not* tightly, but loosely, so that it swings completely round in the hand at each pull.

The bow describes an almost complete rightabout, or rather, left-about face. This used to cut my hand to pieces; but now I get on by using a handwrap of soft cotton — in case of shooting for any length of time. I recommend the archery-exercise chiefly because of its coolness, compared with tennis or cricket. The chest, back, and arm-muscles are fully exercised; but the body has to be kept very steady, and one does not feel heated.

It strikes me that there is a good deal of unwritten folk-lore to be got about bear-hunting; and I have just heard some facts which again suggest to me something I wrote you long ago, about a possible parallel to be found in Japanese customs for almost everything generally said or believed to be purely Aino. What I wrote at the time alluded to was my suspicion that there must have been a common origin for the Ainu *inao* and the Japanese *gohei*. But now I want to talk about bears. In the mountain district of Goka in Yatsushiro, not very far from here, and in Ichigo (I think the place is in Ichigo), the people hunt bears. In the latter place they used to be employed by the Tokugawas to hunt bears — especially the "golden bear;" when a bear was killed, an officer was sent to the mountain village to receive the skin, etc.; and this officer used to read a document which the people believed to be a sort of *Kyo*, or religious address, which had the effect of giving peace and contentment to the soul of the bear. But since the passing away of the old customs the people of the bear-hunting villages referred to, say that unless certain religious measures be taken, the spirits of the bears cause deformed children to be born and other sad things to happen. So lots are cast, and every year or so two men are sent, according to the lots, to travel as pilgrims through all Japan to obtain repose for the souls of the bears. I have at least had evidence that pilgrims travel as pilgrims both from the Ichigo place and from Goka in Kyūshū to lay the ghosts of the bears. Some carry with them a few hairs of a "golden bear" or part of a bear's dried stomach, said to be a panacea, and give these to those who treat them well. Now is n't this exactly like the Ainu custom after a bear-hunt — so far as the idea goes? However, the same desire to placate the souls of animals killed while hunting is followed, I believe, by many primitive peoples, — among others, even by some American Indian tribes.

(I am just through with my examinations, but have been so overworked that I must postpone finishing this letter till to-morrow.)

Shooting at a paper lantern at night is a very amusing kind of Japanese archery. Contrary to expectation, however, I found it was fearfully difficult to hit. The great art is to aim an inch or two below the light, when the cup being shattered, the light at once goes out. My father-in-law destroys a lantern this way every time, — so I take care to tire myself shooting at it before he gets a chance. For at his first or second arrow — good-bye, lantern! . . .

My boy now seems to fill the larger part of this world, and is going to give me piles of occupation for the rest of my earthly career. How people can bear to have more than one or two now puzzles me really. One is almost too much for us all to attend to. Curiously, he takes to me more than to anybody, notwithstanding that I rarely play with him; — he has learned to give me my papers and letters, ride on my shoulder, and express his wishes without words. He is really remarkable in that he never cries. "Perhaps he *shall* become a Buddha" — unless I can take him to Italy and drown him with music, and take him to France to learn something about life. I want to do wonderful things for him. And I really think I shall be able to.

I got a beautiful set of compositions at the summer examinations on the theme "Home." There is, after all, delicious poetry in the boys. However, they will soon become selfish and hard, I fear; and will love nothing. What a humbug Government Education is! The Government is a mother, perhaps, but a stepmother only. The old terakoya was infinitely better in some points of view than all their detestable higher schools.

I will not write again till I get nearer to you.

Ever faithfully,

LAFCADIO HEARN.

YOKOHAMA, July 15, 1894.

DEAR CHAMBERLAIN, — This is a very bad letter, because written under difficulties. I hope to run up to 19 Akasaka Daimachi to-morrow, for a couple of days.

I have been intimately acquainted with Mason for more than a million years, and understand, I think, just why you like each other. Mason is what Goethe would have called "a beautiful soul." I have been to his charming little home, and felt quite in Paradise there, and love everything and everybody in it. We passed to-day at Kamakura swimming and indulging in debaucheries of beefsteak, whiskey and lemonade, gin and ginger ale and beer. His son was with us — and I like the little man very much; we soon became friends. — Well, you understand how very, very delightful things were. I should not trust myself to say exactly what I felt about our holiday. We are to take a trip together presently.

Coming out of my solitude of nearly five years to stand on the deck of the *Kobe Maru* on the 10th,

I felt afraid. I saw myself again among giants. Everything seemed huge, full of force, dignity, massive potentialities divined but vaguely. A sudden sense of the meaning of that civilization I had been so long decrying and arguing against, and vainly rebelling against, came upon me crushingly. In another few hours I had new friends.

The first man I spoke to was an engineer. He and I felt each other at once. He had been, like myself, a wanderer, — had seen Mt. Everest from a bungalow in Nepaul, — and studied many things.

The twin bits of our race-souls touched at once. What no Japanese could feel, that rough square man knew, — and he seemed to me a deity, or a demideity, — and I felt like one about to worship Western Gods.

Another day, and I was in touch with England again. How small suddenly my little Japan became! — how lonesome! What a joy to feel the West! What a great thing is the West! What new appreciations of it are born of isolation! What a horrible place the school! — I was a prisoner released from prison after five years' servitude!

Then I stopped thinking. For I saw my home, — and the lights of its household Gods, — and my boy reaching out his little hands to me, — and all the simple charm and love of old Japan. And the fairy-world seized my soul again, very softly and sweetly, — as a child might catch a butterfly.

Still, I am rather inclined to look forward to Tokyo. I can't dislike it any more. I have seen Mason's home, — so Tokyo seems to me very beautiful after all. — What queer experiences these! — how they make a man feel himself a creature of the forces of life — moved and moulded by that which is outside of himself!

How would it be were I here for a couple of years? Just now, you know, I seem to be in Scandinavia. Never did I see so many blond men with accipitrine noses, Berserker eyebrows, etc. I did not know how fair Englishmen were till now. I give up many notions. I must write of disillusions, and speak respectfully of the open ports.

Faithfully,
LAFCADIO HEARN.

Excuse this letter. The room is awfully hot, and I'm writing on a washstand.

TOKYO, July 17, 1894.

DEAR CHAMBERLAIN, — The banks were inaccessible for three days after my arrival in Yokohama, and it was only yesterday afternoon (Monday) that I was able to wind up my little business in Yokohama, and wire to Toda. (By the way, the bank manager, a very nice fellow, — after giving me a lecture for not having settled the business a year ago, — practically made me a present of fifty yen. I don't think bankers are such terrible people after all. Certainly no American banker would have done it — at least not for an insignificant school-teacher.)

Well, now for what would have been written last night had I not been very tired.

On the way from Shimbashi, I stopped at Hasegawa's, gave him two stories, and liked him. At your house all was in waiting for me; but the dog first made my acquaintance, — running before to the gate. He is now watching my every movement as I write, — and we are good friends.

Mr. Toda is too kind, and takes too much trouble for me. He was not in at the moment I came, — but making preparations for me on the strength of the telegram. He speaks English — which is delightful, as I can express all my wants. The charm of the home lacks but one thing — your presence; but I am not selfish enough to wish you to leave the mountains even for a day while this prodigious heat lasts. (I like heat; but I doubt if many do; and the heat in Tokyo is tropical.) I can't yet write my impressions about 19, — as I am still confused with kindnesses. Only — that delightful casket in the room upstairs with the medallion on top enclosing a picture of some structure that might have been the stately pleasure dome of Kubla Khan — what a fairy-thing it is! . . .

And now for confessions. I am glad my paper on jiujutsu was not published; and I am grateful to the Gods for having been obliged to visit Tokyo and Yokohama. The jiujutsu paper must be remodelled; and my ideas of the open ports reconstructed, repaired, renovated, and decorated. I have received from the Gods inspiration for a paper, — the Romance of the Open Ports, — or, perhaps, the morality of the open ports. If I had Michelet's divine gift of uttering tender surprises, I could startle the world with a paper on the ideas that came to me the other day. Perhaps there are illusions among them, too.

But, after all, what are all high ideals but illusions, and all high thought and sentiment lives by them, and ascends by them, — as by those golden fairy-ladders of legend, — whereof each step vanishes as quickly as the foot passes it? Really, I was totally unfitted to make any judgments about the ports when I left them. I had had my ugly experiences with American business men and American trick-sters, who played the rôle of friends for a purpose; I had seen infinitely too much of the black side of life as a journalist of long standing; I was uncomfortably situated and had Hinton in my thoughts as a co-lonial type. In short I had seen nothing which I ought to have seen. Then, by contrast, the caressing atmosphere into which I entered on going to Izumo — where secret orders had been given "to make the foreigner happy" — affected my judgment still more. Now comes the turn. The hospitable open-ness, the sympathies, and the abnegations light up for me all at once.

But here is the principal fact that impressed me about the moral question, — *entre nous;* for I don't want anybody else to get on the track of the idea till I develop it.

Morality is not shown by any unavoidable obe-dience to codes — indeed, it's often shown in the breaking of them. It is shown best, I think, when men, in defiance of traditions, conventions, and prejudices, — without any obligation, and in utter disregard of their own interests, — follow the guid-ing of their hearts on the path of what they feel to be eternally right and true. Race prejudice and cruelty *do* exist: they exist everywhere a little; and the unfortunate quality of goodness is that it remains invisible and silent. Love and generosity do not get themselves talked about: they never "advertise," — as Kipling would say. And, indeed, the fact that they are taken as a matter of course suggests their commonness. In connexion with all this, there is a beautiful subject — requiring very delicate handling — that has never been touched. What of the numbers who have given up England, France, Italy, — all the large Western life, — all that made them, and all that must in silent hours pull at their heartstrings as the sea pulls at the soul of a boy, — for pure love of duty? Never again will they dwell with their kindred, — never visit the scenes they dream of in sick hours, — when the Past floats back to say, hand in hand with the Shadow of Death, — "We are waiting, Come!" They have wealth; they have no obstacles or laws to hinder them. Only moral obligations they need not perforce obey. But even these have little to do with the matter. It is simply love — the purified affection, from which every atom of selfishness has been sifted out ages ago. In the brief time since I got on the *Kobe Maru* I have learned so many astonishing things, that it really seems to me I must have been guilty of blasphemies in other days — may the Gods forgive my ignorance! — And then the tales of prejudice! Numbers have given their whole lives and brains and means not merely to do what is right and good, but what is extraordinary and generous to the uttermost limit of their human capacity. My imaginary hard-

fisted and cold-hearted business men of the colonies
vanish away — phantoms only; and in their places
what warm human realities appear! — Really there
is a vast romance to be written here in a few words
— with help of thoughts and illustrations from
evolutional philosophy. — How you should smile to
compare this letter with other letters written long
ago! But in a few years more, how will I be writing
to you again? Truly we have not permanent opinions until our mental growth is done. The opinions
we have are simply lent us for a while by the Gods
— at compound interest.

Really, I must try later to get into this exiled
Western life, and love it, and study it, — and tell
all the beautiful things there are in it, leaving that
which is not beautiful to be related by its enemies.

"Read *all* my books!!" — I have n't been able to
read anything yet. I may be able to take a few
glimpses at some one corner of this wilderness of
good things. — I will read the titles, though, as
knowing what you have may help me later to pick
up for you something you have not.

Mason and I project a trip to Nagano for a few
days. I will leave my valise with your kind Toda,
and seek Zenkoji, — whither all the dead must go
before their journey to the Meido. Mason is a man
awfully fond of movement. I could not live as he
has to do. Had I such a sweet little home in Tokyo,
nothing could pull me out of it except at vast intervals of time. He needs exercise, however, and reminds me of a Targui (the plural "Touareg(s)"
is always used by the papers, in spite of the books

about that extraordinary race). You know they are very tall fair men with blue eyes (when the race is pure). "They can be known far off by their walk, — *long and measured, like the stride of the ostrich.*"

Ever with best regards and — but I can't thank you on paper for all this, you know! I shall try to revenge myself at some future day —

LAFCADIO HEARN.

19 AKASAKA DAIMACHI, July 20, 1894.

DEAR CHAMBERLAIN, — Yesterday, just after posting some lines to you, there came from Miyanoshita one of the very prettiest letters I ever got: I certainly shall follow your advice, — even to the matter of title, *probably*. The book is already, you know, half-done, eight papers having been finished.

Did any philologist ever before, in this mortal world, coolly tell his friend, — "Just take along with you any of my books you wish to read"? I don't think so. You are really too kind to me; — however, I think I can consult them here, in this cosy room, for all I need to look up. I have been mining extensively; but you will find no volume out of place when you return. Here are a few notes on what I have been doing: —

After Charlevoix the other literature and letters of the Jesuits interest me little. I glanced through some volumes in French and Spanish, and through Satow's monograph on the mission-press. (What a world of unfamiliar things you have!) Then I read three volumes of Tolstoi, full of tender deep caressing melancholy; I *re*-read (third time) Loti's Kyoto

("La Ville Sainte"), and judged it more kindly.
Lowell's papers on "Esoteric Shinto" greatly disappointed me. He utterly fails to feel the emotional
significance of oracles, — their relation to human
life from ancient times, their consolatory value,
their infinite poetry behind the poor little mask of
necessary fraud. So with the calling back of the
dead, the messages from the underworld: for what
myriads have these wrought peace of heart! — I
read Wepfner, and gnashed my teeth: what a
beastly little woman! I did not read "The Japanese
Bride," but I read all your delicious comments on
the margin. I looked through Dickson (not Dixon),
and admired him. He has art and taste. I glanced
at the Italian of the Avaloketesvara Sutra — it
seems less beautiful than in its embodiment in the
Saddharma Pundarika (Kern's version); — there is
a sublime invocation in the English, beginning, "O
Thou whose eyes are beautiful, whose eyes are kind,
whose eyes are full of sweetness and of pity . . ." or
words to that effect.—Nitobe's book on the United
States and Japan I liked very much. The curious
"Memorials of the Empire" is of supreme literary
value for *effective* references. Besides this, I have
turned over the leaves of scores and scores of books
on Japan, — and am not halfway through making
acquaintance with the legion. I was delighted with
the little volume of quotations from Schopenhauer:
a masterpiece of editing. I was delighted with the
pretty pictures to Ayame-San, and greatly vexed to
think such fine work should have been wasted on
such disgusting trash as Murdoch's text. — To-day

I expect to look over many more books. I admire
your impartiality as much as anything; — you seem
to have read and commented upon such a host of
things on Japan that try one's patience; and your
notes make the humorous side of the work the apo-
logy for its being. — I really had no idea until now
how much had been done in certain lines; and feeling
that all I could do would be only to add a few bricks
to the great Babel, I have become properly humble,
— I hope. But all this only to show you that I have
not been idling my time.

Upstairs, where on the *tansu* "the shadow of the
dome of pleasure floateth midway on the waves," —
I have been greatly taken by the mosquito-house. I
never saw anything resembling this outside of the
marsh country in Southern Louisiana; but even
there the arrangement is not adapted for bedrooms,
but for office-work, and the netting is wire. Along
the Lakes, near the mouth of the Mississippi, and
along the Gulf coast, wire netting is used for all the
openings of the house in summer. The structure at
19 Akasaka Daimachi is more simple, ingenious,
and effective than any I have met before. — The
work on that stove in the library is a wonderful
thing in its way: indeed, I am constantly finding
wonders. At night, curiously enough, I hear exactly
the sounds that I hear at night in Kumamoto — the
calling of the bugles, the chorus of military song. I
could fancy myself at home. But the night before
last I dreamed of robbers. The robbers became
transformed into something nameless and awful. I
did not see them — only felt them. Something

entered the house; and the stairs groaned under a hideous weight: I wanted to rise, but could not. IT was coming, coming. I suddenly awoke; *and felt the whole house shaking.* Imagine the momentary sensation! An earthquake,—and a very, very long shock. Did n't I think about the Meido!—Then the force of the old Scripture verse came to me, — about "the thief in the night;"—earthquakes are certainly the weirdest things in human experience.

At Mason's last night,—a Japanese dinner, very elegant and dainty,—Koto-playing by Mrs. M. and her sister (one of the sweetest little women I ever met),—a display of fireworks by the boys,— a great big warm moon. One of those evenings that never die: — But I fear all these experiences will demoralize me. After rescue, a castaway enjoys too much the food offered; a physician stands by to prevent him eating enough. My ghostly part was really too hungry for such experience, and feels longings not wholesome for it; — sympathy is the supreme delight of life. I ought now to meet some horribly disagreeable foreigners, — so as to have my pleasure checked a little. Besides, I am much too happy to write essays and sketches.

The heat is great. — The dog sits by me at dinner, comes to bid me good-morning regularly, and if I am not up by a decent hour, he utters a little plaintive cry outside the fusuma. He knows the hours for everything as well as if he studied the clock. — Mason and I *probably* will start on Saturday for a short trip to Zenkoji. The heat is still mighty —

equatorial. This is a poor letter; but intended only as an indication of how all is with your small question. . . .

Ever very faithfully,

LAFCADIO.

TOKYO, July 21, 1894.

DEAR CHAMBERLAIN, — I am stealing a few sheets of your note-paper until I can supply myself, which I hope to do to-day.

And here is Mason putting off our trip for three days more on account of his friend. So I am likely to torment Toda until Tuesday. He is very good. We went out shopping together yesterday. The *Atlantic* has come, but I have not received my copy yet, and only saw the number belonging to the *Mail*. I shall mail it as soon as it comes from Kumamoto. Somehow or other I don't feel that my story is a success.

Kuroda's "Outlines of the Mahayana" and Munro's pamphlet on the "Physical Basis of Mind in Relation to Evolution" are both interesting me much. I have got several strong suggestions from the former — nothing new from the latter, but the sensation of a soul that I should like to know better. — The most mysterious thing about any germ or sperm-cell, but especially about the human one, is that it contains potentially all the future idiosyncracies and capacities of the individual, as well as all the tendencies of the race. Now every material explanation of this has been demolished. Supposing the *atom*, or *force* centre itself, to carry the secret modification, the mathematician has very plainly proven that the number of atoms in the cell could not possibly be adequate for such enormously complex hereditary transmissions as take place. Spencer suggests a sort of polarity, and Munro tries to follow him. There is a world of suggestion in the mere fact of this impossibility to explain the transmission. Polarity, etc.,—all ghostliness,—who knows what it is? If these tendencies which make individuals and races belong, as they seem to do, to the life of the cosmos,—what strange possibilities are in order! Every life must leave its eternal records in the Universal life,—every thought of good or ill or aspiration,—and the Buddhistic Karma would be a scientific, not a theoretical doctrine. All about us the thoughts of the dead, and the life of countless dead worlds, would be forever acting invisibly upon us.

How touching Tolstoi is! Still, the fault of the beautiful religion of the man is simply that it is unsuited to the real order of things. Resentment, as Spencer has not hesitated to point out, is not only essential to self-preservation, but is often a moral duty. Altruistic characters may be regulated by Buddhist or Christian codes of action—but what about anti-altruistic characters, the Ape-souls and tiger-souls whose pleasure is in malice or destruction? The number is few;—but which of us has not met some, and recognized their capacity for evil? I believe the mass of humanity is good. I think every man must so think who has suffered much, and reached middle life. Nevertheless the sum of this goodness is not so preponderant that we can practically adopt either Tolstoiism or Buddhism to our Western civilization. Indeed no general course of action will suit. The dynamics of ethics must be varied according to class and time. The great fault of all religious systems is their application of a single code to many widely different conditions. — For all that, Tolstoi is certainly a light of the world, — a practical Christ in his own life. Curious that in Russia and England, in the same generation, two poets, Ruskin and Tolstoi, should have attempted to follow in practice the teaching, "Sell all thou hast, and give it to the poor." The most religious men of the nineteenth century are the infidels — the "atheists and blasphemers."

I wish you could get Minnie Hauk to sing you a *Habanera*, or the *Seguidilla* (seducing word!) from "Carmen." I heard her sing it, and the little eddies it made in my soul still thrill. — I cannot tell how glad I was to find that Mason had not read Prosper Mérimée's "Carmen." The opera, lovely as it is, does not give the awful poignancy of the tale — simple and clear beyond description. I am going to send it up to you, with a bundle of other things, as soon as I get back.

This reminds me of a dream I had a few months ago. I was sleeping, after reading "Carmen" for the fifth time, I think — quite a tropical afternoon it was. I entered a patio, — between lemon-coloured walls, — there was a crowd and music. I saw no face in the crowd — only felt people were there; — all my eyes and soul were for a gypsy dancing in the

midst; — poising, hovering, balancing, tantalizing
with eyes and gestures, — and every click of the
castanets went into my blood. I woke up and found
the clicking of the castanets was only the ticking
of the little clock, — strangely exaggerated in the
heated silence of the afternoon.

The enormous laughter of the crows every morning amuses me very much. I had not heard anything like it since leaving Izumo. The only striking
bit of weirdness in "Shuntoku Maru" is that about
indicating the time of the apparition of the boy's
dead mother as "the hour when the crows first fly
crying abroad, before the breaking of the day."

Let me entreat you, if you have it not already
as an experience, to procure yourself the curious
sensation of the "Kalewala," in Léouzon Le Duc's
complete prose-version. (A partial translation in
two volumes appeared in '55; a complete one, at
five francs, one volume, 1884.) The episode of the
dead mother is one of the most touching things in
all literature. "Then the mother arose from the dust
of her rest, and said: — "My son, for thee I have
kept the dog to be thy guide and friend; thou
wilt find the dog tied to the tree" — perhaps you
remember the lines.

The Tokyo Club (Rokumeikwan?) was a great
surprise to me. Architecturally and otherwise, it
would be a credit to any city in the world. The
reading-room is an invaluable advantage. Still, I
could never accustom myself to that kind of life. It
has occasional high value for me: just a dip into its
atmosphere. But were I able to live in the capital, I

should try to live very, very quietly — just as I have
been doing. One could never do any literary work,
and belong to society life in the real sense of belonging. And to mingle at all with that existence, without losing one's own rights to seclusion and quiet,
requires a character and experience much superior
to mine. It is a constant wonder to me how you can
be yourself, and yet give yourself so much to others,
— despite all the leisure you can have.

On your writing-desk there has been placed for
me, at my request, a little *tabako box*, and, dressed
in only a yukata and slippers, I write, smoking my
Japanese pipe betimes — taking a cigar only after
meals (small cigars I always carry with me when
travelling). The dictionary laid aslope on the table,
with the blotting-paper upon it, exactly suits me for
writing upon. — Upstairs, in the mosquito-house,
I use the hard pillow only — it is nice and cool.
They give me a bath every morning. Toda cooks
exquisitely, but gives me too many good things: I
have to tell him not to take so much pains, and to
restrict him as to dishes. His coffee (I take it black
only) is divine. — How shall I get even with you for
all this? I don't yet know, but I shall pray the Gods
to help me find out.

I am both glad and sorry for knowing Mason.
Why glad I need not say. But I shall feel sorry when
I am separated from him; — and anticipate regrets
of various kinds. What a delightful thing Schopenhauer says in that little book of yours — comparing
men to porcupines, trying to huddle together for
warmth, and presently repelled again by the contact

of their prickles! Mason has no porcupine-quills for me. It is such an experience to be close to a man like that.

Surely you are bored by this time.

Ever faithfully,

LAFCADIO HEARN.

July 22, 1894.

DEAR CHAMBERLAIN, — Yesterday at Otsu with Mason, — but would rather far have passed the day in his house. Still we had a glorious swim, and the sight of a fishing-net pulled in, — what splashing and spraying of prismatic colours! Otsu is not Japanese, however, — except the background of sky and mountain and sea. It has been spoiled — become a mere trap for foreign flies — saucy girls — rough proprietor — huge straggling spaces of *"ramshackle"* rooms — as one of the guests called them. There is, however, a glorious beach, and a great warm wind like a trade-wind.

After all, I am not going to Nagano! — After glancing over my passport, Mason came to the conclusion that we could be only one day together; and as the anticipated pleasure depended largely upon his company, I gave up the notion. I am getting ready to say good-bye to Tokyo, and shall disappear as soon as he flits. I shall go to Yokohama, however, and pass there a few days, feeling pulses — as I want to provide if possible against being compelled to leave Japan. What may happen *next March* none of us can guess. One sure thing is that if the Department conclude to do without us for a spell, we shall

never be taken back again upon the same terms.
This uncertainty (which Mason well calls the sword
of Damocles) poisons every pleasure, and paralyzes
every undertaking.

Still mining in your library. I envy you the glorious sets of Transactions, of the various Asiatic Societies; and the " Lettres Edifiantes " have finally got
hold of me. I took the liberty, also, to cut with the
horse-hoofed paper-cutter the pages of a book you
had not read —the bard of the Deinbovitzu. I found
queer inexpressible beauties and originalities in
them — a sort of savage tenderness and fierce grief
such as reminded me of the Servian poetry. The
Servian poetry seemed to me, however, far more
interesting, and, with all its strange ferocities, more
perfectly natural. A half-suspicion clings to this collection: its tone seems due to individual taste in setting, pruning, and decorating. What a curious half-
Eastern world is this world of Eastern Europe! I
suppose you have read the Unwritten literature of
the Caucasus: — the same indescribable mingling
of bloody ferocity with tenderness and lamentation.

I have not yet found among your books the pretty
translations of Japanese moral tales made by Turre-
tini (I think) which I used to possess (Romaji text
and French version), and some of the charming
prints of the Musée Guimet. Perhaps you have
them stowed away. If you have not, I think you
might like to add them to this glorious collection.
My library of ancient days was chiefly folk-lore. I
had the *Arabic* poets in many editions, the whole
Bibliothèque Orientale Elzevirienne (Leroux) up to

date, — the larger Bibliothèque Orientale, containing Burnouf's great essay, etc., etc., — "Les Littératures Populaires" (Maisonneuve), and hosts of such things. Except that their perusal enriches fancy, and gives glimpses of other race-souls, however, they are of small use to men not serious scholars or finished poets. To you I fancy some of these French series would be highly valuable. The genius of the race shows itself even in the serious work of their philologists: they select, curiously enough, just those subjects which English translators rarely touch. It seems to me that the really human side of Oriental literature in the Transactions of your own Asiatic Society has been appreciated only by Aston, Satow, and yourself. Such papers as "Mistress An's Tale," and "A Literary Lady of Old Japan," and three or four others, form so striking a contrast to the work usually done by the mass of the contributors. This literary sense strikes me as being shown in a more general way by the French Orientalists, — however defective their work may be in other respects. Comparing, for example, Lenormant and Maspero in Assyrian and Egyptian studies with English studies in the same line, — how much greater is the charm of the former for one able to understand the literary side only. . . .

Mason said a pretty thing the other day in the train. Opposite to us were sitting little mothers with their children. Both mothers and children were good to look at, — and the little white feet in snowy *tabi* seemed scarcely of this world. Mason looked at the dainty picture with a caress in his eyes, and said: — "If those people could only feel for us the sympathy we feel toward them —!" Indeed the whole question of life in Japan to a sensitive Westerner was summed up in that half-utterance. The unspeakable absence of sympathy, as a result, perhaps, of all absence of comprehension, is a veritable torture. Consequently, the entering into relations of sympathy again temporarily is for me like an electric bath. The charm is something like the first sensation of the tropic world. Really I have been a great blasphemer, and am well punished therefor. Now the idea of returning into the life of Japan is a growing terror to be overcome. I have been partly demoralized by my Tokyo days. I need a little medicine of unkindness — want to be sickened for a time of Yokohama, etc.

Hasegawa gave me a cheque of twenty for my first story, and seems extremely anxious to get more. This will please you, I know.

LAFCADIO HEARN.

July 24, 1894.

DEAR CHAMBERLAIN, — Mason is gone, — leaving a great void in my psychical atmosphere. I linger awhile, hoping to-day or to-morrow at latest to have the *Atlantic* for you, and to arrange a little matter in connexion with the Boston firm.

I never had the experience before of coolly taking possession of a friend's house during his absence, — and feel a slight remorse of conscience which I can't get over, no matter how many kind things you may say. If I did not hope to be able to give you some day an almost equal amount of pleasure, I should really feel very bad — and there is no use reasoning about the thing at all, because feeling is quite independent of reasoning. Indeed reason is the most tricky and treacherous thing in the world; and the Shinto formula, "obey your own heart," is much more satisfactory. — There are several pleasures in having been here which I did not speak about yet. First it is nice to know a friend's home — in which something of him always lives wherever he be; — to comprehend his pleasures and habits through the kindness of servitors who try to make the guest as happy as their own master (placing the lounge for him where the breeze blows, and all these little attentions); — to get an idea of the geography of his intellectual world, and glimpses of the favourite literary paths; — to notice and sympathize with his comments on margins; — to be instructed by the mere names of the volumes he has collected in all places; — to understand something of his tastes, and so to take pleasure in all his happiness; — in short, to have the definite sensation of what we might call "The Soul of the House." For every dwelling in which a thinker lives certainly acquires a sort of soul — there are Lares and Penates more subtle than those of the antique world; — these make the peace and rest of a home. And besides, there are memories of England which bring back visions of my boyhood — suggestions no American home furnishes. The English crest on silver plate, — the delicious little castors, — the "homey" arrangement of articles which represent the experience of generations in search of good solid comfort, — all created for me a sort of revival of old, old, and very intimate impressions. Therefore, I suppose, some ghosts of very long ago came soundlessly about me once or twice in twilight time, — and portraits of another era, forgotten for thirty-five years, faintly shaped themselves for me in the dusk before the lighting of the lamp. In thought I sat again upon the floor of a house which no longer exists, and shot at armies of tin soldiers with cannon charged with dried peas. For, just as the faintest odour of fresh tar recalls visions of unnumbered days of travel, — decks and faces and ports and horizons of which the names have faded out altogether, — so it requires only a very little suggestion of England to resurrect home-days.

I have almost stopped mining in sheer despair. It would take me ten years to work through all these veins — I mean the veins I *could* work a little; for one large section would ever remain for me incomprehensible as a *grimoire*. — I never saw the work of Captain Basil Hall before, — though his name, attached to translations of his books, has been long familiar to me in French catalogues. Looking over the beautiful little volumes in calf, I could not help thinking that our English prints of to-day are, on the whole, quite inferior to the choice texts of that time — when type, paper, and binding possessed a durable solidity and beauty that latter-day competition is destroying. To-day, our best English prints seem like imitations of French work.

Since you thought enough of the Creole Grammar to bind it, I must send you a couple of Creole prints I have at home. Should I ever be able to recover my library, I could give you an almost complete set of works relating to all the French-Creole dialects. What I regretted was my inability to procure the Catechism of Goux (Père). I had it in my hands, but could not persuade the owner to part with it. I think my next letter will be from Yokohama.

Ever faithfully,

LAFCADIO.

August 9, 1894.

DEAR CHAMBERLAIN,—After five—no, six—days at sea, and eight hours rail (*Kato* — with the thermometer at 96!), I am home again, naked, cool, and able to write. I found all well, and my boy crawling about and opening drawers and developing terrifying capacities of rapid growth and mischief. I delivered your kindest message, which gave no small pleasure; — and, full of those pleasant memories, which are wholesome regrets, I sit down to chat with you. Not so pleasant as under the stars among the shrubbery shadows at Miyanoshita, —but that was a luxury, and might happen only once in a lifetime.

What shall I chat of? I think you would be most interested about my experiences with men and women on board. The experiences of travel are usually among the most pleasant in our lives — ugly ones being comparatively rare. The general rule would seem to be that human nature in any normal condition of a purely temporary kind throws off its armour of reserve, abandons its ferocity of egotism, and exposes to the best light whatever of kindness it owns. I have made a few acquaintances of whom I hope to hear again.

My roommate *was* a mate — a steamboat mate in the N. Y. K.'s employ, — a long hard man, very young, built like a greyhound, representing the swarthiest type of swarthy Englishman. His heavy black brows, hawk-nose, and heavy chin were lighted up by a wonderful smile, however, as we met; and that smile made us friends at once. I expected to find him rough and straight, and I did. Very soon I learned all his life, — his ideas of right and wrong, plain and good, — his sacrifices for others, — his hopes about the sweetheart waiting at home. It was pleasant as a cool strong sea-wind on a burning day. He liked rough jesting, and spared me instinctively, but teased the other passengers considerably, who seemed to allow his domination without regret. Samples of conversation ought to have been written down, — but I laughed too much at the time, and next day forgot them. Only a few fragments are herewith submitted: —

Mate. — "Is that lady your sister?"

Passenger. — "Yes."

M. — "Can't see the resemblance."

Pass. — "Well, that's not my fault. Still, I'm younger than she is."

M. — "Young! — you'll never see fifty-nine again!"

Pass. — "I'm only thirty-three."

M. — "Good Lord! You'll be a nice-looking brute, won't you? — at sixty. Why, you're half-dead now!"

Pass. — "Just out of the German army."

M. — "Well, well! — Many soldiers like you?"

Pass. — "Not many so good. I took all the prizes for shooting."

M. — "With what?"

Pass. — "With a gun."

M. — "What gun — *your* gun? I don't think you could shoot much with that." . . .

Pass. — "Those are pretty good shoes — what number? Mine's five."

M. — "Five! I should n't like to be lying down in the street when you're walking around with that number five! — That's eleven — or fourteen!"

Pass. — "Well, it's too large for me. But I like that — because number five and number fourteen are just the same price: you see I like to get the worth of my money."

A very sweet-faced elderly woman, who adapted herself to the seaman's rough ways with gentle success, attracted me pleasantly. She was on her way to Vladivostok. She was an expert in electro-metallurgy, kinetics, and mineralogy. Her husband, a Frenchman who looked like a front-page drawing by Cham out of the *Charivari*, was rightly proud of her, — and told her to explain to me the defects of triple-expansion engines and other things, — which she did very shyly and sweetly. I learned to almost love the old lady, told her all I could about Japan to interest her, and about my own affairs. She gave me her ideas about things delightfully, and with that perfectly straight natural sympathy which is essentially German. "The future," she said, "is to natural science. The old professions are being more and more overrun. If your boy has a good head, give him a scientific education — there is a sure future for the man having practical scientific knowledge." As we passed the high cliffs, — she would point out streaks of colour, and tell me the names of metals that could be extracted from them.

Her brother — a fiery red — one of those men who look as if ready to break into flame — was all good-nature and honesty. He had a curious way of gazing at you with half-shut eyes — letting only the least steely glimmer filter out between the eye-lids: I had only once before seen that sort of gaze, in a Spanish fencer — a decidedly dangerous man. But this, I felt sure, was due to other causes. The Spaniard had teeth in his eyes: this German gaze was pure fine steel. At Kobe, we all tried with glasses to read the name of a hotel from the deck: he read it at a glance, with the naked eye. He was the crack-shot of a German corps, — and long prac-tice had given him that singular manner of looking at things and people, as if taking aim. He got up in the night to see me off — so did his nice old sister. I took their address, and they promised to write me, and want me to visit them, if I can, at Vladi-vostok. The three belong to some electrical com-pany, — the woman, curiously enough, being the scientific head of the undertaking.

The fifth acquaintance was a globe-trotter, — a

Swiss ex-officer of artillery, — on a three years'
journey. Curious! he had just come from New
Orleans! He was a man of the world — hard and
cold as a glacier, — and it took some time to make
him thaw. The thawing was pleasant — because he
was a thoroughly well-informed man on everything
relating to Switzerland, — and he almost induced
me to study some means of settling there in future
time. He spoke Russian, Italian, French, and German as well as English; and he had been in the West
Indies and Spanish Honduras. He was not a man
one could ever make friends with, but he was a
highly interesting acquaintance, — all precision and
exactness, — a mathematical machine, highly polished, and running noiselessly. I thought it strange
that he paid little attention to Japan, — which he
had only touched at on his way to India. But short
as was his stay at Yokohama, he knew all about the
principal mercantile houses there.

Now, don't you feel bored with all this? Well, I
just wanted to hint of my experiences, as typical.
I discovered something else, too. — Since my hair
has turned grey, I find I get along better than I
used to do among absolute strangers. Grey hair
gives a suggestion of wisdom, of experience which
may or may not be true, but always secures a little
consideration. — And one other thing struck me —
when all of us second-class passengers were ordered
rather coarsely to keep away from the first-class
deck — that it is good to be *very* poor, and good to
be *very* rich; but that to be neither rich nor poor is
the unforgivable sin. For the steerage passengers,

— Chinese especially — were allowed more privileges than we.

To-day I am sending some books to you, and some, separately, to Mason. The wonderful study of Napoleon, by Taine, is in that volume (5) of the "Origines" entitled "Le Régime Moderne." I would advise you to begin the set with that. I send also "La Cité Antique;" and the last volume written by Maupassant ("L'Inutile Beauté") just before his madness. It is noteworthy that there are two studies of insanity in this volume, — one of which, about *le monstre à crâne-de-lune*, might have been written in an asylum. But neither of these compares with the awful sketch "Le Juge" — in "La Petite Roque."

I would like you to read the whole of these stories line by line. Maupassant may sometimes be disgusting, but he has splendid psychological perceptions at times, — and his commentaries and arguments are, I think, the most valuable part of his work. But I must stop for to-day, though I have much more to say.

With all pleasant and grateful memories,

Faithfully,

LAFCADIO HEARN.

August 12, 1894.

DEAR CHAMBERLAIN, — Yours of the 8th just at hand. By this time you will have my letter and the books. I did not get home for just a week, you know, — leaving on the 31st (Monday) and reaching Kumamoto only on the night of Saturday.

The heat has been terrible, and night before last

we had thirty-five (!!) shocks of earthquake — the
first of which was violent enough to break the *kabe*.
We had to pass the night in the garden. All this is
atrocious.

I don't mind tropical heat, — because there is
ample consolation in the splendour of tropical light
and colour, and wondrous vegetation. But this dead
oven heat is tiresome, — prevents thinking. To
write the name Kumamoto now is disagreeable —
the feeling is that one has toward the names of certain unpleasant people one tries to forget, and dislikes the mention of. The old sensation of nervous
lonesomeness enveloped me just like a black atmosphere after my return, and stays with me. I am
tortured by the mere repetition of this question,
always recurring," How long can I bear this?" But
what else can I do? — except leave the country.

Enough of this, however. — Let me disagree with
you. I think you are perhaps strongly under the
influence of the 18th century in poetry, — you are a
classic, I am not. I detest the 18th century, and I
cannot believe that one true line of poetry could be
found from the first page of Pope to the last. I
should call everything Pope ever wrote tiresome
bald prose. I am speaking, of course, a little strongly
—would modify the last statement in respect to
values, if considering the literary influence of
Pope at length. But I cannot think Pope ever felt
an emotion. To me emotion, uttered with power,
touched with natural rhythm and colour, *is* poetry;
and form is not poetry at all. The prose of the English Bible; the prose of Kingsley's "Heroes;" the

prose of Ruskin betimes, is the noblest of poetry. Or take the prose-line of the translated Arabian thought about the desolate site of the camp "when the north wind and the south have woven the twisted sand,"—in all Pope what touches it? Now "The Song of the Camp" contains true feeling; and though you are quite right in judging all Bayard Taylor's work as second-rate (indeed you might have said third-rate), I think there is fine emotion all through the book,—gold strands to be picked out here and there. Don't you think that if we keep to the masterpieces only, we must lose a great deal of that which is most beautiful and original in human utterance? For all deep-souled men—however unlettered—are betimes poets, and utter poetry worth remembrance; and the second-rates and the third-rates, if sifted, give us pearls and rubies and emeralds. Miller has written much trash,—nevertheless to read Miller is to receive a world of new sensations.

It is true that much of Pope cannot be thought of out of the form in which he cast and froze it. But is not this true even of proverbs in rhyme?—which are prosy enough—especially the musical Spanish ones—

Con la mujer y el dinero
No te burlas, compañero.

Byron was strongly under Pope's influence; but he had passion, enormous force, a colossal imagination. Therefore, in the true sense of poetry, I would think the "Siege of Corinth"—even fifty lines from it—worth more than all Pope's work.

Well, I suppose we really agree at bottom — except about the value to literature of inferior poets.

With kindest remembrances,

LAFCADIO.

August 21, 1894.

DEAR CHAMBERLAIN, — I can't quite understand about Welsh being written phonetically — how about "CWRW"? — beer, is n't it? I used to live in Wales. As a child my folks passed all their summers at Bangor, — where we used to hire donkey-phaetons and bathe and have a good time. Retired Indian officers in multitude used to be visible there, — and some used to tell me queer stories. I was then regarded as a pampered little heir to wealth and luxury, and I got wonderful petting from beautiful ladies, who would not like to see me now. — Carnarvon Castle was a favourite visit. I used to climb the Eagle-tower, and look down upon the crawling of the ships. I remember a *white* peacock there. — In Carnarvon also I had my first knowledge of the farther East. One year I lived there all alone with my nurse in the cottage of a seaman of some sort, — he was on the Chinese run; and every time he came back he used to bring all sorts of curious things from China, — porcelains, grotesques, gods. These were piled upon a great "dresser" reaching nearly to the ceiling. I used to look at them with awe, and dream about them at night. — My nurse used to be able, though a Connaught girl, to understand the speech of the country folk. These would come into town in their witch-hats, — a fashion preserved from the sixteenth century, I think, — wearing frilled caps under the hats. — What *very* happy times those were! —they gave no augury of the years of nightmare to follow.

I am trying to prepare those ballads for the A. S., but it goes against the grain. The ballads are all right, but should be well supplied with notes, which I am not competent to make; and I've lost all interest in the material. It appeals to no feeling. It is folk-lore of the baldest narrative kind. However, I'll try to make some sort of an introduction, and then send you the thing by parcel-post — or, if you don't wish to look at it, I'll send to Mason — for though very clearly written, the MS. might tire your eyes.

I am sorry you have so much trouble with your eyes. I fear you must lose the chief part of pleasure in reading, by having a student read to you — especially the French. I can't help thinking this may have been a reason for disliking Gautier's tales. They are not adapted, I think, for being heard, — the blaze of colour, the ghostly delicacy of word-mosaic, and the whole rhythm of the sentences, address themselves best to the eye and to silence. — Were I independent of teaching, and nearer to you, what a pleasure it would give me to read something wonderful to you occasionally. I had a dear old friend in America, who taught me printing. He had a great big silent office, and every evening for two years, it was our delight to have such reading. I read nearly all the old *Atlantic* stories to him — at that time, you know, the *Atlantic* was the medium

of Emerson, of Holmes, of every man distinguished
in American letters. The old man was something
of a Fourierist. In his office I made acquaintance
first with hosts of fantastic heterodoxies, — Fourier
himself, Hepworth Dixon ("Spiritual Wives"), the
Spiritualists, the Freelovers, and the Mormons, —
the founders of phalansteries and the founders of
freelove societies.

I don't know whether my fellow travellers were
anarchists. They might have been, though. They
spoke very eloquently about the religion of humanity and the atrocities of modern civilization. I
sympathized with them. I shall always sympathize
with anarchy and nihilism while I am unable to get
large chances in life. — You remember the story —
the fact rather — about the Nihilist or Anarchist
sheet published some years ago. One morning the
paper appeared in mourning with a farewell edition.
saying: —

"We are sorry to announce our inability to continue the publication of the ——. The editor has
decamped. A vile traitor to the cause, a selfish
hypocrite; — having been left by his uncle the
sum of £300 a year, he has declared that his sentiments have changed, and that he sympathizes
with the bloated bondholders and aristocrats. Fearing our just vengeance, he has fled."

Ever faithfully,
LAFCADIO.

DEAR CHAMBERLAIN, — So glad to get your letter — I was a little uneasy, fearing that some

sudden change in temperature might have had unpleasant consequences: for the weather is terribly
treacherous now, and we shall all have to be very
careful indeed at the fall season. — Here the heat
is thick and solid at night, but the land-breeze blows
twice a day — and I have the privilege of living
naked, with only a *koshimaki*. To wear any costume now would be decidedly disagreeable, and
signify a constant drenching.

Oh! I am so glad you liked the "Red Bridal," —
an awfully dangerous experiment, and one I know
you would not have encouraged in advance. I shall
attempt very little in that line, though. Perhaps
you are right about the metaphysical conversation,
though nearly all the thoughts are based on notes
taken from Japanese conversation. I have struck
out a few lines for the book-form — lines or touches,
thrown in by myself.

The little Creole pamphlets I send you, and the
"Flying Trip round the World," and the Lotis and
the novels, are for your library, of course. Don't
think of sending them back. I read "Au Maroc"
through, with a sort of half-scared pleasure; and the
impression is lasting. Although purely personal
work, it seems to me a very perfect book of travel.
I slipped into it a note from Pierre Loti. Perhaps
you would like to keep a specimen of his chirography.

What you said about the Welsh was very illum-
inating: I could understand many things at once
through those few lines of yours. How very curiously the value of letters changes in certain tongues!
— By the way, when I was in Wales, excellent daily

papers were published in Welsh. Perhaps these still exist. If you study Welsh, as a living tongue, perhaps it would interest you to see a few copies of those curious papers.

Yes, indeed, there is an astonishing parallelism between the classic French and classic English — the Drydens and Popes with their satellites, and the Racines, Corneilles, and Boileaux, etc., with theirs. Boileau seems to me most worthy of comparison with Pope. But what a delight to turn from these fettered giants to wild freedom of the Romantic schools, and the later imitations of it in England! The monotony of Pope and Boileau tire me awfully — like the perpetual beating of a drum without orchestra.

By the way, did you ever wonder how the old English Bible translators ever managed to get that splendid hexameter (is n't it?) —

God is gone up with a shout, the *Lord* with the sound of a trumpet!

And is n't it greater than any line in Pope?

Have you read Murger's "Scènes de la Vie de Bohème," Kompert's "Scènes du Ghetto"?

All of Kompert is good, — but I only suggest one for trial: the greatest Jewish story-writer of the age. Murger, I think, you have read; but should you have missed it, please get it, and have a delightful mixture of humour — uproarious humour — and profound but simple pathos. It also is one of the great books of the century — not perfect in style — but so human: it is to prose what much of Béranger's

TO BASIL HALL CHAMBERLAIN 375

work is to French song. All the works of these two
writers (Lévy Frères) are issued at one franc each.
And pray, *pray* don't forget, when you order books
again, Gérard de Nerval's "Filles de Feu." (Lévy,
one franc.) One of the Daughters of Fire (a dream)
inspired what has entered into French literature as
one of the most perfect of all essays on the romantic
ballads of mediæval France. Let me suggest also
Maupassant's "Des Vers." I have not read them,
but I trust Saintsbury's enthusiasm about them.

I am just finishing a little paper "Yuko," story
of the girl who cut her throat that the Emperor
might cease to sorrow (May, 1891), mere narrative,
with philosophical reflections. — I fear you will be
disappointed with my "ballads" — the work was
altogether beyond my powers. I sent to 19 Akasaka
— so that you should not have the trouble of looking at them till the weather got cool. — Should you
condemn them, however, I may try to offer, later,
a decent version of a rather dry but very curious
Buddhist book — "The Story of the *Humming* of
the Sainokawara." Curious phrase. There is a
Polynesian song, quoted by Giles, which has in
a refrain the words, "Listen to the *humming* of the
ghosts." And curiously also, I found the word used
in the same sense by the blacks of Martinique.
(Earthquakes every night nearly.) Have discovered
a new weird Shinto God — *Shinigami.*

Faithfully,   LAFCADIO.

P. S. I have *stacks* of MS. Creole compositions
taken down from dictation — folk-songs, stories,

samples of conversation. All these are at your disposal, to keep, if you ever want them.

Note. — The essay by Dr. Mercier (now dead) is the best, and I believe the only good paper in the Louisiana patois. I don't like Fortier's article, and I don't think it is correct. He elaborates Creole into a complexity the spoken tongue never possesses in black mouths.

September 6, 1894.

DEAR CHAMBERLAIN, — The Imperial gift came, — through the Governor of Shimane and through the kenchi of Kumamoto, — a very handsome sake-cup of red lacquer with the Kiri-mon therein in letters of gold. This was accompanied by a very handsome document from the Governor of Shimane, stating the why and the wherefore. — Pleasant, of course, — but probably the last pleasant thing that I will have in Japan.

My robber had very large feet: "stately stepped he east the way, and stately stepped he west," — and the Junsa took a proof of his soles on a piece of paper, and we burned many *moxa* upon the tracks, that his feet might become sore. Perhaps this is why he was riding all over town yesterday in a kuruma, trying to sell my watch. Curious, the police have not caught him yet.

The soldiers are being addressed by Buddhist priests, and consecrated to Amida by the laying of a razor on each head — symbolic tonsure. The sword and helmet of Kato Kiyomasa are said to have disappeared from Homnyoji and to have been sent to Korea.

Autumn has begun. I hope your throat is better. It occurred to me, since my last, that the long conversations in the raw mountain air, on the porch at night, might have been as tiring as they were pleasant. When I have to talk in the class for an hour without stopping, I feel it afterwards in hoarseness and fits of coughing.

Yours very faithfully,

LAFCADIO HEARN.

September 11, 1894.

DEAR CHAMBERLAIN, — Glad to get even a line from you — though it has not brought me as good news of you as I could wish. Perhaps it is only the unsettled weather: the clear autumn may bring back strength.

I was interested by Lowell's letter. Since I first read of Schiaparelli's discovery, I had always wondered why different astronomers could not agree on the character of the so-called canals, — many pronouncing them double, others single. Lowell would seem really to have hit the cause. — What are the canals? *Are* they canals, or only the lines of a monstrous planetary breaking-up?

I have just sent off another sketch, "A Wish Fulfilled" — the story of one day of a Japanese soldier.

Lord! Lord! what *is* morality? Nature's law — the cosmic law — is struggle, cruelty, pain — everything religion declares essentially immoral. The bird devours the fly, the cat the bird. Everything has been shaped, evolved, developed by atrocious immorality. Our lives are sustained only by murder. Passions are given, which, if satisfied, would stifle the earth with population, were there not other passions of cruelty and avarice to counteract them. Perhaps it is the higher morality that the strong races should rob the weak — deprive them of liberties and rights — compel them to adopt beastly useless conventions — insult their simple faith — force upon them not the higher pleasures but the deeper pains of an infinitely more complicated and more unhappy civilization.

There certainly is no answer to this. It is contrary to all our inborn feeling of right. But what is that feeling? Only the necessary accompaniment of a social state. Does it correspond to any supreme law of the universe? — or is it merely relative? We *know* it is relative; we don't know anything about the ultimate laws. The God of the Universe may be a Devil, — only mocking us with contradictions, — forcing us through immeasurable pain to supreme efforts which are to end in nothing but the laughter of skulls in a world's dust. Who knows? — We are only what we can't help being.

From remote time all my ancestors were in the army. Yet to kill the fly that buzzes round me as I write this letter seems to me wrong. To give pain knowingly, even to one whom I dislike, gives more pain to myself. Psychology tells me the why — the origin of the feeling. But not by any such feeling is the world ruled — or will so be ruled for incalculable time. Such dispositions are counted worthless and weak, and are unfitted for the accomplishment of large things. Yet all religions teach the cultivation of the very qualities that ruin us. Clever men always follow the forms and laugh at the spirit. — Out of all this enormous and unspeakably cruel contradiction, what is to come? A golden age, some say. But what good will that do us? — and what good will it do any one — since it must pass according to inevitable laws? — I understand the laws, their results. But what is their meaning? What is right? What is wrong? Why should there be laws at all?

(I must try to get James Hinton's "Mystery of Pain," to see if he can throw any light on the matter.)

We are all tired of Kumamoto. I must try to get out of it this year or next year. I am almost certain, however, that I had better go to America for a time. One does not isolate one's self from the Aryan race without paying the penalty. You could not know what it means, unless you had borne it long; — the condition is unspeakable. You say I work well. If I did not, I should go insane, or become a prey to nervous disease. Perhaps the suffering has been good in this — that it has forced me to literary discipline which I could not otherwise have obtained. To write three volumes in five years (for my new book is almost done) really means a good deal — teaching besides. But Kumamoto, what with earthquakes, robbers, and thunderstorms, is my realization of a prison in the bottom of hell. I would be glad of half the salary with half as much more peace of mind.

Is it selfish to tell you my feelings? It would be, perhaps, if you were feeling gloriously well, — but as you also have some trouble, — perhaps more suffering from illness than you ever speak of, — you will have the grim comfort of knowing that one not sick at all thinks of your existence as the seventh heaven, — as the life of Haroun Al Raschid, — as the luxury of the most fortunate of the fortunate khalifs of Bagdad.

Faithfully, with best wishes,

LAFCADIO HEARN.

DEAR CHAMBERLAIN, — I did a man unwittingly injustice — gross injustice! — in my last letter to you. Fardel's handwriting is so bad, that I really mistook his meaning, and am delighted to find that his declaration of position was exactly the opposite to what I had made him say, and what vexed me at the time so much that I drafted a protest. He has not yet, as I feared, been devoured by the Philistines. But the prejudice of which he spoke, and my comments thereon, seem to be as I put them.

This was really all I meant to say, and I hope no one but you saw my horrible mistake. You might scold me severely for it, and I should be as submissive as Kipling's "Mowgli" when he took his whipping like a man.

I've learned nearly all of Kipling's ballads by heart, and am every day more and more amazed at their power. If you have only read them once, try a second reading, and see how they strike you. They gain every time. I must have read them over ten times. The way they get into memory comes in sleep. I wake up repeating such lines as —

There's a wheel on the Horns of the mornin', an' a wheel on the
     edge of the Pit,
And a drop into nothing beneath you, as straight as a beggar can
     spit . . .

What a curious sense of individual knowledge
the thing gives. Every man in these ballads is a
different character, and yet intensely real. The
"Mandalay" ballad is the utterance of a dreamy,
good-natured trooper, — "Gunga Din" is that of an
aggressive brute, — "The Widow's Party" is that
of the sullen, hard, bulldog soldier, — "Troopin'"
and others represent totally different, light, jolly
characters. Great is K.

L. H.

September 12, 1894.

DEAR CHAMBERLAIN, — Your letter certainly
does place the treaty in a most unfavourable light,
as regards Things-as-they-are. And I suppose that
is the only way to look at the matter after a generation: Things-as-they-should-be having gone to
oblivion. Also you rather quickly dispose of my
supposition about the supreme future power of
invested foreign capital. Well, I suppose it is the
last grip of the *jiujutsu;* and my article still holds
good, in that event. But there are two strong possibilities — no, three — against the treaty going into
operation: —

(1) That other European powers will agree to
no such terms, — and that the United States will
very energetically oppose them.

(2) That the foreign colonies will make their
claims heard to some purpose in an effectual protest.

(3) That the sense of the Japanese nation, the instinct of the masses, will oppose the treaty as on former occasions — blindly — in spite of any and all reasoning.

Besides, there is the war-sphinx whose questions have not yet been answered.

No, I did not intend to take part with the officials. I did not even think of them. I thought emotionally of the common people only — those who would suffer — the fairy-folk who perform miracles on a diet of rice, with their "pathetic pleasures" (Pater), their innocent faith, their love of the dead, their little shrines, their temples — the antique world which has not yet vanished, nor been injured by ridicule of shallow-pated missionaries. I thought of these toiling in stinking factories, under foreign employ; — I thought of utilitarian transformation and destruction (artistically) of the porcelain and lacquer industries; — I thought of all the horrors of American industrial life forced into Japan. . . . I shall always love the common Japan: there is plenty of it — 40,000,000 of it. — You should really live among it alone for a year, — and you would not feel lonely. It is only after a long time that the lonesomeness comes. If the treaty could save this life intact, I should be glad. But I fear that the future demoralization of Japan is to be effected by Japanese in frock-coats and loud neckties. That will be infinitely worse.

I can't stand them. I must get out of the country for a time. I feel, much more than you could have thought, your words about "white men." Yes, I would rather work for white men of almost any kind — though there are mean kinds enough — than under these. . . .

I'm glad I have a young man in the house. He is wonderfully handy, and makes the most beautiful toys for the child I ever saw.

You did n't congratulate me on the sake-cup. Perhaps such presents are very common. Don't tell me the missionaries get them, or I shall "howl a whoop, and with the howlment of the whoop shall yip a yawp!"

How is this definition by a Japanese student? — "A friend is one person to whom we can tell *all our suspicions.*"

Faithfully, with best wishes,

LAFCADIO.

September 22, 1894.

DEAR CHAMBERLAIN, — If I did not feel a certain awe of you, I should say "What a dear fellow you are!" You knew that sake-cup was a farce — it is No. 5 and cost $1.25. But you were too sweet to tell me. The Japanese friend to whom I wrote an exquisite message for the Governor of Shimane, couched in high-court style, was much less considerate. He frankly laughed at me and at the sake-cup, and told me also about an Evangelical *temperance* society having been embarrassed by the Imperial gift of a sake-cup of silver. . . . Ah bah! all this world is illusion.

I have definitely accepted the Kobe offer, and anticipate misery. Still, any sort of change is a relief. After the Prophet lay upon his left side for three hundred and ninety days to bear the iniquity of the house of Israel, he was quite glad to lie three hundred and ninety days on his right side to bear the calamity of the house of Judah; and he was grateful to the Lord.

I have just sent off my eleventh paper, finishing my second book on Japan, as I am limited to 70,000 words. I suggested for a title, "Out of the East." (*Ex Oriente lux?*) . . .

And now I shall *try* at least to get material for open-port sketches.

"In Yokohmam" is a Buddhist paper, — a conversation with an old priest. Amenomori helped me magnificently with it — answering questions in the most beautiful way. His MS. is a wonder in itself. Any man who can write such English as Amenomori, and think so profoundly, ought to be able to render the "Tao-te-king" into perfect French. May the Buddha forgive me for all the wrong I have done others in thought and word, and charge up my sin to the illusions and bewilderments of this beastly universe!

I sent an *Atlantic* the other day. The last instalment of "Philip and his Wife" seems to me almost a miracle. I would also recommend the paper on Plato — conventionally managed, but within narrow limits extremely clever. . . .

If I did not have to work to keep up I should be very unhappy at all this. In the whole United States there is now not one single publication of the first-class entirely under liberal control. Is the case

any better in England, — when Frederic Harrison
must write side by side with the Right Reverend
Jack-in-the-Box, — and an essay by Spencer must
be controverted by His Grace the Archbishop of
Croquemitaine, — and the Gladstone Skeleton must
be dragged into utterance as a respectable denuncia-
tion of Huxley's common-sense? Is the whole world
going back into the dark ages again, — through the
mere demoralizing effect of that centralization of
wealth and of conventionalism following upon the
solidification or stratification of society? How
much better seems to me the wild days of Mormon
evangelization in America, — of the Freelove phalansteries, — of Brook Farm and the Oneida Community, — of Hepworth Dixon's "Spiritual Wives"!
Humbug, of course, but what a finely fluid aspirational condition of society the whole thing meant,
— even with "Mr. Sludge, the Medium" thrown
in! Anything is better than the crystallization of
ideas, the hardening of conventions, the recognized
despair of thinkers to oppose the enormous weight
and power of Philistinism. *"You!"* — said a Jew
to me long ago (a Jew with Heine's soul, and
therefore now dead and double-damned) — *"You*
fight society. Oh, you fly! the elephant's foot will
crush you *without feeling you."* — What matter!
In those days being supremely an ass as well as
a fly, I thought I could overturn the universe. I
was a new Archimedes: the lever was enthusiasm!
all radicals were my brothers, and had I been
in Russia I might have tried to blow up the
Czar.

All this reminds me that Fardel, replying to a letter as to whether he could take my place here (he says he can), writes to me quite needlessly about the Eurasian question and about his "martyrdom in fighting seven years against a social wrong," — the Eurasian party representing the *wrong*. He has become evidently *fige*. . . . Thinking over the matter, I cannot help admiring the d—d Jesuits. There race-feeling is trampled out of a man's soul; — there the conventions of society are subjected utterly to one spiritual though fanatical idea; — there is religious democracy — equality — fraternity; — there no moral question is caught up as a hypocrite's mask for race-hate. I almost wish I could believe, and hie me to a monastery, or preach Rome on the banks of the Amazon.

Oh! this is a blue letter, — and you have been so kind, — sending telegrams and everything! Never mind, I 'll try to make it up to you some day. I am going to try to flee soon.

With best regards and ever so many warm thanks,
                                    LAFCADIO HEARN.

                                        October 2, 1894.

DEAR CHAMBERLAIN, — Thanks for the *Spectator*. I liked the poem, and would like to read that interesting book by Crooke. I used to get everything of that kind.

Writing now about Watson, I can only remember the impression of the poem thus: —

(1) Attention — (2) concentration of mind on subject — (3) impression of commonplace correctness

with certainty of a last surprise — (4) surprise in last stanza — little ghostly thrill of pleasure.

But — I could not remember what the pleasure was without reading the poem again. I have the memory of a sensation, not the memory of a thought. And this is the way Watson generally impresses me — except in the "Dream of Man," which is a masterpiece of fancy, but a weak piece of verse. (I think there are fully a score of bad lines in it.) Wherefore Watson seems to me one of those that will never reach beyond the verge of greatness. Really, we have no more great poets now. Swinburne only reëchoes himself in the frost of his age. Henley approaches Watson in power, — but power of a different sort, rather realistic. Lang and Dobson are exquisite — but it is all rococo — stucco and paint. Civilization is stagnant: there are none of those motions which stir below the vast surface, — no race-feelings, — therefore none of the large sensations which made the song of the past. America has no poets of high degree, — nor France, — nor any other country just now. The beauty is going out of human life — only tones, faint shades, faint ghostly thrills remain, betimes to make one remember that which has departed.

The book on India might suggest a book on Japan. I think there would be no money in it, though: — there is no money in anything but fiction, — and that only for a few. However, what struck me after reading the article was this: — "What a book I could NOW write about a Roman Catholic country, like Mexico, after having lived in Japan." In order to write well about Catholicism, one must have studied paganism *outside of it*. The whole poetry of the thing then appears. Who can really feel the poetry of the Bible except the man who is not a Christian? Well, is n't it the same way with other matters? Roman Catholicism in some Latin countries, — with its vast world of ghosts, saints, evil and good spirits at each man's elbow, — its visions, its miracles, its skulls and bones enshrined in silver and gold, — its cruelties and consolations, — its lust-exasperating asceticisms that create temptations, — surely to understand it all one must have felt either the life of the pagan or polytheistic Orient, or understand profoundly the polytheism of the antique West. A book on Latin life — studied through polytheistic feeling, sympathetic feeling — would certainly be a novelty. Strange sensations might be evoked, — new even to the nineteenth century. Ever faithfully,

LAFCADIO.

We're beginning to pack up. I'm sick — not attending school, just pleasantly sick. I thank the Gods therefor.

Oh! I am rather angry with the Gods. I have been fighting their battles; but they don't listen to me any more. Perhaps they are all *rusu* — away in Korea — and did not hear.

October 9, 1894.

DEAR CHAMBERLAIN, — Having a moment's leisure, permit me to say that your last letter is, according to synthetic philosophy, contrary to scientific position. The examples you cite by Dr. Tylor would prove exactly the contrary to the theory they are intended to sustain. The incoherent character of the myth in New Zealand folk-lore, compared with the coherent character of a similar myth in Sanscrit folk-lore, would argue the priority for New Zealand, if it argued anything at all — that is to say, at least, it would argue that the myth retained its primitive form among the savages and lost it among the civilized — supposing a community of origin, which is disputable and improbable.

The fact seems to me to be simply this, that modern philology — seriously to its own cost — still ignores the application of evolution to sociology. Tylor has been severely criticized on this head; but nearly all the big philologists and no small number of the folk-lorists remain in the same position. Philologists as a special class have not had until within very late years any reason to trouble themselves about the tendency of modern philosophy; and they have stuck to the theories of the Middle Ages: the idea of an Eden-centre, whence radiations of development, and the absurd theory of a degradation of man from a high state of arm-in-arm-walking-with-God knowledge. All this must be changed; for the philologist of to-day who undertakes the serious mastery of the new philosophy gains power to smash out of existence ninety-nine of every hundred theories brought up by men of the Edkins species. It is a great pity that Tylor and others will stick at the spiritual side of evolution —

like Max Müller. The fact necessarily delays progress, compelling a process of investigation as contrary to the natural order of things as looking through the large end of a telescope. To accurately judge any folk-lore or myth, we *must* begin with the evolutional order of fancies, — the beliefs about shadows preceding all beliefs in ghosts, — and the beliefs in ghosts preceding the belief in Gods. And the proofs of the truth of this system are in Japan all about us.

Of course I do not mean to say that the study of borrowings is not of the highest importance. I think the introduction to your "Kojiki" is most probably right in every particular as to the unrecorded antiquity of Chinese influence. Still, I am not sure. Coming from a common stock, the resemblance of a Japanese to a Chinese myth would not involve the belief that the one was borrowed from the other. Let me cite an example. The belief in the *Nukekubi* I myself discovered in Japan (not first, perhaps, but I found it and studied it). Well — in a little French book (translated mostly from ancient Chinese) "Les Peuples Étrangers comme des Anciens Chinois" (Leroux's "Bibliothèque Orientale") I find the same superstition mentioned, illustrated with curious Chinese engravings. Must I infer that the Japanese borrowed this myth from China? Certainly not, — and I believe the contrary. Such superstitions are of the most primitive class, and were probably held by this people ten thousand years before coming to Japan. I use big figures. But we must now accept the fact of man's existence on the planet, as *Man* (not ape) for more than 500,000 years.

I am sure that if you would read systematically Spencer's first volume of Sociology you would find reasons for agreeing with me. But of course you would have to confess all religions as religions mere evolutional growths out of childish fear and fancy. Hence it requires courage to take the position publicly.

LAFCADIO.

P. S. . . . Wrote note to Aldrich — hoping you will see him. Gave him your address. He is all that you would like and nothing that you would dislike.

(His first letter from Kobe on taking up newspaper work there. Rec'd at the Yaama Hotel, Kyoto, 14th Oct. 1894.)

DEAR CHAMBERLAIN, — I can't guess whom to be vexed with — you or Mason; but I have been feeling resentful. Both of you knew, or ought to have known, that I was in the Kwakto-Jigoku for two years, but neither of you would move a pen to help me out of it. Well, I suppose you consulted over together (unfair! — two against one!) and concluded it was best to let me stick it out. And it was, — since it forced me out of a service which has become unbearable. Still, I feel a little mad at you both. For either of you I should have broken my back to help if necessary, without waiting for finely detailed explanations.

Yes, and I hold the black end of the poker always in correspondence! Ay de mi! Still, *you* are much better in that regard than Mason and others. Mason writes monthly, — with business regularity, though happily not with a business soul. You *do* write oftener, much oftener; but not often enough. I am getting exacting, you see.

My associate in the *Chronicle* is *Secularian*. He is a young, vigorous Scotchman, of the half-dark type, — grey eyes and black hair. I liked him at first shake-hands, which is a great thing. We shall get along socially. About the financial question, I can't see glory ahead, — but I am with clean-souled Englishmen anyhow.

I met a missionary on the boat running to Kobe and liked him — the first of his kind. A great big fellow, six feet three — and fresh-hearted, and frank, and innocent as a boy. I explained some things to him, and showed him some which he had never looked at (such as Japanese *sake*), and almost felt fond of him. What a pity such men can find no better calling! He had had his troubles, too, — tried to win hearts, and learned to wonder whether gratitude existed in the Japanese soul.

Hotels here infernally dear — four to seven dollars a day. Still, if you pass Kobe after I am settled here, I shall expect a call. In another fortnight all will be arranged; and I shall be well able to make you cosy with us.

I cannot think less of Loti's genius. . . . Cold-blooded he seems of course, and personally detestable he very probably is, and his life not at all limpid by our standards. But what matter! Drop the shell of the man, — the outer husk, on which the vices are mere lichen-growths; — and within glows the marvellous, subtle, luminous-winged soul of the Latin race, — of Latin art, — of Latin love of life and youth and all things beautiful. I will select pages from the "Fleurs d'Ennui," from "Le Roman d'un Spahi," from "Le Mariage de Loti," — and defy any other living man to equal them. Neither our De Quinceys nor our Coleridges nor our Byrons could have written such things — prose more poetical than all English poetry — prose more luminous and penetratingly sweet than Tennyson's best verse. (De Nerval is the only other who has approached Loti.) Of course I do not mean to say that an art wholly based upon nervous susceptibility is the ultimate art. It cannot be. But we need it. The spiritual is based on the physical; the moral is based on the physical; the aspirational is based on the physical. We need such instrumentation. We need the means. The purification will come later. At present we have the highest aspirations, the deepest potentialities, — we Northern men. But however much better morally we flatter ourselves to be, we are still, all of us, — Russians, English, or Scandinavians, — mere sucking babes in the knowledge of art as compared with the Latins. An Italian fruit-vendor has more sense of beauty than a member of our Parliament, — a beggar of Piedmont more musical sense than the average graduate of an English musical college.

Oh! the book by De Rosny does not belong to the Maisonneuve Collection, but to the Leroux Collection. De Rosny has nothing in the former. The former (of which I sent only one poor sample) has all the Breton literature, including songs and music, — Maspero's translations of the old Egyptian ghost-stories, the Hitopadesa, and a host of things. But both collections are worth having.

Ever yours,

LAFCADIO.

KOBE, October 23, 1894.

DEAR CHAMBERLAIN, — You asked for my other address, which I enclose in Japanese — but I don't think it will be good for more than six months, as I hope to build a house here this winter, — fit even to receive the Emeritus Professor of Japanese in the Imperial University of Japan. My present home is a nondescript building, foreign upstairs and indigenous downstairs — barring the *benjo;* — the upstairs rooms are fixed for stoves and are warm, and I have indulged in a debauchery of cheap carpets, mattings, and furniture. My employer and his wife were very good to us; — Mrs. H. has been petted and helped and invited about, and everything was got for us at a bargain.

I think this a very pleasant position — the most pleasant I ever had in my life; for I am treated not as an employee, but as a directing spirit *in* the office, and as a brother outside of it. Of course I don't know how long I shall feel this way. Human nature is full of surprises. But for the time being it is very pleasant; and I would not exchange the place for a government post at *any* price. Perhaps I shall think differently later. Faut jamais dire, "Fontaine, *Je ne boirai plus de ton eau!*"

Curious. The proprietor began this paper with only 1000 yen, and worked it up to a good property. His little wife helps him at proof-reading; and before I came, they alone ran the whole paper — no reporters or assistants. It was terrible work for one man, and I could not do it. Young is hearty and juvenile in appearance — serious, pleasant face —dark beard—used to be a proof-reader on the *Saturday Review*, for which post some culture is necessary. Is a straight thorough English radical. We are in perfect sympathy upon all questions.

I wrote to Mason yesterday that Thomas Bailey Aldrich is to visit Japan this fall. I should like you to know America's greatest "literary man" (if we except Holmes and James). He is a very polished gentleman; and knows Europe by heart, for he has been a great traveller. You ought, I am sure, to pass a pleasant hour or two with him. He would sit at your feet in the matter of the higher scholarship; and you would enjoy his knowledge of persons and places.

I think your copy of "Glimpses" has been awaiting you at Tokyo.

Faithfully — without reproaches for not touching at Kobe,

LAFCADIO.

November 3, 1894.

DEAR CHAMBERLAIN, — I got your last delightful
letter in its Japanese envelope. You thought it
was a poor letter; but what you generally think
poor I find unusual interest in. There is a deal of
concentrated penetrative observation in those hast-
ily written notes of yours which sinks into my mind,
and is apt to reappear again, after many days, in
some essay of mine — having by that time become
so much a part of my own thought that I find it
difficult to establish the boundary-line between
meum and *tuum*. Of course one must have lived a
long time in the country to feel your letters in this
way.

Aldrich is at the Grand Hotel, or was, until time
of this writing. I dropped him a note, expressing
the hope that he would meet you and Mason.
He can talk Italy to you.

I am glad you agree about the Italian and French
character — the depth, subtlety, and amazing latent
power of the former; the Greek cast of the latter.
Yes, I don't think we should disagree much — except as to my firm conviction of the artistic and
moral value of sensuality. You know in this nineteenth century we are beginning to make war upon
even intellectual sensuality, the pleasure in emotional music, the pleasure in physical grace as a
study, the pleasure in coloured language and musical
periods. I doubt if this is right. The puritanism
of intellect is cultivated to the gain of certain degrees of power, but also to the hardening of character, — ultimately tending to absolute selfishness

and fixity of mental habit. Too deeply fixed in the cause of life are the pleasures of sense to be weeded out without injury to the life-centres themselves and to all the emotions springing from them. We cannot attack the physical without attacking the moral; for evolutionally all the higher intellectual faculties have their origin in the development of the physical. . . .

I send you an *Atlantic*. Tell me how you like it, *my* little dream.

LAFCADIO HEARN.

LETTERS TO W. B. MASON

II

LETTERS TO W. B. MASON

DEAR MASON, — Here I am imprisoned by bad weather. It was lucky for me, however that I resolved after all to make for Kyoto first, as a frightful storm has been raging off the Izumo coast. Still I have till 10th September free, and hope to be in Oki early next month. The exquisite beauty of this little hotel compensates somewhat for the bad weather. The house dates only from the seventh Meiji; but it is a curiosity of beauty and ingenuity. Kano recommended it as the most original hotel in Kyoto. It is too charming to refer any globetrotter to; they could not by any possible chance understand it. The people are rich: the house is small; and only a few choice guests are received.

I liked my Japanese hotel in Kobe, however, — the Tokiwasha. Magnificent double room — one end fronting the harbour; the other dominating the roofs of the city, — and doves nesting in the eaves. How beautiful Kobe is! More than Yokohama. And the more I see of the open ports the more I feel convinced that the Japanese character is too essentially individual and strong to be overwhelmed by foreign influence. Everything characteristically and charmingly Japanese *accentuates* immensely at the open ports, as if in defiance of foreign aggression. Architecture improves by becoming at once larger — yet more Oriental. — It gave me a sharp indescribable sensation to meet Englishmen and Scotchmen again after two years in the interior. Even a rather cheeky clerk who wanted to sell me "a medicated flannel" (may the Gods d—n medicated flannel) seemed to me a superb creature. The old Scotch accent touched me as the sound of Scotch bagpipes touched hearts in India. I took my wife into some of the stores. She had never seen a foreign shop before: it was a fairy world for her. A Scotch merchant was amused at her interest in simple things, and gave her a pretty present. He was a grim man, too; but I liked him for that, and bought many things from him. My wife asked me this question, "Why is it that you only smile when you talk, and all these other foreigners don't smile — only their eyes smile?" "That," I answered, "is because I have lived so long alone among Japanese." And I became aware that my ways must have seemed a little odd to these serious Highlanders and growling Britons. But that day they all appeared lovable. "Absence," etc.

I have been looking at the obi of Kyoto. We have quite as fine kimono-silks in Kumamoto, — Osaka fabrics, I think, — but the obi are wonderful. Still, although far prettier to the eye, and much more costly, they don't compare with the solid enduring rich plainness of Hakata work. I want to see the temples; but I don't want to see them on gloomy days; and it keeps raining; and I am extremely angry to no purpose with the weather.

Do you want to find out anything about Kyoto? If you do, write to me right speedily. I will be here another week. And I want to see that village where the women are all gigantic and rosy and comely, and carry great weights on their heads — the nurses of Emperors. Also Nara. I want to live in Kyoto. And study Buddhism. But I live in a city where they have no temples and no gods — nothing but soldiers and the noise of bugles.

Ever faithfully,
LAFCADIO HEARN.

KYOTO, July 30, 1892.

DEAR MASON, — There is a sickening weight in the air — that kind of atmospheric pressure which makes people despondent and full of the idea that something Awful is going to happen. I can't think; I can't enjoy anything; I can't say that I liked Kyoto as much as I expected.

First of all, I was tremendously disappointed by my inability to discover what Loti described. He described only his own sensations: exquisite, weird, or wonderful. Loti's "Kioto: La Ville Sainte" has no existence. I saw the San-ju-san-gen-do, for example: I saw nothing of Loti's — only recognized what had evoked the wonderful goblinry of his imagination.

And I tried after three days of temples. I had waited until the weather was fine to look at them. Well, I was not much impressed. Doubtless because I have become too familiar with temples. The new Hongwanji I don't care about. It is only large and loud. A Kamakura temple is worth a dozen Hongwanji's. Of course the ropes of women's hair are touching spectacles. But those only interested me.

The finest temple to my mind, in every way, is the Chion-in — where the mighty bell is. The whole is magnificently right and harmonious, without being vulgar. But the finest thing — except the divine gardens — of the Chion-in, is the glorious gate, with the extraordinary images and frescoes upstairs. These are being defaced by brutal visitors: no watch is kept to prevent human beasts from disfiguring the wall-paintings. How hopelessly indifferent Buddhism has become about preserving its own glorious past! Shinto, on the other hand, guards everything with rigid scrutiny, and compels respect. Really, I am not of those (*now*) who regret the handing-over of old Buddhist temples to Shinto. Shinto has been able to preserve what I feel sure Buddhism would not have had the nerve to protect. The more I see of Shinto, the more I respect it.

Then I am tired of looking only at screens — faded out of recognizability — painted by Kano Something, and the chozubachi in which Hideyoshi washed his hands. Vast is the multitude of these. Buddhist temples have lost individuality for me. They resemble each other like the faces of Japanese students. What I am *not ever* tired of seeing — and what is worth, I think, a mention in the Guide-Book, is the beauty of the Buddhist gardens. The gardens of the temples are more interesting than the temples. Also the temple avenues and courts beautify and expand the city — catch and keep the sun, and seem to make the air brighter.

It is at night that Kyoto is most beautiful. The street-scenes, the lamps, the delight of the lantern files viewed from the Shijo-Ohashi along the Shijo-Gawara: this is fantastically beautiful.

As for industries, I took note only of obi-silks, porcelain, and metal-work. The last took my breath away. I could not afford to buy anything there. The house is small. The room in which guests are received is hung with exhibition-certificates and medal-cases containing medals from different European and American exhibitions. Visitors are kindly received and shown everything. One who has not studied the subject should first see the process, in order to appreciate the delicacy and difficulty of the manufacture. I enclose the card.

A visit to the Awata-ware factory of Sobei Kinkozan also pleased me. European taste, I fear, is spoiling the manufacture; but there are lovely things there. What impressed me most was the delicious colour. I bought ten plates for four dollars. Visitors can see everything done.

The great display of obi-silks ought to delight foreigners. There are Kyoto obi worth a hundred yen each. Besides the expensive obi, there is a beautiful cheap stuff for obi, called ito-nishiki, one factory of which I visited (Yoshida, Sangencho). It is a mixture of cotton, silk, and gold thread. Foreigners ought to like this stuff. It is used chiefly for obi for children and young girls; and the best designs are all large, or rather large — storks, flowing water, tortoises, clouds, etc., in gold and colours.

The good folks of the Nikkoya will give you the best pair of rooms in the hotel if you come down here with your family in winter. They will also furnish you, if you desire, excellent foreign cooking from the neighbouring Tokiwa hotel, and good Bass's ale. There are no chairs — but I suppose you don't care; and beautiful low tables are used to serve the food (foreign food) upon, instead of a zen.

I fear this letter is dull, and of no use — even suggestively; but the weight of the air is platinum vapourized.

Sincerely yours,
LAFCADIO HEARN.

P. S. You write most delightful letters; but I have n't the faintest ghost of an idea who you are. I don't know whether I ought even to try to find out. It is more charming to know one's friends as amiable ghosts thus.

Don't be shocked! The force of Lowell's "Soul of the Far East" is daily growing on me. I can't combat his views within myself as I was wont to do: I find so much that only his book attempts with any success to explain. I am about to be converted. There are times I feel so hopeless about everything in Japan that I would like to leave it if I had no one else to care for. Especially when I meet insolent clerks who have learned impertinence and Christianity at the Doshisha, — when I see Christian cathedrals, — when I find Christian teachers among the Japanese instructors of the higher schools.

Therefore great Kyoto pleases me far less than Izumo. One little country village of the west coast delights my soul more. After all, my whole study must be the heart of the commonest people. The educated class repel me. It is impossible to make friends among them, and pure madness to expect sympathy. Did you read Smith's hideous book "Chinese Characteristics"? I sometimes think education is Chinafying the new generation.

My hope for the next two years' work will be to make a *heart*-work on Buddhism. But I must have highly intelligent help. Can I get it? There is the puzzle. The educated Japanese is insulted if asked a question about Buddhism.

L. H.

SHIMAYA; MIONOSEKI, SHIMANE, August 31, 1892.

DEAR MASON, — I have been waiting here for a good steamer to Bakkan, and must wait four days more. After all my discontent with Kyūshū, I am homesick for a little house in Tetorihoumachi, the dogs, the magazines, the books, the letters, etc. After all this wandering, Kumamoto seems very much better than it did before. I pass most of the time here swimming in the harbour. There is nothing else to do except to make the miko dance at the Miojinja, or to listen to the geisha.

A funny thing happened yesterday. A menagerie tried to come to Mionoseki; and among the properties was an alleged *Kudan*. Scarcely had the Kudan arrived when there came a stiff breeze from Daisen, accompanied by sounds of distant thunder. The Kannushi declared the God of Mionoseki was offended by the presence of the Kudan and ordered the people away, and they returned by the same steamer.

I thought Mionoseki was the only place where chickens and hens' eggs were not suffered to enter; but I find at Iya the same custom, inspired by the same tradition. My friends at Matsue sent me yesterday a box of ducks' eggs from Iya — otherwise I should be rather badly off for nutriment. Iya is not far from Yasugo where the same Deity — Koto-Shiro — Nushi-no-Kami — is worshipped with directly contrary observances; — Yasugo is famous for eggs and chickens. The inhabitants declare that the best way of serving the God is to kill and devour his enemies.

All along my journey I have been tormented by an insane desire to steal other people's servants. The temptation was very strong at Kyoto, where the hotel maidens are veritable *Tennin;* but I did not yield to it till I got to Oki. At Oki we found a pretty Shizoku boy working in the hotel as a servant of people who had once been retainers of his family. We stole him, and I am now teaching him how to swim. He is so intelligent that I cannot think of having him only as a servant. When we know more of him, we may do something else for him.

Ever truly yours,

LAFCADIO HEARN.

KOBE (en route to Oki).

DEAR MASON, — I'm writing, as usual, upon the floor, which does not improve the look of a letter.

Nara was a charming experience — all except the hotel at which I stopped (Uoya) and in which I saw some curious things.

While the face of the Nara Daibutz has no such possible beauty as that of the Kamakura image, the whole effect is something never to be forgotten — especially in connexion with the colossal building. I am glad I saw it. Of course I saw Kasuga and fed the deer and beheld the miko dance. The dance is an infinitely more complicated affair than that of the Kitzuki miko, who are not children, but tall young women; but it was very pleasing, and the flower-beauty of the child-dancers sweet beyond expression. No geisha have such charm, — for obvious reasons cannot.

I collected a number of o-fuda, mamori, etc., for the Professor in both Kyoto and Nara, and at the Giant temple also got a couple of ex voto, — grotesquely ugly in themselves, but touching in connexion with the faith which created them. An interesting Nara deity is that one who listens only to one prayer. "O Lord, just grant this little thing, and I'll never trouble you with another prayer of any sort as long as I live!" This shocks Christian superstition; but how deliciously human and natural it is!

I forgot to bring the Guide-Book with me, — so I can't decide whether you wrote about the use made of the bed of the Shijo-Gawara at Kyoto on summer nights. Little bamboo bridges lead from

either bank to the dry spaces, and there much yuki
and lemonade is sold, and all is a maze of lanterns,
like a swarming of fireflies. It is very pretty.

Do you know that the iron cauldron in which Ishi-
kawa Gogemon was cooked alive in boiling oil is
(said to be) exhibited at the Daibutz temple at
Nara? But besides the cauldron you see dried mer-
maids and dragons — wherefore I do not believe.

Another thing worth mentioning about Nara, if
you have not already mentioned it, is the manufacture of what are called Nara Ningyo. These things
are much esteemed by the Japanese and some very
clever bits of rough wood-carving may be occasionally found among them. But to appreciate them the
foreigner ought to be previously acquainted with
the conventional Darumas, Shojos, and other
grotesqueries of Japanese art: then he can admire
the hasty cleverness of the wood-cutting. I bought
some trifles.

The foreigners spoil these places in some respects,
but perhaps they also help to preserve the grand old
trees and groves by their liberal patronage and unaffected admiration of what they *can* understand
and like.

Among my memories of Kyoto are dreams of
sweet faces and voices. There is an inexpressible
gentleness, refined kindness and sympathy about
Kyoto women, I imagine.

Still, I long for the primitive west coast, where
speech is ruder and ways simpler and nothing good
can be had to eat, — but where the ancient Gods
live still in hearts, and the lamps of the Kami are

kindled nightly in every home, and where there are some gods so extraordinary that I dare not write about them at all, lest unkind things be said about the Japanese.

Here Pan is dying.

Ever sincerely,

LAFCADIO HEARN.

MOJI (en route for Oki — wonder if I shall ever get there!)
August 6, 1892.

DEAR MASON, — Here I am at Moji, — landed from Saikyo Maru, and waiting for the Sakai steamer due at 2 A. M. I could not follow my first plan of visiting Miyajima and other places, as the railroad was hopelessly broken. So I have a chance to write.

My second stay at Kobe spoiled the pleasant impression of the first. I saw more of the foreigners and longed to get away from them again. This proved difficult, as I could only go by the N. Y. K. steamer, without waiting; a splendid steamer, but patronized extensively by foreigners, four Chinese foreigners likewise. There were three beautiful deer on board, in large wooden cages, destined for Shanghai; — they made plaintive sobbing noises, and I firmly believe they were Kasuga deer, — though I could not find out. The voyage was pleasant enough; but I prefer the dangerous little Japanese steamers where you can squat down on deck in a yukata and smoke a little brass pipe, and become agreeably acquainted with everybody. The N. Y. K. is a chapter in the modernization of Japan which I am tired of seeing. Professor Chamberlain spoke to me about the variability of one's feelings toward Japan being like the oscillation of a pendulum: one day swinging toward pessimism and the next to optimism. I have this feeling very often, and I suppose you must have had it many times. But the pessimistic feeling is generally coincident with some experience of New Japan, and the optimistic with something of Old Japan. It is a whole year since I had a real thrill of pleasure in people, — such as I could often obtain in Izumo. Everything seems so factitious this side. Even the dancing of the miko at Kasuga impressed me only as a pretty show given for money: the solemn, dignified Kagura of Kitzuki never danced for money, had the charm of religion, as well as the respectability of primitive tradition to recommend it. I liked Kitzuki better than all I saw on this side: though I cannot say why in a short letter. The reading of the Professor's "Kojiki" of course had something to do with it — prepared one's mind for the impressions of the place. A peasants' country temple to the God of Silkworms interested me more than the Kiomidzu of Kyoto. — But with what hideous rapidity Japan is modernizing, after all! — not in costume, or architecture, or habit, but in heart and manner. The emotional nature of the race is changing. Will it ever become beautiful again? Or failing to become attractive, can it ever become sufficiently complex to make a harmony with the emotional character of the West? It is really a very, very, very hard thing to study, is the Japanese soul. And ever so much of what

I wrote in my forthcoming volume of Japanese sketches seems now to me wrong,—now that I have lived so long out of Izumo. I see no literary inspiration ahead. I can imagine no means of consoling myself except by plunging into the study of Buddhism — making a sort of prose-poem that no Japanese will ever look at. But who — not a madman — should try to write a book for Japanese to read, after having acquired some knowledge of things?

Well, they have no reason to love us *en masse*, at least. Here, across the strait, is the city bombarded by us; — and all along the lines of railroad the old gods seem to be passing away; and the people are losing their good manners, their graces, their pretty ways, by foreign contact; and the scale of living is always rising. We bombarded unhappiness into the country — beyond any doubt. Force sowed the seed; the future will gather the black crop. In the eternal order of things, I suppose it is inevitable that every race should be made as wretched as possible; and all who cannot accept wretchedness as a necessary part of life must be exterminated. But again, in the eternal order of things, what is the use? What is even the use of the life of a solar system — evolution, dissolution, — re-evolution, re-dissolution, forever more? Really Buddhism alone gives us any consolatory ideas on the subject; but it is now vulgar to mention Buddhism to the Japanese.

The weather to-day is very gloomy. So is this letter from

L. H.

SAIGO, August 17, 1892.

DEAR MASON, — I am already tired of the island of Saigo or Dogo, and am going to try for better luck at the Dozen Islands. It is very hard to see anything here; and I solemnly suspect there is nothing to see — except natural scenery. That is nice — well, nice is not the word: there is much wild grim beauty. But the roads are so atrocious, and the distances so appalling, that even the inhabitants of Saigo, *as a rule,* know nothing about the interior.

I went to-day to the celebrated lake of Sainoike, where the Bateiseki stone is said to abound. I had to wait two days to go, — because there was a little wind; and with ever so little wind, travelling along this coast in a boat is really dangerous. The rocks rise sheer from the water, and beetle frightfully overhead, and are worn into all sorts of shapes by the waves. We skirted there for about an hour, occasionally passing a pretty cove, with some grey thatched houses, — fishermen's houses, — and then landed at a bank of shingle. The infinity of boulders was disheartening to see, — much more disheartening to walk upon. With every incoming wave, the shingle moved, and when the wave receded, the sound was like heavy volley-firing. After stumbling and swearing for five minutes, we got to the grass beyond the shingle, and advanced into a sort of little circular valley — close to the beach (the crater, I think, of some enormously ancient volcano). There I saw a large shallow pool of fresh water, with a few plants — water-lilies, etc., floating in it. I

wanted to enter it, and try how deep it was; but
the people would not hear of it. They said monsters
and deities guarded it. — All this was very disappointing. I asked about the black stone, and was
told it came from a mountain overhanging the lake
— all covered with scrubby growths and pathless.
So I returned. I heard of a celebrated shrine of
Jizo. I prepared to visit it; and was told it had been
burned *twenty years ago*. But the news of its burning
was known only to some few people — so slow does
news travel here. I enclose a photo. giving one
glimpse of Saigo. *There is one pretty temple, Zen-
ryoji, on a hill above the town* — Jodo-shu-nen —
the gift of a wealthy citizen. I hope to get folk-lore
in Oki; but there is nothing, I imagine, to attract
the tourist — except the absence of missionaries:
that is something.

Very truly,

L. HEARN.

HISHIMURA, — which is in the Island of Nakashima,
in the Archipelago of Oki, August 21, 1892.

DEAR MASON, — Leaving Saigo by a Japanese
sailing boat — could n't catch the nasty little
steamer — we re-entered the harbour called Hishi-
minato day before yesterday. It is very picturesque,
— the entrance to the harbour. First one passed a
lot of extraordinary islands — Komori, "The Bat,"
with a cavern in it or rather through it; — and Sa-
buro and Futamatta and others. Entering from
Saigo, one has Nishinoshima on the right and Nakashima on the left. The scenery on the Nakashima

side is especially impressive, — a sort of natural bastion work, — the mockery of a colossal Japanese fortress.

Anciently there were no robbers in Oki. Quite recently robbers have appeared in Saigo, — strangers from other ports, — but in Dozen, folk still sleep with doors and windows open, holding robbers to be impossible. They believe in foxes, — not in thieves. There are about 1000 people in Hishimura, and only one policeman for this and all the neighbouring villages. There is never any fighting or serious offences, — although immorality considerably prevails, as in all open ports, — whereby public health and good temper do not appear to suffer. But the horrible stories told by the Japanese themselves about Oki morals are not true — any more than the stories about phantom islands and men who walk about without heads.

I went yesterday to Amagori — Nishinoshima — where is the tomb of Gotoba-Temo. It is about one ri by boat from Hishimura, — very pretty scenery, and lonesome. At the Ujigami of the little village of Amamura, I got a queer ex voto for the Professor. At a short distance from the village, you see the tomb of the Emperor, enclosed by a high paling, and shadowed by pine trees. The picture in the Oki book I am going to send you will give a good idea of the scene. Lonely, shadowy, and not without melancholy charm.

In Amamura there is a house called Ama-no-Shikikaro-no-Iye. He was anciently Choja, and the exiled Emperors used to visit him; and in the family are said to be preserved the cups of silver the august guests were wont to drink from, and many other relics, — which, by the way, were on exhibition at the last Tokyo Exposition. But the present descendant and representative of the ancient Choja is very old, poor, and ill, — is expected to die soon, — and visitors cannot see the relics now.

I got some folk-lore here — only a little. Will try to-morrow at Urago.

The highest mountain in Oki is said to be Tako-hizan-Nishinoshima, on top of which there is a shrine of Gongen-sama, very famous. Ghostly fires are said to come from the sea and visit the mountain at certain times. The ascent is not difficult — except for the roughness of the path.

So plentiful is the cuttlefish off these islands that native boats have been broken and swamped by the weight of one catch. . . .

The scenery in Dozen is far more attractive than in Dogo (Saigo). I think it really beautiful — sailing through this group in a small fishing-vessel. I love Oki — with all its barrenness and bleakness, and would rather live there (in summer) than in any part of Japan I know. Everywhere the food is ample and surprisingly good.

There is one drawback, — the atrocious smells inevitable to the cuttlefish industry. They are really awful; and I don't think either you or the Professor would willingly endure them. Only at Hishimura there are no dreadful smells at all — at least none while I was there.

I was disappointed about folk-lore. The best of

any Oki folk-tales I got outside. In Oki the new generation refuse to talk about their old traditions. "Oh!—that was when we were all savages (*yaban*)" — they say. Somehow or other I fancy people are apt to become less good-hearted when they begin to mock their old beliefs, their old gods, etc. . . .

Ever most truly,
LAFCADIO HEARN.

URAGO, OKI, August 24, 1892.

DEAR MASON,—Returning to Urago, of which I wrote you in my first letter from Oki, I had more chance of studying the place. It is very queer, and very primitive. There are two hundred and fifty houses, from which I judge the population to be at least 1500 — children swarm. At Saigo the Oki folk are accustomed to see men-of-war, but nobody ever saw a foreigner before at Urago, wherefore the population climbed upon the roofs to look at me. They were as kind and gentle and absurdly trustfully honest as if the world had only been just made and they were the first inhabitants thereof.

On the way to Urago — from Hishimura — I stopped at the funny little village of Beppu, in Nishinoshima. You can imagine how primitive it is from the fact that at the only Yadoya in the place kwashi are represented by dried peas, and there is *no* real tea in the village — I think. There is a shrine of Godaigo at Beppu, on the top of a small but very steep hill, shadowed by pines. The shrine is only a little wooden miya, containing a metal mirror, and an earthen vessel.

Before embarking on the Oki-Saigo, I have the good luck to find an Oki family in Saikai, who give me much information. I have already got a lot of Oki folk-lore. I must try to include an Oki sketch in my book if I can: the trip will pay me in many ways. I doubt if it would pay the globe-trotter *communis*, or mere sight-seers.

Last night a steamer came and lay before the window, — the *Nagasaki*. Immediately, instead of working, captain and crew sat down on deck to a feast of sake and divers condiments. And a multitude of women went on board into all the cabins and orifices of the ship. And the people did eat and drink right joyously until daylight, — but without ruffianism or much noise. And some queer things were said. At midnight there were still three men on deck, and a mochi-seller. One man had drunk so much sake that he could only enunciate with difficulty words to this effect: — "Women as for, please me not. Sake is the best thing in this fleeting world." Whereupon, another man said, "To eat and drink as for, I little care. Woman is the supreme thing in this temporary world." Then he went below. And the third man opened his mouth and said, — having finished the last mochi in the box of the mochi-seller, and having said words of scorn to the mochi-seller because he had no more, — "Sake as for, and women as for, I care nothing. Mochi are the most excellent things in this miserable world." And the mochi-seller promised to bring more mochi to-night, — when I shall be in Oki.

Now if I had invented this, it would be commonplace enough; but being true, it illustrates human nature quite oddly enough perhaps to make you smile. Wherefore it is written.

L. H.

Tetorihoumachi, Kumamoto, September 10, 1892.

DEAR MASON, — I missed the steamer at Sakai (the agents are liars!), and had to cut across the country for the third time by kuruma. I first tried the Okayama route; but it has been so badly damaged by rains that the police warned me against it, and I shifted to the Onomichi route, via Kurashiki, where I caught a train for Onomichi after three days of mountain travel. The experience was hard, but interesting; — I saw a lot of things that would interest the Professor, and that I will write to him about later on — regarding o-fuda and mamori. Some of the scenery was exquisite. I tried to buy guide-books for you everywhere, but there were none. I got home only two hours ago, to find your charming letter awaiting me.

Before I say anything else, let me protest against that Doshisha correspondent of yours. No foreigner can tell you more about Izumo than I can. The information seems to me intended as a sort of slur upon Mr. Senke — though I may be mistaken. The man referred to is a priest and has simply a reputation as an uranai or fortune-teller: there are lots of such. I have been at Kakeya, but never thought the matter worth bothering about, — only a few peasants know of the man in the neighbourhood of Matsue. My Izumo servant, O-Yone (she is from

Imaichi, not far from Kakeya), knows about him, because her father once got his fortune told by the old priest.

But to mention such a man in connexion with Senke, or a parallel, is an insult to a very refined gentleman, the son of Baron Senke whom you doubtless know. . . . The more I learn of Kitzuki, the grander the old temple seems. All through Iwani, Tottori, Bingo, Hoki, Oki, Okayama, the o-fuda of the mighty shrine whiten in a million rice-fields, and occupy countless Kamidama. The mere fact that I was received at the temple has been a talisman for me. Everywhere Shinto priests treat me with extraordinary kindness. I thought the Kitzuki material worth more than two hundred printed pages for my book. All the famous Shoguns and Emperors left their gifts there. There is nothing so good as Kitzuki in Kyoto,—nothing. It is hallowed by all the oldest traditions of the race. And then to mention its princely chief in connexion with a vulgar country bonsan and fortune-teller, really stirs my bile.—As for the fortune-teller you will find a much more interesting one in Yokohama, in a tiny Jizo-Do, near the hundred steps—an old priest of the Jodi sect, whom I used often to visit. But the idea of Izumo peasants worshipping a bonsan is supremely absurd!! . . .

What I saw at Sakai that charmed me for nearly a whole night was a magnificent bon-odori by the whole population of stevedores and longshoremen—labourers far more robust than you see at Yokohama. Imagine nearly a thousand superb peasants,

men and women, fantastically attired, singing the
weirdest, wildest, sweetest song, — full of quaverings
and fractional notes impossible to write; all the hands
and feet sounding together in the measure of a
dance that never ceased until daylight. I have seen
many bon-odori, — the dance differs in almost every
village, as well as the air. But except the great
Honen-odori at Kitzuki, when Mr. Senke called out
some five hundred dancers, I never saw so impressive a scene as that at Sakai. Even the famous
West Indian dances were far less singular and
haunting. But the music and the movement of the
Izumo and Oki dances are extremely complicated,
and very difficult to describe. Even the Matsue
people and other city folk cannot easily learn the
tunes of these dances. I wish I had had a musician
with me capable of writing down the notes. It
would be very difficult, however, because the notes
are to a great extent *fractions* of notes.

By the way, I forbid my pupils to use the word
"idol." Its original Greek meaning was beautiful;
but it has an offensive missionary-meaning to-day,
and its use in connexion with Buddhism is monstrously unjust. Buddhist priests do not worship
"idols," though they teach respect for the images
in their temples, which are symbols only. Your
correspondent is horrid with his "idol"!

Yes, I think Irving will make a public hit with
Arnold's Japanese drama. What would please you
and me, or at least seem artistically congruous,
would not perhaps have such a chance with the
public. Something purely and perfectly Japanese

and artistic would not be understood. The public taste in theatrical matters is still more incomprehensible sometimes than the public taste in regard to new books. It is a special art — and not a very lofty one — to divine the *plebs* in these things. Whoever has the natural gift to do it while still young, can get rich without much trouble. . . .

I almost forgot to tell you about my travelling with a party of Naval-Academy students from Onomichi to Kure. What magnificent boys! I fell quite in love with all of them. They have a teacher (Norman), and he has very little work. If that place ever becomes vacant, I would sacrifice something to get it. To be able to teach such splendid fellows would be a pleasure indeed. And I fancy the Japanese professors would be good fellows all — being naval men. I have two ex-Doshisha colleagues here and — well, I won't say anything more.

> Ever truly,
> LAFCADIO HEARN.

. . . My stolen boy promises well. He learned to swim in about five days — very nicely. He is now installed in my home.

May 28, 1892.

DEAR MASON, — . . . Since we began to correspond I have also made the epistolary acquaintance of Friend Dening, which is another relief to the utter isolation of the Japanese exile. A fact that impressed me strongly is that neither of you, in writing, seems to have much to say about the personality of the

man, — though Dening's analysis of his work, as
an ethical influence and otherwise, was very interesting. But I suspect Kipling does not show personal peculiarities strongly; — I would imagine
him to be quite an ordinary positive character to
outward seeming, — one of those Lowell talks about
who make themselves strongly felt even without
saying anything when they go into a room. By the
way, I absolutely adore his work. I have read most
of his books four or five times over; and some particular stories much oftener. I like nearly everything;
and even what I don't like, I re-read and wonder at.

I sent some other letters to the *Mail*. One about
Snodgrass was suppressed altogether; and I am
getting tired fighting with my hands tied by their
absurdly unjust "blasphemy" limit. Lecky, whom
Brinkley praised warmly in an editorial note some
months ago, speaks of the theological conception of
God as "considerably worse" than the theological
conception of the Devil. He says also that men "succeed in persuading themselves that their divinity
would be extremely offended if they hesitated to
ascribe to him the attributes of a friend." (Vol. 1 —
pp. 96–97, Appleton's ed.) I wonder what Brinkley
thinks of that. I am very fond of parts of Lecky;
though his theory of intuitional morality leaves him
far behind the colossal intellect of Herbert Spencer,
and though he is by no means wholly impartial. . . .

By the way, I feel quite pleased with that little
address of Sir Edwin's to the Ladies' Educational
Association. It was really very pretty, and large,
and anti-theological. He is not, apparently, in-

clined to pose here as a Christian, in spite of his
"Light of the World," — so that sop to Cerberus
may have prejudiced me too much against him.

In your last letter you referred to Bourget. Did
you ever read "Le Calvaire" by young Octave
Mirbeau? If not, try to get it: I wish I had a copy
to send you. It is the most terrible picture of
physical slavery to a woman I ever read; — Manon
Lescaut turned professional prostitute, with a literary man for *souteneur*. Perhaps it will shock
you a little, — unless you have a dash of Latin
blood in you (I don't mean shock your prudery,
but your Northern manhood). I, who am three
fourths Latin, understand it. A Scandinavian rarely
reaches such an abyss, though his passions are
stronger: — he is more apt to turn upon the sub-
jector, and tear her to pieces. It takes the Latin
to visit Le Calvaire, or to let Daudet's Sapho trail
him through all infamy into ruin. But we all know
there are women neither beautiful nor witty having
a magnetic something, — a sort of sexual electricity,
— that means damnation to whomsoever they touch
even with the tips of a finger.

I have two French novels only, — perhaps you
have not yet read them. Zola's "L'Argent," and
Loti's last "Le Livre de la Pitié," etc. (a volume of
sketches really). The latter contains a piece called
"Rêve," which I made a very rough translation of
for the *Mail*. Would you not like to read it in the
original? The other pieces are not up to his usual
manner. Zola's book is powerful. It is also at your
service if you have it not.

My book is to be called (unless the publishers at the last moment desire another title) "Glimpses of Unfamiliar Japan." I have dedicated it to Mitchell McDonald and to the Professor. Not without some doubt as to whether the Professor would like being thus placed in apposition. But I trust it is all right. If not, let me know. McDonald was a rare friend to me. . . . In the West Indies only I found such another. But these kindnesses make eternal friendships, after the little obligation, or rather the little part of the great obligation has been settled. I thought at first of putting other names in the dedication; but I can't very well. I reserve that for a new book. . . .

The vacation is coming, and I think, after all, I must spend part of it in Kyoto, and part in some sea-village. I love swimming. The best place I know for it is Mionoseki, — where you can jump out of the window into fourteen feet of water. But things are upset. I can't get my contract renewed till the idiotic Diet decides matters; it is being renewed only by patches of months. They want me for another year; but nobody knows what the villains in Tokyo are going to do. It makes one feel like a soshi: every blow given to a member of the opposition evokes from my soul a sympathetic "Ha!"

Ever most faithfully yours,
LAFCADIO HEARN.

DEAR MASON, — This letter is for the Professor, by rights; but as he said to me that you represent him in every particular, I am going to burthen you with it, — as well as with some other things. . . .

I enclose also a ningyo sold at the place, because it represents Inari with the attributes of Daikoku, and although a toy, illustrates the manner in which any popular Shinto Deity can absorb Buddhist influence and steal Buddhist property.

The rest of the things doubtless explain themselves — except the Nobori, or little paper flags.

I took these little paper flags from before wayside shrines on the mountain road between Yonago and Onomichi. They are marked simply with the age of the petitioner — the prayer remains secret in the heart. It is thought sufficient to tell the Deity: "A woman of 22 years." He knows the rest.

These shrines are intensely interesting. I read Eastlake's papers on "Equine Deities" and upon the "Kirin" with considerable disappointment. In the heart of the mountains, Bato-Kwannon explains herself very simply. She is simply the divinity *who protects horses and cattle*. And the peasants erect before her shrine sotoba giving her this rôle, and requesting her to take care of their live-stock, and to protect them from all harm.

Passing through the cholera region, it was touching to see how each parish called upon its ujigami to prevent the advent of the plague. At the border-line between parish and parish the mamori of the local divinity were planted, with a prayer to hinder the pestilence from advancing further. The Japanese language does not personify Death or Plague: yet here was the evidence of a personification in thought. The pest comes by the road: therefore the Gods must guard the road. The Pest will not come by the rice-fields because the road is too bad.

In the rice fields of all the Ken I traversed, the o-fuda of the Izumo Taisha prevailed. However, I saw what I never saw in Izumo — through Hoki and Tottori and Okayama Kens — a sandara placed over the top of each mamori to protect it from the rain. I also saw charms mounted, having a little awning over them. I also saw written prayers for the souls of domestic animals, — requests that the dumb servant might enter into Paradise. This was pretty. Continually on one bit of road, my jin-rikisha men turned aside to avoid hurting *snakes!* In America everybody would be trying to kill the poor creatures. They were so little afraid that they would lift their heads to look at us, after we passed by, — instead of trying to hide. They are excellent guardians of fields too. The passion to kill them abroad has produced evil results — especially in the West Indies. . . .

The temple Kwan-ze-on-dera near Dazaifu is the most interesting which I have seen since leaving Kamakura. The art is the same: the art of a very remote epoch full of force and strangeness.

I don't know if you observed that Herbert Spencer in his recent "Inductions of Ethics: Individual Life" (the concluding part of vol. I, "Principles of Morality") gives "particular hell" to Friend Dening and the Mombusho. However, it is rather a compliment even to get a little hell from Spencer. Moreover, Dening stands on the same plane with

Gladstone, who is savagely criticized for his Hellenic tendencies in the same volume. What consoles one for these severities is the delightful assertion that in order to find the virtues which we imagine to be Christian, we must go to countries which are *not* Christian, and among people who are *not* highly civilized. And this statement is gloriously capped by the declaration that the only hope for future morality is that Western civilization will be able to rise at last to the moral level now occupied by various nations of naked savages! Whoop! Hurrah!!

If you put anything new in the Guide-Book about the Honmyoji temple near Kumamoto, you might add that a very painful spectacle is to be witnessed there almost daily: multitudes of fox-possessed coming to invoke the aid of Kato Kiyomasa. The sight, however, is horrible: I hope never to see it again.

With regards, ever,
LAFCADIO HEARN.

October 18, 1892.

DEAR MASON, — How delightful it would be to see the Professor here! — I think I could make him comfortable (for Kumamoto): with beefsteak, potatoes, roast chicken, and Bass's ale. . . . But I'm afraid the prospect is too good to be true: what we want to happen in this world never happens.

Well, well, — I hope I did not make any serious mistake about the matter of animal-souls. Here is a text from an inscription of Bato-Kwannon by the roadside among the mountains, near Kamamura: "Bato-Kwan-ze-on-Bosatsu-gin-ba-bodai-han-ye." It might have been rendered wrong for me: tell me when you write again how you would translate it. As for the little ceremony at the death of animals, I know only this. At my neighbour's house a dog died which the people were fond of: it was buried under a tree; — a number of incense-rods were set in the ground above the grave, and the women and children of the family joined their hands and murmured little prayers over the grave. I thought it strange and asked my wife, who told me it was not strange: that it was commonly done in Izumo, — and I suppose elsewhere, — by people who were fond of their animals. I enquired of my cook, — who was a long time a yoshi of hyakusho, and came to me in consequence of the death of his people. He said, however, that in his part of the country that was not done. My wife is a samurai, and knows the customs of the country but little. Still, there is the evidence of the Bato-Kwannon inscription, of her assertion that in Izumo the little prayer is often said, and of what I saw done myself.

Moreover, my mother-in-law, who knows much more of the old customs than the rest of my folks, tells me this: When a cow dies, a little drawing of it is made on paper — white — black — or black-and-white, — according to the colour of the cow, — and the age of the cow is written on the paper, — and this is pasted with rice-paste on the door of a Kwannon-do, — and a little prayer is said "*ushi bodai no tame.*"

My servant O-Yone, from Imai-ichi, knows no-

thing about these things, nor my boy from Oki. But
my wife's family (a very illustrious family in old
days in Matsue) knows much about them; and
although I have never seen the performance in the
Izumo country, I saw it elsewhere, and the Bato-
Kwannon in Tottori-Ken. All this would seem to
indicate that the custom was once much more generally practised than now. But other evidence on
the subject is needed, and I shall try to obtain it.
Your wife's statement convinces me that the facts
I obtained are insufficient to base any general statement upon.

Now about another matter of interest to the
Professor. In no part of Oki could I hear of an inu-
gami-mochi, — though I made thoroughly searching enquiries, and even questioned the police. But
the fox-superstition takes curious shapes there, and
is very strong.

Therefore, the statement printed in "Things
Japanese," from a Japanese physician, on the authority of an alleged Oki peasant, puzzled me. I
have been making enquiries since, and my mother-
in-law tells me this: There are no "goblin-dogs"
in the beliefs of the west coast; but in Iwami (and
perhaps in Oki) the term inu-gami is used for hito-
kitsune. I take it to be a euphemism. There is among
the peasantry an idea that the fox (hito-kitsune)
takes shapes something like an itachi (weasel),
sometimes like other creatures; keeping its other
form invisible. But it is very difficult to define the
beliefs — not merely because there are *at least* three
varieties of ghost foxes, but because the beliefs

about them differ everywhere; and scarcely two peasants tell the same thing. I was helped in these researches in Izumo by a fellow teacher, who questioned numbers of peasants for me.

I am told the name of the main island of Oki is simply Dogo, not Saigo, as I imagined and heard in Oki. Saigo is only the town. I can only decide these contradictions by the book. Rein calls the big island Oki, but he was never there. I have written an enormous mass of stuff about Oki: it is nearly finished, but I am in doubt about its value.

With best regards ever from

LAFCADIO HEARN.

November 1, 1892.

DEAR MASON, — . . . You delighted me with a hope of seeing you here at No. 34. I think I can make you cosy. Are you accustomed to a Japanese house? I have no chairs and tables à l'Européen; but everything else is possible. I can give you good *seyoryori*, whiskey, Bass, or Guinness. And I would like very much to see your son. Besides, I want to know you. I have asked Mr. Kano about you: he does not remember the name. I have never seen anything of you except your charming letters; and I am beginning to doubt whether you exist except as a Soul. To talk of retiring into your "former obscurity," when the Professor returns, means of course silence, — for the mystery of you has always been. But I have become too much accustomed to your letters, and it would be quite bad of you to stop them. So I hope you won't.

JAPAN

From a sketch by Hearn

I am horribly sorry you did nothing with your book-material. You ought to do something lovely. Who can do justice to Japan without sympathy; and how many writers on Japan have a grain of it? Conder perhaps has, and there the line stops. Even the author of "Japanese Women and Girls" has no deep comprehension of things. But what a horribly difficult thing it is to write about Japan. The effort in itself dries me up. I'm afraid you'll find my book heavy. I can't venture to imagine soul-play: the motives and thoughts escape me as individualities; I get glimpses of them in generalities only. I'm trying now to write stories: it is the hardest work I ever tried to do, and I fear the result will be flat. — And you, who know so much more about the Japanese than I, hesitate. That is not encouraging.

I saved at least four fifths of my first impressions; but in correcting them, they began to contract and dry up in a way that told me I had let emotion run away with me. Self-restraint is very hard at first in Japan: later on all impulse and inspiration fail, and there is only a dead grind. Yet the result of the grind has more value in certain ways. What worries me is the absence of feeling, — the want of something to stir one profoundly when his knowledge of the country is sufficient to prevent illusion. And it won't come. I'm afraid it will never come any more. I must content myself with the queer, the curious, the artless, — or attempt a work on Buddhism, which, as you say, would require much time and money.

It occurred to me, however, to ask you to help

me in an easy way — by writing me a few lines
about anything touching or noble in common every-
day life which you might happen to see without
wishing to use. A maidservant, a child at school,
an aged man dying among the memories of the past
and the disorders of the present, a bit of kindness
by the roadside, — any "heart-thing," — I would
like to know. I collect all I can, and write them,
and put them in drawers. In time they work themselves out. For instance, I have a servant's death
written, — but I want to get a beginning for it, —
a sacrifice if possible. What I mean is this: In an
idle hour if you hear or see something in Japanese
real life that would suggest to you, — "Hearn
would like to see that," — then a line or two might
inspire me with a whole sketch.

I can't get much chance to study life in Kumamoto. I don't like the Kyūshū people — the common people. In Izumo all was soft, gentle, old-
fashioned. Here the peasants and the lower classes
drink and fight and beat their wives and make me
mad to think that I wrote all the Japanese were
angels. . . .

Ever faithfully, with a strong protest against the
sin of vanishing into obscurity,

LAFCADIO HEARN.

DEAR MASON, — . . . I have just read that most
frightful book by Kipling, "The Light that Failed,"
where he speaks of the horror of being in London
without money. Nobody can even dimly imagine
— no, not with a forty horse-power imagination —

what the horror is, if he has n't been there. And I
have — in London, Cincinnati, New York, Mem-
phis, New Orleans, Savannah — not to speak of
other places. Repeated experiences make it worse:
you never can get used to it. I would not return to a
great civilized city again without money to save my
life from a tiger. Hell is realized there. No: if ever
I have to leave Japan, I shall sail straight south into
some old tropical port; — any crumbling Spanish
town, any village of half-naked savages, any im-
aginable land of cannibals and pagans, where the
winter is not, is a million times better to live in than
a world's capital without money. "What a fool I
was not to go and live among savages when I was
nineteen years old," was my first thought when I
passed my first week in a West Indian cabin in a
mountain district. Money! — And yet I must look
sharp after money now; for whatever happens, I
must fix my little woman and her folks all right first.
It will puzzle me, too. They are Izumo samurai —
old-fashioned — know as little about business as I
do, which is a most awful thing to say about them.
I suspect real estate is the only thing — and that
in their own country of Izumo, where things have
less changed. . . .

I understand your horror of Zola; but I think it
is a literary duty to stomach the horror, and discern
the curious mental phenomenon behind it — the
mind that sees and hears vice as Dickens saw and
heard eccentricity. Now, if you have not read
"Germinal," there is a treat for you: the tremendous personifications of machinery, devouring hu-

man life. And if you have not read "L'Attaque
du Moulin" (in "Les Soirées de Medan") there is
another treat for you. I am going to send you a
third treat — "Le Rêve" — by Zola. Read it: it
will not shock you at all. It is full of curious
beauties.

In which of Kipling's books is "The Finest Story
in the World?" — I never read it, though I ordered
Kelly & Walsh to send me everything that Kipling
ever wrote or will write (only, not American pirated
editions). I feel I still underrate Kipling. He grows
bigger every day to me, — looms up colossally, —
reaches out like a stupendous shadow, over half a
planet at once. But oh! the hardness of the tone —
the silent cynicism of facts — the self-repression
— the "matter-of-course" way of seeing things —
the extraordinary objectivity and incomprehensible
subjectivity cruel as fate! What a most damnable
thing civilization is! — must be, *to create such a
writer*. What complexities of suffering, of knowledge,
of penetration, of toleration, of all accursed experience, and all diabolical intuition are summed up
in that one young life! What a revelation of the
ghostliness of matter! . . . Goodness! how small it
makes me feel to read that man; how blind I am,
— how stupid I am, — what an egregious ass I am
to waste a page upon what that mind hurls into
half-a-line!

Don't read "Fantôme d'Orient:" I got it the
other day, and have been disgusted astonishingly.
Something is now the matter with Loti. I don't
know what. For all such men there is one certain

danger. Their work depends for its value upon marvellous super-sensitiveness to impressions: thus it is rather physiological than psychological — in the higher senses. Now feelings begin to dull as we glide away from "the tropic clime" of youth. Then, unless the mind has been trained to higher things, there is only dust and ashes. And there is only dust and ashes in "Fantome d'Orient," — nerves morbid, feeling turned in upon itself, no longer responding to the spiritual ghostly touch of cosmic things.

I think the novel by Mirbeau you refer to is the *sequel* of the other ("Le Calvaire"); but I never saw it. I expect enormous things from Zola's forthcoming "Débâcle." He is stupendous at painting battles.

I hope to write a Buddhist book within the next two years — something quite different from anything ever before attempted. But the obstacles are colossal. It is so difficult to reach the people — to get at the popular heart with system. The more a Japanese is educated, on the other hand, the further he is from you. The delicious Japanese child's life globes into yours, vibrates with it: the distance between the European and the schooled adult is vast as the interspaces between suns. I despair betimes.

With best regards,
Ever yours,
L. HEARN.

LETTERS TO MRS. HEARN

III

LETTERS TO MRS. HEARN

July 12, 1904.

LITTLE MAMMA, — To-day we have not much sun-light, but I and Kazuo swam as usual. Kazuo played a torpedo in the water. [Hearn means a play of his boy, who pulled his legs from under the water while swimming.] He is growing clever in swimming, to my delight. We had a long walk yesterday. We bought a little ball and bell for the cat whose life I had saved and brought home. The stone-cutter is showing me his design of the Jizo's face. Shall I let him carve the name of Kazuo Koizumi somewhere on the idol? I can see how glad the Yaidzu people would be to see the new idol.

We have too many fleas here. Please, bring some flea-powder when you come. But this little delight-ful cat makes us forget the fleas. She is really funny. We call her Hinoko.

Plenty of kisses to Suzuko and Kiyoshi from
PAPA.

July 25, 1904.

LITTLE MAMMA, — Your sweet letter at hand. I am glad of it. So Umé San [Professor Umé of the Imperial University] has built his own new house. We shall go together to see him at his home. Kazuo swam into a deeper sea first yesterday; he swam five times toward a boat at quite a distance. He is grow-ing more strong and clever in swimming every day.

He is terribly black now. The weather is lovely and cool. We gave a name to Kazuo's boat, "Hinoko Maru." Osaki San [Otokichi's daughter] made little flag for the boat. As I informed you already, the cat is called "Spark," and her little eyes burn like sparks. Sweet word to everybody at home from

PAPA.

August 1, 1904.

LITTLE MAMMA, — Yesterday we had a real big wave, of the height of summer season. Otokichi swam with Kazuo, as he was afraid for Kazuo to go alone. The sea began to groan terribly since noon; and at evening the billows grew bigger, and almost reached the stone wall. It is difficult to swim this morning also, but I expect that the sea will be calmer in the afternoon.

The little baby sparrow which I already wrote you about had been pretty strong for the last three days; but under the sudden change of weather it was taken ill.

Last evening Otokichi bought two sharks. Kazuo studied their shapes carefully; and it was the first experience for him. Otokichi cooked nicely for our supper shark's meat, which was white and excellent. I take some milk in the morning.

August 10, 1904.

LITTLE MAMMA SAN, — This morning we had a pleasant swimming, the sea being warm. Kadzuo did not swim so well as before, but I think he will improve in a few days. I noticed his wearing a tiny charm, and asked him what it meant. He answered that mother, from her anxiety for him, had told him to wear it whenever he go a-swimming. Iwao swam a little. He will become a good swimmer.

Ume [Otokichi's son] is now a grown man and even married. His wife is kind and lovely. This year Otokichi looks a little older than before. As to the rampart here, it was the old one that had got some damage; the new one is very strong. It is a pity that those ducks and doves are seen no more.

Loving words from Papa to dear Mamma and Grandmother.

August 13, 1904.

LITTLE MAMMA SAMA, — The weather is good always. The other guest at Otokichi's has gone; I am glad of it. The wife of Otokichi is ill, and moved to Tetsu's house. I believe she is getting better. Otoyo called on us. Her husband, I am told, was called to the front, and also the tobacco-shop keeper whom you know. Yaidzu has sent her seventeen soldiers out to Manchuria.

To-day the sea is high, but rather calm. Kazuo and Iwao with their Papa swam. Iwao is improving in swimming; he has learned how to float well. I am sure he will soon master the art thoroughly. I felt so hot and lazy; but Papa's belly, like Hotei-sama's [the big-bellied God of Comfort], is growing rather small.

The festival is held to-day. "Yarei, yare, Haya," we hear the musical voice. The sacred car of the festival I expect to pass by the house this afternoon. Sweet word to Kiyoshi, and kisses to "Aba, Aba" [so he called Suzuko, his last girl, as she muttered "Aba, Aba"], from their

PAPA.

August 14, 1904.

LITTLE MAMMA SAMA, — The festival is over. It was interesting last evening. But they did not give the dance. In view of the war, they withheld this year to raise fund for such kind of merry-making.

It was with great delight that I received your lovely letter last night.

This morning the waves were so high that Oto-kichi San helped me in my getting into the water; and it was too difficult to take the boy with me.

We shall walk to Wada this afternoon. The day is fine indeed. The boys are regular in their daily study. I teach Kadzuo reading only. In the morning I teach him and Niimi teaches Kadzuo. In the afternoon we exchange our pupil.

My kisses to dear Suzuko and Kiyoshi, and kind words to Mamma and Grandmother.

August 15, 1904.

LITTLE MAMMA, — We had an Extra last night. Great victory! We had our own celebration here, drinking lemonade and eating ice. But we had no other extra after that. To-day we had a little wave, but plenty jelly-fishes. We — Kazuo, Niimi, and I — were bitten by them. Last night we took a short walk, and went to the shrine of the Yamatodake god. Kazuo caught a black dragon-fly. We have too many fleas here, but not many mosquitoes. The boys are happy. Otokichi goes always with them into the water. Iwao is learning how to swim, but it is rather difficult, as the waves are pretty big. The road toward Wada has been ruined by the rush of waves. "Osemi" [big cicada] is singing. I think Kiyoshi must be lonesome at home. Kisses to "Aba, Aba" from

PAPA.

August 16, 1904.

LITTLE MAMMA, — The weather is fine lately, but there are large waves. Kazuo is always happy. The baby of Otetsu grows big and strong. It tumbles down, and often tries to fly. "Osemi" sings only at morning, and not when the sun is very hot. It is not like the cicada at Okubo Mura. Papa and his boy grow perfectly brown.

I fancy that Okubo Mura must be fine with the new leaves of the banana tree, and also with the new bamboo leaves.

"Tsukutsukuboshi" [a kind of cicada], I think, must be singing in the home garden. Sweet words to everybody at home.

August 17, 1904.

LITTLE MAMMA, — Your welcome letter at hand. It reached me this morning to my delight, and I can explain my joy with it in my Japanese. You must never think of any danger which might occur to your boy; I hope you do not worry about him. I have n't gone to the sea at night this year yet. Otokichi and Niimi take good care of Kazuo. He is perfectly safe, although he often swims in deep water. He is so afraid of the jelly-fishes this summer, but he swims and plays all the same. It was such a lovely thing, this charm of the Narita temple. I feel lonely sometimes; I wish I could see your sweet face. It is difficult to sleep on account of the thick fleas. But as I have a delightful swim in the morning, I usually forget the misery of the night. I take a little hand bath in a ridiculously little tub for the last two or three evenings.

Good words to everybody at home from

PAPA.

August 18, 1904.

LOVELY LITTLE MAMMA SAMA, — The charm of Narita Sama [a famous Buddhist temple at Narita] to hand. I gave it to Otokichi, who was very glad. His wife is now a little better.

Thank you for the shirts you kindly sent me. But please rest assured that I do not feel cold any more; I am now quite strong; I have got a fresh layer of skin by virtue of the salt water.

I beseech you, Mamma Sama, that you will take care of your own self. You must be so very busy to look after the masons and carpenters engaged in the repair-works.

I was busy to-day, because the publishers sent me the proofs. But I have finished the work. The boys are strong and lovely. They enjoy themselves much in the sea and have become black. Otokichi is kind to them. They study every day.

Good-bye! loving words to lovely Mamma and Grandmother. Kisses to the children.

August 19, 1904.

LITTLE MAMMA SAMA, — Your lovely letter to hand. I am glad to hear that the carpenters and masons are at work. This morning the sea was very rough, and I could not go for swimming. So we intend to take walk to Wada with Otokichi.

Do you remember that little lame girl in this village? What a pity it was to see her! She has now much grown up. Then the boy in our next-door neighbour has become as big as I was and goes to school. He learns very well. It is two years since. Is n't it wonderfully rapid that all young people grow up?

Iwao will finish his first English book very soon; there but remain *4 or 5 pages* more to be studied. I have ordered Kadzuo to write these underlined letters.

I am giving just a moderate work to Kadzuo and he does it well. It is just the reviewing, not the new lesson. When we return to Tokyo, I shall give him new lessons. At present he is diligent in penmanship, letter-writing, writing his diary, and English reading, so I do not press upon him. Nor do I force Iwao, for he does his half an hour's study very well. It is simply lovely to see them learn well.

We have collected a great number of pebbles and put them on our window-sill. Every day Papa's pocket in the sleeve is filled with pebbles. What lovely, innocent, and pitiable creatures the children are!

Good-bye! and looking forward to the time of seeing Mamma's lovely face,

KOIZUMI YAKUMO.

August 20, 1904.

LITTLE MAMMA, — Yesterday we went to Wada, where we had our lunch; and there I taught Kazuo. He was delighted to catch the crabs. Iwao is beginning to learn how to swim. The house at Wada has been mended a little. The tea we had there is always good; and I am told that the tea is home-made, which might be the reason of its excellence. Fuji was seen clearly last evening. We cannot swim this morning, as the sea is so high. It was so hot last night we could not shut the doors. But the weather is always good. Iwao let his crabs walk on the roofs of Otokichi's house; and they walked and walked. During the night those crabs tried to bite into the box of our soap, but it was beyond their power to open the tin cover. How sorry! From

PAPA.

August 21, 1904.

LITTLE MAMMA, — Otokichi gave us plenty of pears in a tray yesterday, as it was the day of *Bon*. I believe it was to thank you for your gift of the charm the other day. We went to Wada to-day and had lunch there. Iwao learns well how to swim; and he has no fear whatever, and takes delight in

Just this moment I received your big letter. I am very glad to hear how you treated the snake you mentioned. You were right not allowing the girls to kill it. They only fear, as they don't understand that it never does any harm. I believe it must be a friend of Kami-sama in our bamboo bush.

Mr. Papa and others wish to see Mamma's sweet face. Good words to everybody at home.

YAKUMO.

LITTLE MAMMA, — *Gomen, gomen:* [Forgive me:] I thought only to give a little joy as I hoped. The Jizo I wrote you about is not the thing you will find in the graveyards; but it is the Jizo who shall guard and pacify the seas. It is not a sad kind; but you do not like my idea, so I have given up my project. It was only Papa's foolish thought. However, poor Jizo-sama wept bitterly when it heard of your answer to me. I said to it, "I cannot help it, as Mamma San doubted your real nature, and thinks that you are a graveyard keeper. I know that you are the saviour of seas and sailors." The Jizo is crying even now.

PAPA.

Gomen, gomen:
"The Jizo idol is shedding stone-tears."

[The letter, as usual, was illustrated with his own picture; this time the picture was a broken idol shedding bean-like "stone tears." The Jizo he took such an interest in was not a graveyard keeper, but it stood on the shore as the calmer of the wild sea, as the Yaidzu Sea is always.]

INDEX

Accent, in connection with rhyme, 208, 209.

Ainu, the religion of, 25.

Akasaka, 328.

Akizuki of Aidzu, Professor of Chinese, birthday festival of, 73, 88, 89; a visit from, 258; a type of the ideal old Samurai, 315.

Aldrich, Thomas Bailey, 165, 391, 395, 396.

Amamura, Japanese village, 416.

Amenomori, Nobushige, 384.

American, magazines, 34; physiognomy, 46.

Amiel, Henri Frédéric, 72.

Anarchists, 372.

Ancestral, memories, inheritance of, 213; tendencies, influence of, 221, 222; tendencies, genius explained by, 256; ghosts, 267.

Andersen, Hans Christian, 201.

Anderson, William, 156.

Animals, souls of, 338, 429–431.

Anstey, F., *pseud.* *See* Guthrie.

Archery, Japanese, 304, 305, 337, 339.

Architecture, Gothic, Hearn on, xxvii; Gothic and Greek, 24; in Italy, 160; at open ports, 402.

Arnold, Sir Edwin, 110; his Japanese drama, 422; address of, to the Ladies' Educational Association, 424.

Arnold, Matthew, his criticism of Wordsworth, 218.

Arrows of prayers, 13.

Art, Japanese, snow in, 56; idealism in, 109, 110; Japanese, old and new, 118, 119; Eastern and Western, some peculiarities in, explained by sexual idea, 122; Japanese, contrast presented in, 217; Japanese and Greek, anatomy plays no part in, 228, 229; of the Latins, as illustrated by Loti, 393.

Artist, the, his duty to extract the gold from the ore, xlvii.

Artistic sensitiveness conjoined with ferocity, 289–291.

Asakichi, Yasukochi, student, 310, 315–318, 326.

Aston, William George, 358.

Atheists, 330.

Atlantic Monthly, editor of, condemns use of Japanese words, 105; a criticism in, 160; articles in, 293, 330; the pay given by, 210; goes in for fine work, 210; stories of, 371.

Autograph-hunters, 295, 296.

Avaloketesvara Sutra, the, 348.

Awata-ware factory at Kyoto, 405.

Ayame, 348.

Babies, Japanese, 177.

Bacon, Alice, 96, 433.

Bacon, Francis, 287.

Baissac, Charles, his Grammar of the Mauritian Creole, 7.

Ballads, Daikokumai, 196, 335, 371, 375; rhyme in, 207, 225, 234; of Kipling, 380, 381.

Balzac, Honoré de, compared with Zola, 157; his *Contes Drôlatiques*, 188, 189; his *La Belle Imperia*, 199.

Bamboo, Missy, 178.

Bamboo curtains, 163.

Batchelor, John, on the religion of the Ainu, 25.

Bateiseki stone, 414.

Bates, Henry Walter, indifferent to poetical aspects of Nature, 151.

Bath, household, use of, in Japan, 148.

Bathing resorts, Japanese, 13.

Baths, public, Japanese, singing in, 250.

Bato-Kwannon, Japanese divinity, 427, 429, 430, 431.

Baudelaire, Pierre Charles, his use of language, xliv; the wonderful insanities of, 135; quoted, 186; third among the Romantic poets, 187; his *Fleurs de Mal*, 224; his poem on an albatross, 228.

Bears, Japanese custom about, 338.

Beauty, the worship of, 197, 198; of eyes and skin, 268–272.

204; his *La Morte Amoureuse*, 223, 224; his tales adapted to the eye rather than to the ear, 371.

Gayarré, Charles, 130.

Geisha, 171, 301, 407, 409.

Genius, that a book should gain with every reading, the sign of, xlv, 192; Hearn a believer in, 256; want of, the literary curse of the century, 256; explainable by the ancestral hypothesis, 256.

Ghosts, Hearn's belief in, lv, 212–215.

Gladstone, William Ewart, 429.

Globe trotters, 91, 92, 365, 366.

Goblin-dogs, 431.

Goblins, 26, 27.

God, some Japanese views on, 334, 335; what he is, unknown, 378; Lecky on the theological conception of, 424.

Gods, Japanese, 8, 28, 29, 46, 47, 100, 181, 375, 408–410, 413, 427–429.

Goethe, Johann Wolfgang von, 195, 263; quoted, 238; his *The New Melusine*, 264, 265.

Gogol, Nikolai Vassilievitch, 200.

Goka, district in Yalsushiro, 338.

Gothic architecture, xxvii, 24, 160.

Government schools in Japan, 225, 226.

Greek, architecture, 24; church, the, 49; art, 198; sculpture, acquaintance with anatomy plays no part in, 228, 229; fables, 308, 309.

Greslon, Robert, 50, 52.

Griffis, William Elliot, 328.

Griswold, Rufus Wilmot, biographer of Poe, v.

Guthrie, Thomas Anstey (F. Anstey), his *Giant's Robe*, 86.

Gypsy matters, 259, 260.

Hachimau, 170.

Hakodate, Japanese city, 311.

Hall, Captain Basil, 361.

Harper's Magazine, 5.

Harte, Bret, 165.

Hasegawa, 342, 359.

Hattori, Ichizo, 4.

Hauk, Minnie, 353.

Haunters in Japan, 173, 174.

Hayward, Abraham, his translation of *Faust*, 137.

Hearn, Lafcadio, Stedman on, v; mis-

statements and legends about his life, vi-x; summary of the facts of his life, x; number and richness of his letters surprising, xvii, xx, xxi; contrast of his life at Izumo and Kumamoto, xviii; conditions combined to make of him a creator of famous letters, xx; his letters a revelation of himself, xxi-xxiii; his letters the record of a Man, xxiii-xxv; his capacity for sacrifice and for fury, xxv; shrunk from publicity of personality, xxv; the salient qualities of his personality, xxvi; his life's purpose same from the first, xxvi; his literary models, xxvii; on Gothic architecture, xxvii, 24, 160; on Victor Hugo, xxvii; Noguchi on, xxxi, xxxix, xl; his integration of purpose for an ideal end, xxviii, xxix; his sensitiveness, xxix–xxxviii; expended great labour on his writing, xxx; on the colour, form, character, etc., of words, xxxi-xxxiii, 105–107, 113; his sense of colour, xxxiii; his quickness of observation, xxxiv; his sensibility to sounds, xxxvi; his sensibility to smells, xxxvii; his sensibility to touch, xxxvii; his timidity and shyness, xxxvii; his lack of capacity to fit easily into the social organization, xxxviii; sought peace in solitude, xxxviii, xxxix; compared to Akinari Uyeda, xxxix; the innate beauty and sensuous imagery of his work, xl-xliv; his attitude toward the tendency of the school of decadence, xliv-xlvi, 307, 308; on the artist, xlvii; Osman Edwards on, xlvii; his reproductions of humble beauties, xlviii; sample of his style on sterner matters, xlix; why he first went to Japan, l; his first impressions of Japan, li, lii; his interpretation of Japan, liii, liv; his belief in ghosts, lv, 212–215; a mystic, lvi; in sympathy with Oriental faiths, lvi, lviii, lix; born too late for an anthropomorphic vision of a deity, lvii; a believer in Spencer's theories, lviii, 221–223, 231; desirous of writing a good book upon Japan, 3; desirous of obtaining a place in a private family, 3, 5; enchanted with Japan, 5, 13; desirous